Resident Alien

Resident Alien

Rian Malan

Jonathan Ball Publishers
JOHANNESBURG & CAPE TOWN

The pieces in this collection first appeared, some in a different form,
in *The Spectator, Esquire, Rolling Stone, Maverick, Sunday Telegraph,
The Observer, Noseweek,* (London), *Sunday Independent, Empire,
Fair Lady, Condé Nast Traveller, Best Life* and *Frontiers of Freedom.*
The original publication dates appear at the end of the relevant pieces.

Published in 2009 and reprinted in 2010 by
JONATHAN BALL PUBLISHERS (PTY) LTD
PO Box 33977
Jeppestown
2043

ISBN 978 1 86842 356 9

Cover photograph by Guy Tillim
Cover design by Michiel Botha, Cape Town
Text design by Triple M Design, Johannesburg
Printed and bound by CTP Book Printers, Cape

ISO 12647 compliant

Set in 11/14pt Rotis Serif Std

Contents

Acknowledgements

IIIIIIIIIIIIIIIIIIIIIIIIIIIIIIIIIIIIIIIIIIIIIIIIIIIIIIIIIIIIIIIIIIIIIIIIIIIIIIIIIIIIIIIIIIIIIIIIIIIIIIIIIIIIIIIIIIIIIIIIIIIIIIIIIIIIII

I'd like to doff the hat to all the brave and patient editors who assisted at the birth of these pieces, especially Bill Tonelli at *Rolling Stone*, Rosie Boycott at *Esquire* UK, Allan Jenkins at the *Observer*, Stuart Reid at *The Spectator* and Graham Boynton at the *Sunday Telegraph*.

I'd also like to thank three men whose whose efforts on behalf of local magazine journalism deserve monuments – Branko Brkic of *Maverick*, Denis Beckett of *Frontline* and Martin Welz at *Noseweek*.

Sincere thanks to Kevin Bloom for an astute reading, and to Ann Seldon Roberts for the WABI.

Finally, thanks to my South African publishers Jonathan Ball and Jeremy Boraine for taking on this project and to production manager Francine Blum, editors Frances Perryer and Valda Strauss, and designers Kevin Shenton and Michiel Botha.

Introduction

||||||||||||||||||||||||||||||||||||||||||||||||||||||||||||||||||||||||||||||||||||||||||||||||||||||||||||||||||||||||||||||||||||||||||||||

Once upon a time in America, I worked for a semi-underground news-paper that had offices on a seedy stretch of Hollywood Boulevard and at least one great writer on its masthead. Michael Ventura was a New Yorker who'd somehow reinvented himself as a straight-shootin', hard-drinkin' cowboy from the lonesome plains of Texas. I guess that was the Larry McMurtry part of his complex persona. He also had a Kerouac aspect and broad streaks of Mailer and Hemingway, but on the page, the spirit he most often channelled was Thomas Wolfe, whose incantatory rhythms he could mimic with uncanny accuracy. Ventura started out as a reporter, but he'd decided that 'nobody can write fast enough to tell a true story' and moved on to movie reviews. If we were lucky, he'd pitch up on a Tuesday morning with black rings around his eyes and two days' stubble on his chin, bearing a searing 5 000-word essay on whatever Hollywood blockbuster had irritated him that week. The best of those reviews began, 'This is a chickenshit movie.'

So then – let's get on with it. This is a chickenshit collection, and the best I can offer is some lame excuses as to why. Let's begin with Ventura's aphorism about the alleged impossibility of writing a true story. This is of little consequence to news reporters who glance at the charge sheet and produce a dry recitation of the basic facts, but some of us had other dreams. I suppose the ideal was a piece of non-fiction so carefully observed and exhaustively reported that reading it was as good as being there.

This was a fiendishly difficult thing to pull off, even in America, where people speak the same language, share most values and un-derstand with a reasonable degree of certainty the boundaries of the matrix they inhabit. The laws of cause and effect are known. The narrative may twist and turn, but the forces that drive it are quantified. Even so, your chances were slender. You could set the words down and polish them until your fingers bled, but Ventura was generally right: the ideal was beyond attainment. *Nobody can write fast enough to tell a true story.*

In America, this was an artsy verdict on the limitations of the form. In South Africa, it's like a law of nature: there's no such thing as a true story here. The facts might be correct, but the truth they embody is always a lie to someone else. My truths strike some people as racist heresies. Nadine Gordimer's strike me as distortions calculated to appeal to gormless liberals on the far side of the planet. A lot of South Africans can't read either of us, so their truth is something else entirely. Atop all this, we live in a country where mutually annihilating truths coexist entirely amicably. We are a light unto nations. We are an abject failure. We are progressing even as we hurtle backward. The blessing of living here is that every day presents you with material whose richness beggars the imagination of those who live in saner places. The curse is that you can never, ever get it quite right, and if you come close, the results are usually unpublishable.

I would say, looking back, that the only worthwhile writing I've done over the past two decades appeared in letters to friends in whose company I could ignore the crushing racial taboos that govern public discourse and just call it as I saw it. Beyond that, I don't know. I think it was TS Eliot who said the end of all exploring is to return to where you began and see it as if for the first time. When I came home from America, everything seemed different to me; I saw that I was in Africa, and that changed everything. Those I'd left behind remained obsessed with apartheid. I became obsessed with what replaced it. They thought apartheid was the source of all SA's pain. I thought we were doomed unless we figured out what had gone wrong elsewhere in Africa, and how to avoid a similar fate. I was an atheist in the great revival tent of the New South Africa; the faith on offer was too simple and sentimental, the answers too easy.

We'll probably disagree here, but if you ask me, the most telling creation of apartheid was not the *dompas*, or the *veiligheidspolisie*, or the mines and factories that generated the taxes that paid for repressive measures. It was not the sjambok, or the whites-only signs that once hung on everything from toilet doors to the portals of higher education. Apartheid's great triumph was the creation of a generically Western moonbase on Africa, where whites lived exactly like whites in the capitals of the great white empire.

It follows that apartheid's greatest glories were actually suburbs like Parktown, where English-speaking liberals lived in a bubble that resembled nothing so much as the more civilised parts of Boston or London. Parktown had it all. It had Nadine Gordimer, who won a Nobel for her fashionable literary critique of the empire that largely tolerated and sustained her. It had the Linder Auditorium, where civilised whites gathered to hear other whites playing the music of Dead White Men. And finally it had that great university on the far side of Empire Road, where white professors faithfully propagated doctrines laid down on the far side of the planet by the High Priests of white civilisation.

By the time Mandela came out of prison, those doctrines were generally of the variety called 'progressive,' which rejoiced in the downfall of white males. Practitioners of this doctrine saw themselves as part of, sometimes even heroes of, the uprising of the natives. They thought the wrath of the masses would fall on the bad white males who controlled the land and the mines, while 'good' whites merged into a smiley-face culture of interracial harmony and soft socialism. I said, bullshit, dudes, the laws of poetic symmetry call for another outcome entirely. The wind of change will eventually sweep everything away – your job, your illusions, your university as presently constituted, the wires that bring light at the flick of a switch, the pipes that discreetly remove your turds, the freeways on which you drive, the high-tech chemical farms that put food on your table, the investments intended to sustain your comfortable old age, and the clean, efficient hospitals in which you plan to expire. All these things are creations of the empire, and when it fades, they will too.

That was more than two decades ago. Every day since has brought thunderous confirmation of the rectitude of my prognostications. Every day also brought irrefutable proof of the fact that I was mistaken. I cursed Mandela when he refused to shake De Klerk's hand during some televised debate during the peace talks era. A few months later I was fighting back tears at his inauguration. I claimed vindication when the rand began its great collapse, ate my words when it bounced back again. Every farm murder seemed to herald the onset of generalised ethnic cleansing. Every visit to Soweto left me believing in the brotherhood of man again. And so on.

There was a time when I thought these howling ambiguities could only be resolved by a great cleansing apocalypse, but the apocalypse never came. Instead, we had the delirious triumph of the 1995 rugby world cup, where *dik* Boers wept and said, 'That is my president,' as Mandela raised the golden trophy into the blue heavens celebrated in *Die Stem*. The resulting goodwill was obliterated by the one-sided maunderings of the Truth Commission, but it made a comeback when the economy started growing under Mbeki. Five years later, Zimbabwe put catastrophe back on the agenda, and by the time the lights went out in 2008, the end seemed nigh. Everything seemed to be disintegrating: Eskom, the parastatals, the sewerage system, the highways, the hospitals, the putative moral integrity of the Rainbow Nation. But even as the rot deepened, we saw the rise of the only force that could check it – black people who said, fuck racial solidarity, this cannot be tolerated.

Which brings us back to Michael Ventura. I imagine him shaking his head in disbelief as he reads this. 'Chickenshit,' he says. 'Malan can't make up his mind. He's been sitting on the fence so long the wire is cutting into his pompous and cowardly arsehole.' I agree entirely, but if there is an overarching truth here, I can't see it. The only true line I've ever written about South Africa is this one: 'We yaw between terror and ecstasy. Sometimes we complete the round trip in just fifteen minutes.' If you share the feeling, thanks, but there's a significant difference between us: I am a journalist, which means that I leave a trail of prophecies and judgements, several of which are mortally embarrassing in retrospect. There is no excuse for such failings, but if this was a trial, I'd waltz my way to an acquittal.

In the past two decades, South Africa has been stricken almost weekly by scandals that would have toppled governments in the West but seem almost meaningless here. Who stole the funds donated to help resettle ANC exiles? Who asked the Zambian government to throw Katiza Cebekhulu into a dungeon so that he couldn't testify against Winnie Mandela? Did Thabo Mbeki really negotiate the arms deal on a 'government to government' basis and pocket the resulting commissions? Did he really tell Bulelani Ngcuka to bring him the head of Jacob Zuma, even if that entailed fabricating evidence and setting honey traps? When these stories break, you think they're going to tear the country apart and alter everything forever. But they don't. They linger for a week or two and then fade into oblivion, blown off the front pages by the next dumbfounding scandal. The ordinary laws of cause and effect don't seem to apply here. The boundaries of the matrix we inhabit remain unknown.

But what the heck, there's something to be said for practising journalism on the edge of an abyss, trying to follow your targets into the murk that surrounds. In the pieces that follow, I often miss, but there are a few passages that come close to disproving Michael Ventura's dictum. For the rest, I tried my best, and provoked reactions as richly varied as the reality we inhabit. A few people said nice things, of course – 'a born story-teller,' according to the judges on some American awards jury – but the reactions that lodge in my memory are mostly the angry ones. Some said racist, but that's so commonplace it's barely worth mentioning; any South African journalist who hasn't been called a racist or self-hating black is a *kak* one whose lips are chapped from sucking the unmentionable appendages of those in power. The more interesting accusations were incest, homosexual tendencies, heterosexual debauchery, incompetence, deceit, murder, sissiness, 'carbuncular' practices, a secret alliance with the diabolical President Mbeki, spying for Inkatha, drinking too much, taking drugs and smelling bad.

What can I say? My name is Rian Malan and I called it as I saw it.

1

Politics

Nemesis

||||||||||||||||||||||||||||||||||||||||||||||||||||||||||||||||||||||||||||||||||||||||||||||||||||||||||||||||||||||||||||||||||||||||||||||||||

Is it chaos theory which holds that a butterfly flaps its wings in Tasmania and causes an enormously complex chain reaction that eventually results in a devastating hurricane on the far side of the planet? This story opens with just such an event. It takes place outside international arrivals at Johannesburg International Airport on a hot morning in March 2000. A South African Airways' flight has just arrived from Germany. Passengers are edging out into the sun. Among them is a 45-year-old businessman in a black suit, carrying two suitcases. He puts them down, lights a cigarette. Spots his driver approaching, steps off the curb to wave him down.

Just then, a loiterer dashes forward, grabs one of the unattended cases and runs. The man in the black suit looks an easy victim, balding and a bit soft in the middle. He isn't. He runs the felon down, drops him with a rugby tackle. An accomplice leaps into the fray, but by now the driver is out of the car and coming towards them, so the second hoodlum flees, leaving his buddy and black suit wrestling on the pavement. Black suit sees security guards across the road, shouts for help, but they ignore him.

At this, black suit strips his proverbial *moer*. He gives the struggling felon 'a few taps' and warns that if he doesn't come quietly, he'll get seriously hurt. Then he hauls the felon to his feet, twists his arm behind his back, and frog-marches him towards justice. The driver picks up the suitcases, follows. Onlookers shrug, go on their way.

The butterfly has flapped its wings. Eight years hence, this minor event will result in an enormous scandal that reveals the outlines of a master plan to take control of the South African criminal justice system, causes mortal damage to President Thabo Mbeki, and leads

3

ultimately to the arrest of Jackie Selebi, the nation's – in fact, the world's – top policeman. It's a story that reveals more than you want to know about the dark side of South Africa, and it all began, improbably, with a bungled petty crime at the airport.

The improbable Mr O'Sullivan

Paul O'Sullivan is a cautious man. You send him an email inviting him to dinner in Rosebank. He fires back a response saying, sorry, I can't, try another date. Seconds later, he phones to say this is just a ruse; he can make it, but suspects that sinister forces are intercepting his email and wants to be sure they don't show up too. O'Sullivan has many enemies, and he's reluctant to say too much about his survival strategies. 'If I tell you what precautions I take,' he says, sliding into a booth and ordering a Guinness, 'I'm telling you how to defeat me.'

In his fifties, O'Sullivan has the fleshy face of a prosperous banker. The blond hair is thinning, jowls forming. His skin is almost translucently pale, and his eyes a wary, washed-out blue-grey. Tonight, he's wearing a bomber jacket and jeans, and there's a bulge on his hip that looks like a handgun. In this guise, he resembles the veteran detective sergeant in some British TV crime series, but appearances can be deceptive. Four days hence he'll be wearing a suit and tie, playing the polished toff at a Chamber of Commerce gathering. A week after that, drinking beer and chowing tripe in Soweto with black empowerment luminaries. Next afternoon, sunning himself at a Houghton poolside in the company of a hauntingly beautiful Russian who turns out to be his third wife, Irina, aged 32.

O'Sullivan says he's Irish, but his accent shifts chameleon-like from British midlands to hardcore Johannesburg southern suburbs and even Afrikaans. He says he visited South Africa in the 1980s but was never comfortable because of apartheid. When Mandela was freed in 1990, however, 'I came screaming down here with the wife and kids.' He was an electrical engineer by profession, but he'd made some sound investments and when he liquidated everything in the UK he was worth a shade over a million pounds; nice money when converted to rands at the preferential rate offered to immigrants. He bought a faux Cape Dutch mansion in Bedfordview and dabbled in property development before taking a job with Highmoon Properties. His starting salary was R100 000 per annum, but O'Sullivan was a driven man; by the end of the decade, he'd held senior executive positions in a string of firms like Chubb or Sage Properties, and his salary had risen tenfold.

That's the mundane part of his extraordinary CV. O'Sullivan describes himself as the son of a 'post-war colonial police officer' who taught him to pull his weight and do his duty. So he'd pull weight at the office, and then pull a second shift as a volunteer for worthy causes. He was a director of the Johannesburg Tourist Board, chairman of the inner-city Community Policing Forum, director of the Tourism Business Council and founder of Johannesburg City Watch. According to the CV, he was the man who persuaded sponsors to install closed-circuit cameras throughout Johannesburg's crime-blighted downtown. The man who felt it was an insult for the city's main police station to be named after apartheid premier John Vorster and organised for it to be renamed Johannesburg Central. The man who raised R16 million to build a museum at the spot where schoolboy Hector Pieterson died in the opening minutes of the 1976 Soweto uprising.

O'Sullivan loved South Africa. He thought of it as 'paradise on earth.' He liked the sun, enjoyed the company of Africans, even liked crime, if only in the sense that it provided opportunities for high adventure. He joined the police reserve in 1992, and spent 30 to 40 hours a week pulling his weight there too. He lectured at the Police Reserve College, assisted in the prosecution of white-collar swindlers, patrolled the streets as a beat cop. One night, on the East Rand, he and his partners stopped a car that had just been reported hijacked. O'Sullivan took three bullets in the ensuing shootout, but lived to tell the tale. One of the bad guys didn't.

Three bullets would dampen most people's enthusiasm, but not O'Sullivan's. He remains the sort of oke who gets a faraway look in his eyes and says things like, 'My old man taught me that if a country is worth living in, it is worth fighting for.' Or, 'I firmly believe that the world's next great civilisation will rise right here in South Africa.'

In pursuit of this vision, O'Sullivan flies to a tourism conference in Berlin in March 2000, representing the Soweto Tourism Development Association. He spends three days handing out glossy brochures and assuring apprehensive Europeans that no harm will befall them if they visit South Africa. Then he steps off the plane back home, and someone scales his suitcase. This does not amuse him, and there is worse to come.

'What happened,' he says, 'is that we arrive in the charge office and the sergeant behind the desk says, "Ah, thanks, man, we'll take care of it from here."' Being a part-time cop, O'Sullivan knows the sergeant can't do anything without a statement, so he insists on making one. Then he insists on being given a case number, or at least a cell register number. The sergeant says he can't help. By now, O'Sullivan's bones are telling him that this cop is planning to cut a deal with the thief as soon as his back is turned, so he whips out his camera, pops a flash in the sergeant's face and says, 'Right. If you don't phone me in 24 hours with a case number, I'm going to make sure you get fired or locked up or both.'

After that, the law takes its course and the thief goes to prison, but the experience sets O'Sullivan thinking that someone ought to do something about the gauntlet tourists have to run after their jets touch down. Their baggage is sometimes rifled or stolen. In the concourse, they're besieged by dodgy taxi drivers. Petty thieves and armed robbers lurk outside, and from what he's seen, policing is pretty slack. So he arranges a reservist transfer to the airport's border police unit, and a year or so later accepts an offer to become group executive for security at the Airports Company of South Africa (Acsa), the parastatal that manages the country's ten largest airfields. It's the perfect job for a man of his skills and inclination. He dusts off his hands and says, 'Right, let's get stuck in.'

Nature of the beast
'All international airports,' says a study by criminologist Mark Gurkel, 'are sites of struggle between justice and criminality.' Johannesburg International (as it was in 2001) holds its head high in this regard. In the course of the 1990s, South Africa became one of the planet's great marijuana-exporting nations, as well as a major trans-shipment point for Europe-bound cocaine.

An unknown proportion of this contraband is passing through JIA, which is also a hotspot for human traffickers who fly Third Worlders into Johannesburg, kit them out with fake identity documents and ship them on to the UK, where a South African passport allows visa-free entry. Policing this zoo requires the services of 1 200 people per shift: customs officers to inspect cargo; clerks to check passports; cops and intelligence specialists to watch out for smugglers, terrorists or wanted criminals; security guards to patrol the perimeters. In theory, it's the most tightly policed 40 square kilometres in the country. In theory.

Five days after O'Sullivan starts his new job in July 2001, a truck rolls up to a perimeter gate that is supposed to be locked at all times. It isn't. There are supposed to be two guards on duty, but there's only one. He's supposed to be armed, but he isn't. Gunmen overpower him and proceed to the precious goods cargo terminal, where a Swissair plane is unloading a $16-million consignment of cash and diamonds. The gunmen help themselves and leave without being detected. This fiasco sets the tone. There will be five similar robberies before the year is out.

'Security was useless,' says O'Sullivan. He catches guards sleeping on the job, or accepting bribes to escort illegal immigrants around passport control; customs agents being paid to overlook containers full of counterfeit goods; cops who would, for a fee, smuggle a suitcase full of hot cash or contraband through security and hand it back to you in the departure lounge. According to O'Sullivan's reports, you'd see airport workers lining up outside exchange bureaux after every shift change, waiting to convert their foreign currency bribes into rands. His boss, Acsa chairman Mashudu Ramano, shares his concerns, describing airport crime as 'unbearable' and backing the Irishman's efforts to fight it.

O'Sullivan has no authority over policemen or customs agents, but he and Ramano can crack the whip over the Airports Company's private security contractors. The largest of these is Khuselani Security, the outfit whose *slapgat* guard let the Swissair robbers through the gates in the first week of O'Sullivan's tenure.

After that, the Irishman keeps an eye on Khuselani's operations, and discovers dismaying shortcomings. Guards absent from their posts. Guards so ill-trained they barely understand their standing orders. In some instances there are guards who don't exist at all: the Airports Company is being billed for their services, but when O'Sullivan makes surprise checks in the dead of night there's no one there. He starts documenting these lapses. Each time one occurs, he sends a letter to Khuselani's owners. By 5 October 2001, O'Sullivan has sent 23 such warnings and he's ready to take it to the next level: a legal letter informing Khuselani's owners that he's converting their contract from a yearly to a monthly basis and giving them 30 days to shape up or ship out.

A few days later, a giant Mercedes-Benz ML glides into Acsa's parking lot. It's a so-called Yengeni Benz, one of the luxury cars offered at steep discounts to figures positioned to ease approval of South Africa's purchase of some very expensive German military equipment. Out of it steps your proverbial fat cat – a giant Zulu, weighing at least 150 kilograms. He says to O'Sullivan, 'I understand you want to alter my contract.' O'Sullivan assents. The visitor seems amused. He says, 'You don't know who you're dealing with.' Paul O'Sullivan has arrived at the base of a steep learning curve.

The Battle of Jo'burg Airport

Professor Noel Ngwenya is a comet who blazed brightly for a year or two and then vanished into the obscurity from whence he came. Some say he once taught at Rand Afrikaans University, but that could not be confirmed. He apparently spent time in Canada, and when he returned was given a seat in the senate of Mangosuthu Technikon in Durban. In the late 1990s, he comes into focus as an executive at arms manufacturer Denel's Isando facility. While there he comes to realise that vast opportunities are opening up in the security field: every national key point requires protection, and the ANC government is determined to swing the business to black-owned entities. So Ngwenya quits Denel and becomes chief executive of a company called Khuselani Security, which tenders in 2000 for a giant contract put out by the state-owned Airports Company. The incumbent is Fidelity, an old-guard firm that stands little chance against a bright and shiny empowerment outfit whose shareholders include Noel's brother Jerome, an eminent lawyer, and Vuyo Ndzeku, described by the *Mail & Guardian* as a man who could 'open doors' and 'take you to minister level, to premier level.'

Khuselani has little experience in the security field and only 60 employees, whereas the airports contract calls for 3 700, but these are minor problems. The political climate favours Khuselani, and it winds up winning a contract potentially worth R280 million over the next five years. Noel Ngwenya celebrates by throwing a victory bash at which the guest of honour is his friend Jacob Sello Selebi, the recently appointed national commissioner of police.

A few months down the line, Ngwenya discovers that he's underbid on the contract and there's too little money left to do the job properly. Khuselani pressures rank-and-file guards to accept minimum wage. Newcomers are given little or no training. 'If they were short-staffed,' says O'Sullivan, 'they'd just go out into the street and hire anyone who fitted the uniform.' Some of the guards thus dragooned are good men, but others are bent or incompetent, and their managers are 'useless,' in O'Sullivan's estimation. This leads, as we have seen, to an avalanche of complaints about Khuselani's performance and ultimately to a visit from the corpulent Ngwenya, who smiles and says, 'You don't know who you're dealing with.' O'Sullivan registers the implied threat, but it doesn't faze him, not even when two eminent empowerment wheeler-dealers come to warn him to tread carefully.

Lungi Sisulu is a son of the illustrious Walter, who spent 26 years on Robben Island with Nelson Mandela. Sisulu tells O'Sullivan that Khuselani Security is actually his baby; he founded the firm and laid the groundwork for the Acsa bid before moving to New York, where his wife had been appointed South Africa's consul general. On his return, he says, he discovered Ngwenya had cut him out entirely. His companion, the aforementioned Vuyo Ndzeku, says he was similarly treated and then thrown into prison – on the personal orders of Jackie Selebi, no less – when he threatened to cause a fuss. This strikes O'Sullivan as wildly implausible. The commissioner of police misusing his position to settle a business dispute? He offers Ndzeku a cup of tea, but secretly dismisses him as a nutter.

The very next morning, O'Sullivan receives a phone call saying Commissioner Selebi wants to see him. Selebi is an avuncular struggle veteran who served as a diplomat before being deployed to the police force. Friends describe him as a charming bon vivant and raconteur. Underlings dread his temper. O'Sullivan is impressed by his uniform, a gold braid-encrusted affair that steals the show in the VIP lounge where their meeting takes place. Selebi tells O'Sullivan he's unhappy to hear that Acsa is thinking of changing its security arrangements. This is reinforced the following morning by a call from Selebi's deputy, André Pruis: don't touch the Khuselani contract.

O'Sullivan declines to follow these orders, pointing out that the police have no right to intervene in a dispute between Acsa and one of its contractors. In subsequent court papers, the police will claim that they were acting pursuant to a cabinet-level re-evaluation of airport security in the wake of the September 11 terrorist attacks. O'Sullivan counters that if this is indeed the case the order should have come from Transport Minister Dullah Omar, under whose control the Airports Company falls. He asks the cops to make their case in writing, but nothing materialises, so O'Sullivan, with the backing of his board, proceeds with his plan to oust Khuselani.

On 29 October, Ngwenya is formally notified that Acsa intends to revoke his contract on grounds of non-performance. Back comes a letter accusing O'Sullivan of 'violating the direct instructions of the National Commissioner of Police.' The Airports Company's lawyers respond by again raising the issue of legal authority: on what grounds does Commissioner Selebi presume to issue orders to Acsa? Nothing more is heard on this score, and the game moves in a new direction.

Mashudu Ramano is a financier who rose to prominence as general secretary of business federation Nafcoc in the early 1990s. After the fall of apartheid, he rocketed to the top of the business world, becoming chief executive officer of Nafcoc's investment vehicle, chairman of African Harvest and, in August 2000, chairman of Acsa. On 21 November 2001, this corporate star sits down in front of a tape recorder to tell an extraordinary story.

'The name is Mashudu Ramano,' he begins. 'Over the past four months, I have had a security problem.' It all began, he says, when a disgruntled former employee warned him that 'the ANC is doing an investigation of Mashudu' and that 'he knew people who would put bullets in my head.' Such talk initially struck Ramano as absurd, but as the Khuselani dispute intensified, he began to wonder. Strange things were happening around him. Spurious salesmen made calls to his home, asking questions about his family. Armed men came piling over his garden wall one night and traded shots with his security guards, an event that left Ramano so shaken he moved into a hotel and took the precaution of making this recording.

'Some time during October,' he continues, 'we changed the contract of Khuselani Security, headed by a gentleman named Noel Ngwenya, who apparently has certain relationships with certain politicians. When we cancelled the contract Noel appealed for help to the commissioner of police.' Ramano notes that Selebi has approached employees with a view to getting the Khuselani decision reversed, but refuses to meet Ramano himself on the grounds that 'he has instituted an investigation into my affairs and within two weeks he would have a report exposing whatever their findings are going to be.' Ramano observes that these threats are 'almost identical' to earlier warnings and concludes, 'Perhaps there is a link between the security problems I am experiencing and the events that are now beginning to unfold.'

He leaves the tape with his secretary, who is instructed to release it should any harm befall him. Five days later, policemen rock up at Ramano's hotel and haul him off to Pretoria, claiming they have discovered he is an illegal alien living in South Africa on forged identity documents. This is bizarre, given that Ramano was born and raised in Soweto, but it doesn't stop police spin-doctors from leaking the story to the media.

Said spin-doctors launch a simultaneous strike against O'Sullivan, using credit card and bank statements allegedly stolen from his office. These are handed to an investigative reporter at the *Mail & Guardian*, along with a briefing to the effect that they contain proof of corruption. Reporter Evidence wa ka Ngobeni is particularly interested in a R400 000 deposit into O'Sullivan's bank account. O'Sullivan says he'd sold a tranche of shares, but Ngobeni has been told the money is a bribe from the security company angling to replace Khuselani. Ngobeni is also interested in a credit card transaction involving the purchase of a voice-stress lie detector from the US Federal Bureau of Investigation. 'You impersonated a law enforcement officer here,' he says. 'You claimed you were with the border police.'

'But I am with the border police,' protests O'Sullivan. He pulls out his badge. 'Detective-sergeant O'Sullivan, reservist attached to the border police.'

O'Sullivan's explanations notwithstanding, the *Mail & Guardian* publishes a story noting that Ramano and his security chief are facing investigation. If this is intended to intimidate them, it fails: the Acsa boys stand firm and at midnight on 30 November, Khuselani's contract is cancelled. This is a crippling blow to Ngwenya and his allies, who go to court to have the revocation overturned.

On 6 December, a red Volkswagen with tinted windows falls in behind O'Sullivan as he leaves the office. As the VW draws abreast, he says, its passenger window slides down and he sees a man in a balaclava raising a gun to take aim at him. The Irishman does a handbrake turn and screams off in the opposite direction. He's initially willing to regard this as just another Jo'burg hijacking attempt, but a month later there's a second incident in which shots are fired. There is no evidence to link these attacks to the police or Khuselani, but this doesn't stop O'Sullivan from feeling someone has declared war on him, and retaliating in kind.

His chosen weapon is a tip-off to tax authorities, who are told that Khuselani is evading taxes. A raid on Khuselani's office reveals irregularities that will eventually lead to a fraud conviction. Meanwhile, Ngwenya has the satisfaction of seeing O'Sullivan booted out of the police reserve, a move that drastically limits his room for manoeuvre. By now, O'Sullivan claims to have established that someone inside Acsa is reporting his every move to Ngwenya, so he starts investigating fellow executives for corruption, fraud and conflicts of interest. They counter by instituting disciplinary procedures aimed at curbing the Irishman's allegedly 'rude and aggressive' behaviour. These developments create an atmosphere so toxic that only one end is conceivable: in January 2003 O'Sullivan is fired.

Five years later, the Airports Company's lawyers sit down with *Maverick* to discuss the firestorm of litigation that ensued. We find ourselves in a boardroom at Webber Wentzel, one of South Africa's largest law firms, facing a panel of six legal heavyweights. We present O'Sullivan's version of events, which rests on the assertion that key Acsa executives conspired with police chief Selebi to save Khuselani's R280-million contract. Not so, says litigator Trevor Versfeld. 'If Paul O'Sullivan's conspiracy claim is taken to its ultimate, you would have expected Acsa to pull the plug on the Khuselani litigation. This didn't happen. I was never told to go easy or give them a second chance. The litigation proceeded expeditiously, and they were in fact fired.'

We grant the point and move on to the circumstances surrounding O'Sullivan's dismissal. An affidavit has recently come to light in which Glenn Agliotti, the noted drug dealer, asks his pal Selebi why O'Sullivan is causing so much trouble. Selebi replies, 'I had him removed from the airport,' or words to that effect. The police chief makes a similar claim in an affidavit of his own, saying that 'O'Sullivan was relieved of his duties after I exposed his incompetence.' Either way, the evidence indicates that police chief Selebi played a leading role in the Irishman's demise.

The members of Acsa's legal team say they have no knowledge of such things; as far as they're concerned, it was an 'incompatibility dismissal.' In July 2002, says labour specialist José Jorge, O'Sullivan and Airports Company CEO Monhla Hlahla signed a memo acknowledging their 'history of conflict and mistrust' and 'the need to create a more positive relationship.' Both parties committed themselves to attending monthly counselling sessions mediated by a consultant, and O'Sullivan undertook to mend his relationship with the police. Towards the end of the year, O'Sullivan sent Selebi a Christmas present, but otherwise, says Jorge, 'He just didn't come to the party. He was not prepared to change his ways.' O'Sullivan, on his part, contends that his anti-corruption activities continued until the day he was fired, 'and if there was an incompatibility issue, this was its root cause.'

The last straw, says Jorge, was an incident on 17 January 2003, when O'Sullivan allegedly stormed into a boardroom where his boss Monhla Hlahla was meeting an advisor to the Minister of Transport. 'Actually,' says Webber Wentzel senior partner Daniel le Roux, 'the door was locked, so he went around outside and banged on the window. I mean, this is extreme behaviour.' The distinguished guest was hauled off to the parking lot and asked to explain a scratch on O'Sullivan's R450 000 Audi. When it emerged that he was not responsible for the damage, O'Sullivan apologised and the meeting resumed. O'Sullivan claims it was all 'extremely cordial,' but CEO Hlahla says she was left feeling 'undermined and humiliated.' She reported the matter to the conflict mediator, who concluded that her relationship with the Irishman was beyond saving and that 'termination is appropriate.'

And so O'Sullivan found himself on the street, his chances of landing another senior executive position fatally damaged. He filed a wrongful dismissal claim, but lost on a technicality. He appealed to the Public Protector to investigate Selebi's role in his dismissal, but his letters were ignored. He asked the police's Independent Complaints Directorate for help, but his plea fell on deaf ears. In April 2004, he convinced a judge to order the ICD to look into his complaints, but the ensuing inquiry was a cursory affair, conducted by a Scotland Yard detective who clearly failed to take O'Sullivan very seriously. By January 2005, O'Sullivan had exhausted all orthodox avenues of redress. 'And that,' he says, 'is when the war began.'

O'Sullivan in the underworld

We are now entering murky territory where hard men carry guns and kill those who threaten their secrets. O'Sullivan is our guide in this netherworld, and when he talks about it, his narratives are so riddled with half-truths, ellipses and evasions that they read like a cut-up William Burroughs novel. O'Sullivan says this is as it must be: 'It's called securing your sources, your assets. If you don't protect them, they get terrified and refuse to testify. Or die.' Almost all his sources are therefore nameless, and the Scorpions, who feature heavily in what follows, are under strict orders not to talk to the press. So then, should we trust our guide?

This turns out to be an interesting question. Over the years, O'Sullivan has built up a chorus of supporters who see him as a self-sacrificing altruist who simply cannot be stopped once he gets his teeth into an investigation. 'He'll work his butt off just for the honour of it,' says Lungi Sisulu. 'A man of the highest integrity,' says former Chamber of Commerce and Industry president Patrick Corbin. Webber Wentzel partner emeritus Ronnie Napier got to know O'Sullivan while they were jointly investigating a giant fraud case in the nineties. 'Paul's a serious operative with a focused and all-consuming passion for justice,' he says. 'God knows when he sleeps. This is a very unusual human being.'

In the middle ground, battered by gales of disinformation, stands a small group of investigative reporters who have known O'Sullivan for years and rate him a reliable source. And in the opposite corner we find the police, who say the Irishman is a liar, an arsonist, a wife-beater, mentally unstable, an arms dealer, a human trafficker, and a sexual predator besides. As for *Maverick*, we yawed between these extremes on a daily basis, our confusion exacerbated by O'Sullivan's reluctance to disclose all the cards he was holding and the Scorpions' refusal to comment on his claims. At times, we were ready to write him off as a fantasist, but we were always checked by the one unassailable argument on view here: the Irishman seems to have got it right. For years, he stood alone in a storm of derision, saying, 'The police chief is a crook.' Nobody believed him, so he squandered millions of his own money on the quest for evidence, and lo: he now stands on the brink of vindication. The tale of how he did it reads like a spy novel, and may in parts be one. But it certainly merits hearing.

Some time in early 2005, we are told, O'Sullivan established an operations room in his Bedfordview home. He says the walls were covered with organograms showing the overlapping structures of half a dozen Johannesburg crime syndicates, with dotted lines linking crime bosses to shadowy intermediaries who were in turn linked in unknown ways to police headquarters in Pretoria. There were also aerial photographs (he's a pilot) of places of interest. A farmhouse where drugs were stashed. A security company's sprawling operations base. A holiday complex on the Indian Ocean where Selebi and his family once spent a holiday. The shelves in this room were laden with lever-arch files containing reports and statements, all meticulously typed by his own hand. All told, he estimates there were around 2 000 names in those files. The names were on his computer too, in a law enforcement software programme designed to find connections that elude human analysis. O'Sullivan also had recording devices, eavesdropping gear and guns, because he was playing a dangerous game.

If you'd been standing outside a certain strip joint in Rivonia on certain nights in early 2005, you would have seen O'Sullivan rolling up in his Audi roadster, wearing his standard jeans and bomber jacket with pistol bulging beneath. O'Sullivan has been hanging out here, trying to get a handle on who comes in, what they talk about. He's particularly interested in the bouncers, steroid-crazed gorillas with shaven heads who do dirty work on the side, like smashing up nightclubs that decline to hire the protection services of an outfit called CNSG – Central National Security Group.

O'Sullivan has a theory. He believes CNSG owner Clinton Nassif is involved in all sorts of rackets, and has police protection. Exactly how this works O'Sullivan has no idea, but he's watching and learning, making friends in dark corners. In fact, he says he's recruited two of Nassif's sidekicks as deep-cover agents, paying them out of his own pocket. O'Sullivan is building a dossier. A dossier, ultimately, on police chief Selebi, who has by now risen to global prominence as president of Interpol.

In April 2005, O'Sullivan buys a cheap pay-as-you-go cellphone, easy to ditch once it's served its purpose. He uses it to call CNSG, posing as a security consultant whose clients are interested in the firm's services. They say, come in, we'll show you around. The tour starts at JCI House, the skyscraper that houses the headquarters of

Brett Kebble, the billionaire financier and art patron. Kebble is CNSG's most famous client, and O'Sullivan is impressed by the work CNSG has done for him. 'It was a sophisticated set-up,' he says. 'Skilled managers, modern control room, closed-circuit surveillance of almost everyone in the building.'

On the other hand, O'Sullivan doubts that this aspect of Nassif's business is generating enough to subsidise the boss's flashy lifestyle. The Mayfair boykie has moved up in the world. He owns two properties in the northern suburbs, a posh weekend retreat at Hartbeespoort Dam, shares in various IT companies, and wristwatches worth around R3 million. Nassif is also a fan of rare and expensive cars. He's been seen driving a Lamborghini, a Mercedes-Benz SC65, a Porsche GT2. He seems to own an entire fleet of Hummers. Where's all the money coming from?

Some potential answers emerge in the next phase of the tour, which features a visit to CNSG's headquarters on Loveday Street. 'It was like a warehouse,' says O'Sullivan, 'a big semi-industrial indoor car park with a suite of offices inside.' As they move around the site, his guide is boasting about the firm's police connections. They have several legendary (some would say notorious) Murder and Robbery Squad veterans on the payroll. Several serving cops are moonlighting for them too. 'They took me into a control room from where they ran dirty tricks and undercover ops,' says O'Sullivan. 'All these people tapping away at computers. They told me, "From here we can do wiretaps, get phone records and police records." The message was, "Between us and this brick wall, you can get anything you want here."'

As he leaves, the guide hands O'Sullivan a glossy brochure hyping CNSG's capabilities. In it, there's a colour photograph of a young woman named Ntombi Matshoba. A caption identifies her as a director of CNSG. The name means nothing to the Irishman, so the guide gives him a nudge: 'Keep it to yourself, but she's Jackie Selebi's mistress.'

At this point in the telling, O'Sullivan's eyes widen comically and he exclaims, 'Hello?' It turns out Matshoba was Selebi's secretary in the early 1990s, when he was in charge of the ANC's repatriation programme. They fell in love, had a child. Selebi still lives with his wife Ann, but he and Ntombi are often seen together in public. What on earth is the police chief's girlfriend doing in a firm that, by Sullivan's reckoning, is involved in protection rackets, money-laundering, in-dustrial espionage and assassination?

Meanwhile, another line of investigation has thrown up the name of Glenn Agliotti, a charming glad-hander who runs an events company in Midrand. The Italian-South African has no record, but O'Sullivan has a connection at police headquarters who tells him Agliotti has an alter-ego nicknamed 'The Landlord,' who runs drugs.

O'Sullivan pays little attention until the late winter of 2005, when a reservist he knows responds to a 'robbery in progress' call on School Road, Sandton. While he's interviewing the victim, a muscular neigh-bour comes over, introduces himself as Glenn Agliotti. When he hears what's happened, Agliotti whips out a cellphone, dials a number and hands the receiver to the cop, who finds himself speaking to police chief Selebi. The commissioner says, 'Glenn is a good friend of mine, take care of him,' or words to that effect. The dumbfounded reservist hands the phone back to Agliotti, who seems very pleased with him-self. He says, 'Ja, Jackie's my mate. We had breakfast just this morn-ing.' Then he hands the cop a business card that identifies himself as an employee of Brett Kebble's company, JCI. It's another 'Hello' moment.

So now O'Sullivan's got Nassif, Agliotti, the police chief and his mistress locked in a mysterious orbit around Brett Kebble. What makes this particularly intriguing is that Kebble has become very big news in recent weeks. On 30 August 2005, the flamboyant young wheeler-dealer lost control of the mining houses JCI and Randgold in a shareholders' revolt triggered by deepening doubts about his in-tegrity. Forensic accountants are beavering in JCI's books, where they will shortly uncover R2-billion missing. In months to come, some will claim Kebble wanted to die rather than face the music, and was beg-ging connections to help him stage an 'assisted suicide.' Others main-tain he'd lost the confidence of his criminal associates, who suspected he was about to cut a deal with prosecutors and sacrifice them all to save his own neck. Whatever the truth, Kebble dies on the night of 27 September 2005, cut down by seven bullets on his way to a dinner engagement.

Newspapers initially portray the murder as a botched hijacking, but O'Sullivan calls his underworld sources the following morning and hears a different story entirely. They tell him the hit was orchestrated by Agliotti in conjunction with John Stratton, Kebble's partner, and Clinton Nassif, whose bouncers pulled the trigger. They say Agliotti was lurking nearby when the hit went down and called Selebi on his cellphone to report its successful conclusion.

O'Sullivan cannot remotely prove any of this. In fact, the story is so big and strange he can't quite believe it himself, but he trusts his sources and the details are compelling. 'I swallowed hard,' he says. 'I mean, put yourself in my shoes. Who do I tell?' Not the police, is for sure. Nassif's operatives were all over the Kebble murder scene, tampering with evidence and chatting happily with police investigators, one of whom has a brother who worked for the Lebanese businessman's security company. Under the circumstances, O'Sullivan is pretty certain that disclosing his informers' scuttlebutt to police will result in bullets in the head for them. So he starts a process he likens to 'planting a trail of aniseed balls and letting the hounds smell them out.'

In early October 2005, eight days after the murder, he sends the Scorpions 'an overview of personalities around Kebble, mentioning Nassif, Agliotti, Selebi, his girlfriend and many others.' He's hoping this will be enough to get the bloodhounds out, but there's no response. Nothing at all. By Christmas, O'Sullivan has come to the dismaying conclusion that Selebi is truly untouchable. He is wrong.

Enter the Scorpions
The Directorate of Special Operations, aka The Scorpions, was established in 1999 to combat corruption and organised crime. In the years since, the 500-person 'hot squad' has acquired a reputation for nailing its targets. On the other hand, it has a knack for making sure TV cameras are on hand whenever it raids a prominent suspect, which leads to heated charges of trial by media. But this is part of the plan. The Scorpions are designed to appear as Hollywood-style super cops who drive fast cars, carry special weapons and strike unexpectedly. They are supposed to be invincible, incorruptible, deadly. On the day of Kebble's death, they are also in deep political trouble, largely as a result of their pursuit of corruption charges against former Deputy President Jacob Zuma. The Scorpions say they are just doing their job, but Zuma supporters believe President Thabo Mbeki is using them to eliminate 'Msholozi' as a contender for the state presidency.

This argument seems to have some merit, but meanwhile, the growing populist clamour for the Scorpions' disbanding is providing cover for a host of other agendas. ANC parliamentarians are still smarting over the Scorpions' 'Travelgate' case, which led to humiliating fraud convictions against 38 MPs. Western Cape militants are angry about the Scorpions' involvement in the jailing of their hero, MP Tony Yengeni. A Durban-based cabal is furiously resisting the Scorpions' investigation of struggle icon Mac Maharaj, and several ANC figures are anxious about the unit's probe into Kebble, who pumped hundreds of millions of other people's money into 80 flimsy 'joint ventures' with politically connected empowerment types. Against this backdrop, the last thing the Scorpions need is another high-profile investigation of a senior ANC leader, which might explain why O'Sullivan's memo about Selebi has gone unanswered. Behind the scenes, however, trouble is brewing.

The Kebble murder investigation is initially a joint police/Scorpions effort, with the rival forces sharing information and apparently pursuing clues with equal zeal. By January 2006, however, Johannesburg chief prosecutor Charin de Beer has come to suspect something is wrong somewhere. A top secret letter to Mbeki expresses it thus: 'In essence, the complaint was that the National Commissioner of the SAPS, Mr JS Selebi, was perceived to be protecting a target of the investigation.' The letter goes on to state that 'analysis of phone call data' shows 'suspicious' calls between Selebi and certain suspects 'on the night of and after the murder,' and that Selebi has warned these suspects to watch their backs. Only at this point – on 28 March 2006 – is an investigation formally authorised.

Within days, O'Sullivan is summoned to a Sandton coffee shop to meet a fast-talking, chain-smoking Scorpions investigator named Robyn Plitt. She tells him the Scorpions are looking into Selebi's organised crime connections, and that she'd like to compare notes with him. O'Sullivan's heart leaps: at last, a real investigation. 'Think of my situation,' he says. 'You're out there doing your thing in the playground and all the other children are spitting and throwing stones at you and nobody's backing you up. Then all of a sudden you've got 500 guys behind you. I thought, we're on the move at last, so I dropped everything else and ramped up the speed of my investigation. I worked seven days a week, flat out, to bring all the pieces together.'

O'Sullivan says he was operating in accordance with the domino theory of organised crime investigation: you start at the very bottom, catch a small fry, force him to roll over on his boss, and so on up the chain of command. In this case, the bottom is easy to plumb: O'Sullivan knows of an East Rand bar owner whose joint was trashed by CNSG boss Nassif's bouncers when he declined to pay protection. The bar owner provided police with the bouncers' names and closed-circuit TV footage of their rampage, but no arrests were made. O'Sullivan visits the injured party and says, 'Want justice? I can help you.' The bar owner agrees to co-operate.

A second aniseed ball involves a brand-new Mercedes E55, apparently totalled in an accident in 2004. The car belonged to Nassif, who insisted that insurer Lloyds pay him out for his loss. According to O'Sullivan, insurance investigators suspected that there was something fishy about the claim but couldn't prove anything, so Nassif walked off with a cheque for R500 000. Two years later, O'Sullivan asks the insurance assessors to reopen their file for him. They refuse. He speaks to their lawyer, who says, 'I have a wife and kids,' and hangs up.

'I realised I had to start again from scratch,' says O'Sullivan, 'so I went to the scene of the accident looking for tow truck operators. I went back night after night until I found a guy who helped load Nassif's vehicle onto a flatbed. He told me the name of the flatbed driver, and that he lived somewhere in Alexandra township. I drove around Alex for days, knocking on doors. Do you know what it's like, looking for an address in Alex? I made six or seven visits, but in the end I found this guy, and he confirmed what we'd suspected: when Nassif's car was loaded onto that flatbed it had a flat tyre with a damaged rim, nothing else.' O'Sullivan says he booked the driver off work, gave him a stipend and sent him to Cape Town, 'where he could not be got at.' Then he went to the Scorpions with his latest aniseed ball. It subsequently emerged that Nassif took the barely damaged Merc to a panel beater and had it dropped repeatedly off a forklift. After this, the car was indeed a write-off and Nassif was able to file a fraudulent insurance claim that he would come to bitterly regret.

A third aniseed ball involves a trucker who has been doing odd jobs for Glenn Agliotti for years, delivering consignments of drugs, untaxed cigarettes and counterfeit goods. When the Scorpions' Robyn Plitt mentions this guy's name, it rings bells in O'Sullivan's brain. 'I realised I'd met him about ten years earlier, so I set out to find him.' The Irishman traces the trucker, wins his trust and documents every delivery he's ever made for Agliotti. The cherry on the cake is a giant consignment of hashish and compressed marijuana, shipped to South Africa from Iran by an international drugs syndicate a year earlier. Part of the consignment is still sitting in the source's warehouse. The rest is parked on a farm outside town. On 27 April 2006, O'Sullivan meets with the Scorpions at an East Rand McDonald's, where he hands over the trucker and his electrifying information. Ten weeks later, South Africa wakes up to news of a R200-million hashish bust near Benoni. Beyond that point, the dominoes tumble. Confronted with video footage of themselves trashing an East Rand pool hall and other evidence, bouncers Mikey Schultz and Nigel McGurk start cooperating. Nassif collapses when investigators tell him he's going to prison for that fraudulent insurance claim. As for Agliotti, the Benoni hashish bust results in charges likely to earn him 15 years in jail unless he cooperates. By the end of 2006, everyone is talking, and the investigation has moved into realms darker than anything O'Sullivan has ever dreamed of.

According to court documents, the conspiracy dates back to December 2002, when billionaire swindler Brett Kebble learned that the Scorpions were investigating him. Incensed that anyone should treat him thus, Kebble 'initiated a project to get Bulelani Ngcuka and Penuell Maduna out of office.' Safety and Security Minister Maduna was the man who'd ultimately authorised Kebble's investigation, and chief prosecutor Bulelani Ngcuka controlled the Scorpions, who'd carried it out.

These targets placed Kebble in alignment with a powerful ANC faction that was also gunning for Ngcuka, largely on account of his pursuit of corruption charges against Jacob Zuma. According to insiders, Kebble felt that the best way to solve his own legal problems was to support Zuma's counter-attack. His motives were 'purely selfish,' says Kebble biographer Barry Sergeant. 'If he could show that Zuma was the victim of a malicious, politically-based smear campaign, Kebble reasoned, he might also be able to discredit the charges he faced as part of a power-play within the ANC.' Kebble thus became an outspoken Zuma supporter, haranguing journalists about the Scorpions' 'sinister machinations' and financing ANC rebels who shared that view.

Glenn Agliotti came into the picture as a result of his friendship with Jackie Selebi. They'd known each other since the early 1990s, when Selebi was just another penniless returned exile, struggling to survive on an ANC stipend of R3 000 a month. Agliotti settled some medical bills on Selebi's behalf, and Selebi never forgot his kindness. When Selebi became police commissioner, Agliotti let it be known around town that he and 'the chief' were close. It was this connection that brought Brett Kebble and his partner John Stratton to Agliotti's door.

'They wanted to know how much it would take to secure a relationship with Jackie, to have him in their camp,' says one of Agliotti's affidavits. 'I made up my own figure – a million dollars.' Agliotti also suggested that Kebble retain the services of Clinton Nassif, and organised the first of several dinners where police chief Selebi and Kebble met face to face.

In early 2004, Kebble deposited R10.7 million into a slush fund, and cash started flowing to the various conspirators. The lion's share allegedly went to Nassif, who was running a dirty tricks operation that reportedly included the attempted assassination of Stephen Mildenhall, an investment analyst who'd come dangerously close to uncovering Kebble's grand swindle. Agliotti helped himself, too, and 'more than R1.2 million' is said to have gone to Selebi, who allegedly made frequent visits to Agliotti's Midrand office to collect his cut.

Among the scores of affidavits filed in court by the Scorpions was one from Agliotti employee Dianne Muller, who said she was frequently instructed to count and package large amounts of cash allegedly destined for Selebi. In at least one instance, she witnessed the actual handover. Muller said she packed R110 000 in cash in a bag and carried it into the boardroom where Agliotti and Selebi were waiting. Agliotti allegedly took the cash and it slid it across the table to the commissioner, saying, 'Here you go, my china.'

In return, Selebi is said to have lobbied for the Scorpions to be disbanded or placed under his command. In fairness, the police chief was antagonistic towards the Scorpions long before these alleged payments commenced, and Agliotti's claims have yet to be tested in court. But if the drug-dealer is to be believed, Selebi wound up deeply compromised. His successful campaign for the Interpol presidency was allegedly financed by Kebble, at Agliotti's instigation. In return, Selebi is said to have shown Agliotti a top-secret British Customs 'activity report' indicating that he and his hash-smuggling associates were under surveillance in the UK. In June 2006, he passed on a document purporting to show that Paul O'Sullivan had a mole in Clinton Nassif's organisation. As O'Sullivan says, 'This was tantamount to putting out a hit on me, my source and my family.'

With evidence like this, the Scorpions had no further need of O'Sullivan's help. Indeed, court papers indicate that Scorpions investigators were instructed to distance themselves from the Irishman in July 2006 on the grounds that his parallel investigation was threatening to muddy the waters. This didn't suit certain parties, who had been intercepting O'Sullivan's communications, tailing him around town and digging into his background. They'd discovered something that threatened to be hugely embarrassing to Selebi's enemies in the Scorpions.

On 5 November 2006, O'Sullivan records a phone conversation with deputy police commissioner André Pruis, one of the few old-guard police generals to survive the post-1994 purges. Pruis has a background in counter-intelligence. He tells O'Sullivan he knows a spy when he sees one, and as far as he's concerned, the Irishman is exactly that. 'The British high commissioner is on his way right here right now,' Pruis barks, 'and I think you should attend the meeting. I want to know, today, what's going on here!'

Pruis is on to something, because O'Sullivan does indeed have an intelligence background. It's right there in his CV – a cryptic reference to 'foreign intelligence work' during his stint with the British military in the 1970s. O'Sullivan says he can't discuss this aspect of his life, other than to say he went to places he can't name where he did things he can't talk about. But there's little doubt that he's had intelligence training. You see it in the way he drives, the cleansing rites he follows to make sure he's not followed, the psychological tactics he deploys to win the trust of informers: all classic British spycraft, straight out of a John le Carré novel. Pruis says, 'I'm not a moron, Paul. I'm not a child. You run sources. You act as a handler. What is that? It's an intelligence role.'

A few days later, the South African Police Service starts circulating a 'top secret' document in which O'Sullivan is portrayed as 'an active MI5 agent.' The report claims there is 'conclusive evidence'. 'O'Sullivan has been handling human resources, debriefing these resources, conducting electronic, physical and aerial surveillance operations and engaging in covert communications.' Conclusion: The Irishman is engaged in 'a concerted effort to undermine the law enforcement agencies of the state.'

On its face, this sounds persuasive, but the underlying logic is defective. Granted, there was a point where O'Sullivan's behaviour resembled a professional spy's, but since the Scorpions took over the investigation, he has confined himself largely to psychological warfare. A deep-cover secret agent doesn't file lawsuits, shout his mouth off on talk radio or share his gleanings with investigative reporters. He definitely does not call a press conference where he stands up in a firestorm of camera flashes and calls on Selebi to 'resign, finish and *klaar.*' These are, beyond reasonable doubt, the acts of a man with a score to settle.

But South Africa is not the most logical country. When it first emerged that the Scorpions were investigating him, Selebi made a joke of it, turning out his pockets at a press conference to show they weren't stuffed with organised crime cash. Now his prospects are less certain. In this context, the spy charges against O'Sullivan are a masterful countermove, especially when the 'top secret' SAPS report is decoded for its racial content. All but one of the seven investigative reporters imputed to be O'Sullivan's agents are white. Same applies to the six Scorpions investigators supposedly 'linked' to O'Sullivan's alleged destabilisation campaign. These pale-faced sleuths are in turn said to be 'linked' to American, British and German spies stationed at various embassies.

In short, the SAPS is playing the race card, insinuating that the ANC government is once again under attack by hostile racists. The spy allegations make their way into the press, into private security briefings by Selebi's deputy, André Pruis, and ultimately, onto the desk of the state president. Towards the end of November, Thabo Mbeki alludes to O'Sullivan's intelligence background in an address to clergymen, 'supposedly to indicate that this man was undermining our national commissioner at the behest of a foreign government,' as the *Sunday Times* put it.

Did Mbeki really believe this? Is that why he blew up when he learned, nearly a year later, that Chief Prosecutor Vusi Pikoli had obtained a warrant for Selebi's arrest and was about to execute it? Pikoli was fired on the spot. Mbeki initially offered a misleading explanation for his action, and when the truth leaked out, seemed to deny the Selebi warrant's very existence – a development that prompted the police chief to boast, 'I will never be arrested.'

The following morning, senior staff at police headquarters received an anonymous email cautioning against premature celebration. 'Hello Sewer Rats,' it said. 'As I have it, the warrant DOES exist, and you will get your collar grabbed very soon. You pricks will rue the day you decided to use tax-payer's resources in messing with me to protect your criminal friends.' The missive was signed, 'The Scarlet Pimpernel,' but director Selby Bokaba recognised it as Paul O'Sullivan's handiwork. A former journalist who at one point handled communications for chief Selebi, Bokaba claims the Irishman was in the habit of 'bombarding' him with letters and phone-calls wrongfully linking him to a supposed conspiracy.

Irked beyond endurance by this latest accusation, Bokaba decided to respond in kind, informing O'Sullivan that he was entirely unconcerned about an investigation conducted by 'unrepentant former members of the murderous apartheid-era police force,' abetted by 'a failed master spy.' O'Sullivan came back with an even ruder retort, and the exchange degenerated into a slanging match, with O'Sullivan fulminating about criminality in high places while Bokaba longed for 16 December, opening day of the ANC's Polokwane conference, where the Scorpions' enemies were expected to demand the unit's disbanding. 'Your handlers will be history,' wrote Bokaba. 'You'll never set foot in South Africa again, not even under a disguise. Your time is running out! VOETSEK!!!'

Bokaba's reading was accurate in at least one respect: six weeks later, at Polokwane, the ANC was taken over by Jacob Zuma loyalists whose ambiguous platform contained but one solid plank: the Scorpions had to go. A resolution to this effect was passed immediately, but the Scorpions staggered on into 2008, mortally wounded but still capable of delivering one final sting.

On the fourth day of the new year, key witness Glenn Agliotti was summoned to a Sandton hotel where a group of extremely senior ANC officials was waiting to see him. Among the heavyweights present at this meeting were police crime intelligence head Mulangi Mphego, a vocal Selebi loyalist, and National Intelligence Agency boss Manala

Manzini, who described himself as 'the most powerful man in the country.' Apparently feeling that discretion was the better part of valour, Agliotti provided these men with an affidavit saying he'd lied about Selebi at the behest of the Scorpions, who were said to be engaged in a 'political game' aimed at causing the demise of Jacob Zuma and Jackie Selebi 'for the benefit of outside forces, namely the CIA and FBI.'

On 10 January 2008, this bizarre claim formed the centrepiece of an urgent High Court application seeking to quash Selebi's arrest warrant. In response, the Scorpions tabled a second affidavit in which Agliotti withdrew all charges in the first, saying he was drunk at the time and had been misled into signing. Then they pulled a move nobody was anticipating: they laid out their entire case against Selebi – 335 pages of sworn affidavits, each more damning than the last, along with the report of an independent panel that had evaluated the evidence and found that Selebi had a case to answer. Rattled by this show of strength, Selebi's legal team abandoned their application, and the drama proceeded to its denouement: on 1 February 2008, in a blinding blaze of klieg lights, South Africa's top cop appeared in court to face charges of corruption and defeating the ends of justice.

An epilogue

It's a hot summer night, and O'Sullivan is saying goodbye to some friends in Soweto. We don't really know where he came from, or where he's going next. Sometimes he talks of flying to Australia to confront the saturnine John Stratton, alleged to be the mastermind behind Brett Kebble's criminal empire and the ultimate puppeteer in his murder. On other occasions, he seems to be calling from England, but background noise suggests he's really in Cape Town. All that's certain is that he is here tonight, sitting under the stars with a beer in his hand, surrounded by men who admire him hugely.

One is Tebogo Motswai, owner of this joint, a restaurant/bar called The Rock. He says he's known O'Sullivan since the mid-1990s, when the latter was managing director of the Randburg Waterfront. He tells you how the Irishman spruced the place up, drove out the bad elements, and offered him a prime restaurant site in the rejuvenated complex. This leads to a story about O'Sullivan's pioneering efforts to get nervous whites to visit Soweto. He erected a spurious 'whites only' bus stop at the Waterfront, whistled up some transport and, next thing, well-heeled honkeys were coming to Soweto to eat Tebogo's tripe (which is very good, incidentally).

The burly figure seated next to me turns out to be aeronautical engineer Zukile Nomvete, a former executive director of South African Airways. He says he met O'Sullivan in some tourism body where a senior employee had fingers in the till; the Irishman sorted the problem, and they've been friends ever since. Bra Zuki spent several years working in Dublin for Aer Lingus and acquired a liking for Irish jokes. O'Sullivan obliges with an hour-long carnival of ribaldry that leaves the gathering gasping for breath, slapping his back and offering drinks on the house. Is this the performance that won hearts and minds in dark bars and led hard men to entrust a stranger with secrets that could have got them all murdered? It seems likely, but the Irishman doesn't volunteer details.

The charges against Commissioner Selebi remain untested, but those who doubt their gravity should read the charge sheet. O'Sullivan's role is not acknowledged. He isn't even listed as a witness. But there is little doubt that his long and lonely battle for justice helped propel the Selebi case to where it stands today, and South Africa to its moment of truth. Selebi is – or was – a beloved member of the ANC's old guard. His present situation must be a cause of anguish for many comrades in government. But justice is blind, as we know, and it is especially in such cases that justice must be seen to be done. Allowing Jackie Selebi's prosecution to be sabotaged or abandoned will extinguish the last vestige of faith in the rule of law in this country.

Paul O'Sullivan, the butterfly who precipitated this tempest, is confident that South Africa will survive the challenge. 'It's problem/solution, innit?' he says. 'This is a great country. We can't let a few bad men ruin it.' His only regret is that his one-man investigation has left him almost bankrupt and living temporarily in exile. Not for his own sake, he says. He just felt it was unfair to endanger his family's lives, so he moved them to the UK two years ago. He says they're all coming home as soon as it's safe.

'You know what I really want?' he says. 'I want my airport job back. I want to be paid for all the years I wasn't there, and then to finish the job properly.'

Maverick, March 2008

Postscript: After this piece appeared, I had a 'secret' meeting with an anonymous Scorpion who claimed that O'Sullivan had greatly exaggerated his role in the Selebi investigation. This person said the critical breakthrough in the case was the turning of Clinton Nassif. 'Someone else gave us Nassif's head on a plate,' said my informant. 'O'Sullivan had nothing to do with it.' Confronted by this charge, the Irishman just chuckled. 'What the Scorpions don't know,' he said, 'is that I was controlling their source from behind the scenes.' There was no way to know who was telling the truth, so I cancelled plans to publish the story in the UK and turned down an offer to make it into a movie.

Eighteen months later, lawyers acting for embattled police chief Selebi turned up a snippet of evidence indicating that my doubts about O'Sullivan might be misplaced – a document in which Johannesburg chief prosecutor Charin de Beer acknowledges that her fateful January 2006 letter to State President Mbeki (the one in which she claimed that Selebi was in regular contact with suspects in the Brett Kebble murder case and seemed to be attempting to protect them) was prompted in part by information from an unnamed outsider. 'Was that you?' I asked O'Sullivan. 'Of course,' he replied.

On an entirely more riveting level, this story forces one to contemplate the hallucinatory possibility that the overthrow of Mbeki at Polokwane was orchestrated from beyond the grave by Brett Kebble. The grand swindler has certainly achieved what he set out to do in 2002. The once-mighty Bulelani Ngcuka is now isolated and powerless. Former police minister Penuell Maduna went down in flames along with his boss, Thabo Mbeki. The Scorpions no longer exist, and Jacob Zuma, who once enjoyed Kebble's backing, is now president of South Africa.

Report from Planet Mbeki

||||||||||||||||||||||||||||||||||||||||||||||||||||||||||||||||||||||||||||||||||||||||||||||||||||||||||||||||||||||||||||||||||||||||||||||||||||||||||

It seems a wonder that I have any friends at all, given the abuse they have endured over the years. After a dop or two, any mention of the ANC's 'struggle for democracy' always gets me ranting about the movement's slavish pro-Moscow policies during its exile years. 'People who saw the Soviet Union or Cuba as models for a free South Africa were not democrats,' I'd say. 'They were Red Fascists who wanted to put all of us into the Gulag.' Someone at the table would inevitably challenge my analysis, usually citing one of the stellar liberals (usually Allister Sparks or Anthony Sampson) who portrayed the ANC as an army of hymn-singing Uncle Toms who just wanted the vote so they could set up a democracy like Great Britain's. At this point, I'd go apoplectic, but I could never quite sustain my case. I am therefore deeply grateful to Mark Gevisser for settling the issue in my favour.

I'd like to dedicate this essay to my ex-wife, a fiery (as they say) Latin American who looked a bit like Bianca Jagger and had similarly left-ish politics. The Contessa (for that is what I called her) was educated at Brandeis and cut her political teeth on the Left Bank of Paris, where she dated a fashionably radical 'tankie' (one who yearned to see Soviet tanks trundling down the Champs Elysées) and was peripherally involved with an underground Marxist group called Action Directe. She wasn't exactly a Marxist herself but would argue spiritedly on behalf of Castro and Ortega and saw the Soviet Union as an essentially benign country that should be judged on its good intentions (a chicken in every pot and so on) rather than its dismal record of oppression, subversion, incompetence and mass murder.

Why did this glamorous and civilised creature marry a Boer whose idea of a good time was discussing the radically anti-Soviet books of René Dumont (*The Totalitarian Temptation*) and Bernard-Henri Lévy (*Barbarism with a Human Face*)? I guess she enjoyed fighting as much as I did. We fought for years before she lost patience and filed for divorce on the grounds that 'the parties argue continuously.' This was true. We got so good at it that I eventually took to sketching the argument she was about to make before she'd actually made it, in the interests of saving time and getting to the point quicker. This drove the Contessa mad. 'Stop it!' she'd shout. 'You're putting words in my mouth and distorting the context out of all recognition!'

I offer this as a sort of truth-in-journalism disclosure because I am about to pull a similar move on Mark Gevisser, author of *The Dream Deferred*, the ground-breaking new biography of President Thabo Mbeki. Before I do Mr Gevisser the dirty, it seems only fair to acknowledge that his book is a very good one, offering some staggering insights into the forces that shaped our enigmatic president.

I particularly enjoyed the opening movements, in which Gevisser sketches the life and times of Mbeki's forebears, ineffably civilised African Victorians who owned land, qualified for the vote and schooled their offspring to become lawyers, mathematicians and classical composers. His maternal grandfather, Jacane Moerane, was even a settler of sorts, sent into darkest Africa by foreign powers (the Basotho king and the Paris Evangelical Mission Society) to colonise territory on the western fringe of the Xhosa empire. Jacane built a forbidding stone mansion that looked out over hundreds of cultivated hectares and lush pastures in which grazed a herd of 130 prize dairy cattle. Almost but not quite as grand was the homestead of Skelewu Mbeki, a headman of the Mfengu, who fought for Queen Victoria in the frontier wars of the nineteenth century and were rewarded with grants of land in the buffer zone between anxious white farmers and the barbarous tribesmen of the Xhosa hinterland.

The Moeranes and Mbekis were devout Christians, so it was entirely natural that their children Govan and Epainette should become Communists. The Contessa would never concede the link, but as I saw it, even a cursory reading of Milan Kundera revealed that the state of 'lyrical delirium' experienced by Marxist converts was closely akin to the bliss on offer in Christian churches; both were redemptive faiths, neither was entirely rational, and both murdered scores of millions in pursuit of their respective utopias. Govan Mbeki was a particularly earnest convert, turning his back on a Durban teaching career and dragging his young wife off to a remote corner of the Transkei to found a cooperative trading store. Their dream, says Gevisser, was to uplift the peasantry and bring light to a place of darkness. In other words, they were missionaries.

And so it came to pass that Thabo Mbeki was born on the cusp of a kingdom he didn't quite understand and never felt part of: the kingdom of the *amaqaba*, the raw Xhosa peasantry. The Mbekis did not mix, as it were. They took a dim view of feudal tribal structures and did not perform traditional rites or send their eldest son to circumcision school. Indeed, says Gevisser, the scholarly young Thabo was usually to be found in his father's study, imbibing revolutionary doctrines, while his mother ran the cooperative. Sadly, it failed to prosper, and by the time Thabo was ten, his father had returned to the city to pursue a career as a journalist and agitator.

Thabo did his A-levels in 1961, and fled the country a year later, one of 25 young students deployed by the ANC to acquire skills and begin the arduous task of rebuilding the recently banned movement in exile. This is Thabo's version, at any rate. One of his comrades, Vincent Mahali, told Gevisser that only seven of the fugitives were committed ANC activists, the rest being PAC or non-aligned civilians who wanted only to escape apartheid and get an education. Alas, poor Mahali: he wound up in the Soviet Union, 'where he found the Stalinist strictures of his new environment even more oppressive than apartheid.' Thabo was more fortunate: as an ANC blueblood and a bright lad besides, he was deployed to the University of Sussex, an experimental left-wing campus where nutty professors gave lectures on subjects about which they knew nothing in order to 'liberate ourselves and the students.'

According to Gevisser, Thabo was initially miffed to find himself at this hare-brained institution, rather than Oxford or Cambridge, but he eventually settled down and spent five magical years studying economics and doing what students do – drinking, partying, listening to jazz and sleeping with girls newly liberated by the advent of The Pill. In Gevisser's account, young Thabo was something of a ladykiller, his allure hugely enhanced by the mystique of the revolutionary engaged in dashing underground work for a fashionable cause. The president-to-be organised anti-apartheid marches, boycotted Outspan oranges and led a delegation to a youth conference in East Germany, where he was photographed demonstrating the gumboot dance and the kwela.

These photographs are a crushing blow to those who joke of Mbeki as the stiffest man in Africa. He was a beautiful young man, lean, lithe and starry-eyed, and very sexy (buy the book, you'll see). Gevisser says these pictures hold a special poignancy for him, for it was the last time in years, perhaps ever, that his subject would look free and happy. The Sussex idyll was drawing to a close, and Thabo was about to vanish into the dark Leninist maw of the ANC underground.

I must stress that I am not even paraphrasing Gevisser here; he's a sweetie who would never dream of saying anything unkind about fellow leftists. Indeed, he'll be appalled to think his fastidious prose should inspire such an uncouth conclusion, but I can't help myself: the ANC in exile was a Leninist organisation, and anyone who says otherwise is flat wrong. During the Cold War, the ANC's liberal supporters took their cues from apologists like Thomas Karis, an influential commentator who repeatedly assured Americans that only three of the 30 men on the ANC's National Executive were Reds, with the balance made up of hymn-singing Uncle Toms and bourgeois democrats. Karis was a useful idiot. Also wrong was the journal *Africa Confidential*, whose seemingly authoritative sources claimed the true number was 12. The Boers in Pretoria charged that 23 of the top 30 were Communists, but nobody took them seriously and they were off the mark anyway: according to Gevisser, ANC records reveal that all but one of the potentates who sat on the movement's National Executive in the seventies were secretly members of the Communist Party.

This is a staggering revelation. You have to be a Cold Warrior to get the joke, so I won't belabour it here, but I will say this: unless you have some sort of understanding of what it meant to be a disciplined Communist in the era of Soviet hegemony, you have no hope of understanding Mbeki. His courage will be invisible to you, and his triumphs will seem as nothing. Even his present political problems will remain opaque, because they too are rooted in the ANC's Leninist genetic code and best understood as the latest phase of an ideological battle that's been underway for decades.

Thanks to Gevisser, we can even pinpoint the very first skirmish. It took place on 14 April 1967, when police were called to a

Moscow youth hostel to save Thabo from a beating at the hands of drunken comrades who accused him of being some sort of counter-revolutionary double agent.

According to Gevisser, the ANC's hardliners disliked Mbeki from the get-go. They saw him as an arrogant toff whose nepotistic connections got him goodies (a scholarship to Sussex and a seat on the National Executive) undreamed-of for the rank and file, who were mostly stuck in grim Russian institutions or forlorn African military camps. They also resented his tweedy, English squire style, his fondness for the better things (good whiskey and debonair suits) and his reluctance to go on active service with MK. In years to come, they would add a much more serious grievance: Thabo was not securely committed to the quasi-religious doctrines of Leninism.

Liberals like the aforementioned Thomas Karis would say this proves their point: the ANC was actually a broadly social democratic movement, full of non-Communists dedicated to fostering Western-style freedoms. Not so: everyone important in the ANC was a Communist, including Thabo himself. According to Gevisser, the ANC's Swedish backers were shocked to hear that the suave, apparently free-thinking Thabo Mbeki was secretly in league with Moscow's troglodytes. Same applies to the legions of businessmen, intelligence operatives and Broederbond leaders who succumbed to Thabo's charm in the talks-about-talks phase of the 1980s. There is no doubt that Thabo presented himself to Westerners as a liberal who cherished all the freedoms they themselves held dear, but there is no way he would have said the same things at a meeting of the SACP's Politburo. Are you mad? They would have locked him up in a mental asylum to be treated for what Russians called 'psycho-social deviationism.'

Gevisser asked Mbeki when his faith in Communism began to waver and got a vague answer about the discontent displayed by an apparatchik who guided Mbeki and his wife around East Germany in the 1980s. As Gevisser says, there was something 'oddly disingenuous and not entirely credible' about this, given that Mbeki had been visiting the Soviet bloc since the sixties and knew all about its food queues, drabness and suffocating security apparatus. It seems more likely that his disenchantment began as early as 1978, when he got into a very nasty scrape in Lusaka.

Having lived in the West, Mbeki understood the power of the media and the ease with which they could be manipulated. He therefore urged his boss, Oliver Tambo, to allow the US television network CBS to make a documentary about the ANC's 'Battle for South Africa.' As Thabo anticipated, the resulting film was a huge propaganda coup, with the ANC coming off as the good guys and the Boers as bigoted McCarthyites. But the hardliners were too rigid to understand this. All they knew was that Thabo was talking to the enemy, and next thing, the ANC's dreaded security service – Mbokodo, the grinding stone – had listed him as a CIA agent and put watchers on his trail. In that dark period, says Gevisser, Mbeki often sought refuge in the home of a friend who got the impression that he feared he was about to be assassinated.

Gevisser will probably say that I am laying undue emphasis on this incident and spinning it for my own devious ends. This is true, but I have justification: he thinks his book is about Mbeki's role in apartheid's downfall, but between the lines, it's actually the story of one man's brave and lonely struggle to outwit Communist hardliners and drag the ANC into the modern era.

In this, Mbeki's chief antagonist was Joe Slovo, the ideologue who ran the military wing and laid down the sacred doctrines that would lead to socialist utopia. According to Gevisser, Slovo and Mbeki's antipathy came to a head in 1982, around the time Pik Botha caused a furore by telling white South Africa he'd be happy to serve under a black president. Meanwhile, a vaguely similar contretemps was brewing inside the ANC, triggered by Slovo's desire to become chairman of the Communist Party. Mbeki disapproved, pointing out that in terms of the movement's two-stage revolutionary theory, the boss of the Communist Party would ultimately become the president of South Africa, and he doubted that the African masses were ready to accept a white ruler.

Slovo was outraged, describing Thabo's position as 'inflammatory' and 'dangerously racist' and ordering him to appear before the SACP's Politburo, an organ so deeply secret that most comrades weren't even aware of its existence. Mbeki ducked the confrontation, but he was disciplined *in absentia* and Slovo had his way. On the day of his investiture as SACP chairman, Thabo turned to a sidekick and said, 'That's the end of the party.'

And so it was, in the long run. Over the years, Mbeki had made himself indispensable to ANC president Oliver Tambo, the only member of the National Executive who never joined the Communist conspiracy. He'd also concluded that the armed struggle was a hopeless affair, and that it was time to start looking towards a negotiated settlement. With Tambo's blessing, Mbeki started meeting anyone with influence.

Hardliners like Slovo and Chris Hani were deeply suspicious. As far as they were concerned, negotiations were fine, so long as the object was to lull the enemy into lowering his guard. But they suspected – correctly as it turns out – that Mbeki was negotiating in earnest, and that was heresy. Luckily, Mbeki was a convincing dissembler, capable of proceeding straight from a meeting in which he assured Pretoria that the ANC was ready to negotiate to a Communist Party conclave where he drafted a resolution calling for 'seizure of power' through 'mass insurrection.'

Asked about such duplicity, Mbeki told Gevisser, 'Some people were hostile to negotiation. They saw it as selling out, treachery.' His solution was to feign belief in the military option while pursuing more promising initiatives behind Slovo and Hani's backs. By 1988, he and the Leninists were living on different planets. When the Soviets asked about prospects for the future, Chris Hani warned them to expect another ten years of armed struggle. Mbeki said, 'We'll be home by 1990.' And lo.

By the time the hardliners' jets touched down on South African soil, the Berlin Wall had fallen and Communism as we knew it was dying. It was a time of agony for true believers. Chris Hani staggered dazed and blinking into the media spotlight, uttering robotic lines about the 'glorious' Bolshevik revolution of October 1917. Joe Slovo presented himself as a born-again democrat, but when Moscow hardliners attempted to overthrow the reformer Gorbachev and restore Communist dictatorship, his party sent the plotters a premature message of congratulation.

Such men were loath to see Mbeki walk off with the laurels, so they staged a 'palace coup' in 1991, axing Thabo's then-ally Jacob Zuma as ANC intelligence chief and toppling Mbeki from his lofty post as head of negotiations. With Cyril Ramaphosa as their point man, they proceeded to play what Gevisser calls 'an intensely dangerous game of brinkmanship,' taking up positions they knew would force a breakdown of peace talks and then launching a campaign of 'rolling mass action,' with uncontrollable crowds replacing Soviet tanks as the weapon that would finally crush the enemy and usher in the socialist millennium.

Thabo warned them that this was a foolish course, but no one listened. 'I was alone,' he told Gevisser. 'I was alone.' Thabo was right; the anticipated crowds failed to materialise, the enemy stood firm, and the hardliners learned their lesson: talk was the only way. Beyond that point, the revolutionaries faded away, and we achieved a happy ending.

Or did we?

Mark Gevisser's book launch at Wits Great Hall was an extraordinary event, not least because of the crowd it drew. It was like a who's-who of Johannesburg's intelligentsia, and their presence spoke volumes about our fascination with the inscrutable and unfathomable Mbeki. The audience was thirsting for insight, but I knew nobody would mention what Gevisser calls 'the two-ton Russian bear' in the room with us. We heard learned talk about history, revolutionary idealism and psychoanalytic paradigms, but not a word about Communism. That's because South Africa's chattering classes are rather like my beloved ex-wife: they think it is bad form even to mention the ANC's long love-affair with left-wing totalitarianism.

I have a wise friend who says, 'Truth has its own sound; we know it when we hear it.' I have read all the major books about South Africa's transition, and most rang false to me, largely because their authors believed (or pretended to believe) that the Communist plot was a bogeyman conjured up by Pretoria's evil racists. Gevisser is the first to put the Red Faith at centre stage, and that's why his book stands head and shoulders above its rivals.

In a way, it's a pity that Gevisser doesn't share my dim view of the Reds, or my glee at the manner in which Mbeki outwitted them, because it could have turned his biography into a thriller. For him, it is more a case of Thabo good, Leninists good too, with rival factions pursuing 'parallel paths' to a similar end. This even-handedness saps his narrative of drama and contributes to its exhausting length, but still: he has put the truth on the table, and succeeded in what he set out to do: 'give Mbeki his rightful place as the primary architect of post-apartheid South Africa.'

I closed *The Dream Deferred* feeling great admiration for Thabo Mbeki. He had the courage to confront an overwhelming Leninist majority, and the brains to see that negotiation was necessary and inevitable. Once in power, he turned his back on failed socialist nostrums and pursued economic policies he knew would make him unpopular with his own constituency and vulnerable to attacks from the left. Willingness to court unpopularity is the only true test of a politician's integrity, and by that reckoning, Mbeki is a great man.

Which is not to say he's not riddled with flaws. My opinion, for whatever it's worth, is that the president is something of a megalomaniac, driven by a vision he's never been able to share. In the bad old days of Red hegemony, it would have got him shot as a traitor. More recently, he had to watch his words for fear of instigating precisely the sort of left-wing backlash now unfolding inside the ANC. The Mbeki vision is what you see when you walk out your front door: a bourgeois democracy with free speech, free markets, a fairly healthy capitalist economy and the emerging trappings of an African welfare state, with 12 million of the poorest poor receiving grants from the state.

I suspect Mbeki expects us to say thank you, and beg him to stay on for ever as our philosopher-king. Instead, we moan about his autocratic style, refuse to forgive his Aids dissidence and the arms deal, trash his judgement as regards Zimbabwe and denounce his handling of corruption scandals. Being a megalomaniac who struggles to distinguish between himself and the state, Mbeki interprets all this as proof of a racist counter-revolutionary plot and reacts accordingly, lashing out at imaginary enemies, using state security apparatus against political opponents and generally spreading poison in our society.

Unfortunately, these recent developments are not covered in *The Dream Deferred*. One gets the impression that Gevisser had excellent inside sources on the rise of Thabo Mbeki, but once he entered the presidency, the doors closed, and now you might as well ask me what goes on in the presidential brain. If you want to know how we got here, Gevisser's book is the one to read. But if you want to know where we're going ...

Empire, January 2008

Return of the Unlikeable Mr Roberts

||||||||||||||||||||||||||||||||||||||||||||||||||||||||||||||||||||||||||||||||||||||||||||||||||||||||||||||||||||||||||||||||||||||||||||||||||||||||

In the early weeks of 2007, an anonymous Deep Throat left an unmarked package on **Noseweek's** *doorstep. It came from the presidency, and contained an unpublished manuscript. Over the next several weeks, it dawned on us that this manuscript was a critical part of Thabo Mbeki's campaign to hold on to power and crush those who were plotting to usurp his throne.*

Newspapers often gave the impression that those usurpers were motivated by admiration of Jacob Zuma, or alienated by Mbeki's haughty leadership style. Some even imagined they were pissed off about Mbeki's policies on Aids or Zimbabwe. Not so. The central issue was 'the class project of 1996,' left-wing jargon for the free market policies adopted that year, largely at Mbeki's instigation. The Communists and trade unionists who once controlled the ANC were not even consulted, and they never forgave Mbeki. As Polokwane neared, it became clear that they were throwing their organisational might behind Zuma, and that Mbeki was seriously threatened.

It therefore became necessary for Mbeki to smokkel with the brains of the ANC intelligentsia, an art at which he'd always been adept. In the 1980s, as we've seen, he convinced the radical insurrectionists that he was one of them, even as he pursued peace talks behind their backs. Twenty years later, the position was reversed: Mbeki had to convince his critics that, appearances to the contrary, he remained a dedicated revolutionary. The presidency found a writer willing to apply himself to this curious endeavour, and Deep Throat had supplied us with the first draft of his efforts.

I wouldn't say Ronald Suresh Roberts is exactly a friend, but I have had the pleasure of sitting opposite him at a few dining tables, and he is outrageously rude and opinionated in a very witty way. Roberts loves ideas, especially his own, but his *pensées* are provocative and there's something totally disarming about the delight he takes in formulating a deadly argument and detonating it in your face. Not everyone's cup of tea, of course, but in my book there's nothing like an uproar to get a party really going. So the truth, then: I like the famously unlikeable Ronald Roberts.

And furthermore: I like the fact that Roberts has rendered himself particularly unlikeable to the pompous and self-regarding English-speaking left-liberal elite. Arriving in SA in 1994, he had the smarts to realise that the Afrikaner horse had long since been flogged to death, so he proceeded to suck up to and then fight with some very prominent English personages – newspaper editor Ken Owen, cabinet minister Kader Asmal and anti-apartheid novelist Nadine Gordimer, who made the mistake of anointing Roberts her official biographer.

Roberts says he reveres Gordimer, but nevertheless found it necessary to disclose some minor inconsistencies and peccadilloes unearthed in her papers. At one of the aforementioned dinners, he spoke for instance of a letter in which The Struggle's literary queen complained that her black domestics were stealing the sugar. The high-minded Nadine objected to the inclusion of such lowly tittle-tattle, and when Roberts declined to excise it, withdrew her blessing, whereupon Roberts's US and UK publishers dropped the book. Roberts charged hypocrisy and censorship. Nadine claimed breach of faith. It was a most amusing literary scandal.

Shortly thereafter, Roberts famously lost his libel suit against the *Sunday Times*, which had run an article describing him as 'unlikeable.' Judge Leslie Weinkove sided with the paper, finding that Roberts was 'venomous,' 'vindictive,' 'grandiose,' 'arrogant' and 'obsessed.' Roberts's enemies were delighted, but I saw no reason to revise my opinion: it is precisely such qualities that I value in the man.

It therefore pains me to say I am disappointed by Roberts's latest endeavour, a corporate-sponsored opus on the thoughts of President Thabo Mbeki. No, you haven't seen it yet. The manuscript that turned up on *Noseweek*'s doorstep was emblazoned with warnings reading, 'Personal and confidential. Strictly no distribution.' One gathers it is a near-final draft of a work commissioned in controversial circumstances in 2003 or thereabouts and delivered to the presidency more than a year ago. According to STE Publishers' website, the book –

titled, *Fit to Rule? Thabo Mbeki's Native Intelligence* – should have been in the shops long ago, but something appears to have gone wrong somewhere. Could it be that Roberts's political sponsors feel he has failed to put the president's critics to the sword in the manner envisaged?

At the outset, Roberts appeared to be the ideal swordsman. He was combative, abrasive and very clever, with degrees from Oxford and Harvard and an almost pathological abhorrence for liberals, especially white ones. His thesis is that the downfall of apartheid forced these hypocrites out of the closet. While the Boers were in power, they could pose as friends of the native, but now they stand revealed for what they really are: reactionaries bent on undermining the Mbeki presidency.

Roberts takes his title from a 2001 editorial in which the *Mail & Guardian* opined that Mbeki's curious views on Aids rendered him unfit to rule. Roberts has conniptions about such statements, ascribing them to a disease he calls 'Eurosis,' short for Eurocentric neurosis. In his view, Eurosis permeates SA's mass media, which 'represents the views, values and interests of the white minority' and therefore denies the native intellectual a fair hearing. Thus stymied, the president was forced to resort to 'cyberspace samizdat' in order to get his views heard. Here we refer of course to the president's weekly internet letter, which Roberts lauds as a noble attempt to defy 'the guile-and-spin culture that has vulgarized politics elsewhere and has enslaved western political leaders to media moguls.'

Roberts is at pains to stress that Mbeki is no mere politician, just as he himself is no mere biographer. 'There are people who are interested in writing what is called Mbeki's "biography,"' he says. 'I am not one of them.' The reason for this is that, 'No soul is knowable by another.' In Roberts's view, it is thus futile to dig into Mbeki's life when all that is knowable is 'his intellectual and political tradition.' Focusing on this is good, says Roberts, because it forces us to turn away 'from personality to discourse, from individuality to lineage, from the sectional to the capacious, and from the parochial to the global.'

This then is a work on the thoughts of Thabo Mbeki, as laid out in his weekly column and elsewhere – a dull idea if ever there was one. The president's writing style is solemn and ponderous. Any writings about the presidential writings were therefore doomed from the outset to be ponderous to the power of ten. Roberts attempts to liven the proceedings with attacks on Mbeki's enemies, but these are so over-cooked and poorly executed that they serve only to irritate. But what the heck, let's give them an airing.

Those who would judge the president are very confused, says Roberts. Some call him 'stubborn;' others say, 'pragmatic.' He is a 'black Englishman,' but also a rabid Africanist. A 'dangerous Marxist,' but also a free-market capitalist. A Stalinist bully and a concilia-tor. On occasion, 'just plain mad.' Roberts undertakes to unravel this enigma and reveal what really drives the man, but his answer is even more complicated than the question posed, so let's turn to DA re-searcher James Myburgh for a pithy summation: anyone who imag-ines that Mbeki is a centrist is 'mistaking patience for moderation.' Roberts loathes Myburgh, but their conclusions are similar: the presi-dent is an unreconstructed leftist, working patiently towards radical transformation.

Roberts believes that whites (including lefties like those at the *M&G*) are very uncomfortable with Mbeki's veiled radicalism, and that some self-loathing blacks don't like it much either. These 'Eurotics' believe that in a 'proper' democracy Mbeki would long since have been thrown out of office, and it irks them beyond endurance that he should continue to head 'a movement that has the largest democratic mandate in the world.' Roberts goes on to compare Mbeki to Franklin Roosevelt, who was also denigrated as a potential dictator and 'clini-cally insane' by his right-wing enemies. But that was just politics. Attacks on Thabo, says Roberts, are a larger crime. 'They are attacks upon the native mind.'

Ouch! What a pompous and stupid thing to say! It occurs fairly early in the draft manuscript, and Roberts never quite recovers. This is a pity, because he makes some telling points in the president's defence. It is true, as he says, that 'Thabo Mbeki is weirdly on trial,' and that some of the charges laid against him are false. Likening his leadership style to Stalin's, as the *M&G* once did, was far-fetched, and *The Economist* erred in calling him 'Africa's Intolerant Leader.' After all, if he was truly intolerant, I wouldn't be writing this, and you wouldn't be reading it. Rising to Mbeki's defence is a worthy endeavour, but Roberts puts a noose around his neck with that re-mark about 'the native mind.' Why? Because it dooms him to argue

Mbeki is beyond reproach, while all criticism is the product of racist dementia.

Consider, for instance, the contortions to which Roberts subjects himself in his efforts to pillory DA leader Tony Leon. We are informed that Tony delighted his mother by proclaiming, at age six, that he intended to be prime minister when he grew up. In time, Tony realised this was impossible. According to Roberts, Leon's life therefore 'looks like a failure from its inside ... unless he can change his goals and prove that it is the world that is out of joint, for only a world that is out of joint could deny him a job that was predestined to be his. Therefore, the post-apartheid world must indeed be out of joint, and this self-appointed Samson must pull its pillars down. Therefore, the agenda is relentlessly negative.'

This is a bit rich, coming from a writer who a few pages earlier was trashing William Mervyn Gumede for resorting to similar pop-psychology 'mind-gazings' in a rival work on Mbeki. Putting such rubbish into print, says Roberts, is 'an exercise in mere invective.' Well, exactly. It would have helped if Roberts cited a few examples of irrational negativity on Leon's part, but the closest we get is a passage where Leon has the gall to demand that government protect citizens from crime. Roberts sniffs, 'I suppose he meant the piecemeal barbarity of suburban crime rather than the far larger and systematic crime against humanity of which his intellectual forefather, Lord Acton, was a notable backer.'

Acton is the man who made up the famous saw about power corrupting and absolute power corrupting absolutely. It irks Roberts no end that white liberals and newspaper editors are forever throwing that line in Mbeki's face, so he starts by noting that they inevitably garble the quote – Acton actually said, 'Power *tends* to corrupt,' not power corrupts. After this pedantic flounce, Roberts explains that Lord Acton was actually a 'grossly authoritarian' fellow who occupied a rotten borough in the British parliament, supported slavery and thought fondly of despots like Frederick the Great. In other words, Acton wasn't a liberal at all, and yet his aphorism has become 'the crux of the so-called liberal agenda in SA.' One concedes this is an amusing irony, but to offer it as a retort to Leon's anxiety about crime is ... demented?

But then Roberts isn't really interested in crime or any other aspect of Mbeki's performance in office. He is interested in Pure Thought. Most of the 'action' in his book takes the form of a theoretical dog-fight between Mbeki's impi (featuring Frantz Fanon, Edward Said, Mao, Marx, Robespierre and kindred 'progressive' intellectuals) and imperialist reactionaries like Churchill, Rhodes and Macaulay. These Tories are the bad guys, while Mbeki exists 'within another leadership tradition, beyond the supposed politics of personal merit, Western spin-culture and parliamentary careerism.' From this lofty position, he looks down on his critics with amused compassion, referring to one as 'our white politician.'

Roberts loves this 'plural possessive gesture,' which serves 'to domesticate that politician as one contains a pet.' It is incidentally insulting, says Roberts, but what is really telling here is Mbeki's 'larger dismissiveness towards the role of mere politician.' When it comes to assessing Mbeki's greatness, says Roberts, 'other criteria are necessary.' And what are these? 'Drawing upon the spirit of Paulo Freire in *Pedagogy of the Oppressed*, Mbeki in fact sees the vocation of the intellectual as a humanizing one in that it is committed to the power of thought to negate accepted limits and open the way to a new future.'

Phew. Okay. Now we know.

It is not nice to critique a fellow writer on the basis of a work in progress. Maybe Ronald is aware that his MS is boring and in parts, impenetrable. Maybe there is a later draft in which these defects are corrected. So why run a story at this point? Because this is no ordinary book. In 2004, the opposition asked cabinet heavyweight Essop Pahad if the presidency had facilitated a book deal for Roberts. Pahad said, 'No.' Now Pahad stands accused of lying to parliament, because it turns out that he did indeed write a letter to Absa inquiring if the bank would be so kind as to pay Mr Roberts a lot of money to write a book about Mr Mbeki. Absa agreed, and a contract was drafted. Roberts was to get an office in the presidency. He was to be allowed 'unprecedented' access to presidential activities, and his work, when done, would be submitted to Pahad for approval. Absa's role was to foot the bill. As of last year, it had paid out a reported R1.43 million

Was the exercise worth it? I think not. If anything, this book is another setback for Mbeki, at least to the extent that it makes him seem a world champion bore. Is he really as drear as Roberts paints him? I doubt it. There is a passage in this book, about five typed pages long, where the leaden procession of ponderous ideas suddenly bursts into technicolour. It is 2004, and Mbeki is on the campaign trail, jacket slung over his shoulder, sleeves rolled up, visiting poor whites in Pretoria. Oddly, they are very pleased to meet their native president. Little old ladies get all tearful and say, 'Jesus went to the poor. It is good that you, like Him, come here.' A *dronkie* runs to fetch a whiskey bottle when he sees the president coming, because he's hoping that he and Bra Thabs can have a dop together. Mbeki even cracks wry jokes at his own expense. 'Do you play golf?' 'In theory, yes.'

Mbeki and the poor whites get along so well that he invites three of them to come with him to meet Charlize Theron at some glitzy function. The sycophantic Roberts strives to read moral grandeur into this gesture, but of course it's just politics as usual. The president has come down from ideological outer space to press flesh and kiss babies, and so help me God, he seems to be enjoying himself. What's more, we like him! For a moment, he comes across as a *lekker ou*, relaxed and charming. But then the clouds of obfuscation close in again, and we return to the leaden plodding.

Let's accept Robert's premise that souls are unknowable, and Mbeki is best judged by writings that offer insight into the processes of his vast mind. If this is indeed the case, there were grounds to hope that Roberts would at last reveal the logic underlying Mbeki's two most famous policy conundrums – Aids and Zimbabwe. For what did Absa pay R1.43 million, if not an explanation of presidential thoughts on these critical issues?

Alas, Roberts fluffs it. By the time he gets to Aids, he's exhausted, prose degenerating into a confused shambles. He makes a half-hearted attempt to show that ANC policy on Aids has always been 'progressive,' tosses in a few quotes about Victorian superstitions regarding Africans as vectors of disease, and then turns the spotlight on RW Johnson, the 'hysterical neo-colonialist' who informed readers of *The Spectator* that Mbeki's utterances on Aids caused some to mutter that the president was 'off his rocker.' Johnson is portrayed as a dubious character who believes that 'relaxed acceptance of things that are crazy, macabre or wildly alarming is very African.' Phew! Can't have that, can we? It's an insult to the native mind. 'This racism,' says Roberts, sidestepping the Aids issue entirely, 'has defined us who are Africans as primitive. It has left us with a legacy that compels us to fight for the transformation of ours into a non-racial society.'

As for Zimbabwe ... by the time he gets there, Roberts has had it; the horse refuses the jump. In the present draft, the Zimbabwe chapter consists of a single quote, spoken by Mbeki in 2002: 'Our peoples across our common border see one another as brothers and sisters,' said Mbeki, 'linked together by history, by a common suffering ... The people of Zimbabwe know we will not abandon them in their greatest hour of need.'

This is entirely fanciful, but I can't help thinking Roberts suffered a nervous breakdown after typing that quote. I imagine him sitting for hours, days, staring at those words and coming slowly to the grim realisation that he would never be able to write his way around them. He'd spent the previous 353 pages shitting on Eurotics and hammering home the message that Mbeki is an unrepentant progressive whose commitment to democracy in its truest, deepest sense is beyond all question. And then comes the moment everyone is waiting for, the moment where Roberts is called upon to reveal how Thabo Mbeki's 'quiet diplomacy' helped the nation that quails under Mugabe's lash. And it simply can't be done.

But what do I know? Ronald is a resourceful chap. Perhaps he took a holiday, returned refreshed, and proceeded to write a masterful passage demonstrating how critiques of Mbeki's Zimbabwe policy are actually attacks on the native mind. Or perhaps he just accepted the consequences of selling out and asked the presidency to dictate the Zimbabwe chapter. We'll see when the finished product arrives on the bookshelves.

Meanwhile, I find myself struggling to reconcile this tedious manuscript with the electric personality on display at bibulous dinner parties. Roberts is not ashamed to liken himself to Oscar Wilde, but man cannot live on *bons mots* alone. He must have funds to maintain his style. Since arriving here, 'Ron the Con,' as columnist John Matshikiza calls him, has proved uncannily adept at ingratiating himself with the rich and powerful and manipulating them for personal advancement. In several cases, the benefactors have emerged sadder but wiser, with bitten hands. But they were relatively small fry, and easily containable, as one might contain a pet. Thabo Mbeki and Essop Pahad are far bigger game.

If it is true that Roberts has occupied an office alongside theirs for several years while enjoying 'unprecedented' access to their activities, one assumes he is now privy to secrets that could truly unravel the Mbeki enigma. Has he shared them? Clearly not. Talking out of turn could be risky, so Roberts did the sensible thing – wrote a load of impenetrable academic hooey, and walked away with nearly R1.5 million.

Clever boy. I look forward to our next encounter.

Noseweek, March 2007

Ugly Scenes in Boer Provence

On the day that Bob Mugabe's genocidal regime acceded to the chair of the UN's Commission on Sustainable Development, I found myself in the lovely Cape village of Franschhoek, once a Boer farming town but now more French and precious than Provence itself. Even as bitter debate broke out in the distant UN, I was checking into a luxurious hostelry and trimming my nostril hairs in preparation for meeting such luminaries as Liz Calder, publisher of the Harry Potter books, and Siri Hustvedt, a glamorous blonde novelist who is apparently world famous in your hemisphere. We had come to participate in the inaugural Franschhoek Literary Festival, but my thoughts were in New York with UK Environment Minister Ian Pearson, who was attempting to convince African diplomats that one could not appoint a malignant regime like Zimbabwe's to the chair of anything, let alone a committee on development. The Africans did not take this kindly. 'It's an insult to our intelligence,' said Boniface Chidyausiku, Zimbabwe's UN ambassador. Most African delegates agreed, and Pearson went down in flames, victim of what the press called an 'overwhelming' snub to the West.

I first saw Robert Mugabe in the flesh at a UN Earth Summit in Johannesburg in 2002. His appearance on the podium was preceded by US Defense Secretary Colin Powell, who was booed and jeered, and by Tony Blair, who met with similar indignities. Mugabe, on the other hand, was greeted by a tumultuous standing ovation. It was shocking to see diplomats according such an honour to a malevolent little shit whose genocidal proclivities were already apparent, but I wrote it off as a passing fad. At the time, black power fanatics were still pumped up over Mugabe's ethnic cleansing of white farmers, and one assumed their enthusiasm would wear off once the consequences of his folly manifested themselves.

Not so. By 2004, Zimbabwe's economy was in freefall and his subjects were growing hungry, but Mugabe was more popular than ever in the black diaspora. He received standing ovations in many African capitals. At President Thabo Mbeki's 2004 swearing-in ceremony he had an entire stadium on its feet. By then, it was clear that Mugabe's 'fast-track land reform programme' had reversed his popularity at home, forcing him to resort to bludgeoning opponents and rigging elections in order to stay in power. His black supporters didn't care at all. Mugabe was giving the whites hell. Mugabe was therefore a hero. 'Mugabe is speaking for black people worldwide,' wrote Johannesburg commentator Harry Mashabela.

One assumes this accounts for the Mbeki administration's reluctance to criticise Mugabe in public. We were told that the situation in Zimbabwe was very delicate, and that 'quiet diplomacy' offered the best shot at staving off anarchy. For a while this seemed plausible, but in time it became clear that quiet diplomacy was mostly a cover for covert support. Western moves to expel Mugabe from the Commonwealth were initially blocked by Thabo Mbeki. He also blocked attempts to place Mugabe's atrocities on the agenda at the UN Security Council and the UN Human Rights Committee. These developments allowed Comrade Bob's popularity in the black diaspora to swell to rock star proportions. Last year, the cocky little psychopath informed an audience of African-American New Yorkers that his rule had created 'an unprecedented era of peace and tranquillity' back home. They gave him a standing ovation.

One understands the wounds of history, but even so, one thought there would come a day when Mugabe's fans realised their hero's behaviour was restoring the reputation of Ian Smith, widely reviled for predicting that Rhodesia would be buggered if blacks took over. Well, they took over, and Smith stands vindicated. Today's Zimbabwe is a very sad place. Eight out of ten citizens are jobless, and those who have work are screwed too, because inflation is 2 200 per cent and they can't afford food anyway. Hospitals and schools are collapsing, factories closing. RW Johnson of the *Sunday Times* recently interviewed a game ranger who said Zimbabwe's hyena were developing a taste for human flesh, the result of scavenging on corpses 'cast into collective pits like cattle.' Johnson concluded that Mugabe's misrule had resulted in as many as two million deaths and that 'the number is now heading into regions previously explored only by Stalin, Mao and Adolf Eichmann.'

It was against this backdrop that the UN's Commission on Sustainable Development met to elect a new leader on 11 May. The chair of this body rotates between regions; this year, it fell to Africa to make an appointment, and African countries were bent on installing Mugabe's man. At first, Western diplomats thought this was some sort of joke, but as the day passed, it emerged that Africans were indeed of the opinion that a body dedicated to fostering development could credibly be chaired by a murderous regime that had reduced a once-thriving nation to absolute penury. The reaction of Western diplomats and journalists was disbelief. 'This is beyond parody,' said an Australian newspaper columnist. 'Preposterous,' said the human rights lobby Freedom House. But Africans wangled support from Latin America and their motion was carried.

News of their triumph cast me into abject gloom, and I made it my business to stink up Franschhoek's rarefied air with predictions of impending trouble here in South Africa. This was not what civilised whites wanted to hear on a lovely autumn day, what with the economy growing at five per cent and surprising numbers capable of forking out £50 a plate to dine with visiting writers. One such dinner took place on an achingly lovely wine estate that calls itself Haute Cabrière, if you don't mind. I was seated alongside Bevil John Rudd, grandson of Cecil John Rhodes's right-hand man, and close to the widow of late *Observer* publisher David Astor. Mrs Astor was eager to tell of *The Observer*'s role in the downfall of apartheid (the Astors were good chums with Mandela and hired Anthony Sampson and Colin Legum to agitate against the dreadful Boers). Bevil Rudd was a genial old eccentric with a mad scientist hairdo, keen to describe his friendship with the African writer Can Themba.

Opposite us, a spiky-haired codger was rattling on in a dismissive way about sceptics who doubt the sustainability of the SA miracle. 'This is a wonderful country,' said Ken Owen, the esteemed former editor of South Africa's dominant Sunday paper. 'I just get richer and richer. Read this week's *Economist*! Our economy is roaring ahead at four times the rate of New Zealand's,' and so on. With several glasses of wine under my belt, I was emboldened to say, 'Pardon me, but your optimism seems unfounded.' My fellow diners looked mystified, so I explained what had just happened in New York. 'You'd have to be blind to misread the writing on the wall here,' I concluded.

The grand personages looked as if a bad smell had reached their noses. Owen said he'd been reading my scribblings in these very pages and hadn't liked them at all. 'I thought you were just playing up to the Brits for the money,' he said, 'but you actually believe this stuff!' Then he explained to the gathering that ANC policy toward Mugabe was entirely rational and designed to prevent Zimbabwe imploding. 'Ah, come on,' I said. 'Zimbabwe imploded years ago.' Jonathan Shapiro, aka the eminent leftish cartoonist Zapiro, intervened at this point, because things were getting nasty. He was willing to allow that the ANC was guilty of double standards when it came to human rights, but I wasn't having any of that. I said, 'Screw double standards. Mugabe's country is ruined and his people are starving, but he smashed the white farmers, so blacks – our government included – support him regardless. These people hate us,' I concluded. Whereupon Owen lost it entirely. 'You're pathetic,' he shouted. 'Pathetic!'

I was heavily outnumbered, so I sallied forth into the night at this point, only to hear that I'd been trashed in absentia at a parallel literary dinner on the far side of town. There, the antagonist was eminent leftish journalist Max du Preez, who told the gathering he'd been pleased to see the back of JM Coetzee, our greatest novelist, now consumed by pessimism and resident in Adelaide. Max opined that the dreadful Malan should leave too. He said he was even willing to pay my ticket.

Ah well, *c'est la vie*, as they say in Franschhoek. I'd picked the wrong time and place to don sackcloth and utter prophesies of doom, and it's just as well I left before they heard what else I had to say about liberals and their craven appeasing of the Mugabe beast.

It seems to me that last week's events in New York render a terrible verdict on well-intentioned do-gooders and the climate of impunity they create for African dictators. These thugs know there is no downside; their own subjects are helpless, and blacks elsewhere don't seem to care what horrors are inflicted on them so long as the great dictator strikes a heroic anti-imperialist pose. As for Western and UN charities, they will happily take any insults dished out to them and come to feed your people anyway, thereby sparing you from the consequences of your criminality.

There can be little doubt that this was an essential part of Mugabe's calculation. I mean, the man has something like eight university degrees. It cannot possibly have escaped his notice that overnight elimination of white commercial farmers would precipitate a food crisis. But why worry? He knew that the UN and allied charities would step in to feed the starving. Indeed, he was so confident of their generosity that he did not scruple to use donated food as a political weapon, rewarding his loyalists with free grub and punishing rebellious villages by withholding same while loudly proclaiming that food shortages were caused by drought, rather than his own deranged policies.

This year, the rains truly failed and millions now face starvation. The response of Mugabe's government was dumbfounding: it announced that it was revoking the licences of every aid group operating in Zimbabwe. The regime has since relented somewhat: donors will be tolerated provided they 'stick to their core business' and otherwise behave themselves. 'Government will not accept food offers from anyone for political purposes,' said information minister Sikhanyiso Ndlovu. Furthermore, offers of help will be accepted only if they are 'not attached with innuendoes of failure.' The reason for this, explained Comrade Ndlovu, is that 'Zimbabwe deserves the same dignity as any other country.'

I read this and think – pardon the language, but I think, 'Fuck you!' This parasite doesn't even have the manners to say please or thank you. But this is beyond etiquette. In the absence of food aid, a ruler who behaves like Mugabe would long since have been torn limb from limb by his starving subjects. One recalls the demise of Louis XVI, of Mussolini and Ceausescu. Is it not time to abandon Mugabe to a similar fate?

Liberals will think this unfair to innocent people, and they are right: hundreds of thousands might die if the food convoys do not start rolling into Zimbabwe soon. On the other hand, as Johnson reminds us, armies of the innocent have already perished at Mugabe's hand, but he continues to thrive. His party recently announced that his reign has been extended to at least 2010. He presumes to dictate terms to charities. Blacks everywhere continue to adulate him and insult the

West by appointing his despicable government to positions of honour. There is only one way to end this farce: cut off the aid, and let Mugabe face the consequences.

The trick would be to tie food aid to acceptance of some very modest preconditions. Let's say, an end to torture, respect for the rule of law, untrammelled free speech and no political interference in the distribution of donated food. In other words, conditions so mild and reasonable that even Mugabe's most ardent fans cannot dispute their justness. If he rejects them, the fans will be left in no doubt as to his moral repugnance, and his long-suffering subjects will know exactly who to blame for their hunger pangs.

The Spectator, May 2007

Postscript: Ken Owen responded to this piece with a letter recalling that he'd once castigated me from the podium at some literary awards banquet. I forget the finer details, but his central charge was racism. 'Malan has hated me ever since,' said the illustrious Mr Owen. 'Hate you?' I replied. 'Come, sir. I didn't even remember who you were until your wife reminded me.' In truth, I've always admired Owen for his vivid opinions and vitriolic turn of phrase, even as applied to me. I was about to tell him this when he bit my head off.

It is also ironic to note that Zimbabwe's 2 200 per cent inflation rate seemed shocking in May 2007. Within a year, it had soared to 160 000 per cent and starving Zimbabwe exiles were swapping five-billion-dollar Zimbabwe banknotes for a crust of bread on the streets of Jo'burg. The black diaspora has yet to take heed and recant.

2

Culture

In the Jungle

||||||||||||||||||||||||||||||||||||||||||||||||||||||||||||||||||||||||||||||||||||||||||||||||||||||||||||||||||||||||||

First the Zulu man made the magic. Then the white man made the money. This is the secret history of popular music, as told through the long, twisted saga of one amazing melody.

Once upon a time, a long time ago, a small miracle took place in the brain of a man named Solomon Linda. It was 1939, and he was standing in front of a microphone in the only recording studio in black Africa when it happened. He hadn't composed the melody or written it down or anything. He just opened his mouth and out it came, a haunting skein of fifteen notes that flowed down the wires and into a trembling stylus that cut tiny grooves into a spinning block of beeswax which was taken to England and turned into a record that became a very big hit in that part of Africa.

Later, the song took flight and landed in America, where it mutated into a truly immortal pop epiphany that soared to the top of the charts everywhere, again and again, returning every decade or so under different names and guises. Navajo Indians sing it at pow-wows. Japanese teenagers know it as TK. The British know it as the theme tune of a popular website. Phish perform it live. It has been recorded by artists as diverse as REM and Glen Campbell, Brian Eno and Chet Atkins, The Nylons and muzak schlockmeister Bert Kaempfert. The New Zealand army band turned it into a march. England's 1986 World Cup soccer squad did a parody. Hollywood put it in *Ace Ventura: Pet Detective*. It has logged nearly three centuries of continuous radio airplay in the US alone. It is the most famous melody ever to emerge from Africa, a tune that has penetrated so deep into the human consciousness over so many generations that one can truly say, here is a song the whole world knows.

Its epic transcultural saga is also in a way the story of popular music, which limped pale-skinned and anaemic into the twentieth century but danced out the other side, vastly invigorated by transfusions of ragtime and rap, jazz, blues and soul, all of whose bloodlines run back to Africa via slave ships and plantations and ghettos. It was in the nature of this transaction that black men gave more than they got, and were often robbed outright. This one's for Solomon Linda, then, a Zulu who wrote a melody that earned untold millions for white men, but died so poor that his widow couldn't afford a stone for his grave. Let's take it from the top, as they say in the trade.

A story about music

This is an African yarn, but it begins with an unlikely friendship between an aristocratic British imperialist and a world-famous American negro. Sir Henry Brougham Loch is a rising star of the British Colonial Office. Orpheus McAdoo is leader of the celebrated Virginia Jubilee Singers, a combo that specialises in syncopated spirituals. The dudes met during McAdoo's triumphant tour of Australia in the 1880s. When Sir Henry becomes governor of the Cape Colony a few years later, it occurs to him that Orpheus might find it interesting to visit. Next thing, McAdoo and his troupe are on the road in South Africa, playing to slack-jawed crowds in dusty villages and mining towns.

This American music is a revelation to 'civilised natives,' hitherto forced to wear starched collars and sing horrible dirges under the direction of dour white missionaries. Mr McAdoo is a stern old bible-thumper, to be sure, but there's a subversive rhythmic intensity in his music, a primordial stirring of funk and soul. Africans have never heard such a thing. The tour turns into a five-year epic. Wherever Orpheus goes, 'jubilee' outfits spring up in his wake and spread the glad tidings, which eventually penetrate even the loneliest outposts of civilisation.

One such place is Gordon Memorial School, perched on the rim of a wild valley called Msinga, which lies in the Zulu heartland, about 300 miles southeast of Johannesburg. Among the half-naked herd-boys who drift through the mission is a rangy kid called Solomon Linda, born 1909, who gets hooked on the Orpheus-inspired syncopation thing and works bits of it into the Zulu songs he and his friends sing at weddings and feasts.

In the mid-thirties they shake off the dust and cowshit and take the train to Johannesburg, city of gold, where they move into slums and become kitchen boys and factory hands. Life is initially very perplexing. Solly keeps his eyes open and transmutes what he sees into songs that he and his homeboys perform a capella on weekends. He has songs about work, songs about crime, songs about how banks rob you by giving you paper in exchange for real money, songs about how rudely the whites treat you when you go to get your pass stamped. People like the music. Solly and his friends develop a following. Within two years, they've turned themselves into a very cool urban act that wears pin-striped suits, bowler hats and dandy two-tone shoes. They've become Solomon Linda and the Evening Birds, inventors of a music that will later become known as isicathamiya, arising from the warning cry, '*Cathoza, bafana*' – tread carefully, boys.

These were Zulus, you see, and their traditional dancing was punctuated by mighty foot-stompings that, when done in unison, literally made the earth tremble. This was fine in the bush, but if you stomped the same way in town you smashed wooden floors, cracked cement and sometimes broke your feet, so the whole dance had to be restrained and moderated. Cognoscenti will recall Ladysmith Black Mambazo's feline and curiously fastidious movements on stage. That's treading carefully.

In any event, there were legions of careful treaders in South Africa's big cities, usually Zulu migrants whose Saturday nights were devoted to epic beer-fuelled bacchanalias known as tea meetings. A tea meeting was part fashion show and part heroic contest between rival a capella gladiators, with a stray white man pulled off the street to act as judge and a cow or goat as first prize. The local black bourgeoisie was mortified by these antics. Careful treaders were an embarrassment, widely decried for their 'primitive' bawling and backward lyrics, which dwelled on such things as witchcraft, crime and getting girls with love potions. They had names like The Naughty Boys or The Boiling Waters, and when World War II broke out, some started calling themselves mbombers, after the dive-bombing Stukas they'd seen on newsreels. Mbombers were by far the coolest and most dangerous black thing of their time.

Yes! Dangerous! Sceptics are referred to 'Ngazula Emagumeni' (on Rounder CD 5025), an early Evening Birds track whose brain-rattling intensity flattens anything played or sung anywhere in the world at the time and thoroughly guts anyone who thinks of a capella as smooth tunes for mellow people. The wild, rocking sound came from doubling the bass voices and pumping up their volume, an innovation that was largely Linda's, along with the high dressing style and the new dance moves. He was the Elvis Presley of his time and place, a shy, gangly 30-year-old, so tall that he had to stoop as he passed through doorways. It's odd to imagine him singing soprano, but that was usually his gig in the group: he was the leader, the 'controller,' singing what Zulus called *fasi pathi*, a blood-curdling falsetto that a white man might render as first part.

The Evening Birds were spotted by a talent scout in 1938 and taken to the top of an office block in downtown Jo'burg, where they saw a machine that cut grooves into spinning discs of beeswax, and a lone microphone on the far side of a glass partition. This was the first recording studio in sub-Saharan Africa, shipped out from England by Eric Gallo, a jovial Italian who started out selling American hillbilly records to working-class Boers. Inspired, Gallo bought his own recording machine and started churning out those train-wreck and dustbowl ditties in local languages, first Afrikaans, then Zulu, Xhosa and what have you. His ally in this experiment was Griffiths Motsieloa, the country's first black producer, a slightly stiff and formal chap whose true interests were classical music and eisteddfodau, wherein polished African gentlemen entertained one another with speeches in high-falutin' King's English. Motsieloa abhorred the boss's passion for cultural slumming, but what could he do? Gallo was determined to find a black audience for his product. When Afro-hillbilly failed to catch on, they decided to take a leap into the unknown and lay down some isicathamiya.

Solomon Linda and The Evening Birds cut several songs under Motsieloa's direction, but the one we're interested in was called 'Mbube,' Zulu for 'the lion,' recorded at their second session in 1939. It was a simple three-chord ditty with lyrics along the lines of 'Lion! Ha! You're a lion!', supposedly inspired by an incident in the Birds' collective Zulu boyhood, when they chased lions that were stalking their father's cattle and managed to kill a cub in the process. The first take was a dud, the second likewise. Exasperated, Griffiths stuck his head into the corridor, dragooned some session cats – a pianist, guitarist and banjo player – and tried again.

The third take almost collapsed at the outset as the unrehearsed musicians dithered and fished for the key, but once they started cooking, the song was glory-bound. 'Mbube' wasn't the most remarkable tune, but there was something terribly compelling about the underlying chant, a dense meshing of low male voices above which Linda yodelled and howled for two minutes, mostly making it up as he went along. The third take was the great one, but it achieved immortality only in its dying seconds, when Linda took a deep breath, opened his mouth, and improvised the melody that the world now associates with these words:

In the jungle, the mighty jungle, the lion sleeps tonight.

Griffiths Motsieloa must have realised he'd captured something special, because that chunk of beeswax was shipped all the way to England, and shipped back in the form of ten-inch 78-rpm records that went on sale just as Hitler invaded Poland. Marketing was tricky, because there was hardly any black radio in 1939, but the song went out on 'the rediffusion,' a landline that pumped music, news and Native Affairs propaganda into certain black neighbourhoods, and people began trickling into stores to ask for it. The trickle grew into a steady stream that just rolled on for years and years, necessitating so many repressings that the master ultimately disintegrated. By December 1948, 'Mbube' had sold somewhere in the region of 100 000 copies, and Solomon Linda was a superstar in the world of Zulu migrants, the undefeated and undefeatable champion of hostel singing competitions.

Pete Seeger, on the other hand, was in a rather bad way. He was a banjo player living in a cold-water flat on MacDougal Street in Greenwich Village with a wife, two young children and no money. Scion of wealthy New York radicals, he'd dropped out of Harvard ten years earlier and gone on the bum with his banjo on his back, learning hard-times songs for hard-hit people in the Hoovervilles, lumber camps and coal mines of Depression America. In New York he joined a band with Woody Guthrie. They wore work shirts and jeans and wrote folk songs that championed the downtrodden common man in his struggle against capitalist bloodsuckers. Woody had a slogan on his guitar that said, 'This machine kills fascists.' Pete's banjo had a kinder, gentler variation: 'This machine surrounds hate and forces it to surrender.' He was a proto-hippie, save that he didn't smoke reefer or even drink beer.

He was also a pacifist, at least until Hitler invaded Russia. Scenting a capitalist plot to destroy what they saw as the brave Soviet socialist experiment, Pete and Woody turned gung-ho overnight and started writing anti-Nazi war songs, an episode that made them briefly famous. After that it was into uniform and off to the front, where Pete played the banjo for bored GIs. Demobbed in '45, he returned to New York and got a gig of sorts in the public school system, teaching toddlers to warble the half-forgotten folk songs of their American heritage. It wasn't particularly glorious, the money was rotten, and atop of that, he was sick in bed with a bad cold.

Came a knock on the door and lo, there stood his friend Alan Lomax, later to be hailed as 'the father of World Music.' Alan and his dad John were already famous for their song-collecting forays into the parallel universe of rural black America, where they'd discovered giants like Muddy Waters and Leadbelly. Alan Lomax was presently working for Decca, where he'd just rescued a package of 78s sent from darkest Africa by a record company in the vain hope that someone might want to release them in America. They were about to be thrown away when Lomax intervened, thinking, God, Pete's the man for these.

And here they were – ten shellac 78s, one of which said 'Mbube' on its label. Pete put it on his old Victrola and sat back. He was fascinated – there was something catchy about the underlying chant, and that wild, skirling falsetto was amazing.

'Golly,' he said to himself, 'I can sing that.' So he got out pen and paper and started transcribing the song, but he couldn't catch the words through all the scratching and hissing. The Zulus were chanting, *uyimbube, uyimbube*, but to Pete it sounded like, awimboowee, or maybe awimoweh, so that's how he wrote it down. A while later, he taught 'Wimoweh' to the rest of his band, The Weavers, and it became, he says, 'just about my favorite song to sing for the next forty years.'

This was no great achievement, given that The Weavers' late-forties' repertoire was full of drek like 'On Top of Old Smoky' and 'Greensleeves.' Old Pete will admit no such thing, but one senses that he was growing tired of cold-water flats and work shirts and wanted a proper career, as befitting a 30-something father of two. He landed a job in TV, but someone fingered him as a dangerous radical and he lost it before it even started. After that, according to his biographer TK, he fell into a depression that ended only when his band landed a gig at the Village Vanguard. Apparently determined to make the best possible impression, Pete allowed his wife to outfit the Weavers in matching blue corduroy jackets – a hitherto-unimaginable concession to showbiz.

The pay was fifty a week plus free hamburgers, and the booking was for two weeks only, but something odd happened: crowds started coming. The gig was extended for a month, and then another. The Weavers' appeal was inexplicable to folk purists, who noted that most of their songs had been around forever, in obscure versions by blacks and rednecks who never had hits anywhere. What they failed to grasp was that Seeger and his comrades had somehow managed to filter the stench of poverty and pigshit out of the proletarian music and make it wholesome and fun for Eisenhower-era squares. Six months later, the Weavers were still at the Vanguard, drawing sellout crowds of fur-coated ladies and tuxedoed refugees from the swell supper clubs of Times Square.

One such figure was Gordon Jenkins, a sallow jazz cat with a gigolo's moustache and a matinée idol's greased-back hairstyle. Jenkins started out as Benny Goodman's arranger before scoring a huge hit in his own right with an appalling piece of crap, 'I'm Forever Blowing Bubbles.' Now he was Frank Sinatra's arranger, and musical director at Decca Records. Jenkins loved The Weavers, returning night after night, sometimes sitting through two consecutive shows. He wanted to sign them up, but his bosses were dubious. It was only when Jenkins offered to pay for the recording sessions himself that Decca capitulated and gave the folkies a deal.

Their first recording came out in August 1950. It was 'Goodnight Irene,' an old love song they'd learned off their friend Leadbelly, and it was an immediate click, in the parlance of the day. The B-side was an Israeli hora called 'Tzena, Tzena, Tzena,' and it clicked, too. So did 'Roving Kind,' a nineteenth-century folk ditty they released that November, and even 'On Top of Old Smoky,' which hit number two the following spring. The Weavers leapt from amateur hootenannies to the stages of America's poshest nightspots and casinos. They wore suits and ties, appeared on TV, rode around in limos, and pulled down two grand a week. Chagrined and envious, their former comrades on the left started sniping at them in small magazines. 'Can an all-white group sing songs from Negro culture?' asked one.

The answer, of course, lay in the song Seeger called 'Wimoweh.' His version was faithful to the Zulu original in almost all respects save for the finger-popping rhythm, which is probably a bit white for some tastes but not entirely offensive. The true test lay in the singing, and here Seeger passed with flying colours, bawling and howling his heart out, tearing up his vocal chords so badly that he was almost mute by the time he reached 75. Audiences were thunderstruck by his performance. 'Wimoweh' was by far the most edgy and unsettling song in The Weavers' set, which is perhaps why they waited a year after their big breakthrough before recording it.

Like their earlier recordings, it took place with Gordon Jenkins presiding and an orchestra in attendance. Prior to this, Jenkins had been very subdued in his instrumental approach, adding just the occasional sting and the odd swirl of strings to The Weavers' cheery singalongs. Maybe he was growing bored, because his arrangement of 'Wimoweh' was a motherfucker, a great Vegassy explosion of big-band raunch that almost equalled the barbaric splendour of the Zulu original. Trombones blared. Trumpets screamed. Strings swooped and soared through Linda's miracle melody, the one invented on the immortal third take of 1939. And then Pete cut loose with all that hollering and screaming. It was a revolutionary departure from everything else The Weavers had ever done, but *Billboard* loved it, anointing it a 'Pick of the Week.' *Cash Box* said, 'might break.' *Variety* said, 'Terrific!'

But around this time *Variety* also said, 'Scripter names five more H'wood Reds,' and 'Chaplin being investigated.' It was January 1952, and America was engaged in a frenzied hunt for Reds under beds. The House Un-American Activities Committee was probing Hollywood. 'Red Channels' had just published the names of artists with Commie connections. The American Legion was organising a boycott of their movies. And in Washington, DC, someone called Harvey Matusow was talking to federal investigators.

Harvey was a weasely little man who had once worked alongside Pete Seeger in Peoples' Artists, a reddish front that dispatched folk singers to entertain on picket lines and in union halls. Harvey had undergone a change of heart, and decided to tell all about his secret life in the Communist underground. On 6 February 1952, just as 'Wimoweh' made its chart debut, he stepped up to a mike before the House Un-American Activities Committee and told one of the looniest tales of the entire McCarthy era. Evil Reds, he said, were 'preying on the sexual weakness of American youth' to lure recruits into their dreaded movement. What's more, he was willing to name names of Communist Party members, among them three of the Weavers – including Pete Seeger.

The yellow press went apeshit. Reporters called the Ohio club where the Weavers were scheduled to play that night, demanding to know why the Yankee Inn was providing succour to the enemy. The Weavers' show was canned, and it was all downhill from there. Radio stations banned their records. TV appearances were cancelled. 'Wimoweh' plummeted from number 6 into oblivion. Nightclub owners wouldn't even talk to The Weavers' agents, and then Decca dropped them, too. By the end of the year, they'd packed it in, and Pete Seeger was back where he'd started, teaching folksongs to kids for a weekly pittance.

So the Weavers were dead, but 'Wimoweh' lived on, bewitching jazz ace Jimmy Dorsey, who covered it in 1952, and the sultry Yma Sumac, whose cocktail lounge version caused a minor stir in the midfifties. Toward the end of the decade, it was included on 'Live from the Hungry I,' a monstrously big LP by the Kingston Trio that stayed on the charts for 178 weeks, peaking at number two. By now, almost everyone in America knew the basic refrain, so it would have come as no particular surprise to see four nice Jewish teenagers popping their fingers and going ah-weem-oh-way, ah-weem-oh-way on TK beach in the summer of 1961.

The Tokens were clean-cut Brooklyn boys who had grown up listening to Alan Freed, Murray the K and the dreamy teen stylings of Dion and the Belmonts and the Everly Brothers. Hank Medress and Jay Siegel met at Lincoln High, where they sang in a doo-wop quartet that briefly featured Neil Sedaka. Phil Margo was a budding drummer and piano player, also from Lincoln High, and Mitch Margo was his kid brother, age fourteen.

One presumes girls were cutting eyes in their direction, because The

Tokens had recently been on TV's American Bandstand, decked out in double-breasted mohair suits with white shirts and purple ties, singing their surprise Top 20 hit, 'Tonight I Fell in Love.'

And now they were moving towards even greater things. Barely out of high school, they'd landed a three-record deal with RCA Victor, with a $10-thousand advance and a crack at working with Hugo Peretti and Luigi Creatore, ace producers of Jimmie Rodgers, Frankie Lymon and many, many others. These guys worked with Elvis Presley, for God's sake. 'This was big for us,' said Phil Margo. 'Very big.'

The Tokens knew 'Wimoweh' through their lead singer Jay, who'd learned it off an old Weavers' album. It was one of the songs they sang when they auditioned for Huge and Luge, as Peretti and Creatore were known in the trade. The producers said, yeah, well, there's something there, but it's a bit weird, and besides, what's it about? Eating lions, said the Tokens. That's what some joker at the South African consulate had told them, at any rate: it was a Zulu hunting song with lyrics that went, 'Hush, hush, if everyone's quiet, we'll have lion meat to eat tonight.'

The producers presumably rolled their eyes. None of this got anyone anywhere in the era of 'shoobie doo, I love you.' They wanted to revamp the song, give it some intelligible lyrics and a contemporary feel, so they sent for one George David Weiss, a suave young dude in a navy-blue blazer, presently making a big name for himself in yesterday's music, writing orchestrations for Doris Day, Peggy Lee and others of that sort. The Tokens took him for a hopeless square until they discovered that he'd also co-written 'Can't Help Falling in Love With You' for Elvis Presley. That changed everything.

So George Weiss took 'Wimoweh' home with him and gave it a careful listen. A civilised chap with a Juilliard degree, he didn't much like the primitive bawling, but the underlying chant was okay and parts of the melody were very catchy. So he dismantled the song, excised all the hollering and screaming, and put the rest back together in a new way. The chant remained unchanged but the melody – Solomon Linda's miracle melody – moved to centre stage, becoming the tune itself, to which the new words were sung: 'In the jungle, the mighty jungle' and so on.

In years to come, Weiss was always a bit diffident about his revisions, describing them as 'gimmicks,' as if ashamed to be associated with so frothy a bit of pop nonsense. Token Phil Margo says that's because Weiss wrote nothing save 33 words of doggerel, but that's another lawsuit entirely. What concerns us here is the song's bloodline, and everyone agrees on that: 'The Lion Sleeps Tonight' was a reworking of 'Wimoweh', which was a copy of 'Mbube.' Solomon Linda was buried under several layers of pop-rock stylings, but you could still see him beneath the new song's slick surface, like a mastodon embalmed in a block of clear ice.

The song was recorded live in RCA's Manhattan studios on 21 July 1961, with an orchestra in attendance and some session players on guitar, drums and bass. The percussionist muted his timpani, seeking that authentic 'jungle drum' sound. A moonlighting opera singer named Anita Darien practised her scales. Conductor Sammy Lowe tapped his baton, and off they went, three Tokens doing the wimowehs while Jay Siegel took the lead with his pure falsetto and Darien swooped and dove in the high heavens, singing the haunting countermelodies that were one of the song's great glories. Three takes (again), a bit of overdubbing, and that was more or less that. Everyone went home, entirely blind to what they'd accomplished. The Tokens were mortified by the new lyrics, which struck them as un-teen and uncool. Hugo and Luigi were so uninterested that they did the final mix over the telephone, and RCA topped them all by issuing the song as the B-side of a humdrum tune called 'Tina,' which sank like lead.

Weird, no? We're talking about a pop song so powerful that Beach Boy Brian Wilson had to pull off the road when he first heard it, totally overcome; a song that Carole King instantly pronounced 'a motherfucker.' But it might never have reached their ears if an obscure DJ named Dick Smith in Worcester, Massachusetts, hadn't flipped The Tokens' new turkey and given the B-side a listen. Smith said, 'Holy shit, this is great,' or words to that effect, so his station, WORC, put 'The Lion Sleeps Tonight' on heavy rotation. The song broke out regionally, hit the national charts in November, and reached number one in four giant strides.

A month later, it was number one in England, too. By April 1962, it was number one all around the world, and heading for immortality. Miriam Makeba sang her version at JFK's last birthday party, moments before Marilyn Monroe famously lisped, 'Happy Birthday, Mister President.' Apollo astronauts listened to it on the take-off pads at Cape Canaveral. It was covered by the Springfields, the Spinners, the Tremeloes and Glen Campbell. In 1972, it returned to number three in a version by Robert John. Brian Eno recorded it in 1975.

In 1982, it was back at number one in the UK, this time performed by Tight Fit. REM did it, as did The Nylons and They Might Be Giants. Manu Dibango did a twist version. Some Germans turned it into heavy metal. A sample cropped up on a rap epic titled 'Mash up da Nation.' Disney used the song in *The Lion King*, and then it got into the smash-hit musical of the same title, currently playing to packed houses in six cities around the world. It's on the original Broadway cast recording, on dozens of kids' CDs with cuddly lions on their covers, and an infinite variety of nostalgia compilations. It's more than 60 years old, and still it's everywhere.

What might all this represent in songwriter royalties and associated revenues? I put the question to lawyers around the world, and they scratched their heads. Around 160 recordings of three versions? Twelve movies? Five TV commercials and a smash hit musical? Number 7 on Valu-Pak's semi-authoritative ranking of most-beloved golden oldies, and ceaseless radio airplay in every corner of the planet? It was impossible to be sure, but no one blanched at $15 million. Some said 10, some said 20, but most felt that 15 million was squarely in the ballpark.

Which raises an even more interesting question: What happened to all that loot?

A story about money

'It was a wonderful experience,' said Larry Richmond, hereditary president of The Richmond Organization. It was two am in Johannesburg, and Larry was telling me about his company's 'wonderful efforts' to make sure that justice was done to Solomon Linda. I wanted to hear everything, but we were on opposite sides of the planet, so I said, 'Hold it right there, I'm coming to see you.' I hung up, started packing and a few days later, I walked into TRO's HQ, a strangely quiet suite of offices in Manhattan.

The dusty old guitar in the waiting room was a relic of a long-gone era. Back in the forties, when TRO was young, eager songwriters streamed in here to audition their wares for Larry's dad, Howie, the firm's founder. If he liked the songs, he'd sign 'em up, transcribe 'em and secure a copyright. Then he'd send song pluggers out to place the tunes with stars whose recordings would generate income for the composer and the publisher, too. At the same time, salesmen would be flogging the sheet music, while bean counters in the back office collected royalties and kept an eye out for unauthorised versions.

In its heyday, TRO was a music publishing empire that spanned the globe, but it was forced into decline by the seventies' advent of savvy rock & roll accountants who advised clients to publish themselves, which was fairly easy and doubled one's songwriting income, given that old-style publishers generally claimed 50 per cent of royalties for their services. By 1999, TRO was little more than a crypt for fabulously valuable old copyrights, manned by a skeleton crew that licensed old songs for TV commercials or movies.

Larry Richmond was an amiable bloke in an open-necked shirt and beige slacks. We drank coffee and talked for an hour or two, mostly about social justice and TRO's commitment to the same. There were stories about Woody Guthrie and Pete Seeger, the famous radical troubadours in TRO's stable. There was a story about the hospital in India to which the Richmonds made generous donations. And finally, there were some elliptical remarks about Solomon Linda, and TRO's noble attempts to make sure that he received his just dues. I was hoping Larry would give me a formal interview on the subject, but first I had to get some sleep. It was a mistake. By the time I'd recovered, Larry had changed his mind and retreated into the labyrinth of his voice-mail system, from which he would not emerge.

So there I was in New York, with no one to talk to. I called music lawyers and record companies, angling for appointments that failed to materialise. I wandered into *Billboard* magazine, where a veteran journalist warned that I was wasting my time trying to find out what any song had ever earned and where the money had gone. But I'd come a long way, so I kept looking and, eventually, figured some of it out.

The story begins in 1939, when Solomon Linda was visited by angels in Africa's only recording studio. At the time, Jo'burg was a hick mining town where music deals were concluded according to trading principles as old as Moses: record companies bought recordings for whatever they thought the music might be worth in the marketplace; stars generally got several guineas for a session, unknowns got almost nothing. No one got royalties, and copyright was unknown. Solomon Linda didn't even get a contract. He walked out of that session with about ten shillings in his pocket, and the music thereafter belonged to the record company, with no further obligations to anyone. When 'Mbube' became a local hit, the loot went to Eric Gallo, the playboy who owned the company. All Solomon Linda got was a menial job at the boss's packing plant, where he worked for the rest of his days.

When 'Mbube' took flight and turned into the Weavers' hit 'Wimoweh,' Eric Gallo could have made a fortune if he had played his cards right. Instead, he struck a handshake deal with Larry Richmond's dad, trading 'Mbube' to TRO in return for the dubious privilege of administering 'Wimoweh' in such bush territories as South Africa and Rhodesia. Control of Solomon Linda's destiny thus passed into the hands of Howie Richmond and his faithful sidekick, one Albert Brackman.

Howie and Al shared an apartment in the thirties, when they were ambitious young go-getters on Tin Pan Alley. Howie was tall and handsome, Al was short and fat, but otherwise, they were blood brothers, with shared passions for nightlife and big-band jazz. After World War II, Howie worked as a song promoter before deciding to become a publisher in his own right. He says he found a catchy old music-hall number, had a pal write new lyrics and placed the song with Guy Lombardo, who took it to Number Ten as 'Hop Scotch Polka.' Howie was on his way. Al joined up in 1949, and together they put a whole slew of novelty songs on the hit parade. Then they moved into the burgeoning folk-music sector, where big opportunities were opening up for sharp guys with a shrewd understanding of copyright.

After all, what was a folk song? Who owned it? It was just out there, like a wild horse or a tract of virgin land on an unconquered continent. Fortune awaited the man bold enough to name himself as the composer of some ancient tune like, say, 'Greensleeves.' A certain Jessie Cavanaugh did exactly that in the early fifties, only it wasn't really Jessie at all – it was Howie Richmond under an alias. This was a common practice on Tin Pan Alley at the time, and it wasn't illegal or anything. The object was to claim writer royalties on new versions of old songs that belonged to no one. The aliases seem to have been a way to avoid potential embarrassment, just in case word got out that Howard S Richmond was presenting himself as the author of a madrigal from Shakespeare's day.

Much the same happened with 'Frankie & Johnny,' the hoary old frontier ballad, or 'Rovin' Kind,' a ribald ditty from the clipper-ship era. There's no way Al Brackman could really have written such songs, so when he filed royalty claims with the performing rights society BMI, he attributed the compositions to Albert Stanton, a fictitious tunesmith who often worked closely with the imaginary Mr Cavanaugh, penning such standards as 'John Henry' and 'Michael Row the Boat Ashore.' Cavanaugh even claimed credit for 'Battle Hymn of the Republic,' a feat eclipsed only by a certain Harold Leventhal, who accidentally copyrighted an obscure whatnot later taken as India's national anthem.

Leventhal started out as a gofer for Irving Berlin and wound up promoting concerts for Bob Dylan, but in between, he developed a serious crush on the Weavers. In 1949, he showed up at the Village Vanguard with an old friend in tow – Pete Kameron, a suave charmer who was scouting around an entree into showbiz. Leventhal performed some introductions, and Kameron became the Weavers' manager. Since all these players knew one another, it was natural that they should combine to take charge of the left-wingers' business affairs. Leventhal advised; Kameron handled bookings, negotiated with mob-linked nightclub owners and tried to fend off the redbaiters. Howie and Al took on the publishing, arranging it so that Kameron owned a 50 per cent stake. The Weavers sang the songs and cut the records, and together they sold around 4 million platters in 18 months or so.

In the late 1940s, these men found themselves contemplating the fateful 78 rpm record from Africa and wondering exactly what manner of beast it could be. The label said MBUBE – BY SOLOMON LINDA AND THE EVENING BIRDS, but at the time, it was not copyrighted anywhere. Anything not copyrighted was a wild horse, strictly speaking, and wild horses in the Weavers' repertoire were usually attributed to one Paul Campbell. The Weavers' version of 'Hush Little Baby' was a Paul Campbell composition, for instance. The same was true of 'Rock Island Line' and 'Kisses Sweeter than Wine,' tunes the folkies had learned off Leadbelly at Village hoots and reworked in their own style.

On the surface of things, Paul Campbell was thus one of the most successful songwriters of the era, but of course the name was just another alias used to claim royalties on songs from the public domain.

'Mbube' wasn't public domain at all, but it was the next best thing – an uncopyrighted song owned by an obscure foreign record label that had shown absolutely no interest in protecting Solomon Linda's rights as a writer. So the Zulu's song was tossed in among the Weavers' wild horses, and released as 'Wimoweh,' by Paul Campbell.

As the song found its fans, money started rolling in. Every record sale triggered a mechanical royalty. Every radio play counted as a performance, which also required payment, and there was always the hope that someone might take out a 'synch license' to use the tune in a movie or TV ad. Al, Howie and Pete Kameron divided the standard publisher's 50 per cent among themselves and distributed the other half to the writers – or in this case, adapters: Pete Seeger and the Weavers. Solomon Linda was entitled to nothing.

This didn't sit well with Seeger, who openly acknowledged Linda as the true author of 'Wimoweh' and felt he should get the money. Indeed, he'd been hassling his publishers for months to find a way of paying the Zulu.

'Originally they were going to send the royalties to Gallo,' Seeger recalls. 'I said, "Don't do that, because Linda won't get a penny."' Anti-apartheid activists put Seeger in touch with a Johannesburg lawyer, who set forth into the forbidden townships to find Solomon Linda. Once contact was established, Seeger sent the Zulu a $1 000 cheque, and instructed his publisher to do the same with all future payments.

He was still bragging about it 50 years later. 'I never got author's royalties on Wimoweh,' Seeger says. 'Right from '51 or '52, I understood that the money was going to Linda. I assumed they were keeping the publisher's 50 per cent and sending the rest.'

Unfortunately, Linda's family maintains that the money only arrived years later, and even then, it was nothing like the full writer's share Seeger was hoping to bestow. We'll revisit this conundrum in short order, but first, let's follow the further adventures of 'Wimoweh,' which fell into the hands of RCA producers Hugo and Luigi by way of the Tokens in the summer of 1961. In addition to being ace producers and buddies of Presley, these men were also wild horse breakers of the very first rank. They'd put their brand on a whole herd of them – 'Pop Goes the Weasel,' 'First Noël,' you name it. They even had 'Grand March from Aida,' a smash hit for Giuseppe Verdi in the 1870s.

As seasoned pros, these guys would have checked out 'Wimoweh' composer of record Paul Campbell and discovered that he was an alias and that his oeuvre consisted largely of folk songs from previous centuries. They leapt to a seemingly obvious conclusion: 'Wimoweh' was based on an old African folk song that didn't belong to anyone. As such, it was fair game, so they summoned George Weiss, turned 'Wimoweh' into 'The Lion Sleeps Tonight,' and sent it out into the world as a Weiss/Peretti/Creatore composition. They did exactly the same thing a few months later with 'The Click Song,' a Xhosa tune popularised in America by Miriam Makeba: Weiss cooked up some more doggerel about jungle drums and love-lorn maidens, the Tokens sang it, and it landed in record stores as 'Bwanina,' another 'original composition' by the same trio.

But they had made a mistake. 'The Click Song' was indeed a wild horse that had been roaming Africa for centuries, but 'Wimoweh' was the subject of a US copyright, and 'Wimoweh' was clearly the lion song's progenitor. When 'The Lion Sleeps Tonight' began playing on America's radios, Howie Richmond instantly recognised its bloodline and howled with outrage. He set his lawyers on The Tokens and their allies, and what could they say? It must have been deeply embarrassing. On the other hand, Howie was on first-name terms with Hugo and Luigi, and deeply respectful of George Weiss's talents. Howie was thus willing to forget the whole thing – provided the publishing rights to 'Lion' came back to him.

Within a week there was a letter acknowledging infringement on Howie's desk, and urgent settlement talks were underway. Why urgent? Because 'The Lion Sleeps Tonight' was soaring up the charts, and the Weiss/Peretti/Creatore cabal was desperate to avoid a dispute that might abort its trajectory. This put Richmond and Brackman in a position to dictate almost any terms they pleased. Pete Seeger says he had informed them that he didn't feel entitled to composer royalties, and would prefer any benefits to flow to Solomon Linda, author of the underlying 'Mbube.' If they'd seen fit, Richmond and Brackman could have forced Luigi, Hugo and Weiss to share their spoils with the Zulu. But they had no legal obligations towards Linda, and besides, taking a hard line might have soured an important business relationship. So they allowed three men they were later to describe as 'plagiarists' to walk away with 100 per cent of the writer royalties on a song that originated in Solomon Linda's brain.

And why not? It was no skin off their teeth. TRO received the full 50 per cent publisher's cut. Huge and Luge and Weiss were happy. The only person who lost out was Linda, who wasn't even mentioned: the new copyright described 'Lion' as 'based on a song by Paul Campbell.'

The paperwork was finalised on 18 December 1961, just as the song commenced its conquest of the world's hit parades. It was Number One in the States on Christmas Day, and reached South Africa two months later, just in time to bring a wan smile to the face of a dying Solomon Linda. He'd been ailing since 1959, when he lost control of his bowels and collapsed onstage. Doctors diagnosed kidney disease, but his family suspected witchcraft.

If true, this would make Linda a victim of his own success. Sure, he was nothing in the world of white men, but 'Mbube' made him a legend in the Zulu subculture, and to be a legend among 'the people of heaven' was a pretty fine destiny in some respects. Strangers hailed him on the streets, bought him drinks in shebeens. He was in constant demand for personal appearances and earned enough to afford some sharp suits, a second bride and a wind-up gramophone for the kinfolk in mud huts back in Msinga.

A thousand bucks from Pete Seeger aside, most of his money came from those uproarious all-night song contests, which remain a vital part of urban Zulu social life to this day. Most weekends, Solly and the Evening Birds would hire a car and sally forth to do battle in distant towns, and they always came back victorious. Competitors tried everything, including potions, to make their voices hoarse and high like Linda's, but nothing worked. The aging homeboys would take the stage and work themselves into such transports of ecstasy that tears started streaming down Solly's face, at which point the audience would go wild and the Evening Birds would once again walk off with first prize – sometimes a trophy, sometimes money, sometimes a cow that they slaughtered as the sun came up, roasted and shared with their fans. Blinded by the resulting adulation, Linda wasn't particularly perturbed when his song mutated into 'The Lion Sleeps Tonight' and raced to the top of the world's hit parades.

'He was happy,' said his daughter Fildah. 'He didn't know he was supposed to get something.'

Fildah is Linda's oldest surviving child, a radiant woman who wears beads in her hair and a goatskin bangle on her right wrist, the mark of a sangoma, or witchdoctor. Her sister Elizabeth works as a nurse in a government clinic, but she announced, giggling, that she was a sangoma, too. A third daughter, Delphi, had just had surgery for arthritis, but she was also using ancestral medicine under her sisters' direction – a plant called 'umhlabelo,' apparently. Elizabeth thought a water snake might be useful, too, and wondered where she could obtain such a thing. They lived in an urban slum but were deeply Zulu people, down to the cattle horns on the roof above the kitchen door – relics of sacrifices to the spirits of their ancestors. Only Elizabeth spoke fluent English, but even she didn't flinch at the talk of witchcraft.

Their aunt, Mrs Beauty Madiba, was the one who brought it up. A sweet old lady in her Sunday best, she remembered meeting Linda in the late forties, when he started to court her sister Regina. The singer was at the peak of his career at the time, and he had no trouble raising the ten cattle their father was asking as the bride price. The wedding feast took place in 1949, and Regina went to live in Johannesburg. Beauty joined her a few years later and had a ringside seat when Linda was brought down by dark forces. 'People were jealous, because all the time, he won,' she explained. 'They said, "We will get you." So they bewitched him.'

Elizabeth muttered something about renal failure, but even she had to acknowledge there was something odd about the way her father's disease refused to respond to treatment. He grew so sick that he had to stop singing. By the time 'The Lion Sleeps Tonight' was released, he was in and out of the hospital constantly, and on 8 October 1962, he died.

Everyone sighed. Rival a-capella groups were to blame, growled Victor Madondo, a burly old warrior whose father sang alto in the Evening Birds. 'They were happy, because now they could go forward nicely.'

But they went nowhere. Linda was the one whose influence lived on, becoming so pervasive that all Zulu male choral singing came to be called 'Mbube music.' Ethnomusicologists dug up the early Birds recordings, and Linda was posthumously elevated to godhead – 'one of the great figures in black South African music,' according to Professor Veit Erlmann of the University of Texas. Latter-day Mbube stars like Ladysmith Black Mambazo sent gifts to this very house when they made it big, a tribute to the spirit of a man they venerated. And then I came along asking questions about money.

It soon became clear that Linda's daughters had no understanding of music publishing and related arcana. All they knew was that 'people did something with our father's song outside,' and that monies were occasionally deposited in their joint bank account by mysterious entities they could not name. I asked to see documents, but they had none, and they were deeply confused as to the size and purpose of the payments. 'Mister Tucker is helping us,' they said. 'Mister Tucker knows everything.'

Raymond Tucker is a white lawyer with offices in a grand old colonial mansion on the outskirts of Jo'burg's decaying downtown. On the phone, he explained that intermediaries had contacted him on Pete Seeger's behalf some decades back, asking him to act as a conduit for payments to Linda's widow. Tucker was honoured to help out, he said. As we spoke, he flipped through his files, assuring me that royalty payments were 'pretty regular, with proper accounting' and that everything was 'totally and absolutely above board.'

Solomon's daughters didn't contest this, but they rejected Seeger's claim that royalties had been flowing through the Tucker channel since the 1950s. According to their recollections, their father's 1962 death was a catastrophe that left the family destitute. Their mother, Regina, was an illiterate peasant with no job and six children to feed. She illegally brewed and sold African beer to make ends meet. Her girls went to school barefoot, took notes on cracked bits of slate and went to bed hungry. Critical Zulu death rites went unperformed for years, because the family was too poor to pay a sangoma to officiate.

'This house, it was bare bricks,' said Elizabeth. 'No ceiling, no plaster, no furniture, just one stool and one coal stove.' Her eldest brother left school and started working, but he was murdered by gangsters. Her second brother became the breadwinner, only to die in an accident, whereupon Delphi took a job in a factory to keep the family going. 'There was suffering here at home,' said Elizabeth. She was adamant that the mysterious money 'from outside' started arriving only much later, perhaps around 1980. That's when they erected a tombstone for their father, who had rested in a pauper's grave since 1962. That's how they remembered.

I asked Tucker if I could see his files, but he balked, citing his clients' confidentiality. I obtained a letter from the daughters and called to discuss it, but Tucker slammed the phone down, so I wrote a note, pointing out that the daughters were legally and morally entitled to information. In response came a series of letters accusing me of misrepresenting myself as a 'white knight,' when I was clearly just a devious muckraker intent on 'writing an article for your own gain.' 'I have absolutely no intention of cooperating with a journalist of your type,' he sniffed.

Defeated on that front, I sent an e-mail to Larry Richmond, asking him to clarify the size and nature of TRO's payments to Linda's family. 'It will take some time to review your letter,' he wrote back. 'I hope to get back to you in due course.' Months passed, but nothing happened, so I appealed to Harold Leventhal, the grandfatherly figure who had once managed the Weavers' affairs. 'You're in a void,' he said, sounding sympathetic. 'All you can do is describe it, or you'll never finish your story.' A wise man would have heeded his advice, but I plodded onward until someone took pity and provided me with a few key documents. Ambiguities remained, but at least I found out why the publishers and their cronies were so coy about making disclosures: it looked as if Linda's family was receiving 12.5 per cent of 'Wimoweh' royalties, and around one per cent of the much larger revenues generated by 'The Lion Sleeps Tonight.'

The payments on 'Lion' were coming out of 'performance royalties,' jargon for the bucks generated when a song is broadcast. The sums in question averaged around $275 a quarter in the early nineties, but who are we to raise eyebrows? Solomon's family was desperate and grateful for the smallest blessing. The money 'from outside' enabled his widow to feed her children and educate the two youngest, Elizabeth and Adelaide. After Regina's death in 1990, Raymond Tucker set up a joint bank account for the daughters in which small sums of money continued to materialise – never much, but enough to build a tin shack in their back yard and rent it out for extra money, and even start a little shop at the front gate. In American terms, their poverty remained appalling, but in their own estimation, this was a happy ending – until I showed up, and told them what might have been.

The annals of a curious lawsuit
It's November 1991, and we're in a bland conference room in the American Arbitration Association's New York headquarters. At the

head of a long table sit three veteran copyright lawyers who will act as judges in these proceedings. Ranged before them are the warring parties: the entire cast of the 1961 'Lion Sleeps Tonight' plagiarism contretemps, either in person or legally represented.

Hugo Perretti died a few years back, but fortune has smiled hugely on the rest of the guys since last we saw them. Howie Richmond published the Rolling Stones and Pink Floyd for a while and is now rich beyond wild imaginings. His sidekick Al Brackman (who got ten per cent of all Howie's deals) is rich, too, putters around in boats on weekends and winters at his second home near San Diego. Luigi Creatore has retired to Florida on the proceeds of his many hit records, and George Weiss is a successful composer of movie scores and musicals. So why are they cooped up here, flanked by lawyers? It's another long story.

In the fall of 1989, just as the initial copyright on 'The Lion Sleeps Tonight' was about to expire, Howie and Al were notified that George Weiss and his fellow writers wanted a handsome bonus. Failing this, they'd renew the 'Lion' copyright in their own names and thereafter publish the song themselves, thus cutting Howie and Al out entirely. The publishers were incensed, pointing out that 'Lion' would never have existed if they hadn't allowed Weiss and Co to 'plagiarise' the underlying music. To which the 'Lion' team responded, in effect, how can you accuse us of stealing something you gave us in 1961? The fight went to court in 1990 and wound up in this arbitration months later – two rival groups of rich white Americans squabbling over ownership of the most famous melody ever to emerge from Africa.

The music industry is riveted, because these men are pillars of the showbiz establishment. Al sits on the board of the Music Publishers' Association. Howie founded the Songwriters' Hall of Fame. George Weiss is president of the Songwriters Guild of America and a tireless champion of downtrodden tunesmiths. As such, he can't possibly say that 'The Lion Sleeps Tonight' infringes on the work of a fellow composer, so he doesn't. Sure, he says, we 'threw the music together' using a 'few themes from this Weavers' record,' but so what? Weiss said he'd been told that 'Wimoweh' was just Pete Seeger's interpretation of 'an old thing from Africa,' so they hadn't really plagiarised anyone. To prove his point, Weiss produces the liner notes of an old Miriam Makeba record in which 'Mbube' is described as 'a familiar Zulu song about a lion hunt.'

TRO counters by presenting a yellowing affidavit in which Linda swears that 'Mbube' was wholly original. At this juncture Weiss backs down, saying, in essence, gee, sorry, all this is news to me, and the hearing moves on to the real issue, which is the validity of the 1961 contract between TRO and the 'Lion' trio. Drawn up in a spirit of incestuous back-scratching, the contract allows the Weiss parties free use of 'Wimoweh' and 'Mbube' in 'The Lion Sleeps Tonight,' with no royalty provisions for the author of the underlying songs. The judges seem to find it a bit curious that TRO should now start shouting. 'Hold on! Our own contract's inaccurate!'

Apparently worried that they might not be taken seriously, the men from TRO develop a sudden and barely explicable concern for Solomon's descendants. 'The defendants seek to deprive Mr Linda's family of royalties,' cries Larry Richmond, directing the brunt of his attack at George Weiss. The president of the Songwriters Guild should be 'protecting the poor families of songwriters,' Larry declares, not robbing them. Stung by these accusations, the Weiss parties say that if they win the case they'll give a share to Solomon's estate. The TRO boys then raise the ante, declaring that the family is rightfully entitled to up to a half of the 'Lion's' enormous spoils.

Amazing, no? If TRO had enforced such a distribution from the outset, Solomon's daughters might have been millionaires, but nobody had informed them that this dispute was taking place, so there was no one to laugh (or cry) on their behalf.

The arbitrators weren't very impressed, either – they awarded 'The Lion Sleeps Tonight' to Weiss and Co, with the proviso that they send 'ten percent of writers' performance royalties' to Soweto. The order came into effect on 1 January 1992, just as the song set forth on a new cycle of popularity. That very year, a new recording rose to the top of the Japanese hit parade. Pow Wow's version made Number One in France in 1993. Then someone at Disney wrote a cute little scene in which cartoon animals prance hand-in-hand through a forest glade, singing, 'In the jungle, the mighty jungle ...' The song had been used in at least nine earlier movies, but *Lion King* turned into a supernova. Every kid on the planet had to have the video and the vast array of nursery CDs that went with it. George Weiss could barely contain his glee. 'The song leads a magical life,' he told a reporter. 'It's been a hit eight or nine times but never like this. It's going wild!' The great composer came across as a diffident fellow, somewhat bemused by his enormous good fortune. 'The way all this happened was destiny,' he said. 'It was mysterious, it was beautiful. I have to say God smiled at me.'

I was hoping to talk to Weiss about God and Solomon Linda, but his lawyer said he was out of town and unavailable. On the other hand, he was visible in the *New York Times'* Sunday magazine, which had just run a six-page spread on his awesome retreat in rural New Jersey. I drove out to Oldwick and found the place – an eighteenth-century farmhouse in a deer-filled glade, with a pool and a recording studio in the outbuildings – but Weiss wasn't there. Maybe he was in Santa Fe, where he maintains a hacienda. Or in Cabo San Lucas, Mexico, where he and his wife were building a house on a bluff overlooking the sea. Defeated yet again, I returned to my hotel and wrote him a letter. Weiss faxed back, saying he was 'distressed' to hear that Solomon had been shabbily treated in the past. 'As you can see,' he continued, 'none of that was our doing. While we had no legal obligation to Mr Linda whatsoever, when we gained control of our song, we did what we thought was correct and equitable so that his family could share in the profits.'

A nice gesture, to be sure, but what did 'Lion' earn in the nineties? A million dollars? Two? Three? Ten? And what trickled down to Soweto? Judging from tattered scraps of paper in the daughters' possession, ten per cent of writer's performance royalties amounted to about $12 000 over the decade. Handwritten and unsigned, the notes purported to be royalty statements, but there was no detailed breakdown of the song's overall earnings, and Weiss's business people declined to provide one, despite several requests. Twelve grand was nice money in Soweto terms, but split several ways it changed little or nothing. Solomon Linda's house still had no ceilings, and it was like an oven under the African summer sun. Plaster flaked off the walls outside; toddlers squalled underfoot; three radios blared simultaneously. Fourteen people were living there, sleeping on floors for the most part, washing at an outdoor tap. Only Elizabeth was working, and when she moved out, most of the furniture went with her.

Last time I visited, in January, the kitchen was barren save for six pots and a lone formica table. Linda's youngest daughter, Adelaide, lay swooning under greasy bedclothes, gravely ill from an infection she was too poor to have properly treated. A distant relative wandered around in an alcoholic stupor, waving a pair of garden shears and singing snatches of 'Mbube.' Elizabeth put her hands to her temples and said, 'Really, we are not coping.'

All the sisters were there: Fildah, with her sangoma's headdress swathed in a bright red scarf; Elizabeth and Delphi in their best clothes; Adelaide, swaying back and forth on a chair, dazed, sweat pouring down her gaunt cheekbones. I'd come to report back to them on my adventures in the mysterious overseas, bringing a pile of legal papers that I did my best to explain. I told them about Paul Campbell, the fictitious entity who seemed to have collected big money that might otherwise have come their way, and about Larry Richmond, who wept crocodile tears on their behalf in a legal proceeding that might have changed their destiny if only they'd been aware of it. And, finally, I showed them the letter in which George Weiss assured me that his underlings were depositing a 'correct and equitable' share into the bank account of their mother, 'Mrs Linda,' who had been dead and buried for a decade.

The daughters had never heard of any of these foreigners, but they had a shrewd idea of why all this had happened. 'It's because our father didn't attend school,' Elizabeth said. 'He was just signing everything they said he must sign. Maybe he was signing many papers.' Everyone sighed, and that was that.

In which a moral is considered

Once upon a time, a long time ago, a Zulu man stepped up to a microphone and improvised a melody that earned in the region of $15 million. That Solomon Linda got almost none of it was probably inevitable. He was a black man in white-ruled South Africa, but his American peers fared little better. Robert Johnson's contribution to the blues went largely unrewarded. Leadbelly lost half of his publishing to his white 'patrons.' DJ Alan Freed refused to play Chuck Berry's 'Maybellene' until he was given a songwriter's cut. Led Zeppelin's 'Whole Lotta Love' was nicked off Willie Dixon. All musicians were minnows in the pop-music food chain, but blacks were most vulnerable, and Solomon Linda, an illiterate migrant from a wild and backward place, was totally defenceless against sophisticated predators.

Which is not to say that he was cheated. On the contrary, all the deals were perfectly legal. No one forced Linda to sell 'Mbube' to Eric Gallo for ten shillings, and if Gallo turned around and traded it at a profit, so what? It belonged to him. The good old boys of TRO were perfectly entitled to rename the song, adapt it as they pleased and allocate the royalties to nonexistent entities. After all, they were its owners. Linda was legally entitled to nothing. The fact that he got anything at all seemed to show that the bosses were not without pity.

So I sat down and wrote long letters to George Weiss and Larry Richmond, distancing myself from pious moralists who might see them as sharks and even suggesting a line of reasoning they might take. 'The only thing worse than exploitation,' I mused, 'is not being exploited at all.' And then I enumerated all the good things old Solomon gained from making up the most famous melody that ever emerged from Africa: ten shillings, a big reputation, adulation and lionisation; several cool suits, a wind-up gramophone, a cheque from Pete Seeger and a trickle of royalties that had spared his daughters from absolute penury.

'All told,' I concluded, 'there is a case to be made against the idea that Solomon Linda was a victim of injustice.'

I sat back and waited for someone to make it.

Rolling Stone, May 2000

Postscript: As this article was going to press, Howie Richmond phoned to say he wanted to make peace with Linda's ghost. The blame for this 'tragic situation,' he continued, lay with the long-dead Gallo Records executive who'd replied to the New Yorkers' initial query about 'Mbube's' legal status. Alec Delmont wrote something along the lines of, 'It's a traditional Zulu song, but it belongs to us.' It's hard to say what Delmont was up to here. It's possible that he didn't understand the legal meaning of 'traditional,' using it as synonym for rural. It is also possible that Delmont foolishly imagined he'd hit on a way to avoid awkward questions. After all, if 'Mbube' was traditional, Solomon Linda wasn't entitled to composer royalties and nobody could object if Delmont's company didn't pay any.

Either way, Gallo Records had made a blunder from which it would never recover. The instant Howie Richmond and his sidekicks saw the word 'traditional,' they thought, aha, another wild horse; we can adapt this one as we please. When the Jo'burg boys realised what was happening, they hastily reversed themselves, but it was too late: the New Yorkers just shrugged off their attempts to recast 'Mbube' as an original composition.

As it happens, Gallo had irrefutable proof of this contention in its vaults – all three acetates recorded during the fateful 1939 session. Played consecutively, they showed beyond all doubt that the miracle melody was Solomon Linda's creation. But 40 years would pass before archivist Rob Allingham rediscovered these treasures. Back in 1951, the Gallo boys thought their case was unwinnable, so they settled for the right to administer 'Wimoweh' in territories like Northern Rhodesia and Portuguese East Africa and grumbled their way out of the picture.

But anyway, Howie Richmond's heart seemed to be in the right place. A week or so later, I received a call from Linda's daughter Elizabeth, who said thugs had barged into her house a few nights earlier, terrorised her family at gunpoint and looted her possessions. Her front door was still hanging off its hinges, so she couldn't leave home to check out a rumour she'd heard from her bank. I investigated on her behalf, and called back an hour later. 'Money is pouring into your bank account from America,' I said. 'Nearly $15 thousand in the last ten days.' At the time, currency speculators were making a run on the rand, so the total came close to R150 000, a mountain of cash for someone in Elizabeth's position. She said nothing for the longest time. I couldn't be sure, but I think she was crying.

The windfall arose from the use of 'Wimoweh' in a US TV commercial for a hotel chain. Some of the money had initially gone to Pete Seeger, who'd turned it back. It seemed he'd been receiving royalties on the song all along. 'I just found out,' he told me on the phone. 'I didn't know.' Seeger and his publishers later agreed to cede all future royalties from 'Wimoweh' to Linda's family. That left unresolved the far greater earnings of the 'The Lion Sleeps Tonight.'

After the *Rolling Stone* article was published, I introduced Linda's daughters to a young Johannesburg lawyer named Hanro Friedrich, who took up the cudgels on their behalf. Hanro convinced Gallo Records to finance some research by Dr Owen Dean, the heaviest copyright lawyer in Johannesburg. Dean spotted an obscure clause in the Imperial Copyright Act of 1911 that offered a cause of action, and the Department of Arts and Culture agreed to finance litigation. One morning in 2005, the world woke up to hear that Dr Dean had taken Donald Duck and Mickey Mouse hostage. Or more accurately: that he'd attached Disney's trademarks on the grounds that the giant American corporation was making unauthorised use of Solomon Linda's music in *The Lion King* and its many lucrative spinoffs.

Dean's ploy had the desired effect. Disney had no stomach for an embarrassing court case, so it brought pressure to bear on George Weiss and his partners. In 2006, the parties reached an out-of-court settlement, the precise terms of which remain secret. Let's just say it involved a fair chunk of money, even after taxes and legal fees, and that it included a provision entitling Linda's daughters to a reasonable share of 'The Lion Sleeps Tonight's future earnings. The daughters traded their sangoma braids for fashionable hair-pieces and commenced a turbulent but no doubt pleasurable adjustment to life in the middle classes.

The Beautiful and the Damned

||||||||||||||||||||||||||||||||||||||||||||||||||||||||||||||||||||||||||||||||||||||||||||||||||||||||||||||||||||||||||||||||||||||||||||||||||||||||||||||||||||||

I didn't take the early 1990s World Trade Centre peace talks very seriously, in part because I doubted that South African politicians could control their followers even if they really wanted to. Also, I'd been watching Yugoslavia degenerate into an orgy of ethnic butchery. Those Muslims, Serbs and Croats were very civilised, at least in relation to us. They looked alike and had a language in common. Decades of authoritarian socialism had flattened the class differences between them. But when the crunch came, they fell on each other like animals. If Yugoslavs couldn't check their slide into race war, what hope had we? There was none, as far as I could see.

So I failed to join in the general rejoicing when the politicians announced that they'd agreed on an interim constitution and set a date for free elections. On the other hand, I was not above clutching at straws and the optimistic shift in the nation's mood was entirely agreeable. Besides, it was summer, and a free trip to Sun City seemed just the thing.

Friday, 26 November 1993: not a red-letter day in South Africa, exactly, but sandwiched between several of same. Last week, negotiators signed off on a constitution that's supposed to bring us peace. Yesterday, US sanctions were repealed and now the sky is dark with flying investors. Next week, the last white parliament convenes to vote itself into oblivion and after that it's all aboard for free elections, uhuru, State President Mandela, etc. The long dark epoch of apartheid is finally ending and all I can say, being white, is hallelujah! Liberation from Guilt! Redistribution of responsibility! The freedom to board a private plane, fly off to King Sol's regal hog-trough and not feel in the least shit about it. I think I'm going to love the New South Africa.

The plane is a ten-seat turbo prop, laid on by Sun International. It takes off from Midrand airport, hops over Hartbeespoort Dam and sets down on the bushveld airstrip near Sun City. The sun is hot, the veld is green and my heart is full, but my friend The Botanist is feeling a bit queasy. She has a past, you understand. She used to edit *Spare Rib* and owns an entire library of weighty feminist tomes. In the seventies, she demonstrated against Mrs Julia Morley's grotesque cattle show, so she's vaguely uneasy about being a guest at Miss World 1993.

Last beauty contest I attended was in Jo'burg City Hall in 1972 or thereabouts. The girls came on one by one and did their go-go dancing bikini thing. Then they were all brought back on stage and the winner chosen by acclamation. The MC walked down the line, holding his hand over the head of each contestant and yelling, 'Let's hear it for Sandra! Let's hear it for Debbie!' Pretty girls drew lewd cheers, which was gratifying, I dare say, but plain ones with plumpish thighs were booed and hissed and humiliated so horribly that I bled for them, but that was long ago, when I was a callow left-winger who believed quite passionately in tearing down what was and replacing it all with something cleaner and brighter and better. Now, hey – now I just go with the flow, which carries me into a Sun International minibus, through the portals of Sun City and up to the top of the valley, where an astonishing sight awaits: a tumble of ancient, weathered ruins, rising from the savannah like the set of some wildly improbable Hollywood movie.

A turbaned Nubian in flowing robes steps forward to greet us. Another Nubian takes my luggage, leads me through the massive wooden gates and into the Palace, where the air is filled with the perfumes of Arabia. Water drips off ancient stone masonry. Rivers leap from the living rock and flow away into mysterious underground passages. You pass through a hall the size of a cathedral and under the shadow of a rampaging bull elephant. Then a door opens before you and the bellboy says, 'Sir, your suite.'

He's about eighteen. This is his third week on the job and he just loves it. He shows you how to work the TV, the safe and the wooden ceiling fan. He draws your attention to the silver bowl full of luscious fruits and bon-bons, the rich bathrobes in the closet, the French champagne in the mini-bar. He draws back the drapes to offer a view of the magical ruins. The temple of Courage, the Gong of the Sun

Lion, the Royal Arena. A dark green lake lies at the foot of the valley and all around, tawny hills rise into a blazing blue sky. All this splendour and the bellboy's alone to display. He turns, bursting with pride, and says, 'Isn't it wonderful?'

Well, yes, it is. I came willing to be facetious, but this spectacle defeats me: all the clever remarks in the back of my mind suddenly seem so blindingly obvious as to sound stupid. So, the truth then: the Palace of the Lost City is magnificent.

The Palace is a grand hotel, as you have no doubt gathered, completed a year or so ago at a cost of almost £200 million and situated somewhat precariously in Bophuthatswana, one of the tribal republics created by apartheid. Until a year or two ago, we used to crack jokes about Bop's 'so-called' independence and the tragic-comic pronouncement of its strongman, Chief Lucas Mangope, but we're not laughing much any more. Mangope is refusing to rejoin a united South Africa and knuckle under to Nelson Mandela. And Mandela, for his part, is threatening to send in the tanks if Mangope refuses to come to heel. But we don't want to talk about that, do we? Nah, it's too depressing.

Let's rather pop the cap on a Perrier and sit down to read the Official Miss World Press Kit. Hmm. One gathers that it's a caring, sharing event these days, gender sensitive and politically progressive. The girls – sorry, women – are judged less on their bodies and faces than on their intellect, personality and commitment to fighting Aids, saving the planet or whatever. What's more, proceeds from this year's ticket sales are going to feed starving black children, and Variety Club International is getting a rake-off from the satellite TV fees. In short, we're going to preen and pose, ogle flesh, sip Veuve Cliquot, and benefit the previously disadvantaged. Gee whiz. I can't wait.

But first, we must pay tribute to King Sol, the man who made all this possible.

Friday 12:30 pm. I'm sitting on the terrace under crumbling buttresses and ancient copper domes talking to Sol Kerzner, schlockmeister, schmoozer, mensch, tycoon. I love this man. He's one of the all-time great white South Africans, a schlemiel from Bez Valley who grew up with almost nothing, and now look at him, lounging on the terrace in Gucci loafers, drawling in a fake American accent, master of an international empire of resort hotels and casinos. Sol's spent most of the past two days talking to foreign media and I am curious as to the drift of their questions. 'Tell me,' I say, 'do they still think you're a moral leper?'

Poor Sol. He's so used to being reviled and spat upon for making a buck off the back of apartheid that he automatically assumes I'm challenging the morality of doing business in the Bantustans. He's five minutes into a justificatory monologue before I can stop him. I tune him, relax my bru. Relax. Nobody cares any more. We've buried the hatchet. The revolution has been postponed. Let's talk about girls, man. Let's talk about the Miss World competition. Let's talk about this press release from the ANC's Women's League, which strongly objects to 'the reduction of women to objects of beauty,' and accuses you of complicity in 'on-going gender oppression.'

'There's nothing wrong with a beautiful girl,' says Sol, and nothing wrong with staging a contest that celebrates beauty, especially if your heart is pure, as is his. He is at pains to stress that he is not staging this beauty pageant because he's into beauty pageants *per se*. He is doing it for promotion – not just for himself or Sun International, but for all of us; the nation. 'Around 700 million people will be watching,' he says. 'They're going to see Cape Town, game reserves, beaches. The exposure is incredible.' In theory, a certain percentage of these international TV viewers will rush to South Africa, clutching fistfuls of hard currency, at least some of which will trickle down to the hard-done-by masses.

All this is offered somewhat shamefacedly, as if to concede that the staging of beauty pageants cannot really be justified in its own terms. And I'm sitting there thinking, hey, Sol, wise up! This is the New South Africa! You're being Mau-Mau'd by a tiny cabal of over-educated feminist mission girls! Forget the Women's League! South Africa's black masses are massively into beauty pageants. There were seven beauty pageants *in Soweto alone* last weekend. Seven! Countrywide, there may have been as many as 50, for all I know. We're talking serious commitment to beauty pageant culture here. We're talking about a country in which the oppressed African majority has exacted the right to give bossy Euro-feminists the finger and hold as many beauty pageants as it pleases! You're a hero, Sol! You're finally doing right by black people!

Yes? No? On balance, no. Sol seems to think I'm a bit cracked, so I toss him a normal question about Lost City.

How did it happen, Sol? I mean, when did the inspiration actually inspire you? It was January 1990, he says, a week or two before Nelson walked to freedom. There was a certain madness in the air, a sense that the worst was over and that the good times were about to roll. Addled with optimism, King Sol stood on a barren hillside in the bushveld of Bophuthatswana and said, here shall arise a Ziggurat, a Xanadu, a pleasure dome to which pilgrims will stream from all corners of the planet. He summoned his minions and bade them begin. 'Whatever you do,' he told them, 'it has to be African.'

And lo, here it is; The Lost City, an instant ruin, celebrating the African authentic: African murals designed in Italy, African artwork conceived in LA, and the music of Dead White Men, performed in the great vaulted tea-lounge by the Soweto String Quartet. It's magnificent! I love it!

Unfortunately, it costs almost £200 a night, way beyond the reach of 98 per cent of South Africans. Only foreigners can afford such prices and most of them are too scared to come here on account of the terrible violence they see on TV – mobs ransacking cities, burning buildings, burning each other. But we really don't want to go into that, do we? Nah. We want to laze in the sun all afternoon, preparing for the evening's rigours.

Friday 6:00 pm. We're in the Superbowl, Sun City's 7 000-seat auditorium. The Miss World logo is suspended above the stage, upon which a dress rehearsal is unfolding. Eighty-one strong young women with well-developed intellects are teetering around in knock-me-down-and-fuck-me pumps, trailing choking clouds of perfume and hairspray, trying out their Little Bo Beep speeches in the microphone. 'Hi, I'm Miss Indonesia! If I become Miss World, I will work for world peace!' Or, 'I'm Miss Paraguay, and I'm seriously worried about the rainforests.' Whales are mentioned, along with the poor, the orphaned and the maimed. Charmain Naidoo and I are giggling. We're writing it all down dutifully, but we're giggling. Wouldn't you?

Charmain works for the local *Sunday Times*, 'the largest newspaper in Africa.' She's been here all week, keeping tabs on celebrities. She has a pretty shrewd idea of who's been sleeping with whom and doing which drugs in what quantity, and it's all absolutely fascinating. Not to you, maybe, but Charmain and I are survivors of the brutal celebrity drought inflicted on South Africa by apartheid. We spent our youths reading about foreign celebrities in magazines, listening to their records and watching their movies, but they never set foot in our pariah state. In my teens, the only rock stars who showed up to be adulated were Barclay James Harvest, who were boring, and the Byrds, who were by then so far gone on acid that they could barely tune their guitars.

But now ... now the skies have opened and it's raining celebrities: Joan Collins, Jerry Hall, Yasmin Le Bon, Ursula Andress, La Toya Jackson, Phil Collins and Elton John are on their way and there are at least ten genuine, world-class celebrities here already, including Twiggy, Christie Brinkley, Lou Gossett Junior, Pierce Brosnan and George Benson. Charmain sighs. She's had a mild crush on George Benson for the last decade. Yesterday he materialised before her in an elevator doorway. He smiled. He stepped inside. She was so excited she could barely breathe. The door closed and by the time they reached the ground floor, Charmain had formed a close relationship with a boil on the back of George Benson's neck. 'It's weird,' she says. 'You spend your whole life dreaming about these people, but when you see them up close they are so ordinary and frail. In a way I wish they'd just stayed pictures on the wall.'

Friday 10:00 pm. The Botanist and I are in the casino, contemplating a thousand myriad reflections of ourselves in the mirrored walls. We're losing heavily, but we're not crying. We are watching a bronzed bloke with gold chains, throwing money away on a roulette table. He signs a cheque, buys a mountain of chips and carpets the bottom third of the table – five grand on a single turn of the wheel. Whirr, click, he loses it all. He clicks his fingers for the floor manager, signs another cheque and repeats the procedure, again, and again. He drops £10 000 before our eyes. '*Ag*,' he says, 'it's only paper and plastic.'

Friday 10:30 pm. The media centre is deserted. The hacks have filed, the phone banks are silent, and there is no sign of Miss South Africa, the lovely Jacqui Mofokeng of Soweto. I had an appointment to interview her here, but I tarried too long at the gaming tables and Jacqui has retired to her beauty sleep. Alas, alas. I was so looking forward to a stimulating discussion of beauty pageant politics, South Africa-style.

Everything in this country is a zone of intense political/racial conflict, even the humdrum world of beauty pageants. For years, the Miss South Africa contest was dominated by blonde Aryans, and black girls weren't even allowed to enter. This odious colour bar was done away with in the late eighties, but the title still went to the sort of girl who'd appeal to a Eurocentric bigot, which is to say: a blonde, or a coloured girl with straight hair, aquiline nose and at least a passing resemblance to Whitney Houston. It was not fair. It would not do, not in a country where 80 per cent of the population is African and passionate about beauty pageants.

The distressed cries of all the disenfranchised Miss Afro Paragons and Miss Benetton Sowetos were heard in high places. The ANC brought pressure to bear on *Rapport* and the *Sunday Times*, sponsors of the Miss South Africa pageant. These days, one does not argue with the ANC. One cuts a deal. The capitalists set up a fund to foster beauty pageant culture among the oppressed masses. In return, the ANC gave the Miss South Africa extravaganza its blessing.

Matters might have rested there were it not for the cynics who claimed there was a secret codicil to the deal. Jacqui Mofokeng is a good-looking girl, but she was also the first full-blooded African to seize the Miss South Africa title, and white racists didn't like it. The instant the crown descended on her head, they started yelling, 'Fix!' Some accused the sponsors of deferring to the ANC and rigging the outcome. Others called radio talk shows and said, 'How can you call her a beauty queen? She's got thick lips and a flat nose.'

I wanted to tell Jacqui how sordid I found all this, and how ashamed I was for my fellow white South Africans. I wanted to tell her that I for one found her extremely sexy, but perhaps it's as well that I blew the opportunity, because she would probably have slapped me. Jacqui's a feminist who takes no shit. Just yesterday, she ripped the head off a British TV presenter who used the phrase 'glitz and tits' in her presence. The poor English girl was reportedly reduced to tears.

Jacqui and I went to the same school, incidentally, a rather expensive private establishment called Woodmead. In my day, Woodmead was whites-only, but it was integrated in the late seventies, in bold defiance of apartheid. Now it's predominantly black and widely regarded as a model of racial harmony and integration. The headmistress's office was petrol-bombed by rioting students the other day, but we don't want to go into that, do we? Nah, fuck it. Let's party.

Midnight. The lobster is done for, the salmon are skeletal and the Veuve Cliquots lie upside down and dead in ice-buckets. The massed hacks, having hogged, are partying in the courtyard under that statue of a towering elephant. And in their midst ... Grace Jones! Grace Jones, in person at Sun City! It's amazing. Grace seems to be a very good sport. She lifted the skirt of a prim local TV newsreader to see what nature of panties she was wearing, if any. She did lewd dances with Marcus Schenkenberg of Sweden, 'the highest-paid male model in the world.' She commandeered a mike in the discotheque last night and got fans to join her in a hypnotic chant of 'Sex! Sex! Sex!' And through all of this, she's extremely friendly to everyone. She'll talk to anyone, kiss anyone, dance with anyone – pimply teenagers, obscure locals, even waiters.

Tonight she's dancing with Christina, King Sol's present paramour. They're doing this very stylish semi-Latin shimmy to the music of George Benson, who's jamming with the cocktail band. After a song or two, George wipes the sweat from his brow and yields the spotlight to the Soweto String Quartet, four scholarly African gentlemen in evening dress who usually play chamber music in the tea lounge. Tonight, however ... tonight they're letting their hair down. Tonight they've playing mbaqanga, township jive, the bassist and cellist sawing out repetitive three-chord phrases while the violinists cut loose with wild solos. They're so good they bring tears to my eyes.

Ah, this country, this country. It's pathetically fucked-up for the most part, but tonight I survey the jiving racial all-sorts, and an outrageous idea takes root in my brain: maybe we really can do it; synthesise rich and poor, black and white, Europe and Africa, and create something so blindingly lovely that the rest of you fall in awe and dismay. Maybe Bill Clinton's right. Maybe we are living in the midst of a miracle. Or maybe it's just a surfeit of champagne.

Saturday, 27 November. The Big Day dawns hot and blue. I wake to find a newsletter stuck under my door announcing the results of an overnight poll taken among the hacks. Odds-on favourite to win the crown is Miss Puerto Rico, with Misses Italy, Chile and Sweden hot on her trail – all Aryans, you'll note, or Latinate Barbie dolls with jet-black hair and golden skin.

Sipho 'Hotstix' Mabuse is ensconced in a corner of the vast dining emporium with his wife and children, eating Eggs Benedict. Sipho is a pop star, inventor of Soweto Afro-disco sound. His wife Chichi owns the local franchise for a line of American cosmetics called Black Like Me. Their little girls are very cute numbers with cornrowed hair and no front teeth.

Sipho says, 'Sit down,' so we do, and soon he's telling us about the bad old days, when it was dangerous to be black and beautiful in small South African towns. Once he was beaten senseless for slashing in a whites-only *pissoir* at a service station. Another time, he and his sidemen were attacked by white thugs and then arrested by white police when they dared defend themselves. Sipho laughs, but the incident left scars on his face, and barely concealed hurt and rage in his heart.

The food is fine, but the talk leaves The Botanist upset and confused. She was just growing to like the New South Africa when Sipho started rubbing her nose in the grim realities of the old. 'God,' she says, 'this country is exhausting. You change your mind all the time.' About what? Well, about Nelson Mandela, for instance. The Botanist regards Mandela as a man of enormous moral gravity, one of the most noble figures of the twentieth century. She was therefore shocked and appalled to see the pictures of him in the morning's paper, resplendent in a penguin suit, opening the new Dunhill boutique in exclusive Sandton. 'I'm so disillusioned,' she says. 'I never thought he'd stoop to that.'

Ja, well. Depends where you stand, I suppose. Myself, I'm elated to see Madiba schmoozing with bankers and captains of industry. Three years ago he was threatening to nationalise everything and plunge us into the antediluvian greyness of total socialist paralysis. I think an interest in luxury leather goods and fine tobaccos is entirely suitable in a future head of state.

Six pm. Excitement is mounting. On distant continents, 700 million viewers are glued to their TV screens. The live audience is streaming down carpets and taking seats in the Superbowl. I survey the crowd and wince for the ANC Women's League, whose righteous denunciations of this gender-oppressive cattle show have clearly gone unheeded. At least a quarter of the seats are occupied by the members of the oppressed masses – sleek, gleaming Sowetans and Nigerians and Zairians in the tribal finery of modern Africa, which is to say, suits by Armani, frocks by YSL or Dior.

One of them is Wally Serote, head of the ANC's Arts and Culture Department and widely regarded as Minister of Culture in waiting. A few years ago, Comrade Serote was writing poems about pouring petrol on white children and setting them on fire. And now here he is in a tuxedo, living it up with the bourgeois pigs. God, I adore the New South Africa. All our sacred cows are keeling over, legs in the air. Nelson Mandela opens boutiques! Apartheid cabinet ministers marry coloured girls! White women anoint a black former 'terrorist' (Tokyo Sexwale) 'sexiest politician in the nation'! Anything goes. I mean, *Peter Mokaba is here tonight!* Peter Mokaba, boss of the ANC's ultra-militant Youth League! Last time I saw him he was on a podium, chanting 'Kill the Boers!' Now it's, All youth to battle! All youth to the frontline! Forward to the Superbowl!

Trumpets blare, music swells, and a dancin', prancin' New Orleans-style marchin' band appears, followed by a forest of waving pennants and banners and scores of glamorous misses. Around the auditorium they come, so close I can almost touch them, not that I would dare.

They seem to fall into three fairly distinct categories. Girls from rich white countries slouch along half-heartedly, as if to say, I'm not really into this, you know, I'm much too hip to take it seriously, but there's a lot of money at stake and who knows, maybe I'll wind up a supermodel or something. Girls from the Afro-Asian bloc, on the other hand, carry themselves with a potentially tragic solemnity. One imagines them in humble apartments in overcrowded tropical cities, offering their best profile to the mirror, practising that smile, that walk, that wave. And finally, there are the Latin Americans, who are simply and splendidly sluttish. Their heads are haloed by great fans of ostrich feathers. Their dresses are slit almost to the armpit. Some are virtually naked. What rare pleasure it is to sit within touching distance of such creatures, admiring their intellects and strong personalities.

After the march-past it's all downhill. Ghastly inspirational songs are sung, insipid homilies delivered. Pierce Brosnan of Remington Steele fame pulls some names out of a hat, and 71 losers exit left. Cut to commercial. A few minutes later, there is another winnowing. Miss South Africa makes it into the final five, at which point I am beset by misgivings. Are the judges so addled by New South African euphoria that they're going to give our Jacqui the title? It'd be great for Jacqui and an honour for our old school. On the other hand, it might goad the bigots beyond endurance and start a race war.

Fifteen minutes later, the final verdict: Miss Philippines comes third, Jacqui is runner-up, and the crown goes to Miss Jamaica, a TV presenter from Kingston. A clean sweep for the Third World, with not one of the media favourites showing. Feminists might be on to something when they complain that the media are dominated by Eurocentric males who harbour secret prejudices against the exotic.

Ten pm, and the Coronation Ball is commencing. We're sharing a table with three inscrutable Mayans from *Vogue* Mexico and a tabloid reporter from Fleet Street, aflush with liquor and clearly confused by the 'authentically African' ambience of his surroundings. He claims to have a scoop, the hottest story of the entire week. 'I've filed already,' he whispers conspiratorially, 'so I'll share it with you. It happened in a town called Krugersdorp, that's K-R-U-G-E-R-S-D-O-R-P...' He proceeds to tell a harrowing story about two unfortunate Chinese, waylaid en route to Miss World by carnivores. 'It happened yesterday,' he whispers. 'That's why there were two empty front-row seats at the pageant.'

Poor fellow. Krugersdorp is a suburb. The last predators there were shot circa 1860. Someone's pulled his leg right off, but who am I to intervene? I hold my tongue and the story appears in the next day's *Sunday People*: 'Miss World Fans Eaten By Lions.'

Four am. The Botanist and I are rolling home, our pockets bulging with swag – a thousand pounds, count 'em, the consequence of a lucky streak at the blackjack and roulette tables. Poor old Sol. We drink his booze, eat his lobsters, sleep in his beds, pose mocking questions in an interview and then cash in our chips and take his money home. Must be tough to own a casino.

Sunday, 28 November, early afternoon. I am drifting on an inner tube through an ancient stone canyon, created 18 months ago by one of Sol's cunning landscape architects. The maw of a tunnel gapes before me. I sail over an artificial waterfall and into pitch-black freefall. An eternity later, the sun explodes above my head and I splash down on a designer-made blue lagoon. In the distance, bikini girls are sipping daiquiris on a designer beach, in the shade of designer palm trees. Something goes whoosh in the wall behind me and a tall wave rushes forward, clearly man-made in its curling blue perfection. I strike out, catch it before it breaks, and body-surf into the concrete shallows. Ah, yes, the sweet life in the Valley of Waves, the Lost City's own Tahiti.

The Botanist is sitting on the beach, reading the Sunday papers. Each front page features the dusky lovelies, Miss Jamaica and Miss South Africa, arm in arm like sisters, flashing blinding smiles. Do we really want to turn the page and examine the horrors that lie within? Nah, not really. Who wants to hear about attacks on police stations and ongoing butchery among the desperate in squatter camps? Who wants to hear about fascist plots and failed peace talks, about small towns where all the talk is of race war? Not I. One loses stomach, eventually. One shrugs and turns to the business pages, where optimism reigns.

The stock market is booming. A new elite is coming into being. Former revolutionaries are moving into boardrooms. Almost 70 per cent of white capitalists now back Mandela. The men in suits say we're heading for a happy ending, that countless jobs will soon materialise, along with houses for the homeless, food for the hungry and hope for the teeming millions of utterly wretched. Who knows, maybe they're right. Maybe it'll all come true. And maybe it's just a fantasy, like this place.

Esquire, February 1994

The Prince of Darkness

||||||||||||||||||||||||||||||||||||||||||||||||||||||||||||||||||||||||||||||||||||||||||||||||||||||||||||||||||||||||||||||||||||||||

Once upon a time, quite a long time ago, the literary editor of a London Sunday newspaper prevailed upon JM Coetzee's agent to persuade the reclusive author to grant an interview, an exercise to which Coetzee was known to be totally allergic. But an understanding was reached and a date was set, and I was deputised to ask the questions. This was a great honour, given that Coetzee was to my mind the greatest living author in the English language. I'd read all his books in a single sitting, engaged on a psychic level so deep I can only liken it to hypnotism. They were awesome, those early Coetzee works, lit from within by a cold and terrible light, haunted by unanswerable questions. I could make a case for Conrad's *Heart of Darkness*, but otherwise, these were the greatest novels ever written about what my friend Jessica used to call, 'Our expedition of consciousness,' by which she meant the struggle of whites to figure out their destiny in Africa.

We met in his office, the great novelist a pale and austere presence in his grey slacks and tweedy sports jacket, and I under strict instructions from his agent to avoid questions about his personal life. We were to talk only of literature, but my opening question was answered by dead silence. Coetzee was writing the question on his notepad. He pondered it for a minute or two, then proceeded to analyse the assumptions on which it was based, a process that offered penetrating insights into my intellectual shortcomings but revealed nothing about Coetzee himself. All my questions were similarly treated, and I wound up sounding like a reporter for a fanzine. 'What kind of music do you like?' I asked, desperately. The pen scratched, the great writer cogitated. 'Music I have never heard before,' he said.

Ja, well, what can I say? I wasn't the first to come short on the hard rock of Coetzee's aloofness. He never did public signings or book tours, kept his political opinions to himself, kept his private life secret. Maybe there wasn't much to reveal anyway. He worked, he cycled, delivered the odd lecture at the University of Cape Town, lived quietly in Rondebosch with fellow academic Dorothy Driver. Beyond that, his privacy was impenetrable, his distaste for the limelight so extreme that he failed to turn up to receive either of his two Booker prizes. Anyone who wanted to understand John Maxwell Coetzee was forced to turn to the books, an area in which the master was kind enough to offer some guidance: 'True interpretation,' he has written, 'is inseparable from true understanding of the cultural and historical matrix' from which any writing emerges.

At the time of that interview, I thought I understood Coetzee's matrix pretty well. I was white and half-Afrikaans, so was he. We both lived in Cape Town. Yonder was a freeway bridge that bore a striking resemblance to the one under which Mrs Curren lay dying in *Age of Iron*, drifting in and out of consciousness while street children probed her mouth for gold teeth. A few miles in the opposite direction was Sea Point, surely the white suburb ransacked in the opening chapters of *The Life and Times of Michael K*. Over the mountain was UCT, where Coetzee had recently taken a brave stand against leftists who wanted to bar Salman Rushdie from speaking on campus on the grounds that the cultural boycott should not be violated.

It was this act, as much as anything he had written, that caused me to think of Coetzee as something of a kindred spirit, a Suzmanite white liberal, disgusted by apartheid but not particularly enthusiastic about the revolution, either. People get upset when I say things like that, but it's true. Coetzee was never anything so mundane as a sloganeer, a trendy shouter of Viva Mandela. His dark, veiled parables usually gave you the sense that our problems might be beyond solution, and that we were heading into a nightmare of burning cities, roadblocks, barbed wire and concentration camps.

This wasn't the future envisioned by Nadine Gordimer and André Brink, but then they were at pains to present South Africa in a way that made sense to outsiders, often peopling their novels with black characters who spoke perfect English and subscribed to fashionable ideas about democracy. Coetzee always offered something more disturbing.

Consider the story of Susan, an Englishwoman cast away on a desert island in *Foe*, Coetzee's 1986 retelling of the Robinson Crusoe fable. On the beach, she encounters an African slave. She is eager to talk to him, but Friday's tongue has been cut out, so he can't answer. Susan becomes obsessed with Friday's silence. Who is he? What is he thinking? In the closing passages, she pries his jaws open and presses her ear to his mutilated mouth, but still no sound emerges. Foreign critics thought *Foe* was a clever commentary on the evolution of the novel, but I discerned something else in its depths – an unbearably painful parable about a country where most whites and Africans had no language in common, and hence no way of reaching understanding. 'Is this not what you are saying?' I demanded in our interview. A pen scratched on paper, the great writer cogitated. 'I would not wish to deny you your reading,' he said.

Coetzee was equally opaque about Mrs Curren, the central character in *Age of Iron*, then his most recent fiction. Mrs Curren is a decent woman, a white liberal of the sort everyone seems to disparage these days. Whenever an apartheid cabinet minister appears on her television screen, Mrs Curren stands up to listen; otherwise it is like being urinated on while kneeling. She loathes the 'savage, unreconstructed old boars' who run the country, but she's never really done anything about them (other than be 'nice' to everyone) and now there is a price to pay: 'I have cancer from the accumulation of shame I have endured in my life,' she says. 'That is how cancer comes about: from self-loathing.' Do you and Mrs Curren have anything in common, I asked Coetzee. 'My position is as confused as hers,' he replied.

That is the most revealing quote I was able to wring out of him, but I counted myself quite lucky – in a previous interview, he'd refused even to disclose his middle name. I went home and wrote a piece in which Coetzee came across as coldly intellectual and possibly a bit weird. His friends were not impressed. 'You got him wrong,' they said. 'He's great company if he's among people he likes. Cooks great vegetarian dishes, cracks jokes. You should have met him in the old days, before he gave up drinking; he could be incredibly funny.'

Others thought my sketch was quite accurate. A writer described dinner parties ruined by Coetzee's ominous silence. 'He just sits there,' she said, 'listening, judging.' An artist told of a three-day trek into a mountain range during which Coetzee said not one word to anyone.

An academic wrote to say he sympathised with my attempts to extract a coherent set of positions from a man he called 'the Great Elider.'

'There are legions of stories to back you up,' he continued. 'A friend of mine was an MA student of Coetzee's. She had to deliver a paper to his home. As she approached the door she noticed the blinds moving, but her ring remained unanswered for a long, long while. When she finally gave up and was walking away, she turned around to find the crocodile-eyed genius contemplating her implacably from a window. She became a lesbian, but I am not sure if there is any connection.'

Do we detect a streak of cruelty here? Well, yes. Coetzee has published two slim volumes about his early life. *Boyhood* was about growing up in Worcester. 'An undistinguished rural family,' he writes. 'Bad schooling.' Boring parents who dance to 'clodhopping' music at the Metro Hotel with 'goofy' looks on their faces. At the age of 15, John decides he will become an artist, and beyond that point, anyone who offers comfort or causes distraction is shoved ruthlessly aside – cloying girlfriends, backward Afrikaans relatives and even his mother, who refuses to understand that young John is 'remorselessly' determined to extinguish the very memory of his family.

In *Youth*, the second volume of autobiography, an entire country is dispensed with. 'South Africa was a bad start, a handicap,' he writes. 'If a tidal wave were to sweep in from the Atlantic and wash away the southern tip of Africa, he (John) will not shed a tear.'

John wants to be an artist, you see, and to his mind, artists have certain characteristics. They understand that 'civilization since the 18th century has been an Anglo-French affair,' and live in London, New York or Paris. Ideally, they should be able to read the classics in the original Greek or Latin, but above all, they must suffer agonies of loneliness and alienation. In *Youth*, Coetzee describes himself sitting in a bitterly cold London flat, eating bread and apples, writing dreadful adolescent poetry and dreaming of making love to film stars. Not Hollywood stars, of course. Exotic creatures in European art films with subtitles. 'Is true art born only out of misery?' he asks himself. The answer is yes, but misery somehow fails to ignite his creative fire.

Some reviewers found *Youth* depressing, but I thought it was full of witty self-deprecation, as if Coetzee was amused to remember what a pretentious little twit he had been, and how awkward his first sexual gropings. But as always in Coetzee, things turn dark towards the end.

John turns 24. John is a failure as a lover and a writer. His soul is 'cold, frozen.' He's so miserable he might as well die.

Alas, poor John, always drawn to darkness in much the way that helpless spacecraft are sucked into black holes in science fiction. At some point in the seventies, he was sucked back into the darkness of South Africa, and the rest is history – a string of eight terrible and beautiful novels, each darker than its predecessor. When the apartheid drama began to lighten, after 1990, he turned towards darkness in his own life for inspiration. His ex-wife Jubber died of cancer, and he created Mrs Curren, who visualises the tumour as a crab inside her body, eating her alive. His son died in a mysterious fall from a building, and he produced *Master of Petersburg*, a novel about a father similarly stricken.

This relentless bleakness eventually began to worry me. I did my own share of agonising, but after the long dark night of the soul there was usually a bright sunny morning followed by a nice braai and a *dop* with cheerful rugby fans in short pants. It pained me that Coetzee was too civilised to enjoy such things. As critic Shaun de Waal observes, 'He cracked a joke in the opening line of his first novel ("My name is Eugene Dawn. I can't help that.") and never laughed again.'

In fact, looking back over Coetzee's writings, I can pinpoint only two moments when he appears to be happy. One came in the summer of 1964 or thereabouts. Coetzee is lying on the greensward of Hampstead Heath. The air is warm, birds are singing. He drifts into a state of consciousness he has never experienced before. '*At last*,' he thinks. 'At last it has come, the moment of ecstatic unity with the All.' Thirty years later, in the delirious aftermath of Mandela's election, Coetzee goes on a bicycle tour of France, and experiences a second epiphany. I can't find the article where he describes it, but the way I remember it, he says something like, 'I am so deeply grateful to be alive.' I got tears in my eyes. I thought, heck, the oke is finally coming right.

Alas, it didn't last. A year later, Coetzee came forth with a caustic dissection of the folkloric spectacles staged around the 1995 world rugby cup. These were supposed to celebrate the birth of the Rainbow Nation, but Coetzee found them farcical, a parade of ethnic cliches designed to promote the interests of 'an international cartel embracing a "philosophy" of growth no more complex than that of a colony of bacteria.'

In retrospect, this was the first sign that Coetzee was not entirely at ease in the New South Africa. It was a common feeling among those of us buried in the matrix of white maleness. Our ancestors bestrode Africa like giants, slaughtering game, digging holes for gold, subjugating everyone. When the tide turned, we steeled ourselves for Armageddon, but nothing happened. The enemy came to power, but no vengeance was taken. They were even willing to forgive us, provided that we fell to our knees and said sorry. I experienced this as totally humiliating. White males had become ridiculous, and we were heading towards irrelevance.

Since I still considered Coetzee a potentially kindred spirit, I wondered how the changes were affecting him. One gathered that the wind of change had begun to buffet UCT. A black woman became vice-chancellor, new ideologies swept the campus. The classics were out, 'outcomes' were in. For a writer who once feared that Europeans might regard him as a 'barbarian' if he couldn't read Aristotle in the original Greek, things were not necessarily moving in a favourable direction. Coetzee took to spending much of his time abroad and to referring to the University of Chicago as 'my intellectual home,' an insult to UCT, as far as I could see. Something was brewing inside him, something unforeseen.

It burst forth in 1999 in the form of *Disgrace*, the story of a Cape Town academic who falls out with university administrators who want him to apologise for a sexual indiscretion with a young student. This would save his job, but Lurie is arrogant and secretly contemptuous of the new order, so primly gender-sensitive and smugly PC.

So he walks away, intending to devote himself to writing an opera about Byron, only to be hammered into cringing abjection by murderous blacks. His daughter is gang-raped, Lurie himself doused with methylated spirits and set afire. Left harrowingly vulnerable on an isolated smallholding, the daughter has no choice other than to offer herself and half her land to her former boss boy in the hope that he will 'take her under his wing' and protect her against further attacks. Lurie himself winds up a nobody, feeding the corpses of stray dogs into a furnace.

On its face, *Disgrace* is a withering dismissal of the fragile hopes on which the Rainbow Nation is based. Had the real Coetzee finally revealed himself? The African National Congress thought so, denouncing the novelist for portraying blacks as 'savage, violent' and 'propelled by dark, satanic impulses.' Whites responded by turning *Disgrace* into a best-seller. Academe was convulsed by debate, and there was almost a fist-fight around my braai one night. My china Ernest shouted, 'Lurie is an effing coward. He should have taken up arms and gone to fight for a Boerestaat.' My china Dan said, 'No ways! Something religious has happened! Once Lurie loses his suburban baggage, he's, like, free, like, on his way to enlightenment.' I stood between them, marvelling at the uproar a good book could cause.

As for Coetzee, he naturally said nothing, and nobody was particularly surprised when he quietly left a year or two later.

Now he lives in Australia, and I sit in his abandoned matrix reading *Elizabeth Costello*, his first post-South African novel. It is a very odd book, a novel about a famous novelist and literary critic who goes around the world delivering lectures informed by a cold distaste for almost everything – journalists, fans, people who eat meat, people who write about violence, who indulge the pretences of second-rate African novelists, who carry on ceaselessly about literary theory, and worst of all – people who keep inviting the writer to award ceremonies that have become pointless and unbearable. In this novel about a writer, the writer is 'old and tired,' 'an old, tired circus seal,' a 'dying whale,' surrounded by parasites, disenchanted by the entire literary/academic enterprise. 'We are just performers speaking our parts,' says the writer. 'The core discipline of universities is money-making. The lecture hall itself may be a zoo.'

Is this the voice of Coetzee, emerging from the mouth of one of his characters? When he stepped up to receive his Nobel last December, was he secretly thinking, all this is nonsense, I wish you'd just sent the cheque in the mail?

Because Coetzee is Coetzee, we will never know. He is a grand master of the literary game of truth and illusion, inclined to speak, if he speaks at all, in riddles and codes that I'm far too dense to decipher. Besides, it's a game that spares everyone the ordeal of confronting reality. I suspect the truth is quite simple: Coetzee has written many great novels, but *Disgrace* is the one they will talk about for decades, because it cuts so dangerously close to the bone. I think Coetzee was saying it will take centuries for whites to live down the consequences of centuries of oppression. Might not be the sort of thing anyone particularly wants to hear, but it's true, isn't it?

All that seems odd is that Coetzee has chosen to remove himself from the drama while it's still underway. I'm sure Australia is very nice, but it is said to be bland and boring. Any reading of *Elizabeth Costello* confirms this impression: a place where an intellectual has nothing better to do than pick silly fights about vegetarianism.

Perhaps Coetzee should have listened to his own Mrs Curren. Midway through *Age of Iron*, she takes up a snapshot of her grandchildren, two little boys who have been taken away from the terrors and ecstasies of Africa to live in America, where they are playing in snow. She studies this little tableau of life in a place where almost everyone is safe and secure, and curiously, she shudders. 'They will die when they are 75 or 85,' she says, 'as stupid as they are today.'

Fair Lady, February 2004

Postscript: After this piece was published, a friend of Coetzee's told me he was experiencing a little problem in Australia: his new home stood on an old landfill that was emitting methane gas, causing health authorities to wring their hands anxiously about bad smells and the remote possibility of an unwanted explosion. In a country stupefied by generations of peace, progress and political rectitude, this is about as exciting as it gets, I guess.

Jewish Blues in Africa

||||||||||||||||||||||||||||||||||||||||||||||||||||||||||||||||||||||||||||||||||||||||||||||||||||||||||||||||||||||||||||||||||||||||||

What follows is a labour of love written at the behest of Benjy Moodie, a record guy who spent his youth following the same Jo'burg longhair rock bands as I. Decades later, he called to say he was planning to reissue a certain seminal LP on his Fresh label, and would I please write some liner notes.

I was in Standard Seven when it happened. The Beatles were banned on state radio. Haircut regulations were merciless. Life in the white suburbs was a hell of boredom and conformity, but help was on its way. They came from the north in the summer of '69, armed with axes and Scarab amps, long hair streaming behind them, and proceeded to slay the youth of the nation with an arsenal of murderous blues-rock tunes, synchronised foot-stomping and, on a good night, maniacal writhing in advanced states of rock'n'roll transfiguration. The masses roared. The establishment was shaken. They were the biggest thing our small world had ever seen, our Led Zeppelin, our Black Sabbath, maybe even our Rolling Stones. They were the Otis Waygood Blues Band, and this is their story.

It begins in 1964 or so, at a Jewish youth camp in what was then Rhodesia. Rob and Alan Zipper were from Bulawayo, where their dad had a clothes shop. Ivor Rubenstein was Alan's best mate, and Leigh Sagar was the local butcher's son. All these boys were budding musicians. Alan and Ivor had a little 'Fenders and footsteps' band that played Shadows covers at talent competitions, and Rob was into folk. They considered themselves pretty cool until they met Benny Miller, who was all of 16 and sported such unheard-of trappings as a denim jacket and Beatles-length hair. Benny had an older sister who'd introduced him to some way-out music, and when he picked up his guitar, the Bulawayo boys were staggered: he was playing the blues, making that axe sing and cry like a Negro.

How did the music of black American pain and sufferation find its way to the rebel colony of Rhodesia, where Ian Smith was about to declare UDI in the hope of preserving white supremacy for another 500 years? It's a long story, and it begins in Chicago in the forties and fifties, where blues cats like Howlin' Wolf and Sonny Boy Williamson cut '78s that eventually found their way into the hands of young British enthusiasts like John Mayall and Eric Clapton, who covered the songs in their early sessions and always cited the bluesmen as their gurus. Word of this eventually penetrated Rhodesia, and sent Benny scrambling after the real stuff, which he found on Pye Records' Blues Series, volumes one through six. Which is how a nice Jewish boy came to be playing the blues around a campfire in Africa. The Bulawayo contingent reached for their own guitars, and thus began a band that evolved over several years into Otis Waygood.

In its earliest incarnation, the band was built around Benny Miller, who remains, says Rob Zipper, 'one of the best guitarists I've ever heard.' Rob himself sang, played the blues harp and sax. His younger brother Alan was on bass. Bulawayo homeboys Ivor and Leigh were on drums and rhythm respectively, and flautist Martin Jackson completed the lineup. Their manager, Andy Vaughan, was the dude who observed that if you scrambled the name of a famous lift manufacturer you came up with a monniker that sounded authentically black American: Otis Waygood. Rob thought it was pretty witty. Ivor said, 'Ja, and lifts can be pretty heavy too.' And so the Otis Waygood Blues Band came into being.

By now, it was 1969, and the older cats were students at the University College of Rhodesia, earnest young men, seriously involved in the struggle against bigotry, prejudice and short hair. By day they were student activists, by night they played sessions. Their repertoire consisted of blues standards and James Brown grooves, and they were getting better and better. They landed a Saturday afternoon gig at a bar called Les Discotheque. Crowds started coming. When Rob stood up to talk at student meetings, he was drowned out by cries of, 'You're Late Miss Kate.'

'Miss Kate' was the band's signature tune, an old Deefore/Hitzfield number that they played at a bone-crunching volume and frantic pace. Towards the end of '69, Otis were asked to perform 'Miss Kate' on state TV. The boys obliged with a display of sneering insolence and hip-thrusting sexuality that provoked indignation from your average Rhodesian. These chaps are outrageous, they cried. They have 'golliwog hair' and bad manners! They go into the locations and play for natives! They aren't proper Rhodies!

Indeed they weren't, which is why they were planning to leave the country as soon as they could. Rob graduated at the end of 1969. He was supposed to be the first to go, but it was summer and the boys were young and wild and someone came up with the idea of driving to Cape Town. Benny Miller thought it was a blind move, and refused to come. But the rest were *bok*, so they loaded their amps into a battered old Kombi and set off across Africa to seek their fortune.

South of the Limpopo River, they entered a country in which a minor social revolution was brewing. In the West, the hippie movement had already peaked, but South Africa was always a few years behind the times, and this was our summer of love. Communes were springing up in the white suburbs. Acid had made its debut. Cape Town's Green Point Stadium was a great milling of stoned longhairs, come to attend an event billed as 'the largest pop festival south of and since the Isle of Wight.' It was also a competition, with the winner in line for a three-month residency at a local hotel. Otis Waygood arrived too late to compete, but impresario Selwyn Miller gave them a 15-minute slot as consolation – 2 pm on a burning December afternoon.

The audience was half asleep when they took the stage. Twelve bars into the set, they were on their feet. By the end of the first song, they were 'freaking out,' according to reports in the next morning's papers. By the time the band got around to 'Fever,' fans were attacking the security fence, and Rob got so carried away that he leapt off the ten-foot-high stage and almost killed himself. 'That's when it all started,' he says. Otis made the next day's papers, and went on to become the 'underground' sensation of 1969's Christmas holiday season, drawing sell-out crowds wherever they played.

In South Africa, this was the big time, and it lasted barely three weeks. The holidays ended, the tourists departed, and that was that: the rock heroes had to pack their gear and go back home. As fate would have it, however, their Kombi broke down in Johannesburg, and they wound up gigging at a club called Electric Circus to raise money for a valve job. One night, after a particularly sweaty set, a slender blond guy came backstage and said, 'I'm going to turn you into the biggest thing South Africa has ever seen.'

This was Clive Calder, who went on to become a rock billionaire, owner of the world's largest independent music company. Back then he was a lightie of 24, just starting out in the record business. His rap was inspirational. Said he'd just returned from Europe, where he'd watched the moguls break Grand Funk Railroad. Maintained he was capable of doing the same thing with Otis Waygood, and that together, they would conquer the planet. The white bluesboys signed on the dotted line, and Clive Calder's career began.

The album you're holding in your hand was recorded over two days in Joburg's EMI studios in March 1970, with Calder producing and playing piano on several tracks. Laid down in haste on an old four-track machine, it is less a work of art than a talisman to transport you back to sweaty little clubs in the early days of Otis Waygood's reign as South Africa's premier live group. Rob would brace himself in a splay-legged rock hero stance, tilt his head sideways, close his eyes and bellow as if his life depended on it. As the spirit took them, the sidemen would break into this frenzied bowing motion, bending double over their guitars on every beat, like a row of longhaired rabbis dovening madly at some blues-rock shrine. By the time they got to 'Fever,' with its electrifying climactic footstomp, the audience was pulverised. 'It was like having your senses worked over with a baseball bat,' said one critic.

Critics were somewhat less taken with the untitled LP's blank black cover. 'We were copying the Beatles,' explains Alan Zipper. 'They'd just done *The White Album*, so we thought we'd do a black album.' It was released in May 1970, and Calder immediately put Otis Waygood on the road to back it. His plan was to broaden the band's fan base to the point where kids in the smallest town were clamouring for the record, and that meant playing everywhere – Kroonstad, Klerksdorp, Witbank, you name it; towns where longhairs had never been seen before.

'In those smaller towns we were like aliens from outer space,' says drummer Ivor. 'I remember driving into places with a motorcycle cop in front and another behind, just sort of forewarning the town, "Here they come.'" Intrigued by Calder's hype, platteland people turned out in droves to see the longhaired weirdos. 'It was amazing,' says Ivor. 'Calder had the journalists eating out of his hand. Everything you opened was just Otis.'

The boys in the band were pretty straight when they arrived in South Africa, but youths everywhere were storming heaven on hallucinogenics, and pretty soon, Otis Waygood was doing it too. By now they were living in an old house in the suburbs of Jo'burg, a sort of head-quarters with mattresses strewn across the bare floors and a family of 20 hippies sitting down for communal meals. The acid metaphysicians of Abstract Truth crashed there for weeks on end. Freedom's Children were regular guests, along with Soweto stars like Kippie Moeketsi and Julian Bahula. Everyone would get high and jam in the soundproofed garage. Otis's music began to evolve in a direction presaged by the three bonus tracks that conclude this album. The riffs grew darker and heavier. Elements of free jazz and white noise crept in. Songs like 'You Can Do (Part I)' were eerie, unnerving excursions into regions of the psyche where only the brave dared tread. Flautist Martin Jackson made the trip once too often, suffered a 'spiritual crisis' and quit the band at the height of its success.

His replacement was Harry Poulus, the pale Greek god of keyboards, recruited from the ruins of Freedom's Children. Harry was a useful guy to have around in several respects, an enormously talented musician and a Zen mechanic to boot, capable of diagnosing the ailments of the band's worn-out Kombi just by remaining silent and centred and meditating on the problem until a solution revealed itself. With his help, the band recorded two more albums in quick succession (*Simply Otis Waygood* and *Ten Light Claps and a Scream*) and continued its epic trek through platteland towns, coastal resorts and open-air festivals. They finished 1970 where they started – special guests at the grand final of Cape Town's annual Battle of the Bands. The audience wouldn't let them off the stage. Rob worked himself into such a state of James Brownian exhaustion that he had to be carried off in the end. 'Whether you accept it or not,' wrote critic Peter Feldman, '1970 was their year.'

After that, it was all downhill in a way. There were only so many heads in South Africa, and by the end of 1970, they'd all bought an Otis LP and seen the band live several times. Beyond a certain point,

Otis could only go round in circles. Worse yet, conservatives were growing intolerant of long-haired social deviance. National Party MPs complained that rock music was rotting the nation's moral fibre. Right-wing students invaded a pop festival where Otis was playing and gave several participants an involuntary haircut. 'We had police coming to the house every second night,' says Ivor, 'or guys with crewcuts and denim jackets saying, 'Hey, man, the car's broken down, can we sleep here?' They always planted weed in the toilets, but we always found it before they bust us.'

By March 1971, the day of reckoning was drawing nigh. Describing drug abuse as a 'national emergency,' the Minister of Police announced a crackdown that included mandatory (and very long) prison sentences for drug possession. At the same time, various armies started breathing down Otis Waygood's neck. When the SADF informed Ivor that he was liable for military service, the boys sneaked back into Rhodesia, but more call-up papers were waiting for them at their parents' homes. 'Ian Smith despised us,' says Ivor. 'They wanted to make an example of us, so we basically escaped.' At the time, international airlines weren't supposed to land in Rhodesia because of sanctions. But there was a Jo'burg-Paris flight that made an unofficial stop in Salisbury. The boys boarded it and vanished.

Back in Jo'burg, we were bereft. Friends and I started a tribute band that played garage parties, our every lick, pose and song copied off Otis, but that petered out in a year or two, and we were left with nothing but their records and vague rumours from a distant hemisphere. Otis were alive and well in Amsterdam. Later, they were spotted in England, transmogrified into a white reggae band that played the deeply underground blacks-only heavy dub circuit. Later still, they became Immigrant, a multi-racial outfit that did a few gigs at the Rock Garden or the Palladium. But it never quite came together again, and the band disintegrated at the end of the seventies.

Martin Jackson never made it back to the real world. He was last seen drifting around Salisbury in 1974, wild-eyed and tangle-haired, with a huge cross painted on his back. Harry Poulos stepped off a building, another casualty of an era whose mad intensity made a reversion to the ordinary almost unbearable. Leigh Sagar is a barrister in London. The Zipper brothers are also living in the UK, Rob practising architecture and Alan running a recording studio. Ivor Rubenstein returned to Bulawayo, where he manufactures hats.

As for Benny Miller, the nice Jewish boy who started it all, he's still in Harare, wryly amused by the extraordinary adventure he missed by ducking out of that fateful trip to Cape Town. He still plays guitar in sixties' nostalgia bands, and produces African music for a living.

Fresh Records liner notes, 1999

Postscript: Strikes me on re-reading that I underplayed the single most interesting aspect of this story. Let's start with a quiz: who made the most money out of pop music in the twentieth century? Most people say, The Beatles, or Elvis, or Michael Jackson. All wrong. Frank Sinatra maybe? Andrew Lloyd Webber? The Stones? Unfortunately not. The winner was Clive Calder, the fast-talking boykie who walked into Otis Waygood's dressing room in January 1970, promising to make them bigger than Led Zeppelin.

Clive Calder was born and raised in Jo'burg's northern suburbs. The white blues boys from Rhodesia were his first venture as a showbiz manager. When they folded, he signed an array of coloured young-sters with bellbottoms and Afros (Richard Jon Smith and Jonathan Butler among others) in a far-sighted but ultimately futile attempt to create an African Michael Jackson. In 1977 or thereabouts, he moved to London, where one of his first signings was Sir Bob Geldof's Boomtown Rats. One thing led to another, and by the time Calder sold his Zomba empire to the German company BMG circa 2001, he had the world's three biggest-selling teen pop stars (Britney Spears, Backstreet Boys and N'Sync) under contract, along with most of America's semi-nal rap singers and countless thousands of songwriters. The Germans paid a dumbfounding three billion dollars for Calder's business. If Calder was the sole shareholder, as is widely presumed, his cashing-out bonus dwarfs all other contenders.

Unfortunately, we can't be sure, because Zomba was privately held and Calder himself is a Howard Hughes-like figure, reclusive, para-noid, rumoured to be riddled with germ phobias and mysterious al-lergies and totally invisible in the media. Rolling Stone once com-missioned me to do a story about him and his sometime partner, a

Machadodorp boykie named Mutt Lange who learned his chops as a session cat on Springbok Radio's 'Hits of the Week,' a long-running enterprise that issued note-for-note cover versions of international hits that cost less than half of the genuine article. Mutt went on to become one of the twentieth century's most successful songwriters and producers, churning out hits galore for ACDC, Def Leppard and Shania Twain, among many others. But he was also a recluse who never gave interviews. I suspect he and Calder were worried that journalists would discover their background and start asking awkward questions about apartheid. Whatever the truth, Mutt & Clive liked being invisible, and they were sufficiently rich and powerful to keep it that way.

The sale of Clive's Zomba empire to BMG was big news for business editors in Europe and America. They ransacked the world for photographs of the mysterious South African, and were staggered to find that none existed anywhere. Nor was he willing to pose for one. The story ran without a picture, even in the *New York Times.*

Odd to think that it all began in Sandringham, Johannesburg. One Friday night in 1970, me and my pimply 13-year-old friends hitch-hiked across the city to see Otis performing at the club called Electric Circus. I have a dim memory of a slender, pixie-like young man manning the ticket booth. His hair was blond, collar-length and cut just so. He was wearing smart casuals, including a navy-blue blazer. He didn't drink, dance or smoke dope, but seemed pretty glamorous anyway. That was Clive Calder. It was the closest I ever got to him.

3

Disease

The Body Count

||||||||||||||||||||||||||||||||||||||||||||||||||||||||||||||||||||||||||||||||||||||||||||||||||||||||||||||||||||||||||||||||||||

My friend Michelle, a left-wing literary critic, argues that all claims to truth are spurious. 'The mere fact of choosing what facts you report, and what weight you attach to them, reduces all journalism to just another form of fiction,' she declares.

I don't buy her conclusion, but Michelle has a point in one regard: the facts you leave out are often at least as telling as those you set down on the page. So then: the truth about this story. When Rolling Stone asked for a piece about the inside and untold story of President Thabo Mbeki's descent into Aids madness, I did not accept because I was interested in the subject. I accepted because I wanted to moer Mbeki. I had never met the man, but there was a time when the image he projected struck me as quite appealing, all those tweed jackets and single-malt whiskeys and earnest undergraduate probings of the larger significance of almost everything.

By the time Rolling Stone called, the enchantment had faded. I would have moered Mbeki for nothing, but this American magazine was offering me a small fortune to vent my gatvolheid on the presidential person, and I could scarcely believe my luck. I'd been struggling for years to get idealistic and naïve Americans to publish anything even vaguely negative about the South African situation. Now they were offering me serious money to sever the presidential head and serve it up on an elegant literary platter. I said, lekker, I'm your man.

Unfortunately, the facts as I found them failed to justify Mbeki's decapitation, so I veered off on a tangent that fell way outside Rolling Stone's brief, with consequences that will dog me to my grave. What follows is a letter to Rolling Stone editor Bill Tonelli, written in December 2000.

Yo Bill –

You will be saddened to hear that Adelaide Ntsele has died. As you may recall, she featured briefly in my article a year ago about the long, twisted history of 'The Lion Sleeps Tonight,' which was based on a melody composed by her father, Solomon Linda. While I interviewed her sisters about the life and times of their father, Adelaide was swooning feverishly under greasy blankets in the next room. She got up from her sickbed to have her picture taken. She was so weak she could barely stand, but she wanted to be in your magazine.

I took her to hospital afterward. We sat in emergency for a long time, waiting for attention. Her sister Elizabeth was there too. She's a nurse. She looked at Adelaide's hospital card and grew very quiet. Later, she told me there was a secret code on it indicating that Adelaide had lit up an Aids test. Atop that she had TB and a gynaecological condition that required surgery. The operation had already been postponed repeatedly. To Elizabeth, it looked like the doctors had decided, well, this one's had it, she'll die anyway, just let it happen. And so it did.

A year ago, the funeral scene would have written itself. I would have described the kindly old pastor, the sad African singing, the giant iron pots on fires for the ritual goodbye feast. I would have mentioned the eerie absence of any reference to Aids in the eulogies, made some rote observation about the denial it betokened. I would have scanned the faces of mourners, trying to pick out the one in five who were carriers of the virus that put Adelaide in her coffin, withered and shrivelled like a child. And in the end I would have turned sadly away, lamenting a society that allowed a 37-year-old woman to die because she couldn't afford the drugs available to rich white people.

Instead, I spent the ceremony thinking about viral antigens, cell-wall particles, heterophil cross-reactions and other mysteries of what Sowetans call H I Vilakazi, the scourge of the deadly three letters. Midway through the proceedings, the pastor broke my reverie: perhaps the visitors would like to say something? I rose to my feet, straightened my tie and prepared to speak my mind, but courage failed me, so I mumbled a few platitudes instead. 'It is a heartbreak that Adelaide was taken so young,' I said. 'She bore terrible suffering with enormous dignity. We will always remember her as she appears in that picture,' I concluded, nodding toward a framed portrait of a wistful young woman with huge doe eyes and cheekbones like Marlene Dietrich's.

Adelaide wanted to be a model. She never made it. I extended my condolences to the family and sat down again.

It wasn't the eulogy Adelaide deserved, but then it wasn't the right time or place for a great cry of rage and confusion either. But now the mourning is done, and there are things that must be said. Unfortunately, I'm not sure you'll want to hear them.

Africa's era of megadeath dawned in the fall of 1983, when the superintendent of a hospital in what was then Zaire sent a communiqué to American health investigators, informing them that a mysterious disease had broken out amongst his patients. At the time, the United States was convulsed by its own weird health crisis. Large numbers of gay men were coming down with an unknown disease of extraordinary virulence. Scientists called it GRID, an acronym for Gay-related Immune Disease, which in turn prompted Conservatives and televangelists to call it God's vengeance on sinners. American researchers were thus intrigued to learn that a similar syndrome had been observed among heterosexuals in Africa. A posse of seasoned disease cowboys was convened and sent forth to investigate.

On 18 October 1983, they walked into Kinshasa's Mama Yemo Hospital, led by Dr Peter Piot, 34, a Belgian who had been to Mama Yemo years earlier, investigating the first outbreak of Ebola fever. A change was immediately apparent. 'In 1976, there were hardly any young adults there except for traffic accidents in orthopedic wards,' Piot told the *Washington Post*. 'Suddenly – boom – I walked in and saw all these young men and women, emaciated, dying.' Improvised blood tests confirmed Piot's first impression – the mysterious new disease was present in Africa, and its victims were heterosexual. The Human Immunodeficiency Virus itself was identified a year later, and in Africa, it turned up wherever researchers looked for it – in 80 per cent of Nairobi prostitutes, 32 per cent of Ugandan truckdrivers, 45 per cent of hospitalised Rwandese children. Worse yet, it seemed to be spreading very rapidly. Epidemiologists plotted figures on graphs, drew lines linking the data points, and gaped in horror. The epidemic curve peaked in the stratosphere. Hundreds of millions would die unless something was done.

These prophecies transformed the destiny of Aids. In 1983, it was a fairly rare disease, confined largely to the gay and heroin-using subcultures in the West. Now it was reclassed as a threat to all humanity. 'We stand nakedly before a pandemic as mortal as any there has ever been,' World Health Organisation chief Halfdan Mahler told a press conference in 1987. Western governments heeded his anguished appeal for action. Billions were invested in education and prevention campaigns. Aids research started expanding 'as rapidly as we could absorb money and people.' Aids organisations sprang up all across Africa – 570 of them in Zimbabwe, a thousand in South Africa, 1 300 in Uganda. By 2000, global spending on Aids had risen to around $35 billion a year, and activists were urging the commitment of billions more, largely to counter the apocalypse in Africa, where 22 million were said to carry the virus, and 14 million to have died.

And this is about where I entered the picture – July 2000, three months after President Thabo Mbeki announced that he intended to convene a panel of scientists and professors to re-examine the relationship (if any) between the HI virus and Aids. Mbeki never actually said Aids doesn't exist, but his actions begged the question, and the implications were mind-bending. South Africa was said to have more HIV infections (4.2 million) than any other country on the planet, and the death toll was reportedly rising daily. As the truth sank in, disbelief turned to derision.

'Ludicrous,' said the *Washington Post*.

'Off his rocker,' said *The Spectator*.

'A degree of open-mindedness is fine,' said *Newsday*. 'But sometimes you can be so open-minded your brains fall out.'

The whole world laughed, and I rubbed my hands with glee: South Africa was back on the world's front pages for the first time since the fall of apartheid; fortune awaited the man of action. I went to see Dr Bob, a friend who also happens to be an Aids epidemiologist of international stature. He was so dismayed by what he called the 'genocidal stupidity' of Mbeki's Aids initiative that he'd left work and gone home, where I found him slumped in depression. Hey Bob, I said, snap out of it. Let's make a deal. And so we did: he'd talk, I'd type, and together we'd write the inside story of Thabo Mbeki's Aids fiasco. All that remained was to doff the hat to journalistic objectivity and briefly consider the evidence that had led our leader astray.

According to newspaper reports, Mbeki had gleaned most of it on the Web, so I revved up the laptop and followed him into the virtual

underworld of Aids heresy, where renegade scientists maintain websites dedicated to the notion that Aids is a hoax dreamed up by a
diabolical alliance of pharmaceutical companies and 'fascist' academics whose only interest is enriching themselves. I visited four such
sites, noted what they had to say, and then turned to rival websites
maintained by universities and governments, which offered crushing
rebuttals to same. Can't say I understood everything, because the science was impenetrable, but here's a rough sketch of the battlefield.

Let's look at Aids from an African point of view. Imagine yourself
in a mud hut, or maybe a tin shack on the outskirts of some sprawling
city. There's sewage in the streets, and refuse removal is nonexistent.
Flies and mosquitoes abound, and your drinking water is probably
contaminated with faeces. You and your children are sickly, under-
nourished and stalked by diseases for which you're unlikely to receive
proper treatment. Worse yet, these diseases are mutating, becoming
more virulent and drug-resistant. Minor scourges like infectious diarrhoea and pneumonia barely respond to antibiotics. Malaria shrugs
off treatment with chloroquine, often the only drug available to poor
Africans. Some strains of TB – Africa's other great killer – have become virtually incurable. Now, atop all of this there is Aids, the most
terrifying and deadly scourge of all.

According to what you hear on the radio, Aids is caused by a tiny
virus that lurks unseen in the blood for many years, only to emerge in
deep disguise: a disease whose symptoms are other diseases, like TB,
for instance. Or pneumonia. Or running stomach. These diseases are
not new, which is why some of your neighbours are sceptical, main-
taining that Aids actually stands for 'American Idea for Discouraging
Sex.' Others say nonsense, the scientists are right, we're all going to
die unless we use condoms. But condoms cost money and you have
none, so you just sigh and hope for the best.

Then one day you get a cough that won't go away, and start shed-
ding weight at an alarming rate. You know these symptoms. In the
past, you could take some pills and they would go away. But the
medicines don't work anymore. You get sicker and sicker. You wind
up in the Aids ward.

The orthodox scientists, if they could see you, would say your immune system has been destroyed by the HI virus, allowing the TB (or
whatever) to run riot. The Aids dissidents who've captured Mbeki's ear

would say, no way – the virus is a harmless creature that just happens to accompany immune-system breakdown caused by other factors – in this case, a lifetime of exposure to hunger and tropical pathogens.

Incensed by this nonsense, the orthodoxy whistles up a truckload of studies from all over Africa showing that HIV-positive hospital patients die at astronomical rates relative to their HIV-negative counterparts. The dissidents are unimpressed. This proves nothing, they say. You claim this man is sick because he's HIV-positive. We say he's HIV-positive *because* he's sick. Either way, we agree on the outcome: hospital patients who carry the virus are very sick people, so of course they're more likely to die.

The orthodoxy grits its teeth. The dissidents are vastly outnumbered, but they're resolute and pugnacious and their ranks include a Nobel laureate (Kary Mullis) who says orthodox Aids theory is so riddled with errors that anyone who believes it is 'so stupid they deserve to be pitied.' I won't even attempt to summarise Mullis's argument, because I didn't understand it. The rebuttals were equally incomprehensible, so I figured the best way to settle Mullis and Mbeki's hash was to show that Aids has caused a massive increase in African mortality, which is of course the truth as we know it: 22 million Africans infected, according to the most recent reports, and 14 million already dead. If those numbers were accurate, Mbeki was guilty as charged. So I set out to confirm the death toll. Just that. I thought it would be easy. I picked up the phone. It was my first mistake.

There was a time when I imagined medical research as an idealised endeavour, carried out by scientists interested only in truth. Up close, it turns out to be much like any other human enterprise, riven with envy, ambition and the standard jockeying for position. Labs and universities depend on grants, and grant-making is fickle, subject to the vagaries of politics and intellectual fashion, and prone to favour scientists whose work grips the popular imagination. Every disease has champions who gather data and hype the threat it poses. The cancer fighters will tell you that their crisis is deepening, and more research money is urgently needed. Those doing battle with malaria make similar pronouncements, as do those working on TB, and so on and so on. If all their claims are added together, says public health expert Christopher Murray, you wind up with a theoretical global death toll that 'exceeds the number of humans who die annually by two to three-fold.'

Malaria is said to kill two to three million humans a year, but malaria research gets about one dollar for every 50 going to Aids. Tuberculosis (1.7 million victims a year) is similarly sidelined, to the extent that there were no new TB drugs in development at all as of 1998. Aids, on the other hand, is totally replete, employing an estimated 100 000 scientists, sociologists, epidemiologists, care-givers, counsellors, peer educators and stagers of condom jamborees. Furthermore, the level of funding grows daily as foundations, governments and philanthropists like Bill Gates enter the field, unnerved by the bad news, which usually arrives in the form of articles describing Aids as a 'merciless plague' of 'biblical virulence,' as *Time* recently phrased it, causing 'terrible depredation' among the world's poorest people.

These stories originate in Africa, but the statistics that support them emanate from the suburbs of Geneva, Switzerland, where the World Health Organization has its headquarters. Technically employed by the United Nations, WHO officials are the world's disease police, dedicated to eradicating illness and fostering development. They crusade against old scourges, raise the alarm against new ones, fight epidemics, dispense grants and expertise to poor countries. In conjunction with UNAIDS (the Joint United Nations Programme on HIV/Aids, based on the same Geneva campus), the WHO also collects and disseminates information about the Aids pandemic.

In the West, this is a fairly simple matter: every new Aids case is scientifically verified and reported to health authorities, who inform the disease police in Geneva. But most Aids occurs in Africa, where hospitals are thinly spread, understaffed, and often bereft of the laboratory equipment necessary to confirm HIV infections. How do you track an epidemic under these conditions? In 1985, the WHO asked experts to hammer out a simple description of Aids that would enable bush doctors to recognise it and start counting cases, but the outcome was a fiasco – partly because doctors struggled to diagnose the disease with the naked eye, but also because this reporting system produced nothing like the tidal wave of cases anticipated. It was abandoned in 1988 and replaced by an alternative on which Africa's Aids statistics are now 'primarily' based.

The system works like this. On any given morning, anywhere in

Africa, you'll find crowds of expectant mothers lining up outside government prenatal clinics, come for a routine checkup that includes
the drawing of a blood sample to test for syphilis. Aids researchers
realised that serum left over after this procedure could be a rich source
of information on the spread of HIV. So they set up a system whereby
once a year, Aids researchers descend on selected clinics, remove the
left-over blood samples, and screen them for traces of the HI virus.
The results are forwarded to Geneva and fed into a computer model
that transmutes them into statistics. If so many pregnant women are
HIV-positive, then a certain percentage of all adults and children are
presumed to be infected, too. And if that many people are infected,
some percentage of them must surely have died, leaving armies of
orphans behind them. Hence, when UNAIDS says 14 million Africans
have succumbed to Aids, it does not mean that 14 million bodies have
been counted. It means that 14 million people are presumed to have
expired somewhere in Africa's great unknown.

You can theorise at will about the rest of Africa and nobody will
ever be the wiser, but South Africa is different – a semi-industrial-
ised country with a respected statistical service. 'South Africa,' says
UNAIDS consultant Ian Timaeus, of whom more later, 'is the only
country in sub-Saharan Africa where sufficient deaths are routinely
registered to attempt to produce national estimates of mortality from
this source.' He adds that 'coverage is far from complete,' but there's
enough of it to be useful – around eight out of ten deaths are registered in South Africa, according to Timaeus, compared to about one
in 100 elsewhere below the Sahara.

It therefore seemed that checking the number of registered deaths
in South Africa was the surest way of assessing the statistics from
Geneva, so I dug out the figures. Geneva's computer models said that
Aids deaths had surged from 80 000-odd in 1996 to 250 000 in 1999.
But no such rise was discernible in registered deaths, which went from
327 822 to 351 281 over roughly the same period. The discrepancy
was so large that I wrote to Statistics SA to make absolutely sure I had
understood these numbers correctly. An official answered in the affirmative,* and I realised this story was heading for trouble. Geneva's
figures reflected catastrophe. Pretoria's didn't. Between these extremes

---

* The official was mistaken. I subsequently discovered that the 1999 figure excluded late registrations
(see below), which raised the total considerably – although not enough to elimate the chasm between UN
predictions and real-life death registrations.]

lay a grey area populated by local actuaries who privately muttered that the Geneva figures were far too high, but so what? They don't make the running in this debate. The figures you see in your newspapers come from Geneva, and they couldn't be substantiated.

But you don't want to hear all this, do you? Nor did I. It spoiled the plot, so I tried to ignore it. If it was indeed true that very large numbers of South Africans were dying, the nation's coffin-makers had to be labouring hard to keep pace with growing demand. I called two entrepreneurs who'd been in the news in the mid-nineties for inventing cheap coffins made of recycled materials, anticipating a killing in the coming death boom. Oddly, they'd both gone out of business. 'People weren't interested,' said a dejected Mr Rob Whyte. 'They wanted coffins made of real wood.'

So I called the real wood dudes, three industrialists who manufactured coffins on an assembly-line basis for the national market. 'It's quiet,' said Kurt Lammerding of GNG Pine Products. 'Very quiet. We aren't feeling anything at all.' His competitors concurred – business was dead, so to speak. In fact, said Joe Alberts of Poliflora, it was so bad that smaller outfits were going bankrupt. I checked, and lo: two of the four coffin factories listed in Johannesburg's Yellow Pages had recently gone under, and one of the survivors maintained that the plague was a 'money-making racket' aimed at extorting charity from the gullible. 'It's a fact,' said Mr AB Schwegman of B&A Coffins. 'If you go on what you read in the papers, we should be overwhelmed, but there's nothing. So what's going on? You tell me.'

I couldn't, although I suspected it might have something to do with race. The big-time coffin firms were all white-owned, and they said South Africa's death business had undergone major changes since the downfall of apartheid in 1994, with unlicensed backyard funeral parlours mushrooming in black townships. They couldn't discount the possibility that these pirate outfits were scoring their coffins from obscure black businesses in places like Soweto. The only one they knew of was Mmabatho Coffins, but when I called, it had gone bankrupt too. Weird, no? According to a July 2000 news report, South Africa's death rate has almost doubled in the past decade. 'These aren't predictions,' said the *Sunday Times*. 'These are the facts.' And if the facts were correct, someone, somewhere had to be prospering in the coffin trade.

Further inquiries led me to Johannesburg's derelict downtown, where an abandoned multi-storey parking garage has recently been transformed into a vast warren of carpentry workshops, each housing a black carpenter, set up in business with government seed money. I wandered around searching for coffin makers, but there were only two. Eric Borman said business was good, but then he was a master craftsman who made one or two deluxe caskets a week and seemed to resent the suggestion his customers were the sort of people who died of Aids. For that, I'd have to talk to Penny. He pointed, and off I went, deeper and deeper into the maze. Penny's place was locked up and deserted. Inside, unsold coffins were stacked ceiling-high, and a forlorn 'closed' sign hung on the wire.

At that moment, a forbidden thought entered my brain. This will sound crazy, but put yourself in my shoes. You live in Africa – okay, in the post-colonial twilight of Johannesburg's once-white suburbs, but still, as close to the Aids frontline as a honky can get. For years, experts tell you that the plague is marching down the continent, coming closer every year. By 1999, the newspapers are telling you that one in five people on your street is walking dead.

This has to be true, because it's coming from experts, so you start looking for evidence. Laston the gardener at number 10 is suspiciously thin, and has a hacking cough that won't go away. His wife Sacred has a rash on her face, and there seems to be something wrong with her latest baby. On the far side of the golf course, Mrs Smith has just buried her beloved servant. Mr Beresford's maid has just died too. Your cousin Lennie knows someone who knows someone who owns a factory where all the workers are dying. Your newspapers are predicting that the economy will ultimately be crippled by Aids, and that the education system might collapse because so many teachers are dying. But then you wind up staring into Penny's failed coffin workshop and you think, Jesus, maybe this is all a hallucination ...

Is this possible? Hard to say. In my suburb, peoples' brains are so addled by death propaganda that we automatically assume that almost everyone who falls seriously ill or dies has Aids, especially if they're young, poor and black. But we don't really know, and nor do the sufferers themselves, because hardly anyone has been tested. 'What's the point?' says Laston, the ailing gardener. He knows there's no cure for Aids, and no hope of obtaining life-extending anti-retrovirals. As a playboy, with three wives back in Malawi and a mistress in Jo'burg, he knows he's at risk for the virus, but finding out would ruin whatever remains of his life, so he refrains. Last winter, he came down with a bad cough, and everyone said it was Aids, but it wasn't – come summer, Laston got better. Then Stanley the bricklayer became our street's most likely Aids case. Stanley maintained he had a heart condition, but behind his back, everyone was whispering, 'Oh, my God, it's Aids.' But was it? We had no idea. We were playing a macabre guessing game, driven by hysteria.

But you don't want to hear this either, do you? Nor did anyone else. Worried friends slipped newspaper clippings into my mailbox: cemetery overflows, hospitals overwhelmed, prison deaths up 585 per cent. I'd always check the evidence, but there was always a contributory factor that had gone entirely unmentioned, like cut-price cemetery plots, a TB epidemic in scandalously overcrowded jails and government hospitals in a state of 'irreversible decline.' After months of this, even my mother lost patience. 'Shaddup,' she snapped. 'They'll put you in a strait-jacket.' Mother knows best, but I just couldn't get those numbers out of my head: 327 822 registered deaths in 1996, 351 281 five years later. I called Dr Bob, the Aids epidemiologist, and said, listen, I am beset by demons and heresies, can you not shrive me? So we had lunch, and I aired my doubts, whereupon he said, fear not, I know of absolutes that will soothe your fevered brain. He pointed in the direction where truth lay, and I set out to find it.

And here we are on a hilltop on the Equator, overlooking the spot where Africa's first recorded outbreak of Aids took place. It's a village called Kashenye, which lies on the border between Uganda and Tanzania, close to where the Kagera River flows into Lake Victoria. In 1979 or thereabouts, according to legend, a trader named Kainga Bweinda crossed the river in a canoe to sell his wares in Kashenye. Business done, he bought some beers and relaxed in the company of a certain Maria, who lived in that house right there. Some time later, Maria fell victim to a wasting disease that refused to respond to any known medication, Western or tribal.

Not long after, a similar drama unfolded in Kasensero, a fishing village on the Ugandan side of the river. There, the first victim was a certain Regina, and the agent of infection was said to be a visitor from Kashenye. In due course, several of Regina's friends contracted the wasting disease. Her neighbours cried foul, accusing Kashenye of putting a hex on them. Soon, villagers on both banks of the river were discarding objects brought from the other side, believing them to be bewitched. But nothing helped. The contagion spread away to the next village, and then the next. By 1983, it was in all the cities on the western shore of Lake Victoria. The first scientists arrived on the scene in 1985, and by 1988, a disturbing picture had emerged. Around 30 per cent of pregnant women in the lakeside town of Bukoba were HIV-infected. In Lyantonde, 150 miles northward, the equivalent figure among barmaids was 67 per cent. In the venereal clinics of Kampala, every second patient was carrying the virus. Newspapers took to describing Lake Victoria as 'the epicentre of the Aids epidemic.' Ugandan president Yoweri Museveni declared that 'apocalypse' was imminent.

This prophecy was based largely on surveys among small groups of high-risk subjects. Many factors remained unknown – the true extent of infection in the general populace, the rate at which it was spreading, the speed with which it killed. To formulate an effective battle plan, Aids researchers desperately needed more data in these areas. They cast around for a place to study, and lit on Masaka, Uganda, a ramshackle town just west of Lake Victoria and about 100 miles north of ground zero. In 1988, a Dutch epidemiologist named Daan Mulder was sent there to lay the groundwork for what would ultimately become the largest and most significant study of its kind in Africa. Just over eight per cent of Masaka's adults were HIV-infected – not particularly high in the African context, but there were other considerations making it a good place to study. Uganda's government welcomed the research effort. The region was politically stable, and there was an international airport three hours away. Mulder's funders (the British Medical Research Council and the UK government) gave the go-ahead, and an epic mortality study commenced.

Assisted by an army of field workers, Mulder drew a circle around 15 villages, and proceeded to count everyone. Then he took blood from all those who were willing (8 833 out of 9 777 inhabitants), screened it for HIV infections, and sat back to see what happened. Every household was visited at least once a year, and every death was noted and entered into Mulder's database, along with the deceased's HIV status.

The first results were published five years later, and as Dr Bob promised, they were devastating. The HIV-infected villagers of Masaka were dying at an astronomical rate. Young adults with the virus in their bloodstream were 60 times more likely to perish than their uninfected peers. Overall, HIV-related disease accounted for a staggering 42 per cent of all deaths. The Aids dissidents were crushed, HIV theory vindicated. 'If there are any left who do not accept this,' commented the Centres for Disease Control, 'their explanation of how HIV-seropositivity leads to death must be very curious indeed.'

Clearly, only a fool would second-guess such powerful evidence, so I just visited the villages where Mulder's work was done, verified Dr Bob's account, and headed back to the airport, my story about Mbeki's stupidity back on track. But my flight was delayed, so I got to spend an hour or two in Uganda's Statistics Office, and what I found there changed everything.

In 1948, Uganda's British rulers attempted a rough census in Masaka district, and concluded that the death rate was 'a minimum of 25 to 30 per thousand.' A second census in 1959 put the figure at 21 per thousand. In 1969, it was 18 per thousand. By 1991, it had fallen to 16 per thousand. Enter Daan Mulder with his blood tests, massive funding and armies of field workers. He counted every death over two years, and then five, and here is his conclusion: the crude death rate in Masaka, in the midst of a horrifying Aids plague, was 14.6 per thousand – the lowest ever measured.

At first glance, this is exactly the outcome a dissident would predict. Blood tests would pick out people whose immune systems were already failing. They would proceed to die in very large numbers, but the overall death rate would remain more or less normal. But you don't want to hear this, do you? Nor did I, so I decided to take a look at statistics from neighbouring Tanzania, another country stricken in the earliest stages of the Aids pandemic.

In 1992, Tanzania embarked on a mortality study that dwarfed anything previously undertaken in Africa. Again funded by the British government and supported by scientists from the University of Liverpool, the Adult Morbidity and Mortality Project recruited 307 000 participants in various urban and rural settings, each of whom was visited at least once a year over the next three years and interrogated about recent deaths or disease. The final results were rather like Masaka's: Aids (or what participants and analysts assumed was Aids) was by far the leading cause of adult mortality, but the overall death rate was 13.6 per thousand – ten per cent lower than the death rate measured in Tanzania's 1988 census, which was rated 'close to 100 per cent' by Professor Ian Timaeus, the regnant authority on African mortality in the Aids era. When no one else could answer my questions, I turned to him.

'Professor Timaeus,' I said, 'this study appears to show that there was no increase in Tanzania's death rate in the darkest heart of the Aids epidemic.' Timaeus shrugged. 'The survey covered only part of the country,' he said. True, said I, but a fairly large part, with hundreds of thousands of participants. 'But were they representative?' he countered. I had no idea. Timaeus smiled and said, 'I think this is the more critical evidence.'

Whereupon he produced a sheath of graphs and papers and laid them on a table. There was, he began, a 'regrettable' lack of knowledge about mortality in Africa, attributable to inertia, donor indifference and a crippling lack of recent data. These factors bedevilled the Aids demographer, but Timaeus found several ways around them, most important of which was the so-called 'sibling history' technique of mortality estimation. It works like this.

Every five years or so, researchers financed by the US Agency for International Development conduct detailed health interviews with mothers in developing countries. Among the questions put to them are these: 'How many children did your own mother have? How many are still alive? When did the others die?' Timaeus realised that close analysis of the answers would reveal trends that were failing to show up elsewhere. He set to work, and published the results in the journal *AIDS* in 1998. 'In just six years (1989 –1995) in Uganda,' he wrote, 'men's death rates almost doubled, and women's death rates more than doubled.' Similar horrors were revealed in Tanzania, where male deaths were up 80 per cent in the same period.

Again, this seemed to settle the matter, but again, there were complications. For one thing, Timaeus's findings of a massive rise in Ugandan mortality contradicted Daan Mulder's epic study, which eventually ran for seven years without detecting any change in the death rate. The same is true of Tanzania's giant adult mortality survey: the death rate remained stable during the very period when Timaeus says it was surging.

How come? I found a possible answer in a paper co-authored by Kenneth Hill, the ace Johns Hopkins demographer who co-invented the sibling history technique back in 1984. Last year, after a worldwide evaluation, Hill and his team concluded that sibling histories were useless for the purpose to which Timaeus put them. As I understand it, the problem was 'downward bias' – people remember recent deaths pretty clearly, but those that happened years back tend to fade. According to Hill and co, this usually leads to a false impression of rising mortality as you near the present, even in countries like Indonesia or Bolivia where there's little or no Aids. In Namibia, for instance, the sibling history method detected a wildly improbable 156 per cent rise in the 14 years prior to 1992. 'This lack of precision,' said Hill's team, 'precludes the use of these data for trend analysis.'

'I don't agree,' says Timaeus, who maintains that Hill and his collaborators must have got their maths wrong. But this is not an argument he pursues with much vigour, because his own papers acknowledge that the sibling history method is 'untried' and that the results it produces 'could be partly or wholly spurious.'

Weird, no? I'd been reading for years about villages in the Lake Victoria region where nobody was left alive save babies and the aged, and where vast tracts of agricultural land had been abandoned by AIDS-stricken peasants. I thought those stories were gospel. In fact, one of my first moves on this assignment was to call NASA, asking for satellite photographs of areas that had reverted to bush or jungle since the start of the pandemic. NASA seemed to think I was a bit nuts, and now I know why. Something is wrong here, Bill. I struggle to believe science would make a mistake of the magnitude claimed by Mbeki's dissident friends. But I have deepening doubts about the scale of the thing.

I was living in Los Angeles in 1981, when the very first cases of GRID were detected. I knew men who were stricken, and sympathised with their desperation. They wanted government action, and suspected there would be little so long as Aids could be dismissed as a scourge of queers, junkies and Haitians. So they forged an alliance with powerful figures in science and the media and set forth to change perceptions, armed inter alia with potent slogans such as 'Aids is an equal-opportunity killer' and 'Aids threatens everyone.' Madonna, Liz

Taylor and other stars were recruited to drive home the message to the straight masses: Aids is coming after you, too.

These warnings were backed up by estimates such as this one, published in the *New England Journal of Medicine* in 1985: 1.76 million Americans are already HIV-infected, said researchers Spivak and Wormser, and the disease is rapidly spreading. Dr Anthony Fauci, now head of the National Institute of Allergic and Infectious Diseases, prophesied that 'three to five million Americans' would be HIV-positive within a decade. *Newsweek*'s figures in a 1987 article were twice as high. That same year Oprah Winfrey told the nation that 'by 1990, one in five heterosexuals will be dead of Aids.'

As the hysteria intensified, challenging such certainties came to be dangerous. In 1988, New York City health commissioner Steven C Joseph reviewed the city's estimate of HIV infections, concluded that the number was inaccurate, and halved it, from 400 000 to 200 000. His office was invaded by protesters, his life threatened. Demonstrators tailed him to meetings, chanting 'Resign, resign!'

In hindsight, Dr Joseph's reduced figure of 200 000 infections might actually have been an exaggeration, given that New York has recorded a total of 120 000 Aids cases since the start of the epidemic. In 1997, the *Washington Post* reported that the true number of HIV infections in the United States in the mid-eighties was probably in the region of 450 000 – one-quarter of the figure put forth by the *New England Journal of Medicine* at the time.

If the numbers could be gotten so wrong in America, what are we to make of infinitely more dire predictions in the developing world? In the early nineties, experts announced that Thailand's Aids epidemic was 'moving with supersonic speed.' It stalled at 2 per cent. They said Aids in India was about to explode 'like a volcano,' but infection levels there have yet to crest one per cent. The only place where the apocalypse has materialised in its full and ghastly glory is in Geneva's computer models of the African pandemic.

Why Africa, and Africa only? I know a possible reason. Read on.

In many ways, the story of Aids in Africa is a story of the gulf between rich and poor, the privileged and the wretched. Here's one way of calibrating the abyss.

Let's say you live in America, and you committed an indiscretion with drugs and needles or unprotected sex a few years back, and now find yourself plagued by ominous maladies that won't go away. Your doctor frowns and says you should have an Aids test. She draws a blood sample and sends it to a laboratory, where it is subjected to an exploratory ELISA (enzyme-linked immunosorbent assay) test. The ELISA cannot detect the virus itself, only antibodies which mark its presence. If your blood contains such antibodies, the test will 'light up,' or change colour, whereupon the lab tech will repeat the experiment. If the second ELISA lights up too, he'll do a confirmatory test using the more sophisticated and expensive Western blot method. And if that confirms the infection, the CDC recommends that the entire procedure be repeated using a new blood sample, to put the outcome beyond all doubt.

In other words, we're talking six tests in all, doubly confirmed. Such a protocol is probably failsafe, but as you draw away from the First World, health care standards decline, and people grow poorer, meaning that confirmatory tests start falling away. In Johannesburg, for instance, a doctor in private practice will typically want three consecutive positive ELISAs before deciding that you are HIV-infected. But his counterpart in a cash-strapped government hospital has to settle for two ELISAs, and in some circumstances, only one. That's also the WHO's recommended protocol for pregnancy clinic surveys in countries like mine, where the HIV rate is above ten per cent.

In America, one ELISA means almost nothing. 'Persons are positive only when they are repeatedly reactive by ELISA and confirmed by Western blot,' says the CDC. In Africa, however, such precautions are deemed expensive and unnecessary, partly because HIV infections are so densely concentrated, but mostly because the blood tests are held to be virtually infallible.

How do we know? Because commercial HIV tests are evaluated by the WHO as they come onto the market. These safety checks involve a panel of several hundred blood samples from all over the world. Some are HIV-positive, some aren't. The object is to make sure new tests are capable of determining which are which. Among the scores of brands evaluated over the years, a handful have proved to be useless. But those manufactured by established biotechnology corporations usually pass with flying colours, typically scoring accuracy rates close to perfect.

In South Africa, such outcomes are often cited in furious attacks on President Mbeki. 'HIV tests such as the latest generation ELISA are now more than 99 per cent accurate,' opined the *Weekly Mail & Guardian*. 'The tests have confidence levels of 99.9 per cent,' said Professor Malegapuru Makgoba, head of the Medical Research Council. Science had spoken, and science was unanimous: the tests were fine, and Mbeki was an idiot, 'trying to be a *Boy's Own* basement lab hero of Aids science.'

It was a good line. I laughed too, but there came a moment when it ceased to be funny. The story begins in Brazil, in 1994. Dr Marise Fonseca is studying for an advanced degree in tropical medicine. Her professors at São Paulo University suspect that HIV might have gained a foothold in the Amazon, so they send Marise to do some testing in a tough gold-mining camp. Most of her 184 subjects are in high Aids risk categories – miners who scorn condoms and girls who work in saloons or cabarets – so it comes as no great surprise when 21 test positive or borderline positive on at least one HIV ELISA. In other respects, however, the results are inexplicable. A locally manufactured ELISA says two subjects are positive. A British one fingers seven, but different people in almost every case. The French test is all over the place, declaring 14 infected.

Clearly, something in the blood of these people is confusing the tests, and the prime suspect is *Plasmodium falciparum*, one of the parasites that causes malaria: of the 21 subjects who lit up the tests, 16 have huge levels of malaria antibody in their veins. Fonseca and her key collaborator, US Army scientist Lorrin Pang, decide to try an experiment. They formulate a preparation that absorbs malaria antibodies, treat the Amazon samples, and repeat the tests on the blood thus cleansed. Eighty per cent of the suspected HIV infections vanish.

Pang and Fonseca write up their results and submit to *The Lancet*, expecting shortly to become famous. Instead, it's the start of a bitter struggle to have their findings recognised. *The Lancet* says their paper is 'not of interest,' so they try the *Journal of Infectious Diseases*, whose anonymous peer reviewers say the data are too meagre to support the conclusions. Pang and Fonseca concede the point and ask the WHO to finance further investigation.

Pang thinks he stands a good chance of getting funding because he's been a WHO consultant for nearly 20 years, but he's turned down, and worse yet, or so he claims, warned that his line of inquiry is 'inflammatory.' This brings out the bulldog in him, and he resolves to publish or perish. He keeps revising the paper and resubmitting it to new journals, but peer reviewers always point out flaws and shoot it down. The impasse persists until May 2000, when Pang and Fonseca find a sympathetic ear at the Royal Society of Tropical Medicine, a venerable British institution that agrees to publish their findings as a 'short report' in its journal. The response, according to the Royal Society's editor, is dead silence: no arguments, no rebuttals, no letters disputing the outcome or trashing their methods. In terms of scientific convention, this means the finding stands.

So what's a layman to make of this? If Pang and Fonseca's finding stands in Africa – and they are the first to concede that this remains uncertain – hundreds of millions might be at risk of testing falsely positive for HIV. I asked Luc Noel of the WHO's Blood Safety Unit for his opinion. He wasn't aware of the Pang/Fonseca paper, but seemed surprised that anyone should take such claims seriously. He handed me a booklet detailing the outcome of the WHO's evaluation of commercial ELISAs. In it, I found two of the three tests that Fonseca deployed in the Amazon – the very ones that went haywire, second- and third-generation kits manufactured in Britain and France respectively. One was rated 97 per cent accurate, the other, 98 per cent.

So – perhaps Fonseca made a mistake somewhere along the line. On the other hand, I couldn't help noticing that these levels of near-perfection were the end result of a process that involves as many as five confirmatory tests. What happens if you use just one or two, like Fonseca? And what if your subjects are desperately poor people whose immune systems are typically, as UNAIDS head Peter Piot once phrased it, in a state of 'chronic activation' as a result of 'chronic exposure' to hunger and tropical pathogens?

I found an answer of sorts at the Uganda Virus Research Institute, possibly Africa's greatest citadel of HIV studies. Perched on a hilltop overlooking Lake Victoria and generously funded by the British government, the UVRI is a many-splendoured institution with great glories to its name. It employs 200 scientists and support personnel, runs an array of advanced Aids studies, tests experimental drugs, labours to produce an Aids vaccine and has generated hundreds of scientific papers over the past decade. It also publishes an annual report. I found a copy of the latest edition on a coffee table and took it home with me.

This document turned out to be full of fascinating snippets. In one experiment, scientists decided to invert standard procedure and run HIV tests on people who were known to be HIV-negative but were sick with other diseases. Their blood was screened using the sophisticated Western blot method, and lo, the tests lit up. Seventy-eight per cent of hookworm-infested subjects were borderline positive. Malaria caused 81 per cent of its victims to test indeterminate. Unspecified 'bacterial infections' confused the test nine times out of ten.

This phenomenon – false reactions on the Western blot – is well-known in the West, where a smallish (three to 18) percentage of subjects test indeterminate, and some test falsely positive. The US National Institute for Allergic and Infectious Disease acknowledges that previous pregnancies are liable to confuse the outcome. In the early days of Aids, researchers published similar findings in respect of more than 50 diseases, among them such everyday scourges as influenza, hepatitis and measles, and in Africa, bilharzia, malaria and yaws, which collectively afflict hundreds of millions. It is for this reason, among others, that the WHO now recommends that HIV testers drop the Western blot entirely. As Luc Noel explained it, second- and third-generation ELISAs use recombinant or synthetic HIV antigens, whereas the Western blot doesn't. It is these modern ELISAs, rather than the Western blot, that are taken to be almost perfectly accurate.

There was a way of checking this. I looked up the results of the WHO's evaluation of two leading ELISA brands – Recombigen, manu-factured by Trinity Biotech, and Wellcozyme HIV Recombinant from Murex Biotech. Test-driven in the WHO's lab, the Wellcozyme test scored 99.1 per cent, while the Trinity model achieved a perfect 100. In the field, in Africa, it was another story entirely. In the course of 1999, the Uganda Virus Research Institute screened thousands of blood samples with these two tests. Exactly 3 369 lit up at least one ELISA, but only 2 237 (66 per cent) remained positive after confirma-tory tests. In other words: 34 per cent of Ugandans who tested positive on just one ELISA were not really carrying the virus. The outcome is even more intriguing if you consider the 88 who twice tested positive, but only weakly so. When their blood was subjected to Western blot-ting, still held to be the definitive test in America, only 11 (or 13 per cent) turned out to be genuinely HIV-infected.

Whichever way you figure it, this falls short of perfection, which is why the UVRI does rigorous confirmatory testing. The same does not necessarily apply in the pregnancy clinic screenings on which Africa's Aids estimates are based. Here, the WHO says it's okay to drop all confirmatory tests in high prevalence settings. I took this up with UNAIDS epidemiologist Neff Walker, who pointed out that most African countries had 'quality assurance' programmes to guard against foul-ups. 'I feel,' he said, 'that if a government found any evidence of too many false positives in their testing, they would report it. Governments would like to find evidence of lower prevalence (as would we all) and since they have the data to easily check your hypothesis, they would do so and report it.'

Would they? I'm not so sure. In fact, I think some Aids researchers have developed an almost religious attachment to dogma about ever-rising HIV prevalence. Here in South Africa, for instance, the Health Ministry informs us that the results of its annual ante-natal HIV surveys are adjusted 'so as to ensure that predicted prevalence trends are not disrupted.' What manner of science is this, where predictions are allowed to influence or even determine the outcome? Who does the adjusting? What were their findings before predictions intervened?

I don't have answers yet, but I can tell you one thing: high Aids numbers are not entirely undesirable in Africa, or anywhere else, for that matter. High numbers mean deepening crisis, and crisis generates funding. The results are manifest: the skies of Africa are full of safari scientists, flying in to oversee research projects or novel interventions and bringing with them huge inflows of cash, much of it destined for the countries with the highest numbers.

On the ground, these dollars translate into patronage for politicians and good jobs for their struggling subjects. An Aids counsellor earns 30 times more than a school teacher in Uganda. In Tanzania, doctors can double their income just by saving the hard currency per diems they earn while attending international Aids conferences. Here in South Africa, entrepreneurs are piling into the business at an astonishing rate, setting up orphanages and consultancies, selling herbal immune boosters and vitamin supplements, devising new insurance products, distributing condoms, staging benefits, forming theatre troupes that take the Aids prevention message into schools. My buddy Jeremy Nathan is co-producing a slate of 40 TV documentaries about Aids, all for foreign markets. My buddy Shan Holmes, who sells HIV test kits to African governments, describes her industry as 'a wall-to-wall cocktail party.' My buddy Dave Alcock escorted representatives of the Bill and Melissa Gates Foundation around Aids hotspots in the Zulu homeland. 'By the time we got there,' says he, 'the Aids orgs already had so much money they couldn't absorb any more. They couldn't find anyone to donate to.'

Such surfeit is the result of dumbfounding Aids estimates based on the presumed infallibility of blood tests. The guys in Geneva maintain that if there's a problem it would surely have been reported, but by my reckoning it has – the UVRI data speaks for itself, and French Army scientists working in neighbouring Mozambique have just published a paper that raises even more alarming questions about the single-ELISA protocol. The best of the tests they evaluated achieved a 'positive predictive value' or PPV of 57.95 per cent, meaning that the test got it right six times out of ten. A second test was right about half the time, while a third produced false positives at the rate of seven in ten. What if they'd thrown a Western blot into the equation? And some confirmatory tests for good measure? In 1988, the US army ran a battery of seven confirmatory tests on recruits who'd lit up at least one ELISA. After each round, the number of positives dwindled, and in the end barely 16 per cent were shown to be truly HIV-infected. In 1992, a similar exercise in Russia produced an even worse outcome: only one in 100 suspected infections were genuine.

So what happens if you treat Africans as equals, and test them as rigorously as everyone else? I can't say. All I can tell you is that the fate of a continent depends on a clear answer, but there doesn't seem to be one.

And so we return to where we started, standing over a coffin under a bleak Soweto sky, making a clumsy speech about a sad and premature death. Adelaide Ntsele died of Aids, but the word didn't appear on her death certificate. Here in Africa, the three little letters stigmatise, so doctors usually put down something gentler to spare the family further pain. In Adelaide's case, they wrote TB. But her sister Elizabeth had no need of such false consolation. She donned a red-ribbon baseball cap and appeared on national TV, telling the truth: 'My sister had HIV/Aids.' As a nurse, Elizabeth had no qualms with the doctors' diagnosis, and she concurred with their decision to forgo surgery and let Adelaide die. 'It was God's will,' she says, and she was at peace with it. I was the one beset by harrowing doubts.

Some people tell me it's criminal to raise those doubts at a moment when rich countries and corporations are mulling billion-dollar contributions to a Global Aids Superfund. They have been brought to this point by a ceaseless barrage of stories and images of unbearable suffering in Africa, all buttressed by Geneva's death projections. Casting doubt on those estimates is tantamount to murder, or so says Ed Rybicki, a Cape Town microbiologist who caught sight of part of this article and found it appalling. 'Aids is real, and is killing Africans in very large numbers,' he wrote to me. 'Presenting arguments that purport to show otherwise in the popular press is simply going to compound the damage already done by Mbeki. And a lot more people may die who may not have otherwise.'

Rybicki is probably right. If I was poised to contribute billions to the campaign against Aids in Africa, I would be shaken to hear that the statistics driving me towards such an epiphany of altruism might be shaky. Indeed, I would say stop right here, there will be no money until we know what the facts are. But what are the facts? American newspapers keep telling me that Aids in Africa is 'worse than the Black Death,' but I couldn't find rock-solid evidence of this in any of the countries where I went looking.

In the end, only one thing seemed certain: the importance of death data gathered by South Africa's government. When I embarked on this story, as you may recall, no massive rise in registered deaths was discernible. A year later, I returned to my point of departure to see if the discrepancy persisted. UNAIDS had yet to update its figures, but a sister agency, the UN Population Program, projected around 400 000 Aids deaths in the year 2000. How many of these could be confirmed by death registration in the only African country where such an exercise is feasible? I wrote to the Dept. of Home Affairs, which manages the death register, and asked for the latest numbers. In response came a set of figures somewhat different from those initially provided – the consequence, I am told, of late registrations trickling in from deep rural areas. Here is the final analysis:

Deaths registered in 1996 – 363 238

Deaths registered in 2000 – 457 335

As you see, registered deaths have indeed risen rapidly. The rise falls way short of the catastrophe predicted by the United Nations, but there is definite movement in an ominous direction. What's more, deaths are concentrated among sexually active young adults: females in their twenties, and males aged 30 to 39. What would account for this, if not Aids?

But even this is not the end of the tale. In 1998, Nelson Mandela's government launched a campaign to improve death registration in villages and townships inhabited by black people whose hardships and health problems had been largely ignored by the apartheid regime. They introduced a new, user-friendly death certificate, opened satellite government offices in remote areas, even introduced a subsidy for undertakers willing to register the deaths of those they buried.

Last year, demographer Sulaiman Bah analysed five years of death data, and found two factors at work. One is the presumed impact of Aids. The other is rising registration, particularly in rural areas where the government's campaign would have had greatest impact. In an attempt to untangle these influences, Bah stripped the statistics of every death that could possibly be attributed to HIV infection – every bronchitis death, every TB death, every death caused by pneumonia, infectious diarrhoea, and all other Aids-defining conditions. The pattern remained unchanged: deaths were still up across the board, and still concentrated most heavily in the same young adult age groups. Bah's conclusion: increased reporting accounts for an unknown proportion of the apparent rise in mortality.

So that's the story: enigma upon enigma, riddle leading to riddle, and no reprieve from doubt. I have wasted a year of my time and thousands of your dollars, and all I can really tell you is this: ordinary Africans everywhere are convinced that a new scourge is moving among them, a mysterious disease whose symptoms are other diseases, now grown impervious to medication. I've grown sceptical of the Aids industry, but I think these ordinary people should be helped if possible. But how? It'll cost a thousand dollars a year to put one African on Aids drugs – a noble proposal, on its face, but nonsensical if that one lucky person's neighbours are dying of starvation and lack of medicines that cost a few cents. So what's the right policy? The answer, as always, lies in Africa's Aids estimates – 16 million dead, last time I checked, and the toll rising daily. If these numbers are accurate, desperate measures are needed. But what if they aren't?

Feel free to publish this, but if it bored you to death, I'll understand.

> Yours,
> Malan

Postscript: Bill Tonelli was a genuinely nice guy, and I'd put him in a very awkward position. His boss, *Rolling Stone* founder and publisher Jann Wenner, discovered in midlife that he was actually gay, where-upon he left his wife and children and became, among other things, a star in New York's Aids charity firmament. Bill and Jann never said so openly, but this report was not what they wanted. They wanted a piece that would illumine South Africa's Aids tragedy and add to *Rolling Stone*'s lustre as a magazine that stood for justice. They did not want a letter teeming with heresies.

The *Rolling Stone* dudes were good Americans whose commitment to free speech was religious. It was unthinkable for them to censor a writer whose opinions they disagreed with, so they said, okay, we'll publish something, but first, answer this: who agrees with you? And I had to say, nobody. The Aids dissidents who'd captured Mbeki's ear wanted no truck with a writer too feeble-minded to understand that the disease didn't exist at all. By the same token, the Aids establishment was pathologically hostile to any suggestion that its claims regarding megadeath in Africa were exaggerated. I was on my own. I said, 'Truth is not democratic. The facts are either wrong or right. As far as I'm concerned, the facts as stated in this letter embody the truth as I understand it.'

Rolling Stone took this on the chin and did the honourable thing: they published the story, but only after every word had been challenged by the dogged researcher Dave McNally and approved by *Rolling Stone*'s special consultant, Dr David Ho, a stellar Aids researcher who'd recently been anointed *Time*'s Man of the Year for his work on protease inhibitors. The resulting article was dull and lifeless, so full of equivocations and digressions as to be barely readable. This isn't a criticism of *Rolling Stone*. It was courageous of them to publish anything at all. But the process was an ordeal that consumed months of my life and left me restless and dissatisfied.

I was also engaged in an extraordinarily intense conversation with an American named Rodney Richards. Rodney was a microbiologist who'd gone straight into Aids research after obtaining his doctorate, becoming a member of the team that developed the first Aids blood test authorised for use in the USA. Intrigued by the ambiguities attendant upon HIV diagnosis, he went on to develop a diagnostic machine he believed was infallible. Convinced that he'd made a historic breakthrough, he invited two notorious dissidents to work with him. One was Peter Duesberg, a brilliant cancer researcher who'd ruined his career by declaring that HIV science was invalid. The other was Kary Mullis, the Nobel Prize-winning researcher who said, 'Anyone who believes HIV theory is so stupid they should be pitied.'

Rodney thought Duesberg and Mullis's endorsement would crown his discovery with irrefutable credibility, only to find, after six months in the laboratory, that he couldn't sustain his case. Crushed, Rodney resigned his job and retired from Aids research. I met him on the internet, and he struck me as an interesting guy. He believed Aids theory was profoundly mistaken, but he had the grace to be tormented by the possibility that he might be wrong. I guess that's why he responded so strongly to the question I was posing: if Aids doesn't exist, how come the death toll in South Africa is rising? I thought the evidence in this regard was pretty strong. Rodney couldn't accept that, but our lungs hungered for the oxygen of truth, so we threw ourselves into a years-long interrogation of African Aids statistics.

I didn't write about this at the time, partly because I was intimidated by the consequences of getting it wrong, but mostly because my wife saw Aids as a destructive addiction that was ruining our lives. She had a point. Rodney and I were spending almost every waking hour on our quest. There was no money coming in, and I was often absent and abstracted. Like all addicts, I started telling lies and fulfilling my dark cravings in secret. But she found me out in December 2003, when I wrote what follows, first for *Noseweek*, and then for *The Spectator*.

Among the Aids Fanatics

||||||||||||||||||||||||||||||||||||||||||||||||||||||||||||||||||||||||||||||||||||||||||||||||||||||||||||||||||||||||||||||||||||||||||||||||

It was the eve of Aids Day here in Cape Town. Rock stars like Bono and Sir Bob Geldof were jetting in for a fundraising concert with Nelson Mandela, and the airwaves were full of dark talk about mega-death and the armies of feral orphans who would surely ransack South Africa's cities in 2017 unless funds were made available to take care of them. My neighbour came up the garden path with a press cutting. 'Read this,' said Capt David Price, ex-Royal Air Force flyboy. 'Bloody awful.'

It was an article from *The Spectator* describing bizarre sex practices that allegedly contribute to the HI virus's rampage across the continent. 'One in five of us here in Zambia is HIV positive,' said the report. 'In 1993 our neighbour Botswana had an estimated population of 1.4 million. Today that figure is under a million and heading downwards. Doom merchants predict that Botswana may soon become the first nation in modern times literally to die out. This is Aids in Africa.'

Really? Botswana has just concluded a census that shows population growing at around 2.7 per cent a year, in spite of what is usually described as the worst Aids problem on the planet. Total population has risen to 1.7 million over the last decade. If anything, Botswana is experiencing a minor population explosion.

There is similar bad news for the doomsayers in Tanzania's new census, which shows population growing at 2.9 per cent a year. Professional pessimists will be particularly discomforted by developments in the swamplands west of Lake Victoria, where HIV first emerged, and where the depopulated villages of popular mythology are supposedly located. Here, in Kagera district, population grew at 2.7 per cent a year prior to 1988, only to accelerate to 3.1 per cent even as the Aids epidemic was supposedly peaking. Uganda's latest census tells a broadly similar story, as does South Africa's.

Some might think it good news that the impact of Aids is less devastating than most laymen imagine, but they are wrong. In Africa, the only good news about Aids is bad news, and anyone who tells you otherwise is branded a moral leper, bent on sowing confusion and derailing one hundred thousand worthy fund-raising drives. I know this because several years ago I acquired what was generally regarded as a leprous obsession with the dumbfounding Aids numbers in my daily papers. They told me that Aids had claimed 250 000 South African lives in 1999, and I kept saying, this can't possibly be true. What followed was very ugly – ruined dinner parties, broken friendships, ridicule from those who knew better, bitter fights with my wife. After a year or so, she put her foot down. Choose, she said. Aids or me. So I dropped the subject, put my papers in the garage, and kept my mouth shut.

As I write, the madam is standing behind me with hands on hips, hugely irked by this reversion to bad habits. But looking around, it seems to me that Aids fever is nearing the danger level, and that some calming thoughts are called for. Bear with me while I explain.

We all know, thanks to Twain, that statistics are often the lowest form of lie, but when it comes to HIV/Aids, we suspend all scepticism. Why? Aids is the most political disease ever. We have been fighting about it since the day it was identified. The key battleground is public perception, and the most deadly weapon is the estimate. When the virus first emerged, I was living in America, where HIV incidence was estimated to be doubling every year or so. Every time I turned on the TV, Madonna popped up to warn me that 'Aids is an equal opportunity killer,' poised to break out of the drug and gay subcultures and slaughter heterosexuals. In 1985, a science journal estimated that 1.7 million Americans were already infected, with 'three to five million' soon likely to follow suit. Oprah Winfrey told the nation that by 1990, 'one in five heterosexuals will be dead of Aids.'

We now know that these estimates were vastly and indeed deliberately exaggerated, but they achieved the desired end: Aids was catapulted to the top of the West's spending agenda, whereupon the estimators turned their attention elsewhere. India's epidemic was likened to 'a volcano waiting to explode.' Africa faced 'a tidal wave of death.' By 1992 they were estimating that 'Aids could clear the whole planet.'

Who were they, these estimators? For the most part, they worked in Geneva for WHO or UNAIDS, using a computer simulator called Epimodel. Every year, all over Africa, blood samples would be taken from a small sample of pregnant women and screened for signs of HIV infection. The results would be programmed into Epimodel, which transmuted them into estimates. If so many women were infected, it followed that a similar proportion of their husbands and lovers must be infected, too. These numbers would be extrapolated out into the general population, enabling the computer modellers to arrive at seemingly precise tallies of the doomed, the dying, and the orphans left behind.

Because Africa is disorganised and in some parts unknowable, we had little choice other than to accept these projections. ('We' always expect the worst of Africa, anyway.) Reporting on Aids in Africa became a quest for anecdotes to support Geneva's estimates, and the estimates grew ever more terrible – 9.6 million cumulative Aids deaths by 1997, rising to 17 million three years later.

Or so we were told. When I visited the worst-affected parts of Tanzania and Uganda in 2001, I was overwhelmed with stories about the disease locals called 'Slims,' but statistical corroboration was hard to come by. According to government census bureaux, death rates in these areas had been in decline since World War II. Aids-era mortality studies yielded some of the lowest overall death rates ever measured in the region. Populations seemed to have exploded even as the epidemic was peaking.

Ask Aids experts about this, and they say, this is Africa, chaos reigns, the historic data are too uncertain to make valid comparisons. But these same experts will tell you that South Africa is vastly different – 'The only country in sub-Saharan Africa where sufficient deaths are routinely registered to attempt to produce national estimates of mortality,' says Prof Ian Timaeus of the London School of Hygiene and Tropical Medicine. According to Timaeus, upwards of 80 per cent of deaths are registered here, which makes us unique: the only corner of Africa where it's possible to judge computer-generated Aids estimates against objective reality.

In the year 2000, Timaeus joined a team of South African research-ers bent on eliminating all doubts about the magnitude of Aids' im-pact on South African mortality. Sponsored by the Medical Research Council, the team's mission was to validate (for the first time ever) the output of Aids computer models against real-life death registration in an African setting. Towards this end, the MRC team was granted privi-leged access to death reports as they streamed into Pretoria. The first results became available in 2001, and they ran thus: around 339 000 adult deaths in 1998, 375 000 in 1999, and 410 000 in 2000.*

This was grimly consistent with predictions of rising mortality, but the scale was problematic. Epimodel estimated 250 000 Aids deaths in 1999, but there were only 375 000 adult deaths in total that year – far too few to accommodate the UN's claims on behalf of the HI virus. In short, Epimodel had failed its reality check. It was quietly shelved in favour of a more sophisticated local model, ASSA 600, which yielded a 'more realistic' death toll from Aids of 143 000 for calendar year 1999.

At this level, Aids deaths were about 40 per cent of the total – still a bit high, considering there were only 232 000 deaths left to distribute among all other causes. The MRC solved the problem by stating that deaths from ordinary disease had declined at the cumulatively mas-sive rate of nearly 3 per cent per annum since 1985. Where they got this from remains a mystery, but these researchers were experts, and their tinkering achieved the desired end: modelled Aids deaths and real deaths were reconciled, the books balanced, truth revealed.

The fruit of the MRC's ground-breaking labour was published in June 2001, and my hash appeared to have been settled. To be sure, I carped about curious adjustments and overall magnitude, but fell silent in the face of graphs showing massive changes in the *pattern* of death, with more and more people dying at sexually active ages. 'How can you argue with this?' cried my wife, eyes flashing angrily. I couldn't. I put my Aids papers in the garage and ate my hat.

But I couldn't help sneaking the odd look at science websites to see how the drama was developing. Towards the end of 2001, the vaunted ASSA 600 model was replaced by ASSA 2000, which produced esti-mates even lower than its predecessor: 92 000 Aids deaths in calendar 1999. This was just more than a third of the original UN figure, but no

---

*This figure disagrees with the death toll previously cited for 2000. Again, the culprit is late registration.

matter, the boffins claimed ASSA 2000 was so accurate that further reference to real-life death reports 'will be of limited usefulness.' A bit eerie, I thought, being told that virtual reality was about to render the real thing superfluous, but if these experts said the new model was infallible, it was surely infallible.

Only it wasn't. Last December, ASSA 2000 was retired, too. A note on the MRC website explained that modelling was an inexact science, and that 'the number of people dying of Aids has only now started to increase.' Furthermore, said the MRC, there was a new model in the works, one that would 'probably' produce estimates 'about ten percent lower' than those presently on the table. The exercise was not strictly valid, but I persuaded my scientist pal Rodney Richards to run the revised data on his own simulator and see what he came up with for 1999. The answer, very crudely, was an Aids death toll somewhere around 60 000 – a far cry indeed from the 250 000 initially put forth by UNAIDS.

The wife has just read this, and she is not impressed. 'It's obscene,' she says. 'You're treating this as if it's just a computer game. People are dying out there.'

Well, yes. I concede that. People are dying, but this doesn't spare us from the fact that Aids in Africa is indeed something of a computer game. When you read that 29.4 million Africans are 'living with HIV/Aids,' it doesn't mean that millions of living people have been tested. It means modellers assume that 29.4 million Africans are linked via enormously complicated mathematical and sexual networks to one of the women who tested HIV-positive in one of those annual pregnancy clinic surveys. Modellers are the first to admit that this exercise is subject to uncertainties and large margins of error. Larger than expected, in some cases.

A year or so back, modellers produced estimates that portrayed South African universities as crucibles of rampant HIV infection, with one in four undergraduates doomed to die within ten years. Prevalence shifted according to racial composition and region, with KwaZulu-Natal institutions worst affected and Rand Afrikaans University (still 70 per cent white) coming in at 9.5 per cent. Real-life tests on a random sample of 1 188 RAU students rendered a startlingly different conclusion: on-campus prevalence was 1.1 per cent, barely a ninth of the modelled figure. 'Doubt is cast on present estimates,' said the RAU report, 'and further research is strongly advocated.'

A similar anomaly emerged when South Africa's major banks ran HIV tests on 29 000 staff earlier this year. A modelling exercise put HIV prevalence as high as 12 per cent; real-life tests produced a figure closer to three. Elsewhere, actuaries are scratching their heads over a puzzling lack of interest in programmes set up by medical insurance companies to handle an anticipated flood of middle-class HIV cases. Old Mutual, the insurance giant, estimates that as many as 570 000 people are eligible, but only 22 500 have thus far signed up. In Grahamstown, District Surgeon Dr Stuart Dyer is contemplating an equally perplexing dearth of HIV cases in the local jail.

'Sexually transmitted diseases are common in the prison where I work,' he wrote to the *British Medical Journal*, 'and all prisoners who have any such disease are tested for HIV. Prisoners with any other illnesses that do not resolve rapidly (within one to two weeks) are also tested for HIV. As a result, a large number of HIV tests are done every week. This prison, which holds 550 inmates and is always full or overfull, has an HIV infection rate of two to four per cent and has had only two deaths from Aids in the seven years I have been working there.' Dyer goes on to express a dim view of statistics that give the impression that 'the whole of South Africa will be depopulated within 24 months,' and concludes by stating, 'HIV infection in SA prisons is currently 2.3 per cent.' According to the newspapers, it should be closer to 60.

On their face, these developments suggest that miracles are happening in South Africa, unreported by anyone save *Noseweek*, South Africa's *Private Eye*. If the anomalies described above are typical, computer models are seriously overstating HIV prevalence. A similar picture emerges on the national level, where our estimated annual Aids death toll has halved since we eased UNAIDS out of the picture, with further reductions likely when the new MRC model appears. Could the same thing be happening in the rest of Africa?

Most estimates for countries north of the Limpopo are issued by UNAIDS, using methods similar to those discredited here in South Africa. According to Paul Bennell, a health policy analyst associated with Sussex University's Institute for Development Studies, there is an 'extraordinary' lack of evidence from other sources. 'Most countries do not even collect data on deaths,' he writes. 'There are virtually no population-based survey data in most high-prevalence countries.'

Bennell was, however, able to gather information about Africa's schoolteachers, usually described as a high-risk HIV group on account of their steady income, which enables them to drink and party more than others. Last year, the World Bank claimed Aids was killing Africa's teachers 'faster then they can be replaced.' The BBC reported that 'one in seven' Malawian teachers would die in 2002 alone.

Bennell looked at the available evidence and found real-life teacher mortality to be 'much lower than has been suggested.' In Malawi, for instance, the all-causes death rate among schoolteachers was under 3 per cent, not over 14. In Botswana, it was about three times lower than computer-generated estimates. In Zimbabwe, four times lower. Bennell believes that Aids continues to present a serious threat to educators, but concludes that 'overall impact will not be as catastrophic as suggested.' What's more, teacher deaths appear to be declining in six of the eight countries he has studied closely. 'This is quite unexpected,' he remarks, 'and suggests that, in terms of teacher deaths, the worst may be over.'

In the past year or so, similar mutterings have been heard throughout southern Africa – the epidemic is levelling off or even declining in the worst-affected countries. UNAIDS has been at great pains to rebut such ideas, describing them as 'dangerous myths,' even though the data on UNAIDS' own website shows they are nothing of the sort. 'The epidemic is not growing in most countries,' insists Bennell. 'HIV prevalence is not increasing as is usually stated or implied.'

Bennell raises an interesting point here. Why would UNAIDS and its massive alliance of pharmaceutical companies, NGOs, scientists and charities insist the epidemic is worsening if it isn't? A possible explanation comes from New York physician Joe Sonnabend, one of the pioneers of Aids research. Sonnabend was working in a Greenwich Village clap clinic when the syndrome first appeared and went on to found the American Foundation for Aids Research, only to quit in protest when colleagues started exaggerating the threat of a generalised pandemic with a view to increasing Aids' visibility and adding urgency to their grant applications. The Aids establishment, says Sonnabend, is extremely skilled at 'the manipulation of fear for advancement in terms of money and power.'

With such thoughts in the back of my mind, South Africa's Aids Day 'celebrations' cast me into a deeply leprous mood. Please don't get me wrong here. I believe Aids is a real problem in Africa. Governments and sober medical professionals should be heeded when they express deep concerns about it. But there are breeds of Aids activist and Aids journalist who sound hysterical to me. On Aids Day, they came forth like loonies drawn by a full moon, chanting that Aids was getting worse and worse, 'spinning out of control,' crippling economies, causing famines, killing millions, contributing to the oppression of women and 'undermining democracy' by sapping the will of the poor to resist dictators.

To hear them talk, Aids is the only problem in Africa, and the only solution is to continue the agitprop until free access to Aids drugs is defined as a 'basic human right' for everyone. They are saying, in effect, that because Mr Mhlangu of rural Zambia has a disease they find more compelling than any other, someone must spend upwards of $300 a year to provide Mr Mhlangu with life-extending Aids medications – a noble idea, on its face, but completely demented when you consider that Mr Mhlangu's neighbours are likely to be dying in much larger numbers of diseases that could be cured for a few cents if medicines were only available. Around 350 million Africans – nearly half the population – get malaria every year, but malaria medication is not a basic human right. Two million get TB, but last time I checked, spending on Aids research exceeded spending on TB by a crushing factor of 90 to one. As for pneumonia, cancer, dysentery or diabetes, let them take aspirin, or grub in the bush for medicinal herbs.

I think it is time to start questioning some of the claims made by the Aids lobby. Their certainties are so fanatic, the powers they claim so far-reaching. All their authority derives from computer-generated estimates which they wield like weapons, overwhelming any resistance with dumbfounding atom bombs of hypothetical human misery. Give them their head, and they will commandeer all resources to fight just one disease. Who knows, they may defeat Aids, but what if we wake up five years hence to discover that the problem has been blown out of all proportion by unsound estimates, causing upwards of $20 billion to be wasted?

The Spectator, December 2003

Postscript: This article was an act of war against the Aids establishment, and I was repaid in kind. Interested parties might wish to consult the Treatment Action Campaign's 40-page rebuttal, which still dominates the results when you Google my name, or the Pugwash Group's retaliatory carpet-bombing. On a more colloquial level, there was a piece in the *Washington Post* that described me as dirty, smelly and half-deranged, and a profile in *Insig* in which I was held out to be a harmless 'court jester' whose 'Aids dissident clown' routine was causing great amusement in the corridors of Wits University. 'We find Malan no threat,' wrote Muff Andersson. 'When a national fool emerges, rushing in and affronting the angels, we tend to look at the audience's sense of enjoyment. His approach is below the belt, comical, carnivalesque ...' and so on.

The interesting thing about this global outpouring of ridicule and venom is that no one challenged the important facts in my article – all that stuff about UNAIDS' malfunctioning model, perplexing census outcomes, serial downward revisions of South Africa's Aids estimates and embarrassing shortfalls in African teacher mortality. The problem with these claims is that they were true, which is why the Aids establishment and its media outriders had no choice other than to shout me down or dismiss me as a crackpot, an exercise to which I unwittingly lent myself by cracking jokes about the insane folly of spending years on a story nobody wanted to hear, and that nobody was paying me for. 'Malan admits he needs therapy,' said the *Washington Post*. Ah, well. If you live by the sword, you die by it too.

But even as the Aids bwanas and I exchanged insults, a Chinese-American scientist was putting the final touches to a book that began to swing the debate in my favour. Dr James Chin was a giant of Aids research. He'd worked in the field since the disease's discovery, at one point heading the United Nations' global HIV forecasting programme. He was also the creator of Epimodel, the computer simulator used to produce the UN estimates I found so implausible. Turns out that Dr Chin agreed with me, and was about to disavow his own creation. In his book, *The AIDS Pandemic* – subtitled *The collision of epidemiology with political correctness* – Chin acknowledged that 'the story of AIDS has been distorted by activists in order to support the myth of the high potential risk of HIV spreading into the general population. Most policy-makers have uncritically accepted UNAIDS' high prevalence estimates when lower estimates are more accurate. Time, money and resources are being wasted world-wide.' Chin thought global Aids infections had been overestimated by around 30 per cent. Other scientists put the overestimation as high as 50 per cent.

At more or less the same time, American researchers working in Kenya published the results of a so-called population survey, which involved testing blood from a representative sample of the population. Using the system designed by James Chin, UNAIDS had previously claimed 15 per cent of Kenya's adults were HIV-infected. The new study, universally held to be more credible, suggested that the real HIV rate was 6.7 per cent. The implications were staggering. Overnight, the estimated number of HIV-stricken Kenyans plummeted from 'as many as four million' to 'as few as one million.'

After that, Kenya-style population studies were carried out elsewhere in Africa, with similar results. In Ethiopia, for instance, estimated HIV prevalence tumbled by 80 per cent. In Burundi, 64 per cent. In Mali, 57 per cent. In Burkina Faso, 35 per cent. In Zambia, 26 per cent. Such results came as no great surprise in South Africa, where a population study carried out in 2002 by the Human Sciences Research Council revealed an HIV infection rate around 30 per cent lower than UN estimates. This finding was initially trashed by the Aids establishment and downplayed by the media, but the HSRC held its ground and was ultimately vindicated.

Interestingly, the 2002 HSRC study revealed shocking HIV rates among South Africa's racial minorities, with (for instance) six per cent of white adults and 11 per cent of white children allegedly infected. These implausible numbers raised questions about those supposedly infallible blood tests, so a follow-up survey in 2005 featured a battery of previously unheard-of confirmatory procedures. The outcome: HIV prevalence among whites fell to 0.6 per cent, a ten-fold drop. In the coloured community, HIV prevalence plummeted from six to 1.9 per cent. In the Western Cape, five out of six computer-modelled HIV infections vanished.

These outbreaks of good news were generally ignored by the South African press, but the cat was escaping the bag. The *Washington Post* decided to take a closer look at Rwanda, held in the 1980s to be 'the fountain of death' from which Aids flowed out into the rest of Africa. 'Aids deaths on the predicted scale never arrived here,' the

Post reported. *The Lancet* published an article charging that Uganda's advances in the war on HIV were a myth sustained by researchers eager to show at least one success for the billions spent on HIV prevention. The *British Medical Journal* reported that Aids was receiving a vastly disproportionate share of health aid, and that 'billions' had consequently been wasted. 'Aids has been treated like an economic sector rather than a disease,' said Roger England, chairman of the UK's Health Systems Network.

And so the wheel began to turn. In 2001, when *Rolling Stone* asked, 'Who agrees with you?' I had to say, nobody. By 2007, even UNAIDS had acknowledged that its estimates for Africa were flawed, and the painful process of correcting distorted spending priorities was under way. I will refrain from crowing, because Aids is a serious problem in Africa. Almost every article I wrote on the subject acknowledged that point, if only in passing. My enemies and I differed largely on the question of degree.

In South Africa, we also disagreed on the question of timing. At the height of the Mbeki Aids furore, the US Census Bureau stated that SA's Aids problem was so severe that the population would start shrinking by 2003. When 2003 rolled around, however, our numbers were growing at a fairly healthy rate, and experts were beginning to acknowledge *sotto voce* that mistakes had been made. 'The number of people dying of Aids has only now started to increase,' said a note on the Medical Research Council's website.

The MRC was right. Over the next four years, the death toll among people I knew personally began to increase. I remain sceptical of computer-generated estimates, but by 2007, the anecdotal evidence was overwhelming: the phantom catastrophe of 1999 had become real; large numbers of people were dying, and the legions who'd mocked and jeered Mbeki considered themselves vindicated.

This is profoundly unfair. Back in 1999, when Thabo Mbeki first questioned the veracity of HIV science, UNAIDS was claiming that we were already living through an apocalypse, with Aids killing a quarter-million that year alone. This estimate was nonsense. Hindsight reveals that the real Aids death toll in 1999 was closer to 60 000 – less than a quarter of the number claimed by the Aids establishment.

Put yourself in Mbeki's shoes. The highest scientific authorities on the planet were telling him that South Africa was passing through the worst catastrophe in its history, that Aids had in a single year killed more South Africans than all the wars we ever fought amongst ourselves and against Britain and Germany. But when he looked around, there was a yodelling chasm between the UNAIDS's claims and the reality we were all then experiencing.

It's much to Mbeki's credit that he refused to crook the knee and praise the naked emperor's glorious raiment. It was not he who lost his head; it was the army of hysterics who believed every word uttered by the High Priests of HIV in Geneva. Mbeki was right to ask questions. His mistake was to accept the first answer given – Aids could be a hoax – and proceed accordingly. Once he'd taken that position, he was too proud to back down, and a terrible price was exacted.

4

Travel

The Last Afrikaner

||||||||||||||||||||||||||||||||||||||||||||||||||||||||||||||||||||||||||||||||||||||||||||||||||||||||||||||||||||||||||||||||||||||||||||

I stumbled upon this story in late 1993, a time of agonising crisis for Afrikaners. Some were willing to abandon the laager and follow De Klerk into democracy. Others were vowing to fight to the bitter end rather than submit to black rule. Under the circumstances, the parable of Tannie Katrien struck me as a story the Volk needed to hear. Especially the right wingers. Those hard manne thought liberals were laughable, but I thought they might heed the word of a little old tannie whose experience defied at least some of our myths about darkest Africa.

Back in Jo'burg, I tried to convince the SABC's Afrikaans service to flight a documentary about Tannie Katrien, arguing that her story would alleviate Boer paranoia and maybe even save us from race war. My letters went unanswered, and the Volk never got to meet the only living Afrikaner who could make soap out of hippopotamus fat.

Once upon a time there was a British colonial family named Hartley who had a magical farm in Africa. It lay on the slopes of Mount Meru, a cool green island in a sea of sunblasted yellow savannah. Twice a year, monsoon winds deposited heavy rains on Meru's leeward slopes, which were clad in dense rain-forest, full of rhino and buffalo and elephant. Several swift, clear streams came tumbling out of the jungle and meandered across a level plain where the soil was so rich and deep that anything you planted bore fruit in astonishing profusion – peaches, apricots, beans, maize, and the sun so close you got two harvests every year.

The Hartleys bought this farm in 1953. Their homestead lay on the shoulder of the volcano, so high that it was often above the clouds.

Sometimes they would wrap themselves in blankets at night and sit on the *stoep* with the clouds at their feet, watching the moon rise over the glittering summit of Mount Kilimanjaro, 40 miles away. In the morning, it would be burning hot again, and you could sit on the same *stoep* with a pair of binoculars, tracking the movement of elephant herds across the parched plains far below. 'I loved that house,' Kim Hartley told me. 'The *stoep* was 99 feet across. It had big white Dutch gables, and the previous owner had left a portrait of Hitler in the cellar.' I didn't have to ask who'd built it. It had to have been a Boer.

In 1904, in the aftermath of the Anglo-Boer war, disaffected Afrikaners sent a scouting party up the spine of Africa in search of a place where a Boer could live free of British domination and rid his mouth of the bitter taste of defeat. They found Mount Meru. Two years later, the first ox-wagons came trundling across the savannah, carrying Afrikaners who settled in a giant semi-circle around the northern base of the volcano. At first, they lived by the gun, but in time, they cleared the land, and began to till it with ox-ploughs. In the beginning, they dreamed of linking up with Afrikaners who'd settled in Kenya and resurrecting the lost Boer republics, but there were too few of them, so it came to nothing, and what they had was fine, anyway: perhaps the best farmland in the world.

By the time the Hartleys arrived, the Boers had created a paradise under the volcano. The lower slopes of Meru were dotted with white-washed farmhouses, shaded by bluegums and jacaranda trees. Around them lay a mile-wide belt of orchards and wheatfields, segmented by whitewashed wooden fences and criss-crossed by irrigation furrows. Below the cultivated lands, literally at the bottom of the garden, lay the dusty savannah, teeming with antelope and big game, and on the far horizon, Mt Kilimanjaro.

A few days later, I met Kim's mother, a grand old white Kenyan, charming, well-preserved, and full of astonishing tales about good chaps who'd been gored by buffalo or died in light plane crashes. Mrs Hartley was fascinated by the Boers, whom she clearly regarded as a subspecies of noble savage, almost as exotic as the Masai. Their leader was General Wynand Malan, a dapper old fellow with a white goatee, remembered for his suicidal commando exploits behind English lines in the war of 1899–1902. General Malan was rich and fairly civilised. So was Sarel du Toit, the haughty man who built the Hartley's hilltop mansion and dreamed of becoming governor of Tanganyika. Mrs Hartley was more interested in the wild Boers, the biltong hunters and *bywoners* on the community's fringe.

They were tall and strong and very good-looking, she said, but when they smiled, their teeth were black, stained by fluorine in the river. Some had never seen electric light, or talked on a telephone. The men wore funny hats and home-crafted shoes called veldskoens, and women seldom ventured outside without a *kappie* or bonnet. They were full of obscure bush lore regarding edible plants and *geneesblare*, healing leaves. They quarried their own whitewash, made their own soap from elephant or hippo fat. They'd disappear into the bush in battered old trucks and return weeks later with loads of biltong and ivory. On market day, they'd pass by in '30s Fords piled high with wheat, oranges, beans and geese, heading toward Arusha.

Arusha was the nearest town, population 5 000 or so. To get there, you had to cross a plain covered with fever trees, and then follow a rough track through the elephant-infested rain forest. Beyond the rain forest was a region of coffee plantations, and then you came to Arusha, a cluster of white houses with red-tiled roofs, bisected by a rushing stream in which gentlemen cast flies for trout. After market, the richer white farmers would gather at the country club, where the men told hunting stories and drank too much and sometimes played *bok-bok*, an extremely violent form of indoor leap-frog introduced by the Afrikaners.

Meanwhile, the ladies sat in the ladies' lounge, rolling their eyes, sipping gin and tonic and talking about children and servants. 'The Boers had a habit,' said Mrs Hartley, 'of twinning their sons with a black boy. They went everywhere together, a little Boer boy with hair this short and his little black companion. But when they grew up, the white boy was expected to be the master, and take a strong line with the blacks.' Too strong a line, in Mrs Hartley's estimation. 'They thought I was stupid,' she said, 'because I didn't know the golden rule: if they did something wrong, you had to beat them. They were very hard on the natives.'

And yet, and yet. African labourers seldom stayed long with English gentleman farmers, but they often stayed with the Afrikaners all their lives. 'It was curious,' she said. 'They seemed to understand each other better than we did.'

Maybe so, but when the wind of change began to blow in the fifties, the Afrikaners of Mt Meru grew unsettled. They thought of Africa as a place where only the strong survived; where a white man had to stand his ground with gun in hand, or else be overwhelmed. Many were convinced they'd be massacred. As soon as independence day was set, they started packing up and heading south in convoys of heavy trucks, laden with furniture and bedding and prize cattle. Some sold their farms, but the market was collapsing, so many just locked their doors and walked away.

A few dozen diehards stayed on after uhuru, but life grew tougher and tougher, and utterly impossible after 1967, when Tanzania committed itself to socialism. The Red Chinese were invited in. Factories and banks were nationalised. Most remaining white farmers – the Hartleys included – were given 24 hours to quit the country. One of the last Boers to leave was a bearded ancient named De Wet, who had come to Meru as a young boy and could not bear to go. But what could you do? There was no appeal. So he loaded his truck and set out for South Africa, only to die of a broken heart two days down the road. And that was the end of the Mt Meru Boers. 'They all left?' I asked. 'Yes,' said Mrs Hartley. 'They all died, or went back home.'

It might have ended there, but Kim was stricken by longing for the landscape where he'd spent his first years, so he took me on a pilgrimage to Mount Meru. Our first day was dismaying. The Hartley's old house was a ruin. The surrounding farmland was turning in part into dustbowl. The Boers' irrigation pumps lay rusting in the dirt. Their fruit orchards had been uprooted and burned. Here and there, an old Boer farmhouse was still standing, inhabited by people who sometimes had vague memories of the kaBuru. 'This belonged to Bwana Billem (Willem),' they would say, or Bwana Saru (Sarel) or Bwana Bitchie (Pietie). 'He was a kaBuru. We chased him away.'

The kaBuru were not always fondly remembered. 'They were a strong, harsh people,' one man told me. 'Like this!' He balled his fist, and raised his forearm as if to strike me. A greybeard chipped in with an amused demurral. 'I worked for a kaBuru once,' he said. 'In six months, I saved enough to buy a white shirt and a bicycle.' The first man laughed, clapped me on the shoulder and said, 'You are welcome. Do you want to see the kaBuru graves?'

So we piled into the Land Cruiser, our guide and ten others, and headed off through the bush on a goat track. Storm clouds were gathering over the volcano. We came to a narrow bridge that crossed a deep canyon, in the depths of which there was a swift river with deep, dark pools. A little further on was kwaJannie, where Jannie Pretorius had once stayed. His house was still standing in the middle distance, unpainted for three decades and now blending into the dusty grey desolation.

As we stopped, a crowd of young men appeared as if from nowhere, wearing ragged jeans and T-shirts and demanding to know what was happening. I said, I am a kaBuru, I've come to see the graves of my people. This did not go down well. There were scowls and unfriendly mutterings in a language I could not understand. Our guide said, 'Socialism is finished here. Whites and coolies are coming back. Some are reclaiming properties that were nationalised by Nyerere. These people think you have come to take their land away.'

I said, *nooit*, I'm just a tourist, but they weren't impressed, so I produced some snaps of a small farm on the Transkei border in which I owned a one-sixth share. I said, 'I'm not interested in your land, I've got my own, in Afrika Kusini.' The snapshots passed from hand to hand. They were studied very closely. Aha. Nice. Mealies? You know about mealies? Soon everyone was smiling. Their spokesman said, 'Up there is what you want to see.'

So we walked up the hillside, sloughing through deep drifts of powdery red dust, until we reached a tall thorn tree under which lay sixteen old graves. They were buckling and cracking, sliding slowly into a donga. Only one bore a legible headstone: General Wynand Charl Malan, 1872–1953. Three teenaged waMeru girls were standing beside me. I said, do you know anything about these people? They were overcome by shyness. Two little ones hid away behind the biggest, who giggled and said, 'We were not born yet. All we can say is, they were kaBuru.'

And that was more or less that. Kim and I returned to Arusha and wound up in a motel called the Tanzanite. The phones were out of order. The power had failed. Toilets wouldn't flush and there was no toilet paper, but the beer was ice-cold and the company was interesting – a party of Indian diamond-smugglers from Jo'burg, on their way home from an extremely dangerous but lucrative trip to Zaire, and some Zanzibaris who were intrigued to meet a white South African.

They assumed I'd come in search of a deal – diamonds, land, a tourist concession, maybe a bit of Swahili pussy. 'Our girls are taught to play sex from when they're this small,' one told me. 'You should try.' They were perplexed when I said we were actually looking for relics and remnants of the Boers. The Boers? KaBuru? Blank stares. No one reacted save William the bartender, who said he knew someone who'd heard a story that struck me as wildly implausible. I said, 'I don't believe it.' William said, 'Come tomorrow, I'll show you.'

In the morning, we headed out of town on a road clogged with ancient, listing Zolas, all weaving back and forth as if drunk, dodging cavernous potholes. The verges were lined with spaza shops, rickety little wooden shacks with brand-new Coca-Cola signs, vivid splashes of capitalist colour against a prevailing backdrop of socialist grey. 'I hate socialism,' said William. 'Nothing happened in this country for twenty years. Kenya got rich, and we couldn't even eat.'

After a while, we peeled off on a dirt road, crossed a vast state-owned coffee plantation and passed under a derelict archway saying, 'Arusha National Park.' Beyond that, we were in rain forest. The canopy closed over our heads. The light was green. There were still a few elephant, apparently, but they hid away on the volcano, and all the rhino had been shot, apparently by the park's own rangers. That's what William said, at any rate. He waved to a strapping young ranger with dreadlocks and a rifle over his shoulder. 'That man,' he said, 'reported his boss for poaching rhinos. What happened was, they put *him* in jail.'

Thirty minutes later, we emerged onto a broad plain covered with fever trees. The clouds parted, and there was Mt Kilimanjaro, looking just like it does on a postcard, save that there were no elephants or lions intervening. This was not the Africa of coffee-table books. This was the real thing, a densely-populated zone of mud huts, banana plantations and mealie patches. The grass was grazed flat as a billiard table. The limbs of many trees had been amputated by woodcutters. William pointed to a distant clump of bluegum trees, so we left the road and headed in that direction. We forded a shallow river, climbed a short rise and came upon a landscape dotted with mud huts and patches of cultivation. One of the houses was set apart from the others. It was made of mud. It was grey. It had no windows, just planks to keep out prowling night creatures.

Outside the sun was like a hammer. I walked up to the door, upon which someone had scrawled *karibuni* – Swahili for 'welcome'. I knocked but no one answered, so I went around the back, into a dusty yard full of goats, rubbish, emaciated dogs and chickens. In the centre of it stood a smoke-blackened hut roofed with banana leaves – a Swahili kitchen. I peered inside. There was a figure within, a withered old crone, hunched over the fire. She had sharp blue eyes and a long sharp nose, the face of a bird of prey. There was an old doek on her head, and down below, a kanga, and dusty feet in plastic sandals. I greeted her in Afrikaans. She came to the door, squinting at me in amazement. Her name was Katerina Odendaal. She had not heard Afrikaans in three decades. She was the last Afrikaner.

The first recorded use of the term 'Afrikaner' took place in the village of Stellenbosch on a wild night in March 1707. The magistrate, a German nobleman named Starrenburg, was roused from his slumbers to deal with some drunk youngsters who were causing uproar in the town square. When the magistrate ordered them to desist, a teenager named Hendrik Biebouw told him to get lost. 'I am an Afrikaner!' he cried. 'I will not be silent!'

The Dutch colony at the tip of Africa was barely six decades old at that point, but the authorities were already failing in their efforts to stop their minions going native. Biebouw, for instance, came from a family whose European identity was rapidly fading. His illiterate father cohabited for years with a slave named Diana of Madagascar. At least one of his siblings was a half-caste, as were many of his friends. Young Hendrik was flogged for his insolence, a punishment that surely deepened his alienation from polite white society. In the aftermath, he sailed away on a passing ship, but many of his Afrikaner peers wandered off into the interior, becoming semi-outlaws who wandered the subcontinent like nomads, driving their cattle before them, living in *rietdakhuise*, hunting with bows and arrows when their ammunition ran out.

In apartheid's schools, Afrikaans boys were taught to think of those early trekboers as pioneers of white civilisation, carrying the torch of Christianity into places of darkness. This was true for some, I suppose, but for others, it was just the start of a hunting safari that continued for centuries, interspersed with occasional battles against African tribes and nights of ecstatic intoxication on home-brewed liquors. The early wanderings of the Odendaal clan are lost to memory, but the patriarch Piet Odendaal comes into focus in the 1890s, a transport rider and biltong hunter on the wild peripheries of the doomed Transvaal Republic.

When the Anglo-Boer War broke out in 1899, Piet joined President Kruger's forces and saw action in several set-piece battles during the war's conventional phase. After that, he joined General Malan's guerrilla commando, which wreaked havoc on British supply lines in the northern and eastern Cape. Malan's commando fought until all was lost, and then fought on, refusing to give up until the very last day, when they were cut up in what was probably the war's very last skirmish.

Peace did not sit well with *bittereinders* like Odendaal and his General, especially not the bit about crooking the knee to British Empire. They would not hands-up. They would not concede. And so, in the aftermath, they trekked away in search of a place where a Boer could live as he pleased. General Malan loaded his wagons on a ship and set sail for East Africa. Piet Odendaal followed later, heading north in a convoy of four big oxwagons, navigating by the sun and stars. He took a wrong turning in the trackless bush beyond the Zambezi River and wound up in the Congo, where he wandered aimlessly for many years, but that was okay; the life of a trekker was quite sweet in its way; game was plentiful, each day was an adventure, and the land went on forever. A new generation of Odendaals was born on the back of the wagons, among the chickens and gunpowder sacks. They could barely read. Their clothes were made of animal skins. It was 1914 before their father caught up with his old General, who had settled under Mount Meru.

Piet Odendaal got himself a farm not far from the General's, where he planted mealies and pumpkins and tried to settle down. But all those years of trekking and freedom had spoiled him for civil society. After a year or two, he reloaded the wagons and spent the rest of his life endlessly circling the volcanoes with his goats and cattle, following the rain and the game.

Katerina was born in 1929, the youngest of five. Her mother died when she was 12 days old, and she was brought up by her grandmother, who called her Katrien. She spent a few years at the Dutch

Reformed boarding school in Ngare Nanuki, and then rejoined her wandering family. 'We went here, we went there,' she says. 'Sometimes we ploughed and planted wheat for other farmers, but we never stopped long in one place. We had our own sheep and goats and cattle. If there was no meat, we shot game.'

She pulls out some old photographs, yellow with age, the edges chewed ragged by termites. A grinning oaf stands on a featureless plain with a dead buck at his feet, at least eight inches of bare skin between his trouser cuffs and veldskoens. Dashing young men pose with ivory tusks. A young girl sits on the head of a dead bull elephant, surrounded by khaki-clad hunters. It's Katrien Odendaal. She points to some tiny, half-naked figures on the fringe of the tableau. 'These little people we called the Dorobo,' she says. 'They hunted with poison arrows. They got used to the Boers. When they heard our engines, they'd come out of hiding, and guide us to where the big bulls were. They kept the meat, we kept the ivory.'

'This was a wonderful place then,' she says. 'It was the Garden of Eden. There was game everywhere. There was room for everyone.' So the Odendaals kept wandering until 1950 or thereabouts, when the Tanganyika frontier finally closed. The population was growing. You could no longer shoot game as you pleased. Farmers were no longer willing to share their grazing. The Odendaals had to sell their livestock and look for jobs in town. Katrien was about twenty. Both her grandparents were dead by now, and her eldest brother Jan was looking after her. He landed a job in a sawmill at Makuru, south of Kilimanjaro, and took her there to stay with him.

The sawmill had electric power, a great novelty for her, and a luxury she would never see again. It also had an office with typewriters, manned *inter alia* by a handsome young African named Shabani Lulu. He came from the Mbulu tribe, a tall semi-nomadic people, renowned for their high cheekbones and aquiline noses. Everyone liked Lulu, especially Katrien. He was handsome. He made her laugh. She had feelings for him that were absolutely forbidden for an Afrikaner girl. She came from a culture in which, as she put it, 'We were taught to keep ourselves separate. If you were a white girl, you weren't even allowed to talk to a kaffir. That's how we were raised, and what did I know? I was just a child.' But now she was a woman, and falling in love with an African.

It was a difficult thing for the old lady to talk about, even 43 years later. She was breaking a taboo so deeply ingrained that somewhere in her heart she still seemed to see herself as a sinner. But she couldn't help herself. She and Lulu had an affair. It had to be secret, because her brothers would have killed both of them. Brother Coen was a thickset *ou* who drank too much and got in bar fights. Jan was tall and gentle, but even he could not be trusted. Katrien enlisted the help of a kitchen boy, who made his house available for rendezvous. They dug a hole in his kitchen floor. If the brothers showed up, Lulu would duck into it. Katrien would cover his hiding place with a plank and a table, and pretend that nothing was happening.

And then she fell pregnant, an absolute disaster. Lulu ran away, terrified of the wrath of her brothers. Katrien didn't know what to do. When the pregnancy began to show, she had to confess. The brothers went mad. 'They wanted to shoot us,' she says. 'I'm telling you, bwana, a Boer's heart is just like a Masai. They don't worry about killing people.' So she packed a few things in a bag and fled. She slept in the bush, stealing food from kraals to stay alive. She had the baby all on her own, under a thorn tree, and she didn't know what to do with it. 'I didn't know how to cut the cord,' she says. 'I didn't know anything.' An old African woman found her wandering around with the baby boy in her arms and took her home, where the cord was severed, along with all Katrien's ties to her own people. As far as Afrikaners were concerned, she was good as dead.

In the aftermath, she returned to the sawmill where Jan was work-ing, but he was deeply shamed by her and her half-caste baby, whom she named Boetie. 'They wanted to send Boetie away,' she says, 'But I fought. They weren't going to do anything to my boy.' Then one day she got a letter and some cash from her lover. He was back in the dis-trict, but wouldn't come to the sawmill for fear the Afrikaners would kill him. So Katrien joined him in Arusha, where they lived together in bitter poverty and had four more children over the next 14 years – Elizabeth, Christina, Flora and Corneliu.

The children were brought up in the Afrikaans manner, with *borselkop* haircuts and regular hidings. During the week they went to school with Arusha's Indians, and on Saturdays, to church with the Sabbatos, the Seventh-Day Adventists. It was the time of uhuru, time of the Mau-Mau uprising. Two or three isolated farms were attacked, their owners murdered. The Boers grew paranoid, took to posting armed guards at night. Katrien didn't care. 'I said, "Let it happen." The Boers rejected me. They hated me. If someone hates you, you can't have pity. They spat at me, and I spat back.'

As independence drew nearer, the Boers started leaving. Katrien was barely affected. Even her sisters didn't say goodbye when they went home. In the end, there were only three Afrikaners left under Mount Meru – Katrien and her brothers, both bachelors. Coen stayed because he drank too much and knew nobody in South Africa. Jan stayed because he'd promised their dying grandmother that he'd take care of his little sister.

Once the other Boers had gone, Jan and Coen relaxed a bit. There were no more expectations to live up to, no pious aunties to sneer when they visited their disgraced sister. They were taken by Katrien's children, who were half-caste, to be sure, but good looking, the girls slender, light-skinned and high-cheekboned, and boys well-brought-up and dutiful. When Lulu abandoned his family in the late sixties, Jan bought a shamba for Katrien, a tiny chunk of an old Boer farm on the far side of the rainforest, just enough land to subsist on. Soon after, Coen died of a heart attack, and Jan passed away exactly one week later. On his deathbed, he told Katrien, 'Now you're alone. Now you will truly suffer.'

This was true. It was 1971, and Tanzania had just started its long descent into total socialist paralysis. Nationalised factories were dying of inefficiency. Cadres of the Revolutionary Party were stalking the countryside, setting up spy networks and trying to force sullen peasants to collectivise. Commodity prices were set so low that farmers hardly bothered to plant. Even if you had money, there was nothing in the shops to buy. No sugar. No fat. No soap. No cooking oil. No tick dip. No petrol. No toilet paper. No cigarettes. No clothes. Sick people dosed themselves with veterinary medicines. Anything that broke stayed that way, because there were no spare parts, no tools. When Katrien's hand-cranked Singer sewing machine gave in, it had to be thrown away, her son's beloved motorcycle likewise. By 1978, she was washing her clothes with bitter apples, like a Voortrekker in the 1830s.

These ordeals would have defeated others, but Tannie Katrien was in many ways a living fossil, armed with survival strategies from an earlier century. She knew how to cure disease with herbs from the veld, how to turn cow dung into a serviceable floor, how to butcher a hippo and turn its fat into soap. She could plough with oxen, snare birds, spear barbel in the veld when the river flooded its banks. Her vocabulary was full of quaint archaisms, among them the word kaffir, or in Afrikaans, '*kaffer.*' She had no idea that it had become a forbidden term. It was just the name Afrikaners had always used for blacks.

She'd sit there with a pitch-black grandchild on her lap, chatting animatedly about the kaffirs and their idiosyncrasies. Sometimes her judgements were favourable, as in, '*Die kaffer sien nie eers jou kleur raak nie*' – the kaffir is colour-blind. Sometimes they were less so. '*Ek sê jou, bwana, dis 'n ander nasie die*,' she told me one afternoon. 'They eat food you've never heard about – bananas and blood and curdled milk. It's a sin to drink blood, because you're drinking the animal's life. That's why I say, you can't live in the same house as them. I was brought up different. I'll die an Afrikaner.' The baby gurgled. The old lady said, 'This one's called Mannetjie,' and planted a kiss on his plump black cheek.

Any contradictions here were invisible to her, and she seemed bewildered by my South African obsession with race. I kept asking, what have you learned here? And she kept saying, 'What do you mean?' I said, the Afrikaners have always believed Africa is a place where only the strong survive. You were the last Afrikaner, left alone and defenceless in a great sea of black people. Why are you still sitting here talking to me?

Tannie Katrien chuckled and told a story from the darkest depths of Tanzania's socialist debacle, a time when the last Boers had left and trade had collapsed entirely and whites were so rare that people would come from miles around to stare at her. 'Usually they brought children, because some of the young ones had never seen a white before. They'd stand right there,' she said, pointing to a spot ten yards from her kitchen hut. 'But they never did anything to me. They were just curious.'

She said she had no problems with her African neighbours. They helped each other at harvest time, punished each other's grandchildren for raiding fruit trees. If her cattle got taken in a Masai raid, all the local men took up their bows and arrows and shotguns and gave chase. Whenever a woman went into labour, they called the kaBuru auntie, because she had some knowledge of germs and sterilisation. She was afraid of many things, of disease and drought and famine, but she wasn't at all afraid of her African neighbours, perhaps because she owned no more then they did, which is almost nothing. She was the only white I'd ever met of whom that was true, anywhere in Africa.

She was dimly aware that South Africa was heading towards its own uhuru, but didn't find the details very interesting. '*Ag*,' she said, 'it will be just like here. They won't do anything to the whites.' But she was equally adamant that black rule would lead to economic collapse. Her reasoning in this regard was based entirely on food. 'When the Boers were here there was plenty of food,' she said. 'Butter, cheese, boerewors, chickens, peaches, plums, and macaroni cheese. And now look! *Ek sê jou, bwana*,' she concluded, '*die kaffers kan nie boer nie. Hulle breek alles*.' The kaffirs can't farm. They break everything.

We returned to this subject several times during the time I stayed with her. I kept saying, it's not really that simple, and she always said, 'It is!' In the end, she lost her temper. '*Is jy onnosel?*' she snapped. Are you stupid? The subject was clearly closed. I crawled off into my allotted corner and went to sleep, thoroughly chastened.

Tannie Katrien rises long before sunrise. I hear her sweeping the yard outside. I find her in the kitchen hut, where she's brewing tea on an open fire, the kettle perched on three stones. Two calves are tethered to a post in one corner, and huge bunches of cooking bananas dangle from the rafters overhead. She has about five pots and pans, five plates, but only three spoons, which will in due course become a source of agonising embarrassment. She's huddled over the fire like one of Macbeth's crones, staring at the flames. She always sits that way, with her painfully thin knees drawn up against her chest like a Bushman. It's the habit of a woman who's spent her life in houses with virtually no furniture, no running water, no electrical appliances. In her world, even tea is a luxury, so she boils it for ten minutes, and then throws in sugar by the handful, to make a brew that is dark and strong and very sweet. We drink a cup apiece, and go outside to milk the cows.

The sun's just rising over Kilimanjaro, and the landscape is heartbreakingly beautiful. There are three milk cows, tethered to banana trees. Her cows. Even her sons are not allowed to milk them. 'They don't do it properly,' she says. 'The milk dribbles down their forearms and off their elbows, picking up dirt and germs.' If it's to be done properly, she has to do it herself.

She trusses up the cow's back legs, hunkers down with a plastic pail and immediately starts cursing. The udder is covered with ticks, bloated, blue-black, big as grapes. I say, why don't you buy some tick dip? And she launches into an impassioned tirade about the short-comings of the Tanzanian government with reference to agricultural chemicals. 'You can't get tick dip anywhere. The government keeps promising, but nothing happens. I ask the coolie at the shop in Usa River to get some, but he can't get it either. So I walked halfway to Kilimanjaro and talked to some whites at a safari camp. They prom-ised to bring some from Nairobi, but that was weeks ago. It's just like the early seventies, when my son Boetie lost 34 cows to East Coast Fever ...'

When I first came, the old lady and I struggled to find common ground. I was a creature of the twentieth century, my head crammed with irrelevant information. I'd ask about stuff I'd read in books, about Ujamaa and kijiji and the policies of Tanzania's ruling Revolutionary Party, but she'd never heard of these things. When I talked about them, she'd turn to her son and say, '*Was dit hier so gewees, Boetie?*' Did that happen here? The conversations that followed were stilted and seemed to bore her, but she'd go on for hours about her central obsessions: rain or the lack of it, seeds and plant diseases, the tech-niques of Iron Age agriculture. She and her sons had dug a furrow that led water into her banana patch. She was also growing tomatoes, onions, beans and paw-paws. She had 16 orange trees, a guava tree with beehives in its boughs, and on a distant hillside, a mealie field, about 50 yards by 20.

In a good year, Tannie Katrien and her sons earn about $100 dol-lars between them, selling beans, oranges and honey. Of this, $70 goes to keep just one grandson in high school. The rest of the family makes do on what remains. They own almost nothing save the clothes they stand up in and their livestock. 'Christmas is just another day,' she says. 'You eat pap, you work, you sleep.' The old lady has given up ploughing, because the strain of handling the oxen was too much for her, but she still hoes and weeds under the burning sun, still carries water, still staggers for hours across the plains, burdened like a donkey under firewood. She says, 'You have no choice. If you're not tough, you die. You just have to be satisfied with what you have.'

By now the sun is high overhead and it's getting hot. We squat on the bare earth outside her kitchen. The conversation peters out. Every now and then, one of her neighbours emerges, squints at the sky and scans the fields for signs of human activity. The old lady says it's time to plough, but nobody wants to go first. 'If you plough first, your crops ripen before anyone else's,' she says, 'and then the baboons and thieves steal everything.' So you wait. Flies buzz around your head, crawl into your nostrils. The hours pass with agonising slowness. A battered old truck appears, crawling along a distant track. The old lady's eyes follow it across the horizon. When it comes abreast of us, she changes her position, so she can watch it go again.

Over the years, I've sat outside a thousand similar huts or shanties, struggling to communicate with Africans who couldn't speak my language. Tannie Katrien was the first African peasant I'd ever met who understood exactly what I was saying, but it was those interminable silences that provided the most eloquent answer to the question I was posing: what's it like to be you? The answer is: bleak beyond description. The only colours in your world are the colours of nature – the grass, the trees, the various shades of soil beneath your feet. The only stimulation comes from a battery-operated radio. The small pleasures that Westerners take for granted – a cup of coffee, a newspaper, a trip to the shopping mall – are unobtainable fantasies.

After several days, I began to feel claustrophobic, but there was no escape ... Okay, that's a lie. I had a credit card. I could have checked into the nearest safari lodge and treated myself to a hot shower and a cold beer. But it seemed shameful to display such selfishness in the face of my hosts' utter deprivation, so I sat there in the dust while the sun wheeled overhead, counting the hours until the evening meal.

One afternoon, I walked to the nearest village with Corneliu, aka Bushy, Katrien's youngest son. Aged 28, Bushy was trying to work as a carpenter, but he had no tools apart from some chisels and a hammer. We were going to buy a live goat for a braai, but the traders doubled their price when they saw white skin, so we settled for three fly-specked haunches.

On the way back, we ran into an old drunkard who asked my name. When I said Malan, he cried, '*Wragtig*!' and threw his arms around me. It turned out that he'd once worked for a Bwana Malan, a descendant of the pioneer general. 'Take me home with you!' he cried. I wanted to invite him to our braai, but Bushy said no. 'My mother has no time for drunkards,' he said. 'This one she will chase with stones.'

After sunset, we sat around a fire in the banana plantation, listening to the sound of singing and clapping from across the river. When the pap and goat meat was done, everyone just sat there staring at it, looking embarrassed. After a while, I realised there were five of us but just three spoons, so I helped myself and began to eat with my fingers. The old lady, '*Sien jy, hy eet met sy vingers, en hy's 'n Boer*' – look, he's eating with his fingers, and he's a Boer. At that, everyone relaxed and joined in.

Katrien's eldest son Boetie had come to eat with us. He was a quiet, shy man of 43, wearing a baseball cap to hide his receding hairline. 'If I go to South Africa,' he asked, 'will the Boers shoot me?' I said, seems very unlikely. He said, 'No, they'll shoot me. I know the Boers. They'll say I'm a kaffir. Will a Boer eat at the same table as me?' And so on. Boetie's childhood wounds seemed to be reopening, so I told a few stories that might ease his pain. State President FW de Klerk's son is engaged to a coloured girl, I said, and nobody makes a fuss. De Klerk's cabinet colleague Piet Koornhof had a child by a coloured woman, and he didn't hide it away, as if it was a sin. In fact, he stood up in front of everyone and said, this is my child. Then he moved in with his coloured girlfriend, to live as husband and wife.

The old lady cackled. 'No,' she said, 'that can't be. Don't lie!' I said, what do you know? You've never even seen South Africa. She said, 'Yes, but my grandfather told me everything.' Like what, for instance?

Well, she said, 'There in the Transvaal it's bitterly cold, but there's no firewood. That's why the Boers have to walk around behind their cows, collecting dung. They use that dung to make cooking fires that fill their houses with smoke. That's why you can always tell a Transvaler by his blood-red eyes.'

Astonishing. The image was at least 120 years out of date. I cleared my throat and started explaining about skyscrapers, freeways and houses with flush toilets, lights and central heating. The old lady gaped, as if listening to an alluring but vastly improbable fairytale.

Another day, more tribulations. Tannie Katrien is wearing her Sunday best. We're sitting in the dust outside a shop in Usa River, waiting. We have done a lot of waiting in the past two days. We came to town to do some shopping, and to meet her lovely daughters – Tina the schoolteacher, married to a safari driver, and Flora the housewife, married to a mechanic. We have waited for taxis. We have waited for bank clerks. We have waited for shop attendants. Right now, we are waiting for Flora, who has some tropical wasting disease. Flora is at the Catholic hospital, waiting for the doctor, who is somewhere else, waiting for the government to supply him with medicine. A lot of waiting is done in Tanzania.

It's high noon. Trucks trundle by, weaving through the potholes. The sun wheels overhead. The tannie is hungry and extremely short-tempered. Perhaps her kidneys are bothering her again. Perhaps she knows what passed between me and Boetie in the bank. I can't really say. All I know is she's the *moer-in*.

We wait until half-past two, when a bakkie comes that happens to be going our way. But first, we must wait for a full load to accrue. Ten people get on, then twenty, carrying bags of mealies and beans. At last we head off. The old lady sits on a tyre right behind the cab, clinging for dear life to the roll bar. She does not trust '*kaffer drywers*,' and she won't even talk to me.

The bakkie drops us at a crossroad in the middle of a flat and featureless plain. I hold out my hand to help the tannie down, but she slaps it away. '*Los my uit!*' she cries. '*Dink jy ek is al dood?*' Leave me alone! Do you think I'm dead already? She gathers up her purchases and stalks off across the plain, all on her own, like a thin, angry secretary bird. The rest of us straggle along behind. The path winds around a koppie and crosses the river on a precarious suspension bridge. Then it climbs a rise and arrives at the clump of bluegum trees in the shade of which lies her home. By the time we get there, the old lady has already changed into her everyday clothes. She's crouched over the fire, muttering angrily.

Her sons and I sit down in the last of the sunlight and light up some Sportsmans. I say, 'Your mother has a temper, hey.' They laugh. Boetie says, 'Ja, you should have seen her when our sisters were teenagers. She threw stones at their boyfriends. She got a whip and chased them away.' Then he turns serious. He says, 'You know, I wouldn't be alive if she wasn't so tough, if she didn't fight for me. They wanted to send me away, you know. They wanted to drown me. Because of, you know, my father.'

There is something that should be mentioned here, something that sheds light on the old lady's fit of ill-temper. When I first arrived, I asked her husband's name. She thought for a long time, then said, 'Uh, Johannes. Johannes van Reenen. He was a Baster, a half-caste Afrikaner.' And your first-born's name? Johannes too. But while we were in town, I wrote a cheque for Boetie to deposit into his bank account, which is how I discovered that his real name was John Shabani Lulu. His father was an African. It was no surprise for me. I'd guessed the truth anyway. Boetie couldn't understand why his mother had lied, why half an Afrikaner was better than a full-blooded African, after all those years and all that pain, in a country where nobody particularly cared. But I knew. '*Ek sal doodgaan as 'n Afrikaner,*' the old lady said. I'll die an Afrikaner. And she was trying, she was trying.

When the sun went down, she came out of the cooking hut with a crooked smile on her face and a peace offering in her hands. '*De,*' she said. 'Look what I made for you!' I smelled cinnamon and the sharp tang of lemon. I struck a match and peered at the plate. She'd baked *pannekoek* for me. On a dark night, under a volcano, in the heart of Africa.

Fair Lady, August 1994

The White Tribes of Ulster

|||||||||||||||||||||||||||||||||||||||||||||||||||||||||||||||||||||||||||||||||||||||||||||||||||||||||||||||||||||||||||||||||||||||||||||||||||||||||||||||

I think this is actually a story about South Africa's gravitational hold on our imaginations. Wherever we go in the world, we carry it with us.

My friend Jacques de Villiers was photographing a row of cheap wine bottles in party hats for some liquor retailer's Christmas marketing campaign when I popped in to say I was going to Ireland. Jacques put down his Hasselblad and told a story about one Donal McLauglin, Irish expatriate, fashion photographer and man-about-town in Cape Town's 1960s. Jacques spent several years as McLaughlin's assistant, and the experience had left its mark. McLaughlin liked drinking and fighting, he said. So did Brendan, his Irish soul mate. On Friday nights, they'd hit the bars for 15 beers and a brawl. If nobody would fight them, they'd fight each other.

One night they chose the wrong opponents and one of them got drowned in a bath. RIP Donal McLaughlin, aged 36. 'He was a lovely guy,' Jacques said, 'but he was terrifying. If he couldn't find anyone else to fight, he wanted to fight me.' Everyone in the room nodded knowingly, as if to say, there is something odd in the blood of Irishmen.

Forgive the crude generalisation, so typical of white South Africans, and founded, of course, upon ignorance. We know very little about Ireland where I come from. It seldom makes the news unless the IRA blows up something truly spectacular in London, in which case the local papers might carry a brief update on the underlying Ulster troubles – 3 000 dead in 23 years, 14 000 bombings, 34 000 shootings, and all this in a country with barely enough people to fill a single telephone directory.

It's as grim a war as any, viewed from that perspective, and extremely perplexing to white South Africans. We say, what's the problem? They're all white, they all speak English, they're all Christians of some kind or another, and yet there they are, locked in a cycle of violence that rivals Bosnia or the West Bank or even our own Boers-vs-Blacks shindig in terms of sheer bloody-mindedness and absolute intractability.

A few days later I landed in Belfast, where I proceeded to get even more confused. I met a few IRA stalwarts, and I'm afraid I liked them, their bad reputation notwithstanding. They had soul; they had passion. They were full of bullet holes and shrapnel and great mystic visions of a day when the green flag would rise above the bogs and silent factories, and there would be justice at last for slum Catholics. On the other hand, I liked the Protestants, too. They were a bit like Afrikaners actually, solid, sensible, courteous, kind. Everyone was friendly and charming, but they had this odd habit of killing people.

The IRA killed two IPLO members while I was there, and blew up the town of Coleraine. Loyalists butchered five civilians in retaliation. A Catholic rebel was martyred at a roadblock, and a policeman dropped dead in the midst of a rainstorm, felled by a bullet from the far side of the border. Why any of this was necessary I could not fathom. Like so many before me, I fell into the swamp of Irish ambiguities, where I floundered helplessly for many weeks, incapable of formulating a single generalisation that would withstand even my own loose and self-indulgent scrutiny. In the end, it seemed that the only way to attain clarity lay in returning to the very beginning.

Towards a unifying theory of the troubles of Northern Ireland

Let's close our eyes and imagine we're standing on the summit of Black Mountain, looking down upon the landscape of bogs and fens upon which the city of Belfast will one day rise. The year is 1601. The last Catholic barons have just been defeated in battle, and the era of colonisation and genocide is just beginning. A fleet of tall ships appears on the River Lagan, carrying Protestant settlers from the British mainland. They fan out across the landscape, evicting its Catholic inhabitants at sword-point.

In 1641, the Catholics return, a horde of 'vile, caitiff wretches' who attack Protestants with pitchforks and stones. A Cromwellian army marches over the horizon and terrible vengeance is exacted: countless thousands of rebels hanged, beheaded, tarred with pitch and dynamite and set on fire. Now the Catholics are truly broken. They lose almost all that remains of their land. They become untouchables, their religion outlawed, their language forbidden, living like swine in the bogs below walled Protestant towns.

A century passes and then another. Great linen mills spring up. Trade flows up and down the river. Belfast evolves into a thriving industrial centre. Slums appear on the slopes below us. At first, their inhabitants are mostly Protestant, but Catholics start creeping in from the countryside, clustering in hovels around their Roman Catholic chapels. Protestants eye the newcomers warily. They think, these people are different. They speak Gaelic. They are bitter and resentful, for good reason. They might slit our throats if we let them. The first outbreak of violence comes in 1813; thereafter, there is a race riot or pogrom every five years, on average. The violence takes a form that will become all too familiar in the coming century – mobs surging back and forth across the city, barricaded streets, hailstorms of stones, the clubs of bully cops flashing in the mayhem.

In 1912, rival Catholic and Protestant militias appear on the hillside below us, drilling in preparation for a civil war which finally comes in 1920. There is more mob violence, more house burning. Thugs drag innocents into alleys, inquire as to their religion and shoot them if the answer displeases. In 1921, the country is partitioned. The South goes free, and Ulster becomes a self-governing statelet, ruled by its stern and selfish Protestant majority. Life becomes even more unpleasant for Catholics in the slums. Council houses are hard to come by. Factories put out signs saying, 'No Catholics Need Apply'. They're diddled at the ballot box by outrageous gerrymander.

There are more riots in the thirties and forties, but nothing changes. In 1969, Catholics take to the streets yet again, only to be attacked by Protestant policemen and vigilantes, in accordance with Ulster tradition. This time, however, the croppies refuse to lie down; they fight back, and boom, the entire city goes up in flames. Mobs surge hither and thither, 100 000 flee their homes. Aeroplanes descend from the sky, carrying a peace-keeping force of British soldiers. By the time calm returns, the landscape is ethnically cleansed – Protestants on this side, Catholics on that, and the Peace Line between.

Now the British are in charge down there, for the first time in 50 years. They strip the Protestant bullies of all powers save those pertaining to the maintenance of parks and the collection of dog turds. They place most functions of government in the hands of impartial quangos, in the hope that a more just administration will make Catholics happy.

No dice, though. This conflict is far too old and bitter to be resolved so easily.

A new life-form appears on the streets below: the IRA terrorist. His stated enemy is the British Empire, but Protestant businesses get blown up too. The Protestants take this personally, and the IRA spawns a monster in its own image, the balaclava-clad Loyalist gunman, ready to counter terror with terror. A mad cycle of violence ensues. British soldiers shoot an IRA terrorist. The IRA blows up a Protestant-owned bank. Loyalist terrorists shoot a few Catholics. Irked, the IRA mortars a police station. Friends of the slain Protestant constables retaliate by blowing up a pubfull of Papists.

And so on. And so on. Politicians confer, clergymen anguish, but the killing continues. The rest of Northern Ireland is dull and peaceful, for the most part, but over 20 years, more than 1 000 are slain in the 12 square miles of slum at our feet. Every street corner in this landscape is a place of weeping. The people are numb and helpless. The violence is like the weather – rotten, but what can you do? You keep your head down. You try to protect your children from the worst of it. You pray for salvation.

Three years ago, the violence began slowly to escalate. Exactly why is hard to say. Peace talks were underway. The possibility of a British pull-out had been mooted. Perhaps the Protestant paramilitaries felt they were running out of time. So they regrouped, purged their ranks of criminals and began to practise terror in earnest.

They killed 36 in 1991, another 44 in 1992. For the first time in history, they were killing more people than the IRA. The British banned the Ulster Defence Association, but the mood among Protestants was such that the organisation's membership doubled in its first five months underground. The tenor of pronouncements from the Protestant paramilitary underground grew more and more belligerent. There were threats of all-out war against the 'pan-Nationalist front', a grouping so vast as to include all Irish Catholics, including those in

Dublin. There was a series of ghastly 'spray jobs' – incidents in which Loyalists machine-gunned Catholics at random.

By the time I arrived in Belfast, the city was more tense than it had been in 20 years. Consider this editorial from the *Irish News*, Belfast's most thoughtful daily: 'There is a deep and almost tangible sense of foreboding in Northern Ireland today. The entire community has been gripped by fear – a fear that something terrible is about to happen.'

And what might that be? I spoke to scores of Belfast butchers, bakers and taximen, and at least 80 per cent of them thought a civil war was possible or inevitable. Ulster already knows the general shape of the compromise under consideration at the negotiating table, and most residents doubt it will stick. What Dublin wants, what the Brits want, what moderate Catholics and Protestants might just be willing to settle for, is joint London–Dublin sovereignty over Northern Ireland, with power passing into the hands of an integrated power-sharing executive. It's a nice idea, but the odds of getting everyone to agree are slender, and besides, the IRA has already declared its intention to fight on rather than settle for half-measures. If the IRA continues its terror campaign, the Loyalist paramilitaries will continue to retaliate and the Troubles will go on, for ever and ever – unless the Brits throw up their hands and pull out unilaterally.

And this is not necessarily a bad idea, to my revisionist way of thinking. Thanks to the British, Northern Irelanders have had a century of conflict without catastrophe – controlled conflict; with acceptable levels of violence and suffering, a benevolent state to salve their wounds, compensate them for death and injury and saturate their streets with soldiers. They're like a couple trapped in a bad marriage, always arguing, bickering and slapping each other, but staying together out of habit. It might be best for all concerned if the Brits just let them sort it out among themselves – a short, sharp civil war to clear the air, eliminate the accumulated psychic toxins and establish a dominance hierarchy in accordance with the laws of nature, whereafter the winners and losers would probably coexist quite amicably. They are, after all, all Irishmen.

Anticipated reaction to Malan's unifying theory
A million Irishmen will step forth with fists shaking, outraged by such simplifications. Catholics will say, how dare you so blithely exoner-

ate the British? Their soldiers are sitting on our faces! They've slain 300 of our lads! They framed the Birmingham Six and the Guildford Four! They let Bobby Sands die! They gagged Sinn Fein! They set up the Loyalist death squads, in league with the capitalist Protestant establishment and the bigoted Royal Ulster Constabulary – everyone knows that!

And Protestants will say, how dare you reduce our lofty cause to such base principles? All we ask is a little respect for our rights as British citizens who died for the Crown in countless wars in accordance with a bond of honour which perfidious Albion is now thinking of breaking because it lacks the gumption to stand up to a tiny band of Marxist-Leninist terrorists.

And they will all scream: how dare you describe the lot of us as barbarous sectarians when it's only a tiny minority on the other side???

PJ O'Rourke once wrote something funny and true about white South Africans. 'They've never learned to stand up and lie like white men,' he said, reflecting upon the Boers' curious tendency to rise in the court of world opinion and state quite openly that they were racists, at least to the extent of believing in differences between black and white people.

Northern Ireland, on the other hand, is teeming with practised liars. They lie to themselves, they lie to each other, and they certainly confused me for a while. Officially, there are no sectarian political parties in the territory. Unionists do not define themselves as Protestant – they just want to maintain the link with Great Britain. Nationalists do not define themselves as Catholic – they just want the Brits to go. The IRA is stridently non-sectarian, but all its soldiers are Papists. Loyalist paramilitaries slaughter Catholics at random, but even they claim to have nothing against Catholics *per se*. Sectarianism is backward, so nobody is sectarian. Raise the subject with a local politician and you get homilies about tolerance, open-mindedness and the brotherhood of man.

And yet the instant you step onto the streets of working-class Belfast, your nostrils are assailed by a reek of tribalism at least as pungent as any I ever sniffed in Africa. Protestants live on this side, Catholics on that, and between them the Peace Line, a 15-foot wall topped with iron spikes, cutting across roads and through mile after mile of semi-detached housing.

Only lunatics and small children cross the border on foot, and even then it is considered dangerous. Most people live absolutely separate lives. A Protestant shops among Protestants, drinks among them, prays alongside them on Sundays and buries his dead in cemeteries for Protestants only. His children attend segregated schools. He travels to and from work in segregated taxis, which operate from segregated ranks. He may have Catholic friends at his workplace, but they'd never visit each other's homes for fear of being sniffed out as 'one of the other' and having their heads kicked in.

Twenty-three years of sectarian tension and bloodshed have turned Belfast's urban war zone into a virtual insane asylum, full of people with nervous tics and trembling hands and eyes that gleam paranoic-ally at the most innocent of questions. They can't tell the enemy by looking at him, so they've invented all these obscure codes and arcane riddles to distinguish friend from foe. A pigeon fancier is probably Protestant. A hurley player is definitely a Taig. A cricketer could be either, but a Rangers fan is an Orangeman.

A strange face on your street is cause for grave misgiving. Housewives peer at you from behind curtains. Young men follow you at a safe distance, trying to figure out who you are, what you're doing, what you're carrying in your bag. In really bad areas, or streets where there has recently been a killing, people won't answer their doors to strangers and will simply leave you standing outside in the rain.

Belfast is the only place I've ever been where ordinary people be-have like spies, varying their routines and performing cleansing rites to make sure they're not being tailed. If you own a car, you approach it from behind and bounce it on its springs, so as to trigger the bomb which might have been planted under the driver's seat. You plan your journey before you set off, trying to find a route that skirts enemy ter-ritory. If that's impossible, you hold your breath through the danger zone, praying that a child doesn't run under your tyres.

One Protestant described this recurring nightmare: he's had a car accident in a hardline Republican stronghold. A huge crowd has gath-ered. A priest is kneeling on the tarmac, administering last rites to some terribly injured person. The priest crosses himself, the onlookers follow suit, but the dreamer just stands there: he's missed the cue; he's betrayed himself. A thousand heads turn towards him, their eyes say-ing, 'Aha, here's one of the other.' The crowd closes in, and he wakes up with heart palpitations.

Is this a tribal society? I rest my case.

Why the rebels think they are black South Africans, but aren't really

On my first afternoon in Ulster, a Sinn Fein activist told me that I'd just arrived in a police state, and I believed him. We were walking through the Falls Road war zone, where the streets are clogged with armoured Land Rovers and forbidding army fortresses loom against the sky. I'd never seen such overbearing security, and this was only its visible aspect. There were said to be high-powered cameras on the roofs of distant skyscrapers, recording our every movement. There were said to be spies in the ceilings of suspected IRA buildings, bugs on the telephones. My guide said, 'It's a lot like South Africa, isn't it?' This was the first of many references to my country.

The IRA and its splinter groups have killed about 1 800 people in the past 23 years – 635 soldiers, 297 policemen, about 800 local civilians and 108 citizens of the British mainland. Ask why, and they'll often say it's because they are treated like black South Africans, subjected to 'economic and political apartheid' by the Brits and their Protestant stooges.

As a metaphor, this is not without foundation. 'The system' has never been kind to Ulster's Catholics. They are not welcome among the High Orange brethren who control the commanding heights of the economy. Unemployment among Catholic men is more than twice the Protestant average. They have fewer houses, cars, fur coats and telephones, but to compare their lot to black South Africans is pushing it. Under apartheid, blacks were denied a vote, robbed of land, banned from white hotels and hospitals, humiliated on the streets, muzzled by censors, jailed for thought crimes and shot down in large numbers if they protested.

This was indeed the lot of Irish Catholics in previous centuries. English policies were virtually genocidal until 1750 or thereabouts, but there was a change in the Age of Reason, a vague stirring of remorse in the English brain. Catholics were emancipated in 1792, enfranchised in 1832. In 1881, in a fit of altruism, Gladstone dismantled the parasitic Anglo-Irish aristocracy and returned its land to the Catholics from whom it had been stolen at sword-point in earlier generations.

Black South Africans would have traded their proverbial eye teeth for so considerate an oppressor. There's no gainsaying that Catholics continued to be wronged and slighted by Ulster's Protestant majority while mainland Britons stood idly by. On the other hand, the Brits have behaved quite honourably since the imposition of direct rule in 1972. Their first priority was to drain the swamps of Catholic misery in which the IRA virus bred and multiplied. So they flooded the province with grants and subsidies. They financed all sorts of bodies to facilitate reconciliation and discourage discrimination. They poured billions into training schemes, investment incentives, job creation and urban renewal. Today, per capita government spending (excluding military spending) is an astounding 43 per cent higher than on the mainland.

I'm going to get a bullet in the brain for this, but it must be said: Whitehall is not oppressing or exploiting the Catholics of Ulster. If anything, they're spoiled. The ghettoes of Belfast are awash with British money. The entire society is subsidised. Almost everyone I met in the Republican strongholds was on the dole, including every last Brit-hating hardline rebel. They relied upon Her Majesty's Government for life's necessities, and then devoted all their energies to biting the feeding hand. I found that rather ironic – a terrorist army underwritten by its deadliest enemy. Very sporting, very British.

As for the war, it's a nasty business, but President Clinton needs his head read, accusing the Brits of inflicting 'wanton violence' on the rebels. I mean, the IRA has killed nearly twice as many British soldiers as squaddies have slain IRA men. Under the circumstances, the British response seems a model of restraint, especially to the eye of a South African accustomed to ruthless secret policing and the murder of radicals by state assassins.

Consider your average IRA Volunteer, waging his David and Goliath struggle against the British Empire. Odds are, military intelligence knows you. They watch you, follow you, tap your telephone, try to plant spies in your circle, but they can't really touch you unless they catch you with a gun or bomb in your hands, in which case they might just shoot you dead and call it self-defence. This happens, but rarely. Usually, they just keep a close eye on you, pick you up from time to time for questioning.

Where I come from, this would be a prelude to unspeakable horrors, but in Belfast it's a cakewalk, at least relatively – no torture, no electric shock machines, no cattle prods or chemical attitude manipulation. The police aren't even allowed to deprive you of sleep or offer deals, your freedom for the lowdown on that other chap. You just sit there and keep your mouth shut, and in seven days they're obliged to let you go. Why? Because Northern Ireland is a land of law.

But the rebels are so steeped in ancestral memories of martyrdom that they can't see straight any more. You say, this neighbourhood bears no resemblance to Soweto; they say, aye, but you should have seen it 30 years ago. You say, your secret police seem quite gentlemanly, and they say, aye, but in 1973 they pulled me hair out and beat me black and blue. I had a telling exchange on this subject with Martin McGuinness, IRA chief of staff in the eighties, who insisted that the absence of torture in interrogation centres didn't mean that the oppressor was playing fair. As far as he was concerned, they had merely dropped brutality in favour of more sophisticated forms of torment.

How so? I enquired. 'Well,' said McGuinness, 'they detain a lad in, say, Derry, and take him all the way to Belfast, 78 miles away' from his mates and mum and dad. 'That's part of a mental torture, in my opinion.' Then they march him into a forbidding police building and traumatise his delicate sensibilities by locking him in a windowless cell. And finally comes the ordeal of saying absolutely nothing for seven days, in accordance with standard IRA anti-interrogation training. You just sit there and stare at a spot on the wall. 'Some people find it very difficult,' says McGuinness. 'It's just a mirror image of what happens in South Africa.'

Really? In South Africa, you talked. Or died.

A ride into Armageddon in the back of an armoured Land Rover

'We're entering bandit country,' said the driver as we crossed the Peace Line. It was a rainy Saturday morning, and I was accompanying British soldiers on a patrol through the Falls Road war zone. A platoon of heavily armed squaddies was trudging on foot through the cold wetness, watching the skyline, watching each other's backs. The lieutenant and I and some others were circling around them in an armoured Land Rover, 'sterilising' the area. Voices crackled on the radio. The foot soldiers had spotted a 'known bandit', a face someone recognised from a briefing. We came around the corner and there he was, a skinny wee lad in flat cap, hands in the air, being searched for weapons. He was clean. The squaddies seemed disappointed. They'd been in Belfast for three months and they had yet to see any real action. The bandit went on his way, and we moved into a particularly notorious IRA area. A voice on the radio said, 'We're crossing into Armageddon.' I peered through the bulletproof windscreen, but all I saw was rainswept streets, old grannies with umbrellas and young mums with infants in prams. What a boring war.

Why Loyalists think they are Afrikaners, but aren't really

There is an Ulster Protestant on the far side of the wall from the desk where I sit writing, in a friend's London home. He is a psychiatrist, a man of immense sophistication and erudition, rational in all respects save one: he believes Catholics will exterminate his mother and brothers in Northern Ireland if they are ever allowed to take over. Not immediately, but in a while. Something would happen, the Catholic underclass would get upset and pour out of the ghettoes on the rampage and, since the Catholic state would be loath to use stern measures against its own people, the Protestants would be massacred.

I'm a South African. I know all about racial paranoia, about terror of The Other. I try to insert myself into the psychiatrist's imagination, but it's impossible: I cannot see what he sees. The vast majority of Irish Catholics are reasonable people who think the IRA is crazy. In an Ireland-wide election, Sinn Fein would be totally crushed by Fianna Fail or Fine Gael, bringing the Protestants of Ulster under the rule of level-headed Dublin conservatives who loathe the IRA almost as much as they do. White South Africans would have surrendered years ago if blessed with so like-minded an enemy.

But the Prods don't see it that way. Whenever the Brits try to extricate themselves, they start screaming, hey, we're British, you can't leave us to the mercy of the Micks, and back up their tantrums with riots and threats of military action. They did it in 1886, when Home Rule first came up for consideration, and again in 1912, under the same circumstances. In 1919, and again in 1969, they responded to nationalist uprisings by launching bloody pre-emptive attacks against Catholics. In 1972, they crippled their own government with a national strike to stop it going soft on the Papists, and now they're slaughtering innocent Catholics at random in what could well be another attempt to block compromise. Ask why, and they say, 'We're in the same position as Afrikaners in South Africa, or Jews in Israel. There's nowhere else to go.'

These are the words of William 'Plum' Smith, a Loyalist activist who took me on a tour of the Protestant Shankill district one rainy afternoon. The sky was grey, the buildings grimy, the roads lined with shabby shops and shabby people in dark overcoats. As we drove, Smith pointed out the stigmata of poverty and offered the standard Loyalist analysis: Catholics complain about discrimination, but as you see, we are suffering too, and now the Catholics want to take what little we have away. That's what the Troubles are all about – the IRA is the armed wing of Irish Catholic nationalism, waging a terrorist campaign against us. I said, hold on, the IRA is socialist, non-sectarian; it's fighting the British, not you. But Plum Smith just laughed at me.

'It's ridiculous for the IRA to claim that their campaign is non-sectarian,' he said. 'I mean, their bombing campaign, they always target police stations in predominantly Protestant areas. All the death and damage will be done to Protestant civilians. When a policeman is shot, they're shooting a Protestant. The same goes along the border – they say they're shooting soldiers, but they're really shooting Protestant farmers who've joined the Army Reserve to protect themselves. In some cases, they shoot Protestants just because they're Protestant. I mean, they talk about ethnic cleansing in Bosnia or Serbia; we've been doing ethnic cleansing for 20 years.'

I'll say. The various Loyalist paramilitaries have killed about 800 civilians since the Troubles began, about the same number as the IRA. The IRA's violence is coldly scientific; the Loyalists tend to be savage. If they can't get their hands on a real Republican, any Catholic will do – a pedestrian, a shop girl, ageing Dunkirk veterans idling in a bookie's. On occasion, their actions have degenerated into sheer psychopathy – Catholics kidnapped and hung from the rafters, their flesh flensed with butcher knives. While I was in Belfast, they beat a woman to death with baseball bats. A few weeks later, they killed a Catholic Good Samaritan who ventured into a Loyalist stronghold to cook a meal for an ailing Protestant friend.

Primordial tribalism aside, the aim of such murders seems to be to terrify Catholics to such an extent that they force the IRA to lay down its weapons. Since the British share this objective, IRA conspiracy theorists maintain that the Loyalist underground is a creation of MI5, an army of mercenary thugs and hoodlums set up to do Britain's dirty work. I put this to Smith, and it clearly irked him. 'Right now, there are more Loyalists in Crumlin jail than IRA,' he said. 'Do you think they put themselves there? Do you think I did that?' It turns out that he was convicted in the early seventies for an 'act of war' – attempted murder of one of the enemy. He spent five years in prison, but remains determined to smash the IRA in the name of ... of what, exactly? Loyalist is a misnomer in this case. Plum Smith is loyal to his own community, not the Union Jack. If anything, he's like a white Rhodesian – a British subject, yes, but stranded on foreign soil, surrounded by enemies, on the brink of being abandoned by perfidious Albion in the interests of expediency. Any day now, he believes, the Brits will pull out, leaving his community at the mercy of its traditional enemies. And that, he says, is when the civil war begins in earnest. 'I don't think people are prepared to stomach a takeover,' he says. 'We would end up becoming the rebels. We would become the IRA.'

I ask how he sees the future. 'More of the present,' he says. 'More death.'

A failed attempt to obtain comment from the British Army

We are trudging up the hill from Lisburn Station, with nought but a soggy *Irish News* to shield us from the freezing rain. We are on our way to the headquarters of the British Army in Northern Ireland, the massively fortified entrance to which looms ahead in the rain. We are here in search of a briefing about the present state of the Troubles, which are undergoing a bit of an upsurge at present – around 2 000 terrorist incidents last year, up 30 per cent from two years ago.

In fact, a terrorist incident appears to be unfolding around me at this very moment. I'm standing at the guardhouse, proffering my rain-slicked passport to the sentries, when someone yells, 'Red light! Red light!!' The soldiers explode into action – unsling their rifles, sprint hither and thither, deploy in battle position. A car has run the red light at the nearest traffic intersection. It's coming closer. A soldier slams the steel gates. Another grabs me by the shoulder, drags me behind a tree. A blue saloon appears in the middle distance, crammed with Semtex, no doubt, and piloted by an IRA kamikaze. The soldiers raise their rifles. All sound dies away. There's an instant of sheer terror, and then: the car screeches to a halt in the middle of the road, a little old lady peers myopically through its windscreen. She was on her way to the hairdresser, took a wrong turn, and now she's staring up the muzzles of ten British guns. Oh, dear. Another Irish misunderstanding.

Ten minutes later I'm in a Quonset hut, pondering a glass jar that once contained instant coffee, transformed into a hand grenade by fiendishly ingenious IRA arms manufacturers. My host is a ruddy, cheerful sergeant from the bomb squad, no names please, supervised by a major from public relations. This is the fate of bedraggled foreign journalists who call from a phone booth and walk in out of the rain: they give you the idiot bomb briefing, designed to make you say, cor, those IRA buggers are truly bad. Exhibit two is the sweetie jar, many times larger than its coffee bomb cousin and too heavy to be hurled by hand. What the terrorist does is, he drops it from the parapet as the army patrol passes below. Failing that, he will blow you up with a baked-bean can full of Semtex fired from his backyard bazooka, or lie in wait in a hedgerow for weeks before detonating this improvised Claymore under your feet. This here's a car bomb, designed to take off your legs and your genitals, leaving your bowels dangling. This device lobs a bomb the size of a beer keg over a barracks wall. This one can lob a 55-gallon drum over same.

It's all extremely blood-curdling, but I'm researching a piece about Ireland, not an arms manual. I mean, I want to talk about the Big Issues: what is the British Army doing here? How do you respond to charges of collusion with Loyalist death squads? Is it true that the SAS shoots to kill? Sadly, these guys won't even discuss that IRA poster on the wall above the kitchen sink – an honour roll of fallen Republican soldiers, with the words 'To Be Continued' tagged on at the end by some bomb squad wag. I don't think I was supposed to see that. The sergeant winks, produces a sheet of steel and says, 'This is a pusher plate.'

There is also a timing device, a selection of remote-controlled detonators and a slab of Semtex. In the end, there is even a little video depicting the triumph of the British army over unspeakable evil. It shows a group of steel-nerved bomb-disposal experts standing on a deserted motorway, staring at a three-ton truck in the middle distance. They believe there's a gargantuan bomb inside it, and they're about to disarm it by blasting the vehicle apart with a smaller bomb of their own. A remote-controlled robot rolls closer, electronic arms waving, and plants a charge on the side of the truck. A voice yells, take cover, and boom, the truck atomises. As the debris whirls down from the sky, the soldiers turn to me and offer their hands.

Some thoughts about kneecapping

There's a lot of kneecapping in Belfast, at least one case every weekend. The shooters are the paramilitaries, the heavies, the hard men. They don't want policemen on their turf, usurping their authority, but by the same token, they have a responsibility to the community, can't let car thieves and burglars and sex offenders run wild. So they administer their own punishments, and the way it's done is an index of how long and fearful a shadow they throw.

Let's say you're a wide boy, suspected of nicking a car or selling a few tabs of E. Word goes around that you did it, and next thing, the hard men are knocking on your door, ordering you to report to such a house at such and such a time to take your punishment. It's no use crying or begging for mercy, and there's no right of appeal. If you don't show up, something worse will happen, and if you tell the cops, they'll probably kill you. So you get aled up to dull the pain, and take the walk of doom at the appointed hour. The heavies are stern and unbending, but not totally inhuman. They'll allow you to take your pants off, so you don't get bullet holes in your new blue jeans, and when it's done, they summon an ambulance to take you away.

And the ambulance will take you down to the Royal Victoria Hospital, where they might wheel you into the presence of Dr X, an emergency specialist who prefers to remain unnamed. Dr X has seen so many kneecappings in her time that she can gauge from the wound the gravity of your alleged anti-social activity. If you're a petty thief or a minor police informer, they'll do you in the fleshy part of the thigh, or in the ankle with a ladylike .22, too small to shatter bone. A surgeon just repairs the blood vessels, and you'll be fine in a while. If your transgression is more serious, they'll shoot you in the back of the knee with a high-velocity rifle or pistol, in which case the bullet usually severs an artery before smashing its way through the kneecap. In truly bad cases you get 'the six-pack', a bullet in each elbow, ankle and knee, but you still won't tell the cops who did it. In fact, you'll most likely apply for government compensation as a victim of terrorism, and when it comes through, there'll be a knock on your door, and the heavies who shot you in the first place will ask for their share.

I say, is this popular? Is it acceptable to the community? And Dr X says, no, not really, it's abominably cruel, but what can you do? 'Everybody's unhappy with the way things are.' It's not just the punishment shootings, it's everything – the bombings, the killings, the moribund economy, the protection rackets, the atmosphere of siege on the streets. She talks about previous attempts at peaceful settlement, and the way all have failed. She says, 'If you ask me ... honestly, I don't know if there is an answer. We're all besieged, just sitting around being besieged.' She offers me a cup of instant coffee, tells me a bit about herself. She was born a Protestant, grew up in a household where Catholic complaints of ill treatment were dismissed as whining exaggerations. Then she went to university, had a religious experience and converted to Catholicism, which broadened her mind a bit, and enabled her to see that Catholic lives were indeed blighted by discrimination and bigotry. Having spent time in both camps, she has concluded that everyone is a bit unbalanced. She says, 'There's a border in their minds.' She says, 'If you live in a situation like this your ideas about what should be done become muddied and vague.' She says, 'Maybe you can see more clearly.'

I wouldn't know about that.

A note on the wisdom of cabbies

The cabbies of Belfast will talk their heads off so long as you don't ask their names. At first, I assumed they were afraid of being quoted, but it was worse than that: in Belfast, they were afraid I'd shoot them. In Belfast, most Bills and Grahams are Protestant, you see, whereas Michaels and Patricks tend to be Catholic. If your fare doesn't like Paddies, he might kill you. So many cabbies have died this way that the government has had to repeal a law requiring them to display ID on their dashboards.

In any event: Belfast's cabbies don't give their names, but they'll speak their minds, and they all say the Troubles will never end because 'there's too much money in it.' It costs millions to run the various underground armies, supply guns to the shooters and support their families if they're killed or captured. Anyone who owns a business in the ghetto war zones is expected to contribute. A Falls Road cabbie pays around £50 a week to the IRA; his Protestant counterpart pays a like sum to the UFF or UDA. The same is true of builders, grocers, pub owners. One declines such contributions at one's peril.

If the conflict were settled, the heavies who collect these 'donations' would have to work for a living. Policemen and security guards would be laid off. Contractors would no longer earn fortunes rebuilding bombed police stations and shopping centres. Greengrocers and butchers in garrison towns would go bankrupt once the British soldiers went home. Half the country profits indirectly from Northern Ireland's de facto war economy, which is why, in the estimation of cabbies, the Troubles will never end.

An encounter with another Ireland, which suggests that we might be taking this all too seriously

It was a Sunday evening, as I recall. I was walking the streets of central Belfast, thinking gloomy thoughts about ineradicable tribalism and inescapable biological destiny, when I heard the sound of distant rock music. Groups of young people were drifting through the darkness in a certain direction, so I followed, and soon found myself in a university pub where a white soul band was playing. Three young students mistook me for a record company scout (this on account of my notebook) and sat down at my table. They were very disappointed to discover that I was only a journalist, researching a piece about the Troubles.

'That's so boring,' said the boy in the double-breasted red jacket. 'I've lived here for 18 years and I've never even seen a gun.' His mate, a gingery muscle man in skin-tight white T-shirt, said, 'They asked me to join the paramilitaries when I was 16, but I said, fuck you. The only ones who join the paramilitaries are people with ego problems.' The girl said, 'Yeah, all we're interested in is raving.'

Her name was Christine, and she was going out with the bloke in the red jacket. They were students of communication by day, rockers by night, and spent summer nights at Portrush, dancing and doing Ecstasy. They said the rave scene in Belfast was the coolest in Europe, according to some British fanzine, and what was my impression?

I was taken aback, quite frankly, especially when it emerged that Christine was a Mick and her boyfriend a Jaffa and that they lived together in a mixed household on the fringe of a campus that was half

Protestant and half Catholic and generally so bored by the Troubles that hardly anyone paid attention any more. Christine didn't even bother to answer when I asked what her Catholic father made of her sleeping with the enemy. She just rolled her eyes as if to say, what a stupid question, and moved off to another table.

It was a well-deserved snub, and quite helpful, in that it drew my attention to the existence of another Northern Ireland, one you seldom hear about in the outside world. Christine and her friends were from the suburbs, and there are no sectarian butchers in the suburbs of Ulster, no mad bombers and no serious tribal tensions. They probably grew up in houses like the one I'm looking at now – a sturdy redbrick manor on a quiet leafy street, with green meadows in the background. It's on the cover of a government brochure detailing the delights of bourgeois Northern Ireland – uncrowded golf courses, good schools, trout streams, lavish government subsidies and just about the lowest crime and murder rate in the Western world.

When I first read those statistics I thought, this can't possibly be true, but I made some calls, and it was. In 1989, Northern Ireland's murder rate (political murders included) was one-fifth of LA's, one-fourteenth of Washington's, maybe one-fortieth of Johannesburg's. The overall crime rate was less than half of Germany's. I felt betrayed. First impressions are misleading. Northern Ireland is not really the Celtic Bosnia of my ravings. War zones aside, Northern Ireland is a quiet place full of law-abiding, church-going white people, not so different, in the final analysis, from the notoriously boring denizens of mid-western America.

And that, I think, is why the Troubles go on and on, forever: they don't really affect enough people. The ghettoes are awash with blood, to be sure, but life is almost normal elsewhere. The Brits are in firm control, levels of suffering are acceptable, and the middle and upper classes are free to go raving or golfing or fly-fishing for salmon, as the case may be. The Six Counties can be very beautiful. They'd be even better if peace broke out, I suppose, but the populace has learned to live with its absence.

One last word ...

And so I board a plane, and fly home across a planet seething with conflicts between tribes and among small nations – 189 such conflicts, by one tally, and more breaking out almost daily. Wherefrom this tribal darkness, and why is it growing? Humanists believe it can be cured by education and enlightenment, but Northern Ireland says otherwise. I mean, the requisite conditions seem to be present there. Schooling is free, literacy is a given and nobody is truly desperate, thanks to the welfare state. There are no dreadful wrongs to right, no aristocrats to guillotine, no estancias to redistribute to starving peasants. It was a dismaying thing for a South African to contemplate all those civilised, rosy-cheeked, relatively lucky and superficially indistinguishable people, squabbling interminably over which group called the shots and under which flag. It made me think there was little hope for my country, with its chasms of race and class, its Himalayas of ethnic antagonism. Indeed, it made me wonder if the tribal disorder is curable at all.

Esquire, April 1993

Hard Men, Hard Country

||||||||||||||||||||||||||||||||||||||||||||||||||||||||||||||||||||||||||||||||||||||||||||||||||||||||||||||||||||||||||

Eric Gagiano is a tough guy from a frontier town where Saturday nights are for drinking and fighting and just looking at an oke the wrong way is enough to get your ribs kicked in. In his wild youth, Eric was the terror of farm dances and *sakkie-sakkie* jols all across the old Suid-Wes, so widely dreaded that his enemies eventually ganged up on him in the alley behind Otjiwarongo Hotel and *moered* him with fence droppers, leaving him with a pulverised cheekbone and an eye that droops lazily, like the TV detective Colombo's. After that came a stint on the border, where he fought 'terrorists,' and a spell on a cattle ranch near Etosha, where he fought marauding lions. These days, he fights bad roads, bandits and chaos in Angola, which is why he's sitting in the cab of a 40-ton truck at Santa Clara border post, waiting.

You do a lot of waiting in Angola. You wait for cops, for customs officers and border guards, for bandits to be cleared off the road ahead. Right now, Eric (48) and his son Mannetjie (21) are waiting for the third vehicle in their convoy, a pickup stuck on the far side of the border on account of a flaw in its papers. Santa Clara has the feel of a frontier town in the old Wild West. The bars and whorehouses start pumping at ten in the morning. Young hoods roam the dusty border plaza in dark glasses and Nike trainers, trying to flog diamonds and ivory.

On the far side of the fence, in Namibia, traders armed with suitcases of hard currency are buying truckloads of groceries and beer for shipment to Luanda, which has become something of a boomtown lately. Drillers have struck oil offshore – five new fields in the last 18 months or so, with reserves in the region of six billion barrels. Oil production is set to double. Diamonds are pouring out of the eastern highlands. Fabulous mineral deposits await exploitation in the hinterland. Angola is Africa's new El Dorado.

On the other hand, it's also the site of 'the worst war on the planet,' a ghastly conflict that seems to be hotting up again, if near-hysterical press reports are accurate. Angolans have been slaughtering each other since 1961, when locals took up arms against Portuguese colonists. After 1974 came the Cold War phase, with South Africa and the CIA supporting the backcountry rebels of UNITA while the Soviets backed the ruling MPLA, an urban movement led mostly by *assimilados* and *mestizos*. The foreigners pulled out in 1988, but the war continued like an old, bad habit, leaving a once-thriving country devastated beyond comprehension. Now the latest truce between the government and the rebels is disintegrating, or so the newspapers say. There are reports of arms shipments, troops massing, attacks on outlying towns. Eric just shrugs. '*Ag, ek worrie nie,*' he says. '*Ek ry maar.*' I don't care. I just go.

So he revs up the engine and the giant 26-wheelers lurch into motion, Mannetjie leading the way in his red International, his dad bringing up the rear in an ancient Scania, and the pick-up truck sandwiched between, its cab and load bed crammed with construction workers who belong to the tribe known as Basters. We'll be in Angola for at least three weeks, so Eric's cab has all the necessary comforts – orange fur on the dashboard, *sakkie-sakkie* tapes, bunk screened off by a Confederate flag in Yankee rebel trucker style. The freezer's full of beer, Coke and braai meat, and there are several crates of cheap whiskey on the trailer, to be dispensed as bribes to customs officials, difficult policemen and bazooka-toting teenagers. Beyond such inconveniences, there's malaria to contend with, and Angola's stomach bugs are dreaded, especially since a dash into the roadside bush can be very dangerous in a country littered with landmines. Still, says Eric, these things are as nothing. '*In Angola, dis die paaie wat jou werklik laat kak.*' In Angola, it's the roads that really make you shit.

Consider the one we're travelling on. Once tarred, its surface has been cut into knife-like ridges by tank tracks and pitted with bomb craters. The verges are strewn with blitzed Russian troop carriers and tanks, relics of a great battle against the South Africans in the eighties. We're moving at walking pace, the truck creaking and groaning over savage potholes. 'This is nothing,' says Eric. 'There's places north of Lubango where the potholes are so deep the truck in front of you vanishes inside them. There's places where the mud's so deep in rainy season that you can't even open the door of your cab.'

He starts telling hair-raising stories about breakdowns in a country where there are no phones, no spares, and no hope of rescue. 'Who's gonna help you, my man? You just make a fuckin' plan.' Trip before last, he says, the trailer jack-knifed and bent the differential. He and his son hauled the twisted metal into the shade of a tree, found some rocks and sand and ground it back into shape with their bare hands. 'That's four months ago, and it's still working.'

It seems foolhardy to be heading into a war in a truck with a dodgy differential and no weapons save a steel rod that Eric likes to keep handy in case of trouble at a truck stop. But where is the war? We can't seem to find it. United Nations soldiers say that bandits are hitting at least one convoy daily on the road ahead, but truckers coming out of the badlands shrug as if to say, so what? There are always bandits on the road to Luanda. At worst, the situation is '*confusão.*' One driver – a mestizo in a pirate bandana – responds to our questions by brandishing his own AK-47 and yelling, 'No problemsh.' He puts foot and vanishes in a cloud of dust. We pull into a town called Xangongo, where a nightmare of sorts awaits.

Xangongo (pronounced Shangongo) lies 200 km inside the border, but this is where customs are located, for reasons best known to the inscrutable Angolans. Northbound trucks park in the ruins of an old prison and send emissaries to a Quonset hut on a bluff overlooking the crocodile-infested Kunene River. Exactly what goes on there is hard to say. Some trucks go through almost immediately, trailing rumours of connections in high places. Others get stuck for a day or so while 'informal taxes' are negotiated. We fall into a problematic third category: our consignment is owned by an upstanding company that has no intention of bribing anyone.

In fact, they've dispatched an executive from corporate headquarters to pay the necessary taxes. He comes out of the sky in a twin-engined Cessna and hobbles into town with US$30 thousand stuffed down the crotch of his trousers. After they've recovered from shock, Angolan customs officials say there's a small problem with his papers. Next morning, they decide our bill has to be settled in local currency. Ten years ago, one dollar was 29 kwanza. After a decade of hyperinflation, the exchange rate is now 670 000:1 and rising. US$30 000 is 20 billion kwanza, enough to fill a truck. Where do you get a truckload of cash in a town with no banks, no credit system and no communications?

The executive leaps into the pickup and roars off to find out. We sit in the dust all day, sipping Eric's bribe supplies and speculating that this is all a plot to wear us down to that point where we slip the customs boys something under the table. The wind kicks up and blows trash around. Eric regales us with a few battler epics, including a rather good one about the night he came off his bike at 270 kph and his leathers tinkled like a glockenspiel when the medics peeled them off him on account of all the smashed half-jacks in his pockets. Bored out of his skull, Mannetjie gets into an argument with a black man who threatens to stab him. They chase each other around a rusting bulldozer until that gets boring too. Come sunset, we're still sitting. We buy a goat, *slag* it and braai it on a fire. Mannetjie throws open the door of his cab and cranks up his beloved Leon Shuster. A stray Baster named Oupa Sakkie gets *lekker getrek* on Eric's bribe supplies and dances the *langarm* all by himself under a full African moon.

Next day's a repeat of the two previous. All our papers are in order now save for a single stamp from the economic police, but their offices are deserted, today being Saturday, so it's four pm before we roll across the river and out onto the open plains. The road runs straight as a die across golden savannah dotted about with baobab trees. Barebreasted women wander footpaths with water vessels on their heads. A goatherd has an AK-47 slung over his shoulder. Every hour or so, we pass a cluster of pastel colonial mansions crumbling gracefully to dust under the equatorial sun. The road is worse than ever.

Why don't they just send this stuff by sea, I ask, jerking a thumb at the 80 tons of construction material on our trailers. 'Hey,' says Eric. 'You try it.' As he tells it, Luanda's docks are a carnival of chaos and chicanery. Bureaucrats seize incoming consignments pending payment of extortionate bribes. It takes weeks of haggling to secure their release, by which time your containers are likely to have been looted anyway. So it's simpler to send goods overland, and the truckers aren't complaining because they're making a fortune. You can double your money running beer and Coca-Cola to Luanda. The margins in potatoes are even more intoxicating: a pocket of spuds costs about two quid at the border, and sells for five times that in the capital.

'It's mad,' says Eric. 'We haul food across some of the best farming country in Africa that's just lying fallow because of all the fighting and all the landmines in the soil. We haul salt past buggered salt mines, beer past buggered breweries. It's IFA, man – Independence Fucked Angola. Nothing works here any more.' On that note we pull over in a hamlet called Uia and crawl back under the trucks for the night.

Eric's up at sunrise, checking his engine. He says something doesn't feel right, and sure enough, the gearbox is dangling at an awkward angle, four key bolts having been shaken loose by yesterday's vibrations. I want to turn back, discretion being the better part of valour, but the guys make a plan – throw a sling under the gearbox, truss it up and push on.

An hour later, there's an ominous knocking in the engine and the gears freeze. 'Whoa, *fok*,' says Eric. '*Hier's groot kak.*' Here's big trouble. We open the engine again. There's oil everywhere. Eric figures the bearings are about to smash through the block. We can't go on, we can't go back, and we can't raise Windhoek on the radio. The only thing for it is to take the bakkie and hunt down a telephone.

Five hours later, we're in Lubango, a sizeable town loomed over by a mountain topped by a giant statue of Jesus, Rio de Janeiro style. The power has failed, but there's a light on in the back of the central post office. A clerk informs us that the phones have been down for the past nine days, but we're welcome to try again in a week or two.

We're driving around in the dark, trying to make a plan, when the lights suddenly come on again. The whole town whoops and pours out onto the streets. It's Saturday night, and Lubango is bent on partying. We hit a restaurant, order chips and steak. We ask locals about the war. They respond with bemusement. We say, but Angola's in a state of 'meltdown,' which is what we've been reading in the world's great newspapers. The locals don't know what we're talking about. Sure, the generals are manoeuvring for control of the diamond fields near the Congo border, but otherwise, there's 'no problemsh' aside from bandits, and they're no problem, either, provided you stay in convoy and don't travel at night.

Next morning, we call for help on the United Nations' satellite phone system and head back towards the stranded convoy, pausing only to have two tyres fixed. We figure this will take ten minutes, but in Angola, it takes all day, so it's late afternoon by the time we hit the road. The sun is sinking, so the driver puts foot, flying over those knife-edged ridges and potholes at close to 160 kilos per hour. Towards sunset, a tyre blows. We replace it with our last spare, and head on into the gathering darkness. Thirty minutes later, another blow-out, and we're stranded in the night. The guys stand around, scratching their heads. I watch the moon rise over the thorn trees and think about Ryszard Kapuściński, the great Polish foreign correspondent who came to Angola in the seventies but could never quite find the front line of the war he was supposed to be covering. 'The front line is inside your head,' he eventually concluded. 'It travels with you wherever you go.'

Right now, my head is saying that we are in serious danger – stuck in the dark in the bandit zone with few tools, no radio, and little hope of salvation. We're making an enormous racket, trying to lever the tyre off the wheel with sticks and screwdrivers so that we can replace the tube and get going again. Every bandit for miles around is surely zeroing in on us. In the end, we get so desperate that we claw one side of the tyre off the rim with our fingernails, stuff a new tube inside, pump it up and send it.

Back in Namibia, the bosses are rustling up a new 'horse' to replace the crippled Scania. Our instructions are to meet them back at the border, bringing the broken truck with us. One problem: no towbar. Eric makes a plan. He hacks a branch off an ironwood tree and lays it down in the dust atop an angle iron. Mannetjie crushes the branch into the angle iron under the wheels of his 40-tonner. He and his dad strengthen the weld by lashing it with ropes, and *voilà* – an Angolan *disselboom*.

We leave at dawn, heading back whence we came. Our hair is matted with twigs and dust, and the reek of our bodies is unbearable. We've been in Angola for a week, and covered fewer than 300 kilometres. At this rate, it will be a month before Eric sees a cold beer and a hot shower again. The truck bucks through potholes at walking pace. Clouds of powdery dust billow through the open windows. The battler lowers his face into his hands and groans.

Sunday Express, 1996

Postscript: It took another five weeks for the convoy to reach its destination. By then, the rains had set in. Most members of the party contracted malaria. Hospitals along the truck route had no effective drugs, and two men died. Remember them if you ever visit Luanda Sul, the air-conditioned moonbase where expatriates and Angolan politicians live in comfort and luxury. Its foundations were cast with cement hauled across the badlands by Eric Gagiano.

The Land of Double Happiness
Safety Matches

IIIIIIIIIIIIIIIIIIIIIIIIIIIIIIIIIIIIIIIIIIIIIIIIIIIIIIIIIIIIIIIIIIIIIIIIIIIIIIIIIIIIIIIIIIIIIIIIIIIIIIIIIIIIIIIIIIIIIIIIIIIIIIIIIIIII

Photographer Bill was beset by the jitters as we flew into Uganda. A nice suburban guy with three kids, a trophy wife and a propensity to vacation in France or the Bahamas, he'd been trawling the Net for background, and hadn't liked what he had found. The US State Department had issued a travel warning that spoke of troop movements in national parks and banditry in the Mountains of the Moon. Hospitals were primitive, roads dangerous, and the germ threat so intense that members of President Clinton's party, which passed through five days ahead of us, were advised not to kiss anyone and to keep their lips pursed in the shower. On top of this, Bill was reeling from the side effects of tropical disease inoculations and the psychic reverberations of a *New Yorker* article about some crazed rebels on the north bank of the Nile who believed that magic could turn bullets into water and rocks into hand grenades. As we came in to land at Entebbe, his refrain was, 'What the hell are we letting ourselves in for?'

What indeed? Viewed from the sensible perspective of, say, the average European or American, Uganda is one of the last places one would wish to visit, which is probably why so few do. Five years ago, there were hardly any tourists at all. Last year, a mere 4 000 chanced it, and most just climbed a volcano, saw some gorillas and got the hell out again. I mean, we're talking about a country where the power fails every second day, where AIDS is rampant and bugs are known to lay eggs under your skin or crawl up your nose and eat your brain; a country that was once a charnel house in its own right, with the killing fields of Rwanda on one side, the famine grounds of Sudan on the other, and armies of wild Karimojong tribesmen crossing the frontier on massed cattle raids, according to a newspaper we bought at the airport. It was more than enough to invoke in any white man 'a sense of undefinable oppression.'

Those are the words of Winston Churchill, who arrived in Entebbe in 1907 in a frame of mind not entirely dissimilar to Bill's, and to some extent my own. He'd had a splendid time on the trans-Kenya railroad, but something about Uganda unsettled him, something he couldn't quite put a finger on. It could be the altitude, he said, or the insects, or maybe even the unbearable beauty of his first sight of Entebbe, a cluster of red-roofed bungalows on Lake Victoria. 'It was too good to be true,' he wrote. 'It is too good to be true. Behind its glittering mask, Entebbe wears a sinister aspect.'

The young British MP had come at a bad moment, it turned out. There were rebels on the north bank of the Nile, and the countryside was devastated by pestilence. Man-eating leopards prowled the jungle fringes, and the very air seemed full of malignancy. 'A cut will not heal,' he wrote. 'A scratch festers. Even a small wound becomes a running sore.' Pioneer colonists were so depressed that two had committed suicide, and even Churchill was reduced to morbid pronouncements about the curse that seemed to lie over this 'curious garden of sunshine and deadly nightshade.'

That said, Winnie donned his pith helmet, whistled up the porters and set forth on safari. He and his party travelled 500 miles in the next 30 days, trudging across savanna, bicycling down forest paths, steaming across pristine lakes under cool blue skies that were full of waterfowl and fish eagles. He began to notice things that had eluded his first glance – 'birds as bright as butterflies, butterflies as big as birds,' a mad profusion of flowers, forests to rival those that once covered England. He saw great herds of elephant, plains covered with game, thunderstorms 'wheeling in vivid splendour across the night horizon.' The natives were friendly and intelligent, the hunting superlative. By the time he reached Nimule, on the far side of the country, Churchill was enchanted. The rest of East Africa was interesting, he wrote, 'but the Kingdom of Uganda is a fairy tale. You climb up a railway instead of a beanstalk, and at the end of it there is a wonderful new world.'

Ninety years later, we came down from the sky, loaded our misgivings into a Land Cruiser and took off on a journey that carried us to a similar conclusion. Uganda is a happy-go-lucky calypso song of a country where people's pain is enormously sweetened by the bounty of nature. The soils are rich, the lakes teem with fish and the climate is an endless summer. Ugandan peasants harvest three crops a year, where most Africans can't count on any; you can feed an entire family on an acre or so, just sitting in the shade and watching the bananas grow. This eases the desperation that might otherwise obtain in a country so poor and so recently devastated, and makes it possible for people to be nice to each other, and yes, to visitors. We were plied with beer in Kampala bars, given small gifts of fruit by peasants whose clothes were in tatters. We sang in the shower, and never got sick. We ate boo and doo-doo at roadside stands, and lived to tell the tale. We travelled the country from end to end, and everything we saw was beautiful. In Uganda, even the cows are breathtaking.

We began to see them about five hours out of Entebbe, lovely Ankole cattle with horns like lyres, each with its own name, apparently, and a personality much analysed by its doting owner. This I gathered from *Sowing the Mustard Seed*, the autobiography of Yoweri Museveni, cattle farmer, soldier and Uganda's state president. I'd bought a copy in the town of Mbarara, and it was fascinating: an earnest young revolutionary takes to the bush in 1980 with a handful of guns and 29 men, hell-bent on perpetrating yet another socialist catastrophe. But something happens to him during his long fight for power. He abandons the idea that all Africa's miseries are the white man's fault. He becomes an apostle of free markets. He starts talking about discipline, law and order and the need for institutions based on the history, culture and psyche of African people.

After toppling Milton Obote in 1986, Museveni starts dismantling the Ugandan state, or at least whittling away at it. He takes power from the centre, gives it to 'Revolutionary Councils' at village level. He slashes the bureaucracy, privatises state assets, deregulates everything he can. The results are miraculous in African terms: peace returns, inflation vanishes, and the economy starts galloping ahead at ten per cent per annum. Museveni is hailed as Africa's saviour, a Moses come to lead the dark continent out of its nightmare of violence, starvation and economic decay. He's a dictator, to be sure, but Ugandans like Tony Sukuma, our ebullient driver, couldn't give a damn.

'People look around,' he says, 'and they see it's working. They say, this is the right path for the moment. Wherever you go, people are happy.' It turns out that Tony spent a decade in Museveni's army, fighting for a cause that he says came down to common decency: down with the bloody tyrants who stole everything they could lay their hands on, and away with the soldiers who looted your village, raped your sisters and smashed your head in if you stood in their way. He was wounded twice, but remains enormously pleased with the result of his sacrifice. 'I don't want any stupid changes that will take away the peace and stability,' he says. 'If anybody threatens to do this, I will fight again. After all, if it wasn't for this peace, you guys would not be here, would you?'

And what a pity that would have been, because we would never have seen the sight that awaited us at the end of the road, which terminated on the summit of a knife-edged promontory in Queen Elizabeth National Park. Here stood the Mweya Safari Lodge, suspended in the sky between two bodies of water. Porters ushered us through the lobby, past a giant pair of elephant tusks and onto a verandah that commanded one of the most spectacular views in Africa – Lake Edward on one side, the Kazinga Channel on the other, and before us, the Mountains of the Moon, their flanks clad with mysterious forests, their snow-capped peaks lost in cloud today. We collapsed into wicker chairs, struck dumb by the sight of an alpine landscape on the Equator. Waiters brought tall glasses of passion fruit juice. A lanky, bearded fanatic sat down beside us and started jabbering about birds.

Malcolm Watson spent his asthmatic boyhood staring out of fogged-up windows at shivering sparrows in rainy English gardens. From such beginnings grew a life-long obsession that eventually landed him here, where he was trying to establish a bird-watching centre. 'It's a gold mine, if you understand birding,' he said. 'We hold the world record for a one-day species count – 397 species in a single day. There's 558 species in this park alone.' He began to enumerate them: fish eagles, palearctic osprey, goliath herons, the papyrus gonolek, the bare-faced go-away bird, and the legendary shoebill, a huge pterodactyl-like creature with yellow eyes and an imbecilic expression, almost impossible to see on account of its preference for impenetrable swamps. 'I've spent £15 thousand of my own money trying to set this thing up,' cried the birdman, 'and I can't go on alone. I need help and nobody gives a damn.'

Neither did I, quite frankly; birding has always struck me as boring. On the other hand, I'd never met a birder like Malcolm Watson. His description of a fly hatch on the lakes below was inspirational. It happened often, he said, usually in the morning. Flies begin to hatch and rise into the air in clouds so dense that the water appears to be smoking. Soon, an apocalyptic feeding frenzy is underway in the sky above, with millions of swallows snatching insects out of the air and in turn falling prey to raptors that come diving out of the sun like F-16s and thwack – annihilate a lesser bird in an explosion of feathers. 'It's fantastic,' cried the birdman, who was acting all this out with windmilling arms and a grin that was slightly lopsided as the result of an encounter with a buffalo on a footpath a hundred yards away. Irritated, it tossed him a few times, butted him black and blue, and kneeled on his face, knocking his teeth skew.

There aren't that many wild animals in Uganda, but most of them seemed to be converging on our verandah. There were tame warthogs in the flowerbeds. Marabou storks sauntered the lawns like old, stooped men in evening dress, crops dangling down their chests like scarlet cravats. A great rump of reddish brown flesh broke the horizon, and a hippo rose into view, strolling up from the lake to feed on the daisies. We changed tables, ordered beers and watched the sunset. The birdman observed, apropos of nothing in particular, that one of the best things about this place was that you could sometimes sit here at night and watch tracer bullets arcing across the distant mountainside, where government soldiers were hunting rebels and bandits.

But we don't really want to talk about that, do we? Nah, we're on holiday. We want to repair to the dining room, where waiters are serving dinner in uniforms that seem to have been in mothballs since Uganda's fifties' tourist heyday: white shirts, narrow black ties, FBI slacks and black-rimmed spectacles, like a conclave of black Clark Kents. On the menu tonight, as always, there is fish – fillets of tilapia, hauled out of the lake this morning, deep fried, and garnished with lemon. It is an excellent fish, at least the equal of trout or salmon, especially if taken at high African altitude and washed down with cold Ugandan beer. I was groping for a light for my post-prandial smoke when a waiter presented me with a good omen: a box of Double Happiness Safety Matches. I lit up and sat back to savour my coffee, feeling like Winston Churchill at the end of his stay.

Wilfred Megenyi was one of those Ugandans you couldn't help loving. Aged about 30, and a forest ranger by profession, he had two wives to support and hadn't been paid since Christmas. On top of this, his brother had accidentally stepped into a black magic trap that caused his leg to bloat to hideous dimensions. Just this morning, the cook at our camp had lanced the swelling and drawn forth a living snake. These traumas notwithstanding, Wilfred managed a smile, pulled on his boots and led us into the dim jungle, which was full of vines and spider webs and trees that soared to 300 feet, stabilised by side roots resembling the fins of Apollo rockets.

Churchill loved the forests of Uganda, filling pages of his diary with descriptions of their 'awful fecundity' and the 'intense convulsions of life and death' underway in the rich humus underfoot. We were looking for creatures more elevated – our first cousins, the chimpanzees, which abound in Kibale Forest. We trudged through a fairyland of green glens and dells, but alas, the chimpanzees were elsewhere, and Wilfred was reduced to giving us a compensatory lecture on bush medicine: this plant to cool fever, that one to bind the gut; katimboro bark to engender a monstrous erection, and the flowers of the omunyara tree to lubricate the vagina on the receiving end of it. He cupped a hand over his nose and emitted a bizarre nasal whine, imitating a duiker ewe in her birth throes. Moments later, a troop of Colobus monkeys came crashing through the treetops, hoping to feast on the placenta. 'Where did you learn that?' I asked. 'Oh,' he replied, 'I used to be a poacher.'

Wilfred seemed to take the chimp no-show as a personal failure, which is perhaps why he invited us back to his shamba, which lay out on the sun-drenched savanna. He showed us his mud hut, his wives and his many sweet little offspring. We met the neighbours, and inspected his plantation of coffee and matoki bananas, which are picked green and require cooking. In a swamp at the bottom of his garden he'd built a fishpond that was stocked with tilapia. He lopped some leaves off a cassava plant and chucked them in. The water began to boil.

It was a great little fish farm, as fish farms go, but Wilfred had no sure way of getting the fish out of it, save for a hook fashioned from rusting wire. I delved into my luggage and found some tackle for him. He gave me a pineapple, profusely apologising that it was the only one he had. I promised to send some pumpkin seeds. He pressed his precious fish-farming manual into my reluctant hands. Refusing to be outdone, I tried to give him a few bank notes, but he refused them, so I had to slip them to a wife on the sly. It seemed the least I could do for a family that hadn't seen cash since Christmas.

Why not? Wilfred wasn't quite sure, but most national park staff seemed to be in similar straits. I made inquiries when we reached Kampala a few days later, but it was very confusing. Some said the rangers' pay had been diverted into the patriotic frenzy of street cleaning and weed slashing that preceded the recent visit of President Clinton. Others claimed it was lost. A few maintained it had been stolen. Nobody seemed very worried. It was just one of those Ugandan things, apparently, like unreliable phones, atrocious roads and perpetual rebellions on the periphery.

Someone threw a hand grenade into a crowded Kampala restaurant on the night we arrived there, killing three Burundese businessmen. I hastened to the scene the next morning, but most passers-by had no idea who had done it, or why, and the rest shrugged as if to say, relax, man. I walked over to State House, hoping for an interview with President Museveni, but he was in London, so I just strolled around, taking in the sights. Downtown was the standard African jungle of office blocks and traffic chaos, but there was no discernible undercurrent of tension.

On the contrary – the mood of the city seemed astonishingly open and cheerful, considering that Uganda was a one-party state. The newspapers were full of gleeful accounts of the latest government faux pas. Lampposts were festooned with pictures of candidates in a bitterly contested mayoral race. There were seven of them, just about equally divided between 'Movementists,' who supported the government, and 'multi-partyists,' who didn't. The only rule seemed to be that none of them were allowed to run under their true political colours, even though locals knew exactly what these were.

Beyond that, the campaign was a glorious free-for-all. The muckraking *Uganda Confidential* assailed the character of a certain Mr Birriggwa, claiming he'd left a wife and children destitute in America. Mr Birriggwa stormed into the editor's office and 'manhandled' him, whereupon the editor, Mr Cheeye, had challenged Mr Birriggwa to a duel. Another candidate, Mr Sebbaggala, had fallen afoul of hecklers who mocked his lack of education. The result was an inexplicable up-surge in support for Mr Sebbaggala's candidacy. Some said the mock-ery had insulted the city's underclass, who were also poor and illiter-ate. Others said the true reason was that Mr Sebbaggala was a member of the Baganda tribe, which predominates in the Kampala region.

Around lunchtime, I wound up on the shady verandah of a restau-rant called The Lion, where I met A Kadumukasa Kironde II, aged 53, a Ugandan aristocrat whose posh British accent was redolent of Eton, Bentleys and cricket. A celebrated gourmet cook and bon vivant, he was pottering around in a chef's hat when I arrived, experimenting with exotic recipes in The Lion's kitchen. He told me to call him KK, and invited me to sit down for a chat.

The key to understanding Uganda, he said, was understanding Museveni, who was best thought of as 'a master of the art of the impossible' – a quality essential in anyone who sought to rule a country inhabited by 50 fractious tribes and haunted by the ghosts of a million-odd people butchered in the civil wars of the seventies and eighties. Uganda was devastated beyond description when Museveni came to power in 1986, and generally considered ungovernable. Under the circumstances, Museveni did the wise thing: he threw out his volumes of Marx and Engels, and started reading Machiavelli.

'This,' claimed KK, 'is clearly evident in his style of governance.' Nobody gets everything they want, but almost everyone gets enough to keep them quiet. The newspapers are free to say whatever they please. Politicians can pursue their wildest ambitions, provided that they stay inside the broad church of Musevenism. Corruption is ruth-lessly suppressed, but you might get away with it if you're the favour-ite son of a powerful faction likely to cause trouble if you are sent to jail. Tribalism is officially a no-no, but some tribes are a bit more equal than others – a factor, per KK, which might begin to explain rebellions on the periphery and hand grenades in nearby restaurants. Ah, well. At least Uganda was stumbling toward the light, rather than sliding backwards. KK summoned a waiter and treated me to a meal.

'I was most amused,' he said as we tucked into our Goanese chicken curry, smothered in my case with the delectable peanut sauce called boo and the ubiquitous greens known as doo-doo. We were talking about the recent Clinton visit, which culminated in the hallucinatory spectacle of an American president embracing an African strongman who stoutly maintains that American-style democracy is a middle-class indulgence from an alien civilisation. 'It was like a coronation,' observed KK. 'Now Museveni will definitely think of himself as a Messiah.'

KK was a bit disapproving, but this was hardly surprising, given his background. His father was a British barrister, and his first cousin Ronnie was the King of Buganda. A person of his refined pedigree could hardly be expected to endorse Museveni, but myself, I liked what I'd heard. Museveni has a propensity for plain speech – he once dismissed the Organisation of African Unity as 'a trade union for criminals' – and his authoritarian streak has to be seen in context.

At the time, Uganda's state TV service was running a commercial set at a drinking party attended by computer-animated beer bottles, each sporting limbs, a face and the label of a familiar Ugandan beer. Then the door bursts open, and there stands Chairman's Extra Strong, muscles bulging. He walks over to the lesser beers and head-butts them, laying them all out flat. The girl beers swoon, little red hearts flying forth from their breasts, and in the end, Chairman's Extra Strong walks off with a string of them. 'The message seems unmissable,' I said to KK. 'Ugandans surely admire this kind of machismo. Maybe that's why they admire Chairman Museveni.'

KK chuckled. He unearthed a bottle of South African red wine, poured me a glass, and started pursuing the subject I'd raised. 'My entire life has been one of paradox,' he began. He felt too British to be African, and yet England struck him as cold and alien. He had a foot in either culture, and thought it enabled him to see both more clearly than the natives. As KK warmed to the theme, we switched to Ugandan banana gin, and my notes started lapsing into gibberish. By four pm I was so inebriated I could barely walk, so KK whistled up a taxi and sent me on my way, promising to introduce me to his cousin King Ronnie when next I was in town. What a country. What a capital chap. What a day.

Okay, so where are we now? We're up in the wild blue yonder in a twin-engined Cessna, passing over Lake Albert, a vast expanse of greasy green water dotted about with fishing canoes and ominous bits of flotsam that look like crocodiles to me. To the west, the mysterious Blue Mountains rear almost vertically out of the lake, and to the north, lost in a heat haze, lies the Sudanese border – 'a realm of sinister and forbidding aspect,' said Winston Churchill, 'where man is fanatical and often rifle-armed.' It was so in 1907, and it remains thus today. Somewhere in the trackless wastes below, government power peters out, and you enter the fief of the Lord's Resistance Army, or LRA, a band of dreadlocked mystics who seem to specialise in slicing off their enemies' lips and seizing convent girls as concubines. Our destination – Pakuba airstrip, on the north bank of the Nile – is technically under a US State Department travel ban, but the only sign of danger as we come in to land is a herd of impala that refuses to move out of our way until we scream over their heads at full throttle.

A Land Cruiser is waiting. We throw our gear in the back, bounce off across the savanna. Ten clicks down the road, we come upon a patch of charred, blackened sand that marks the spot where a convoy was ambushed 15 months back by the LRA. They executed the drivers, looted their trucks and withdrew into the reserve's northern reaches. They're still out there somewhere, so we take the south fork, which leads through a forest of singing thorn trees to the banks of the mighty Nile, 600 yards wide at this point, its dark waters flecked with yellow foam, rolling towards Egypt at seven miles an hour.

On a ridge above the banks looms a giant wooden stockade of the sort erected by eighteenth-century fur trappers in the wild forests of North America. This is the Paraa Lodge, a relic of Uganda's mid-century tourist heyday, recently refurbished at enormous cost in anticipation of a tourist boom that has yet to materialise. A squad of porters pounce on my luggage and lead me up a grand mahogany staircase. The lime-green walls are covered with etchings – reprints from the *Illustrated London News*, for the most part, showing Victorian explorers shooting elephants, meeting one another in jungle clearings and fending off attacks by 'forest dwarves with poison arrows.' My suite is wood-panelled, with a fan in the ceiling and a mosquito net draped gracefully over the bed. Down in the kitchen, the freezers are crammed with imported delicacies that will shortly be served in a dining room the size of a ballroom. It's amazing, a grand hotel in bush so remote that the only communication with the outside world is by radio.

Outside, the vast tiled terrace is deserted, the swimming pool empty. I drink a cold beer on a cool verandah that commands a broad sweep of the river, and beyond it, the bush stretching low and level to the blue wall of the Rift Valley. This is a richly mythic landscape. Every major Victorian explorer buckled his swash out there among the thorn trees. Theodore Roosevelt hunted rhino at the turn of the century. Winston Churchill passed through in 1907, wearing a beekeeper's veil to protect himself against the dreaded tsetse. Bogart, Bacall, Hepburn and Huston came in 1942 to make *African Queen*. A decade later, Hemingway almost died in a plane crash on yonder hillock, an episode that inspired *The Snows of Kilimanjaro*.

More recently, a smalltown fishmonger named Alice Auma was summoned to a spot just upstream by an ancestral spirit who revealed her new destiny: she was to take up the sword in the name of Jehovah and cleanse the land of evil, beginning with administrators loyal to Museveni. This was the genesis of the Lord's Resistance Army, but we don't really want to dwell on that, do we? Nah, we're beginning to like it here on the wild frontier, poised on a knife-edge between ecstasy and terror. We want to drink gins and tonic and eat beef in a cabernet jus while the sun sets in barbaric splendour over the Nile. After dark, the swimming pool is like a blue jewel in the black African night, and you hear hippos crashing around in the undergrowth below. Lightning begins to play on the northern horizon, a sure sign that the rains are coming.

Next morning, we rise before dawn and go out on a game drive. It's a lovely day, cool and grey. A large herd of kob stampedes across the horizon at our approach. A smudge of black on a distant hillside turns out to be a throng of ruminating buffalo. After a while, we turn back, and see the same kob again, plus five giraffe and a column of ferocious driver ants, heading across the savanna on some inscrutable mission. That's about it as far as wildlife is concerned. We drive home somewhat saddened.

Photographs taken here in the early sixties show a landscape as flat and open as a billiard table, all the trees having been torn down by teeming elephants. The river banks heaved with hippopotami; there were lions and rhino in every second donga; the antelope were too numerous to be tallied. But then the wars began, and rabble armies began to criss-cross the country, living off the land. The antelope were machine-gunned and eaten, the elephants poached for their ivory. Murchison's elephant population had fallen by 90 per cent. Its rhinos had been exterminated entirely.

To be fair, it should be noted that what game is left had dispersed after the rain, so there is far more of it than first meets the eye. It is also true that Museveni's government has restored control over Uganda's reserves, and that recovery is taking place at a heartening rate, with elephant giving birth to twins galore as they expand into empty ecological niches. Still, if you want to see wildlife in splendid variety and large numbers, go to a country where jumbo jets disgorge hordes of tourists who throng to zoo-like parks where they choke on each other's exhaust fumes in traffic snarl-ups around lion kills and waterholes. You'll probably see the Big Five, but you'll never experience anything like the loneliness of the Ugandan wild.

About 20 miles upstream from Paraa, the Nile flows into a funnel of hard rock that narrows and narrows until all its pent-up might is constricted into a channel barely 18 feet wide that blasts over a clifftop and into mid-air, only to thunder down into the abyss below with a din and violence that is almost incomprehensible. The roar of Murchison Falls is audible from ten miles away. Winston Churchill was mesmerised by the sight of them. They were, he said, the highlight of his safari; just seeing them made the long trek worthwhile. Anywhere else, the riverbanks would be covered with resorts and casinos and hippies would be leaping into the chasm with bungees attached, but in Uganda, time has stood still. The road that leads to the falls is a pot-holed abomination. The dusty parking lot at the end of it is absolutely empty. We had the entire magnificent spectacle to ourselves.

By my calculation, I was standing on the exact spot where Winston Churchill stood nine decades earlier, and seeing exactly what he saw, save that the rock on which he spotted a crocodile was under water in this season. Churchill hated crocodiles, so he raised his rifle and shot. At the sound, 'the entire far bank of the river, to the extent of at least a quarter mile, erupted into hideous life.' What he presumed to be a mudbank was actually an unbroken line of basking saurians that rushed madly into the river, where their descendants were presumably still lurking – a probability that began to exercise my mind as I edged towards the foaming water, fishing rod in hand.

And now we come to a confession. Beyond all longing to see new places, this is what I had come for: to stand on this rock and do battle with the giant fish said to inhabit the pool below. They are called Nile Perch, and they are the largest fresh-water game fish on the planet,

400 pounds reputed, 305 verified; fish like whales, and given more than anywhere in the world to lurking right here, in the swirling water at the foot of the falls, waiting to pounce on dazed and stunned prey spat out of the churning cauldron behind me.

My rod was a stout one, suitable for tuna, and the gut on it was thick and strong, terminating in a long wire trace at the end of which a crucified baitfish wriggled. I lowered it into the raging stream and watched in dismay as it snarled on a raft of papyrus that dragged it away to the left, where it snagged in the submerged roots of an overhanging tree. The same thing happened on my next cast, and the next. The river was swollen and full of debris, and I would have been undone had I not happened to pocket the cork from the wine drunk at last night's dinner.

Improvising ingeniously, I like to think, I used the cork as a float on my next cast, and lo, it kept my line aloof from the floating detritus. The cork bobbed around a bit, got caught in an eddy and circled back almost to my feet, where it suddenly vanished, sucked under by a monster. I let the line run, counted to five, and then struck into something heavy. Moments later, the fish came to the surface, a great, thrashing silver thing, mouth agape like a largemouth bass, and dancing on its tail like sailfish. Then it took off across the pool and found the main current, and my line began to sweep downstream like the string of a kite in a gale.

It took ten minutes to win back the lost nylon, and by then, the fish was exhausted. It gave up the struggle and rolled over at my feet, a 30-pounder, to my proud eye. But I was perched atop a rock on account of the saurian menace, and it was in the water, ten feet below. The wire trace snapped as we were hauling it up, and I was left with nothing but a fishing story.

But it was enough, and I went home with a full heart. Back in Entebbe, a cool breeze was blowing off the mile-high lake, and the town which at first seemed so foreboding now looked like a South Sea island, its ramshackle houses tucked away under banana and mango trees and overrun by rioting frangipani. As we rose into the sky, the colours were like a Gauguin painting, the red billboards for Sportsman cigarettes playing off against black Guinness signs, bright yellow phone-booths and pastel-coloured schoolchildren in uniforms of pink and blue. Uganda has terrible problems, to be sure, but it's a special place, the land of Double Happiness Safety Matches. Like Winston Churchill before us, we were beset by the thought that the best was behind us, and that what lay ahead would never quite match. 'Beauty dies out of the landscape,' he wrote as he steamed away, 'and richness from the land.' He was broken-hearted. So were we.

Condé Nast Traveller, circa 1998

5

Truth

The Queen

||||||||||||||||||||||||||||||||||||||||||||||||||||||||||||||||||||||||||||||||||||||||||||||||||||||||||||||||||||||||||||||||||

I met Winnie Mandela once. It was a rainy night in the early 1990s, and I'd been dragged to a primary school concert by a friend. At the time, Sacred Heart was the school of choice for the ANC's senior leaders, and several of the tiny ballerinas twirling around on stage had last names like Sisulu or Mandela. I was standing outside the hall, smoking, when Comrade Winnie turned up to fetch a granddaughter. We fell into conversation, and I wound up bewitched, for lack of a better term. Winnie was beautiful and charming. Her dark eyes danced, and her laughter was infectious. As for hauteur, there was no sign of it. On the contrary, she seemed to derive genuine pleasure from this chance encounter with a grubby white stranger. What can I say? Winnie was a star. When the concert ended and she drove away, the light in that foyer seemed to fade to grey.

This will sound trite, but I found it hard to reconcile the woman I met that night with the monster I'd been reading about for years. I searched her eyes for signs of evil, but none were apparent. I found myself wondering (for the thousandth time) whether the charges brought against her were really the fruit of black propaganda campaigns, as she'd always claimed. As the years wore on, that seemed less and less likely, but the enchantment lingered. When her case came up before the Truth Commission, I persuaded London's Sunday Independent to let me cover it.

'This is witchcraft,' said Governor Mntonga, the house painter from Malawi. It was a hot Wednesday in Johannesburg and we should have been working, but the Winnie Mandela hearings were live on TV, so we'd been glued to the set all morning. Winnie's former henchman-in-chief, Jerry Richardson, was on the witness stand, looking debonair in his dark suit and flashy gold rings, regaling the nation with tales of torture and murder. And then, around noon, the lights went out in the hall where the hearing was underway. I could have sworn it was just a power failure, but Governor thought otherwise. It was, he said, an indication that Winnie's powerful magic was finally kicking in.

Unlikely, I thought, but it was certainly a turning point. The hearings had been underway for eight days, and had hitherto been a nightmare for Mrs Madikizela-Mandela. The erstwhile 'Mother of the Nation' and present-day candidate for the deputy presidency of the ruling African National Congress had been called before the Truth and Reconciliation Commission to discuss the reign of terror perpetrated by the Mandela United Football Club, a loose aggregation of homeless teenagers, guerrillas and struggle fanatics who took up residence in her backyard in 1986, dubbed 'The Year of People's War' by ANC commissars.

Bearing nicknames such as Ninja, Killer, Scorpion and Slash, the youngsters' true function was less to play soccer than to assist Mrs Mandela's drive to render Soweto ungovernable, a noble enterprise which ultimately degenerated into a confused mess of kangaroo courts, gang-style feuds between rival factions and cannibalistic witchhunts for sellouts and spies. As many as 16 people had died at the hands of the Mandela footballers, according to press reports, and several team members had landed up in prison on charges ranging from armed robbery to murder.

Now Mrs Mandela's role in all this was under consideration. Several witnesses announced that they were tired of lying to protect her, and would now tell the truth, which appeared to be hair-raising. Mrs Mandela, it was claimed, had often presided at meetings of the club's 'disciplinary committee,' where offenders were sentenced to torture or beatings in which she and her daughter Zinzi allegedly participated with relish. Two assassins swore that she'd paid them to knock off a potentially troublesome doctor. Three mothers claimed she'd had their children abducted or murdered. Five eye-witnesses alleged that she'd led the assault on Stompie Seipei, the child activist famously butchered by her sidekicks in January 1989.

The climax came on day eight, when former Mandela United coach Jerry Richardson admitted that it was he who had committed the foul deed and three additional murders besides, all at the behest of the woman he called mommy. 'I killed Stompie on the instruction of Mrs Mandela,' he cried, pointing across the hall. 'She does not even visit us in prison! She used us!' Until that moment, the noose appeared to be tightening around Winnie's neck, but then the power failed, and events began to turn in her favour.

Hitherto quite jocular and cocky, Richardson suddenly seemed unnerved. 'I get scared when the lights go out,' he said, peering around apprehensively. They came back on moments later, but Richardson never quite regained his poise. Within minutes, he'd been forced to acknowledge that he was a police informer, an admission that atomised his credibility with black South Africans. Soon after, he began to ramble incoherently, answering in non-sequiturs. At one point, he delved into his briefcase and insisted that the commission study photographs of people who seemed to have no relevance whatsoever to the proceedings. By day's end, Richardson had become a jabbering, pathetic ruin, incapable of answering any questions at all. Things were looking up for Mrs Madikizela-Mandela.

Next morning, she showed up in a pair of rhinestone-encrusted spectacles that gave her face a strangely reptilian aspect. She looked like a turtle, heavy, slow-moving, totally nerveless and inscrutable behind her tinted lenses. Her counter-attack was based on the hallucinatory premise that the Mandela United Football Club had ceased to exist at the time of its reign of terror. Her husband had ordered her to disband it in April 1987, and she had obeyed. How then could she be held to account for alleged club misdeeds that had taken place months or years later?

Lawyers pointed out that she had been filmed as late as February 1989, surrounded by youths in full Mandela United regalia. Winnie conceded that she hadn't the heart to take fancy tracksuits away from poverty-stricken working class lads; otherwise, the point stood: there was no such thing as a football club after April 1987, and as for the disciplinary committee over which she had so arbitrarily presided, this was the first she'd heard of it. For the rest, her accusers were variously lunatic, deluded, mistaken, deranged, drunk, senile, pawns of the secret police, or victims of police brutality, forced to make accusations against her under torture. Anyone who disagreed too strongly was regally censured: 'I will not tolerate you speaking to me like that! I will not!'

There was something hypnotic about these blunt denials and their steady repetition. Winnie didn't counter accusations; she annihilated them with refutations so sweeping that her questioners were left gaping, as if socked in the stomach. She had never even met several of her alleged victims, or else barely remembered them. She had no idea why the ANC's internal wing had found it necessary, in 1988, to set up a crisis committee to curb her behaviour. She had no recollection of this committee begging her to release Stompie and his three fellow captives, because they had never been captives in the first place, or if they had been, it was none of her doing, because she could not – 'for God's sake' – be held responsible for the actions of all the waifs and runaways who had taken shelter on her premises.

Yes, there had been a 'perception' that some of them were running amok, but it had been vastly exaggerated by the apartheid state's disinformation machine and her enemies in 'the cabal,' a grouping within the ANC that was supposedly out to get her. Toward the end, commissioner Yasmin Sooka put it to her that she was forcing listeners towards a rather improbable conclusion: 'If we believe your evidence, everyone else is lying.' Winnie smiled. 'Yes,' she said. 'It's true.'

Appearances to the contrary, Ms Sooka could not have been surprised, because all this was a replay of a closed-door hearing five weeks earlier, where Winnie had countered all charges with similar blanket denials. Why was the Truth Commission allowing her to get away with it? Because the Truth Commission is a sweet and somewhat muddle-headed organism, cast very much in the mould of its chairman, Archbishop Desmond Tutu.

The kindly and forgiving Anglican has been reluctant to use the sword the law has placed in his hands – a pity, since the TRC's most striking successes have resulted from the infliction of terror. Such cases have invariably involved white security policemen and months of rigorous investigation by TRC staff, who have sought out new witnesses and smashed alibis, ultimately forcing the guilty parties to confess rather than face the dreadful certainty of life imprisonment.

No similar efforts seemed to have been made in Winnie's case. The various Ninjas and Killers who once lived in her garden remained names on yellowing police statements. No new evidence was brought forth to break your-word-versus-mine deadlocks of many years' standing. Indications that Winnie had perjured herself in her 1991 Stompie trial were allowed to go unpunished, and alarming allegations of witness intimidation went largely unexamined.

Consider the case of Mike Seakamela, whose testimony might have wiped the smirk off Mrs Madikizela-Mandela's face if he'd showed up to testify as scheduled. Once a driver in Winnie's employ, Seakamela is possibly the only source capable of verifying a story provided to the TRC by Nicodemus Sono. A plump office-worker in his early fifties, Nicodemus once had a son named Lolo, and a nephew named Tebogo, who left the country to undergo military training. When Tebogo returned to Soweto in 1988, carrying a bag of hand grenades and an AK-47 assault rifle, 16-year-old Lolo became his courier, scuttling back and forth between Tebogo and Winnie Mandela, a fellow operative in the ANC's underground army.

On 9 November 1988, Tebogo was betrayed, and he and a comrade died in a fusillade of police bullets. It emerged this week that the real traitor was Winnie's confidant, Jerry Richardson, but at the time, Lolo Sono was the prime suspect. He and a friend were allegedly picked up and subjected to a savage interrogation by Winnie's henchmen. Later that night, a powder-blue microbus turned up outside the Sono home. Nicodemus Sono was called outside. He saw his son sitting in the back of the vehicle, bloodied and shivering. He begged Winnie to let the boy go, but she refused. 'The movement will decide what to do with this dog,' she said as the microbus pulled away. It was the last anyone saw of Lolo Sono.

His father has been telling this story for years, and Winnie has always dismissed it as a fantasy, occasionally imputing that the boy had actually fallen afoul of the security police and been blown up along the border. The only man capable of breaking the deadlock was Mike Seakamela, who was in the blue microbus on the night of Lolo's disappearance and who provided critical corroboration of the father's evidence. Mike made a statement to the police in 1988, but they failed to act on it. He repeated his contention in 1995, but the second statement vanished, along with the original case file. He informed the Truth Commission that he was willing to testify this week, but when the day came, he failed to show. Lawyers said he'd received a visit from Winnie and gone into hiding. Winnie denied this along with everything else, and there the matter ended.

In the hearing's closing moments, Archbishop Tutu was reduced to begging for a display of remorse from the obdurate figure on the witness stand. 'You are an icon,' he told Winnie, 'a stalwart of the liberation struggle. You have no idea how your greatness will be enhanced if you said, "Sorry, things went horribly, horribly wrong." Please,' he concluded, almost sobbing. 'I beg you. I beg you. I beg you.'

Winnie shot a glance at her lawyer, who nodded. Then she turned back to Tutu, smiled condescendingly, and tossed him a crumb or two. 'It's true that things went horribly· wrong,' she said, pausing before adding a critical rider: '... when we were away. For that I am deeply sorry.' She appended a murmur of compassion for the bereaved next of kin, and that was the end of that. The hearing was over, and Winnie had somehow emerged largely unscathed. Pundits were left scratching their heads. Governor Mntonga said, told you so.

Sunday Independent, December 1997

A Truth of Sorts

Truth Commissioner Mary Burton was upset. She wiped a stray lock of hair off her forehead and said, 'The number of people who can say, "I didn't know," is too great to bear.'

It was the final hour of the TRC's hearings on the role of the media under apartheid, and Mrs Burton was nearing the end of her tether. The former Black Sash chairwoman had been sitting there for days, listening to grim testimony about the rape of truth during the apartheid era. Ex-security policeman Craig Williamson had provided an analysis of the apartheid state's propaganda master plan. Two newsroom spies had been unmasked. Colonel Vic McPherson, former head of the dreaded Stratkom mind-control machine, had talked about his network of newsroom sources and informers.

Several black editors recalled the days of segregated canteens, distorted news values and sinister injunctions from white editors to 'tone it down' or be fired. Rashid Seria told of black journalists 'shot, harassed, and tortured.' A media workers' union shop steward added sjambokkings to the list of atrocities. Don Mattera talked about 'a holocaust of truth and of black lives.' Jon Qwelane accused the mainstream press of 'having a hand, directly or indirectly, in the murder of tens of thousands of black people.' Max du Preez fleshed out the contention with a list of Vlakplaas-type stories broken by *Vrye Weekblad* but ignored by the collaborationist bosses of the commercial media, who could, he charged, have stopped the killing and torture if they'd stood up for justice.

All that remained was for a Boer to step forth, heaping the ashes of remorse on his head, lamenting his ignorance and castigating those responsible for it. 'I did not know,' said Professor Arrie de Beer of Potchefstroom University. 'I remained silent when I should have protested. I was an accessory whose inaction allowed the shadow of apartheid to spread across the nation.'

This, it seemed, was what the commissioners had been hoping to hear. 'One can only hope there are more people like you,' said TRC investigations chief Dumisa Ntsebeza, clearly taken by the spectacle of a Boer on his knees. Mrs Burton made her remark about the unbearable extent of apartheid-induced ignorance, and that was more or less that. The commissioners thanked the witnesses and retired to write their report, which will be based, one fears, on the premise that most South African journalists were tools of apartheid, witting or otherwise, and collectively complicit in the suppression of truth on a massive scale – 'denial of the human right to know,' as Jon Qwelane phrased it.

South Africa, as the cliché has it, is a land of contradictions; a place where mutually annihilating truths can be simultaneously valid. It is true, for instance, that we once had – at least on paper – one of the world's harshest regimes of press censorship, and that many people remain justifiably upset about it.

It is also true that the English press was timid and centrist, that the SABC was a state propaganda tool, and that the Afrikaans papers were so many Boer *Pravda*s, slavishly loyal to the government of the day. But whether this adds up to the crime against humanity alleged before the TRC is open to debate.

In fact, I would argue that Jon Qwelane has it upside down: far from being suppressed, the grim facts of apartheid were exaggerated by decades of ceaseless anti-Pretoria propaganda. Indeed, bad press was the primary cause of the National Party's downfall, at least insofar as it triggered a wave of revulsion in the West which in turn led to sanctions and a massive inflow of apartheid-fighting dollars to bankroll the trade unions, churches and NGOs who ultimately brought the tyrants to their knees.

Much of the credit goes to the foreign press, of course, but the staid old aunties of Argus and SAAN did their bit, too, patiently chipping away at the story for decades. The precise details might have remained obscure, but readers of *The Star* and its sister papers were left in little doubt that the police were vicious, the cabinet full of brutes and liars, and dark deeds afoot in secret police cells. In South Africa, the vio-

lence of 'the system' was almost always systematic – every bullet to
be accounted for, every corpse subjected to a post-mortem, followed
by an inquest at which the police would put forth fatuous explanations that were duly ridiculed in editorials, lampooned in cartoons,
raised in parliament by Helen Suzman, picked up by the foreign press
for world-wide amplification and ultimately synthesised into novels
and plays and Hollywood epics of the *Dry White Season* variety. In
the end, there were even pop songs about apartheid on the world's hit
parades. Only the wilfully self-blinded could have failed to notice, and
they have no one but themselves to blame.

As for Colonel McPherson and his Stratkom cronies, they were anything but the diabolical propaganda masterminds of popular imaginings. On the contrary: they were losers, and pathetically incompetent
to boot. By the time their war ended, Pretoria had the most widely
vilified and discredited government on the planet. Nothing it said was
ever believed, even when it was telling the truth. Afrikaners had sunk
so low in the world's estimation that even respectable organs like
Newsweek had taken to opining that Beyers Naudé was the only Boer
worth saving. The rest of us were racists, fascists, genocidal maniacs.
Comparisons between Nazi Germany and apartheid were taken seriously everywhere.

And still are, for that matter. Consider the results of a small and
entirely unscientific poll conducted among my friends and acquaint-
ances, to each of whom the following question was put: how many
political detainees died in the dungeons of the secret police during
four decades of apartheid terror? 'Around four hundred,' said Steve
Sidley, a Johannesburg computer analyst. 'One thousand,' said journalist Philippa Garson. 'Fifteen thousand?' guessed Morgan Entrekin,
a New York publisher. 'Oh, about four hundred thousand,' said Susan
Minot, an American novelist en route to Lesotho.

The correct figure, according to Archbishop Tutu's Truth Commission,
is 72 – an average of just under two a year between 1948 and 1990.
That's 72 too many, and a brutal way to make a point, but still, the
question stands: from whence come such skewed apprehensions? From
the media, of course, a fact at serious and indeed mind-bending odds
with heated charges of truth suppression made before the TRC.

How does one reconcile these contradictions? Perhaps the easiest
way is to acknowledge that the flow of news about apartheid was

controlled by two forms of censorship. One was imposed by Pretoria in a hamfisted attempt to shield its misdeeds from public view. The other was an invisible force that acted on the hearts and minds of apartheid's journalistic enemies. Looking back, it's sometimes hard to say which was the more powerful of the two.

In 1989, an academic quarterly commissioned me to do a study of the US media's coverage of South Africa, and lest it seems that what I am about to say applies only to gormless Yankees, please bear in mind that the Americans' local operation had a rather South African complexion when you looked at it closely. The mighty TV networks hired scores of South African researchers, fixers and cameramen. Allister Sparks (now head of SABC TV news) was writing for the *Washington Post*. The *New York Times* correspondent was John Battersby, now editor of the *Sunday Independent*. Philip van Niekerk, now editor of the *Weekly Mail & Guardian*, was working for the *Baltimore Sun*. Apartheid was an extremely hot story at the time, with the bitingly articulate and enormously telegenic Winnie Mandela always at centre stage.

The American media's love-affair with Winnie began in earnest towards the end of 1985, when she moved back to Soweto in defiance of her banning order. In the ensuing year, she made 70 appearances on network television and merited 22 stories in the hugely influential *New York Times*, more than most heads of state. Scores of flattering magazine profiles were written, and HBO produced a teleplay. She was nominated for a Nobel Peace Prize and showered with honorary degrees. She was one of the most famous women in the world, the brave and selfless Mother of the Nation.

She was also in deepening trouble in Soweto, where her thuggish palace guards were committing atrocities the foreign press dared not touch, even when Winnie's henchmen started appearing in court on sensational criminal charges. Circa 1986, they were accused of hunting down and executing two Soweto men who'd defeated them in a shebeen fistfight. No stories. A few months later, they were accused of etching struggle slogans into the flesh of suspected informers during a torture session at the Mandela home. Again, no stories in any of America's papers of record. On 28 July 1988, they dragged a schoolgirl off the street and raped her, providing journalists with a very big story indeed: a mob burned Winnie's house down in retaliation.

A funny thing happened, though: no one reported it that way. Local papers noted the event, but their stories were extraordinarily elliptical – the consequence, Jon Qwelane once told me, of terror: *The Star*'s bosses feared for their delivery fleet, and black reporters feared the necklace. The *Washington Post* attributed the attack to faceless 'vandals,' while CBS spoke of an amorphous 'black gang.' Nobody mentioned rape and retaliation. As for NBC, it sidestepped the truth entirely and presented the incident as yet another apartheid atrocity in a report so detailed that it took up more than half the prime-time newscast. Trevor Tutu made much of the fire brigade's tardy arrival. Allan Boesak said he knew for a fact that 'the system' was to blame. In the end, NBC's man on the spot knelt solemnly at Winnie's feet and invited her to comment on her suffering at the hands of Boer racists.

And this, I'm afraid, was par for the course for the American media. In fact, it was par for almost everyone else, too; Winnie enjoyed almost total immunity from criticism until the Stompie scandal. The Afrikaans press wasn't interested. The SABC was asleep on its feet. The English press looked the other way, and foreigners buried their heads in the sand lest they damage a myth of their own creation. Only two reporters broke the taboo, and the consequences were unsettling. Peter Godwin of the London *Sunday Times* received death threats after reporting that Winnie was becoming an embarrassment. Nomavenda Mathiane, who provided *Frontline* with an eyewitness account of a kangaroo court at which Winnie presided, wound up trapped in a Braamfontein bank while Mrs Mandela's bodyguards bayed for her blood on the pavement outside.

It seems odd that we didn't hear a bit more of this at the TRC's hearings, especially from black journalists like Jon Qwelane, Aggrey Klaaste and Thami Mazwai, who cut their teeth in the struggle years and are now editors and media moguls in their own right. Almost to a man, they were once supporters of the Black Consciousness movement or the PAC, and they all paid a price for it in 1986, when the ANC's young lions set out to obliterate Azapo's township structures. Around 70 people died in that war, the precise nature of which black reporters were too scared to explain for fear of incurring the murderous wrath of 'a certain movement,' a phrase which became an accepted usage in the *Sowetan* for a while. Azapo members would die at the hands of 'supporters of a certain movement.' Azapo leaders would beg 'a certain movement' to control its unruly youth. American newspaper readers were spared such painful circumlocutions, because American newspapers didn't cover the ANC–Azapo feud at all.

Asked about such lapses, American hacks made lame excuses about 'confusion' and the 'complexity' of South African politics, but the truth is simpler: they didn't want to spoil the plot. Apartheid South Africa was supposed to be the one place on the planet where everything was simple, the one hard rock in a global swamp of relativistic equivocation. There were no Communists in the American portrayal, no revolutionaries who believed it was acceptable to break eggs in order to achieve the desired Sovietist omelette. The ANC was almost always portrayed as an army of hymn-singing moderates in the sentimental American Civil Rights tradition. Anyone who disagreed too strongly was racist or reactionary, if not an apartheid spy. Under the circumstances, the stories most likely to be ignored or suppressed were those that reflected poorly on the forces of liberation.

Consider the case of five ragged young ANC deserters who showed up in Kenya in May 1990, having walked hundreds of miles in search of food, shelter and a sympathetic ear for a story no one wanted to hear. They were about to be thrown out of Nairobi's press centre when Julian Ozanne, a young freelancer who grew up in Lesotho, recognised their accents and invited them to come home with him. Forty-eight hours later, Ozanne filed a story so explosive that the London-based *Sunday Correspondent* declined to run it before checking with their man in South Africa – Shaun Johnson, now editorial director of Independent Newspapers.

Back came a 17-point memo tearing the article to shreds. The tone of Johnson's missive, says Ozanne, was one of amused contempt: 'Your stringer in Nairobi is clearly a naive young chap who has no understanding of South Africa,' and so on. 'His argument was, "I'm an expert on the ANC. I know these guys. The allegations in this story are rubbish."' The *Sunday Correspondent* went back to Ozanne, who filed 35 pages of supporting material. The issue hung in the balance for days before the paper decided to override Johnson's objections and run the story. 'Shaun was furious,' says Ozanne. 'He said, "We're going to be laughed out of South Africa for this. I'm not going to be your correspondent any more."'

And the nature of the story Johnson didn't want printed? It was the first account of life inside ANC detention camps, where guerrillas who'd fallen afoul of the movement's arbitrary and paranoic security system were locked up in coffin-like cages, sjambokked and tortured. The revelations were a mortification for Nelson Mandela, who was about to embark on his first post-release tour of Europe, and also, presumably, for Johnson himself, because his faith in the anti-apartheid movement was palpably sincere and deep-seated.

And this did not necessarily mark him a maverick in the English newspaper culture of the time. On the contrary, his faith was shared by many of his colleagues and even his bosses, who rewarded his generally pro-ANC stance with plenty of space and rapid promotions, which would tend to prove a second point: claims of martyrdom to the contrary, condemning apartheid was a smart option for South African hacks. If you were good at it, you were promoted and praised. If you were particularly good, you might get elevated to the ranks of international TV network fixer or foreign correspondent, in which case the rewards were intoxicating. The downside risk was so small as to be barely measurable – unless, of course, you were working for one of the alternative newspapers, in which case the security police were liable to make your life uncomfortable, or for the underground, in which case you might land up in real trouble.

How many of us were playing that game? It's impossible to say, but one couldn't help wondering as former *Star* reporter Craig Kotze struggled to explain his motives for joining the security police as an undercover agent. 'Everybody was forced to choose sides,' he said, and having had his fill of 'arbitrary revolutionary violence,' Kotze chose the side of the police, the government, and law and order. His link with the state was supposed to be secret, but Kotze wore his heart on his sleeve, and the truth was widely suspected. As a result, Kotze claims he was subjected to 'high levels of psychological intimidation' and occasional anonymous death threats.

His TRC audience rolled its eyes and tittered, but this had the ring of truth to me. South African journalism became a bitterly contested site of struggle in the eighties. I had perhaps a dozen close friends in the profession, about half of whom were common or garden liberals. Another quarter were comrade volunteers, in the sense that they believed in using the pen as a weapon against apartheid and occasionally hid guns or political fugitives in their houses. The last three used journalism as a cover for spying. One worked for the Stasi, the notorious East German secret police. Another ran a small press agency in a neighbouring state while smuggling arms on the side. Howard Barrell (whose name I use because he has already come clean) joined the ANC underground in the early eighties and used his position as a reporter to further the movement's propaganda objectives.

If I knew three, how many reporters were secretly working for the ANC and its allies? Certainly more than Stratkom, which had only two fulltime agents in place in the late eighties, according to TRC testimony. And did ANC agents serve the truth any more than Craig Kotze did? Only if you accept that all propaganda is truth told from a certain point of view, with embarrassing contradictions excised.

Mary Burton believes there was too little truth in our coverage of apartheid. I believe there was too little in our coverage of those fighting to bring it down. The truth probably lies somewhere between.

Frontiers of Freedom, vol 15, 1998

Postscript: An explanatory note seems called for here. In the time of the Truth Commission, every newspaper I read left me feeling as if someone was prodding at my anus with a broomstick with a view to punishing me for being white and male. The only way to escape such indignities was to join the fawning ingrates who pretended that imperialism, colonialism and apartheid were someone else's doing, but I was incapable. I thought my ancestors had done some stupid and vicious things since landing here in 1688. I even accepted the fashionable doctrine of collective guilt, but I wanted the charges formulated with some degree of precision, and I wanted the chance to defend myself. Maybe I was wrong, but it seemed to me that whites who didn't take this line were forfeiting any claim to honour, and worse yet, putting themselves in a position from which they'd never recover politically. So I waged war on the Commission, a campaign that made my name *gat* in many places, among them a village called Boipatong.

A Question of Spin

||||||||||||||||||||||||||||||||||||||||||||||||||||||||||||||||||||||||||||||||||||||||||||||||||||||||||||||||||||||||||||||

This is a story about the Truth Commission, but it properly begins in August 1992, when I authored a shallow and facetious article in *Esquire* magazine about the infamous Boipatong massacre. Anyone who lived through Boipatong and its aftermath will recall that it seemed a watershed; an event of Sharpeville dimensions. Nelson Mandela said, 'South Africa will never be the same again,' and I believed him. It thus seemed terribly important to establish what had really happened in that tiny Vaal Triangle township in 45 fateful minutes on the night of 17 June. I set forth to find out but failed, and then resorted to the classic expedient of the slack reporter: the story of how I tried to get the story. I cracked dumb jokes, remarked on the stupidity of the old SAP and mocked the ANC's conspiracy charges, which 'collapsed under the weight of their own grandeur.' But I never found out what really happened, and never forgave myself.

And so I acquired the habit of clipping newspapers and collecting reports in the hope that the truth might one day emerge. Seven years passed. Four public inquiries were held. I wound up with a crate of documents that travelled with me from city to city. Friends left the room when I began talking about its contents, which were arcane beyond comprehension, boring and irrelevant. By October 1998, I seemed to be the only person left who was interested, judging by the indifference that greeted the Truth Commission's Boipatong finding. Not one newspaper bothered to report it, possibly because it was obvious to everyone save me. Only when someone lent me the TRC report on CD-ROM did I find my way to Volume 3, Chapter Six, where I came upon something strange and disturbing.

This is the story of that disturbing something. It will take many thousands of words to explain it, and you will almost certainly suffer boredom en route. All I can promise is that by the end, you will be better positioned to assess the gravity of a Truth Commission finding that will be with us, as Desmond Tutu says, 'for generations.'

Why should we care?

Most accounts of South Africa's perilous transition hold that the Boipatong massacre caused a breakdown of the Codesa negotiations and almost plunged South Africa into race war. This is untrue. The talks actually died a month earlier, on 15 May 1992, as a result of a deadlock engineered by the ANC's chief negotiator, Cyril Ramaphosa. Several insider accounts published after the event confirm that Ramaphosa had lost patience with government demands for a minority veto and believed he could get a better deal if the ANC returned to 'mass action' – strikes, factory occupations and millions of protestors on the streets. Ronnie Kasrils called it 'the Leipzig option,' in honour of the relentless demonstrations that had toppled East Germany's Communist regime three years earlier. Thabo Mbeki felt that Ramaphosa was playing 'an intensely dangerous game,' but his objections were overruled; on 15 May, Ramaphosa presented De Klerk's team with an ultimatum he knew would be refused, and the peace talks deadlocked.

In the weeks that followed, the ANC started a campaign of rhetorical warfare that seemed aimed at stirring militancy. Residents of Boipatong, for instance, woke one morning to find MK commander Sam Ntsepe on the front page of their local newspaper, vowing to 'arm thousands' and turn the area into a 'liberated zone.' A few weeks later, Communist Party boss Chris Hani informed comrades in nearby Sebokeng that they were 'facing a war situation.' On the other side of the ideological divide, Inkatha politicians were also rattling their sabres, warning the ANC and the National Party that they would resist attempts to drive Zulu nationalists out of the Johannesburg area. The political temperature rose markedly. Stomachs began to knot everywhere.

The ANC's campaign of rolling mass action began on Soweto Day, 16 June. The results were not particularly encouraging. A mere 10 000 comrades turned out to see Nelson Mandela open the Hector Pieterson memorial in Soweto. (Some news reports put the figure as low as two.) In Cape Town, barely 5 000 showed up for the kick-off rally. This fell painfully short of the massive Leipzig-style demonstrations envisioned by Kasrils and his fellow insurrectionists. A spark was clearly necessary to rekindle flagging anti-apartheid passions.

And lo, such came. At 10 pm on the night of 17 June, a mass of armed men fell on the ANC stronghold of Boipatong and its satellite squatter camp, Slovo Park, and perpetrated a ghastly slaughter. Women were raped, babies shot and panga'd, countless houses ransacked and 45 people murdered. Scores more were injured, causing the death toll to rise ultimately to 49.

At first glance, the killings appeared to be a clash between the militant Zulu Inkatha movement and supporters of the ANC. As such, they were of little use to ANC spin doctors. If whites and the police were implicated, on the other hand, they had something to work with. ANC leaders therefore insisted that Boipatong was no ordinary outbreak of 'black on black' violence, preferring to depict it as a 'carefully planned and executed strategic operation,' with white police and soldiers providing logistic support to the Zulu attackers and mysterious white civilians taking part in the killing. In other words, a Third Force operation, organised by FW de Klerk and his apartheid state.

Before Boipatong, De Klerk was riding high, buoyed up by his referendum victory and his rising status in the eyes of foreigners who had come to regard him as something of a statesman. After Boipatong, he was just another racist, vilified in ANC propaganda as a 'Nazi' presiding over a security force of 'beasts.' Ignoring the fact that Codesa had already been forced into stalemate by his own negotiators, Nelson Mandela announced that he was pulling out of peace talks on the grounds that he could no longer justify 'talking to a regime that is killing blacks.' Sam Ramsamy vowed to force the cancellation of a forthcoming tour by New Zealand's rugby team. Archbishop Tutu threatened to sabotage South Africa's planned readmission to the Olympic Games.

In Europe and the US, reliable old warhorses of the anti-apartheid movement lumbered back onto the battlefield, citing Boipatong as proof of De Klerk's malign intentions and demanding a return to embargoes, sanctions and international isolation. Coretta Scott King voiced 'outrage.' Archbishop Huddleston said, 'We in the West have forgotten how to hate.' There was a huge outcry at the OAU and the UN, which devoted a special sitting to Boipatong. On the ground, violence intensified, building to a crescendo with the Bisho massacre.

By September, De Klerk and his negotiators were so exhausted that they just caved in, making extraordinary concessions to get the peace talks going again. Thousands of ANC 'prisoners of war' – including armed robbers, necklacers and kindred figures of the struggle's murky fringes – were set free. Inkatha was ditched to fend for itself. All hope of federalism was abandoned. The ANC began to dictate the pace of change, and wound up a year later with a constitution so weak in terms of minority protections that the comrades (in US author Patti Waldmeier's account) walked away laughing, claiming that the Boers had given the farm away.

It could thus be argued, for better or worse, that Boipatong determined the shape of the society we live in today. That's why we should care. In particular, we should care about the TRC's finding that De Klerk's police and soldiers were involved in the planning and execution of a murderous rampage designed to block progress toward democracy. We will now consider the case for and against.

A grand conspiracy arises

The first reporters to arrive on the scene on the morning after the massacre were confronted by an extraordinary sight – the KwaMadala impi advancing on Boipatong in full view of hundreds of witnesses, and nought to stop them but a thin blue line of nervous policemen. Comrades in the township had regrouped during the night and were threatening to launch a retaliatory strike. The Inkatha impi sallied forth to meet them, armed to the teeth with sticks and spears and drenched with battle medicine, apparently determined to fight a second round in broad daylight, in front of the world's TV cameras. These men were part of a deep, dark Third Force conspiracy? At first glance, it seemed wildly unlikely, but the ANC's propagandists rose to the challenge.

The first claims of white involvement were made around 11 am that day, in the form of a statement released to SAPA by ANC spokesman Ronnie Mamoepa. At the time, nobody had a clear idea of what had happened in Boipatong the previous night. Mamoepa was so ignorant of the facts that he put the death toll at five, but no matter, it was time to join battle. 'The attackers were brought into the township in police Casspirs,' Mamoepa stated. 'There is evidence that police also assisted in the attack.' The police, he continued, had ignored warnings that Boipatong was about to be ransacked. Indeed, they had helped the impi by blasting ANC self-defence units off the streets with 'teargas and live ammunition' before the attack commenced.

'Shortly thereafter,' Mamoepa said, 'police were seen escorting groups of armed men from KwaMadala hostel into the township. Later, they were seen offloading armed men at various points. The armed men attacked the township with an assortment of weapons, including firearms. In those homes where the attackers could not gain entry, police used Casspirs to break down walls and enable the attackers to assault residents and to loot their furniture and other valuables.' In some cases, he concluded, 'the attackers were seen loading their loot onto police vehicles,' or vehicles belonging to the army's Vaal Command.

In the next 24 hours, this theme was embellished and hugely amplified by the press, aided by violence monitors from such ANC-aligned struggle lobbies as the Human Rights Committee and Peace Action. Peace activists took reporters and diplomats around Boipatong and introduced them to eyewitnesses who backed the ANC's claims. Trusted journalists were granted special access to 'hundreds' of witness statements said to contain damning evidence about the manner in which the Zulu attackers were ferried into battle by police armoured vehicles, their ranks swollen by white men in camouflage uniform, in blackface, in white jackets and white gloves, even a white man armed with a spear. By week's end, Boipatong was as famous in its way as Buchenwald or Mai Lai, and observers had little reason to doubt that the security forces had finally been caught red-handed. 'I hold De Klerk personally responsible,' said Cyril Ramaphosa. The entire planet seemed to add, Amen.

The grand conspiracy shows cracks

Let us step now into the mind of President FW de Klerk, who woke up on the morning of 18 June to find himself stigmatised by the ANC as the 'satanic' butcher of Boipatong. Powerless to halt the propaganda juggernaut, he did the next best thing – picked up the telephone and bawled at his subordinates. As soon as the news broke, awed Vaal Triangle detectives began to receive calls from the presidency. Two days later, De Klerk stormed into their offices in person. 'He wanted results,' said an officer who was present. 'He wanted action.' The SAP responded by drafting 200 detectives into the investigation, which proceeded in the traditional manner: suspects were rounded up and subjected to the grimmest conceivable third degree.

Even so, the investigation was a herculean undertaking, with 500 potential suspects and no witnesses, given that Boipatong became a no-go area for police after the massacre. It would be weeks before the first charges were laid, and meanwhile, De Klerk was still twisting in the wind. Desperate to defend himself, he asked Judge Richard Goldstone to draw international figures into his investigation of the killings. Mr P Bhagwati, former Chief Justice of India, agreed to act as an observer. The British government dispatched a team of detectives led by Dr PA Waddington, an eminent criminologist.

Commissioned in crisis and concluded in haste, the Waddington Report was cursory, but nevertheless illuminating. Waddington established that the police were indeed in Boipatong during the massacre. In fact, there was a police station in the heart of the township, staffed by lowly black constables who did nothing to stop the massacre. The same was true of the handful of white soldiers and policemen who congregated at a petrol station across the road while the killings were underway. On their face, these actions seemed shameful. On the other hand, these were ordinary security force members, on foot or in soft-skinned vehicles. As they later told it, these men believed it would be dangerous or suicidal to enter the battle zone in unarmoured vehicles, and besides, their cars and vans wouldn't have made it anyway, because the streets of Boipatong had been trenched and barricaded by comrades. So they just lurked on the outskirts, raising the alarm on their radios.

The first armoured vehicles arrived circa 10.20 in the form of two Buffels from a nearby SADF base. The retreating impi was dimly visible in the dark veld, blowing whistles and firing the occasional shot in the army's direction. A few minutes later, it surged across Frikkie Meyer Boulevard, passing within 50 metres of one of the SADF vehicles. Soldiers could have machine-gunned them at this point, presumably, but no one knew exactly who they were or what they'd just done. So the army simply followed them back to KwaMadala hostel and parked outside to await further orders.

Waddington's assessment of all this was scathing. The police response, he said, was 'woefully inadequate,' poorly coordinated and badly planned, indicative of a disturbing indifference to black lives. On the other hand, he concluded that there was no reliable evidence of police complicity. In fact, he found that several of the ANC's propaganda charges were baseless. Boipatong's high-mast lighting had not been switched off, as alleged, and charges regarding ignored warnings were far-fetched. True, Methodist activist Paul Verryn issued a vague warning to the effect that 'something was going to happen,' but the given location was Sebokeng, 10 km away.

A few weeks later – on 6 August 1992 – the Goldstone Commission began its own Boipatong hearings. The results were a further setback for conspiracy theorists. Sensational allegations of houses rammed by rampaging APCs were reduced to a single garden wall, accidentally knocked down by a reversing Casspir. A critical ANC witness, special constable Ntsietsi Xhaba, who made world headlines in the days after the massacre with a detailed and apparently damning account of gunmen climbing in and out of armoured police vehicles, was taken back to Boipatong on a nocturnal inspection-in-loco. The outcome was embarrassing, with even ANC lawyers conceding that Xhaba could not possibly have seen what he claimed to have seen. In November, Judge Goldstone made some sceptical comments about the veracity of the ANC's allegations, and bowed out in favour of the forthcoming trial.

By now, some 300 KwaMadala residents had been arrested. According to a source involved in the investigation, scores of confessions were obtained by methods that included electric shock and live burials 'in the veld near Parys.' A few years earlier, this would have presented few problems, but the political climate was rapidly changing and prosecutors felt that confessions extracted by torture or the threat of torture were vulnerable to challenge. They thus chose to build their case on the testimony of four accomplices – hostel-dwellers who had taken part in the rampage, but turned state's evidence in return for immunity. On the basis of their testimony, murder charges were brought against 74 KwaMadala inmates, who went on trial before Justice JMC Smit in May 1993.

Staged in Delmas, the trial was a marathon affair that lasted more than a year and produced a record running to 3 879 pages. The state maintained that the killers had acted alone, while the Inkatha defence took a line that surely amused the gods of irony: 'twas not my clients whodunnit, said Advocate Vic Botha, citing the propaganda claims of his client's ANC enemies. It was the police, the army and mysterious Third Force elements.

Given Botha's stance, the court was obliged to devote months to a forensic examination of alleged security force involvement. Indeed, the entire trial came to turn on this issue, with the judge ultimately concluding that the ANC-aligned witnesses were lying. To understand how this happened, two critical factors must be kept in mind. First, the massacre took place in a concentrated time span – around 45 minutes, rather than the five hours initially postulated by the ANC. And secondly, it took place in a tiny township, barely 800 metres from end to end.

At the start of their case, prosecutors set up a giant map and traced the route followed by the attackers. Almost every house along this via dolorosa had its windows shattered. Those that lacked sturdy defences were invaded and ransacked, their inhabitants shot, hacked or speared. Every survivor had a story to tell, and the state called 120 of them. 'Not one,' said Justice Smit, 'witnessed (police) support for the attackers. I cannot believe, if there was such support, that this mass of witnesses would not be aware of it.' As for the handful of dissenters called by the defence, they were invariably bracketed by neighbours who failed to back their stories.

Consider, for instance, the testimony of Abednego Mabuza, whose Goldstone appearance caused a sensation. He was drinking with a friend on the night of the massacre. Just after ten, he left his house to walk the friend home. Outside, they found a small boy named Sibusiso, running from some unspeakable terror. Mabuza took the child by the hand and led him towards his granny's house, which lay diagonally over the road. He heard a noise, saw men approaching, wearing headbands and waving sticks and spears. He ducked into Sibusiso's grandmother's garden and watched in disbelief as a Casspir glided by at walking pace, escorting a host of Zulu warriors who were attacking innocents as they passed down the street.

It was a compelling story, but it failed to survive closer scrutiny. Under cross-examination, Mabuza acknowledged that if his version was correct, 'everyone on Hlubi Street would have seen or heard the Casspir.' But the lost boy's grandmother, Mrs Msibi, looked outside as her windows shattered, and saw only Zulus. The same was true of Mr Siyane, who lived a few doors down, and Mrs Manyika across the way. In all, eight witnesses from that block told the same story. The only person who supported Mabuza's version was Mr Hlubi at number 745, but he was flatly contradicted by his neighbour, Mr Ramothladi, who neither saw nor heard anything of the sort. On the balance of probabilities, the judge concluded that Mabuza was mistaken or lying.

Why would he do such a thing? At the outset, Mabuza described himself as an ANC member. When his partisanship came under scrutiny, he retracted the statement, insisting he was neutral. He was, however, unable to explain a second set of claims clearly intended to cast the police in the worst possible light. The first police to arrive on the scene, he charged, just took some pictures and drove away, leaving the injured to bleed to death. This contention was obliterated by fellow residents who testified that police summoned ambulances immediately, and that most of the injured had been removed by the time a forensic investigator began photographing bloody crime scenes.

Finally, the court demanded an explanation for Mabuza's behaviour at 10.25 pm, when a Casspir piloted by a certain Sergeant Schlebush rolled into Boipatong to investigate reports of shooting in progress. A man ran into his path, waving his arms and shouting for help. The man was Abednego Mabuza. He leapt into the armoured vehicle and guided Schlebush to houses where people had been killed or wounded. The court wanted to know why he did such a thing if he believed the police were killing people. Confronted with this contradiction, Mabuza lapsed into sullen silence and refused to say anything at all.

In the end, Judge Smit found 17 of the accused guilty as charged, but dismissed allegations of direct police involvement as baseless. The left will say that Smit is an old-regime conservative, and that the case before him was prepared by a force with a long history of cover-up and chicanery. This may be true, but it is not entirely relevant. In believing Smit, you were not necessarily believing the police. You were believing the people of Boipatong. Witnesses like Elias Nyokong, a comrade who shadowed the invaders as they butchered their way across the township and swore that there were no whites or police vehicles among them, or ANC-aligned civic leader Ismael Mahasela, who acknowledged that even he had been unable to find anyone who had actually *seen* police among the attackers. These accounts were entirely congruent with the stories told by the accomplices, and in the end, they carried the day.

Did the ANC manipulate the evidence?

This was certainly Judge Smit's conclusion. Here's how he backed it up.

In the hours after the massacre, comrades and street committee members went around Boipatong instructing residents not to speak to police or outsiders. If they wished to make a statement, they were to report to the school, where they could make a statement to 'the ANC.' At the school, they met white people who were attached to the Human Rights Commission or Peace Action, violence monitoring groups with strong pro-ANC sympathies. Statements taken under these circumstances were gathered at the law firm of Nicholls, Cambanis and Sudano, whose clients included Peace Action and the ANC. They were made available to trusted left-wing reporters but withheld from police, who were then accused of failing to investigate the incendiary charges they contained. Police attempts to hold an identity parade had to be abandoned because victims were scared they'd be punished for cooperating with the state.

In the end, the police made a case against the Boipatong killers by other means. Some Boipatong residents had no idea that they'd succeeded in this until they heard media reports about the trial, whereupon a group of them showed up in Judge Smit's courtroom, demanding that their stories be heard. When Smit asked why they had not come forward earlier, they said 'the ANC' had told them not to. Indeed, Mrs Alice Nonjoli told the court she knew of someone who had been murdered for disobeying this edict. Eyebrows were raised, but the trial proceeded.

Eight months later, the defence began to present its case, which was based, as noted, on the notion that white security forces and Third Force elements were to blame. To prove his case, Adv Botha subpoenaed eleven ANC-aligned witnesses who had previously offered first-hand accounts of police complicity to the Goldstone Commission or the anti-apartheid press. These witnesses were horrified to discover, upon arrival, that they had been called to testify on behalf of the Inkatha accused. When Judge Smit asked why, they said, 'We're only allowed to talk to the ANC.' And when Smit asked what exactly they meant by 'the ANC,' many spoke of a white woman they knew only as Caroline – properly, Caroline Nicholls, of the law firm Nicholls, Cambanis and Sudano.

A former student activist and married to Delmas Treason Trialist GM Malindi, Nicholls had been campaigning since the early nineties to have KwaMadala Hostel shut down and razed. In fairness, many of the points she raised were valid. The hostel had indeed become an Inkatha military barracks from which attacks were launched on surrounding communities. It had also become an operating base for criminals who liked the fact that it was a no-go zone for police and ANC-aligned vigilantes.

On the other hand, Nicholls' representations entirely ignored the fact that KwaMadala Hostel was at the vortex of a conflict in which her ANC-aligned clients were anything but innocent victims. Almost everyone inside the fortified hostel had an atrocity story to tell, usually about being singled out for attack on account of suspected Inkatha sympathies. Some were Zulu migrant workers, driven out of a hostel in Sebokeng during a bloody ANC putsch two years earlier. Others were apoliticial township people whose adherence to Zulu custom brought lynch mobs to their doors. These refugees had reason to hate the ANC and seek vengeance. It wasn't just that they'd lost their homes and in many cases, loved ones. Conditions in KwaMadala were unbearable. They couldn't buy food because it was too dangerous to venture outside. Their wounds went untreated, because the nearest hospital lay in an ANC-controlled area. Even going to work was dangerous. In the week prior to the 17 June killings, three stray Zulus were allegedly picked off and murdered in the hostel's vicinity.

Be this as it may, Nicholls regarded the Zulu hostel dwellers as the fount of all evil in the area. She agitated against KwaMadala for almost two years, and when the massacre took place, she was on the scene immediately. As Abednego Mabuza told it, ANC comrades came looking for anyone who could implicate the police. When he offered his services, he was taken to 'Caroline,' who prepared him for his Goldstone appearance. She was similarly involved with Eugenius N Mnqithi, whose surprise appearance was the sensation of the trial.

Mnqithi was a teenager from Small Farms, near Evaton. About a week before the Boipatong massacre, a young woman was murdered on her way home from a drinking party at his parents' house. Mnqithi claimed innocence, but ANC-aligned vigilantes necklaced a friend of his, and then torched his parents' home. Young Eugenius fled for his life, ANC comrades on his trail. Like many before him, he knocked on the gates at KwaMadala, begging for protection. He was admitted after undertaking to join the war on Inkatha's side. A few nights later, a siren sounded, and all males were summoned to the hostel stadium. The Zulus were on the warpath, and Mnqithi was dragooned into participating in the 17 June attack.

The following morning, young Eugenius awoke to find KwaMadala surrounded by hundreds of policemen and soldiers, and realised he'd leapt from the frying pan into the fire. He escaped and returned to Evaton, where his reappearance aroused furious suspicions. Saved from the necklace by a street committee, he was handed over to intelligence operatives from the ANC's Shell House headquarters. They arranged a safe place for him to stay and introduced him to 'Caroline,' who debriefed him. His eye-witness account was considered so important that 'Mr Chaskalson' – presumably Arthur Chaskalson, the famed struggle lawyer and now chairman of the Constitutional Court – was called in to hear it too. Mnqithi swore that he signed a statement, but this document was never seen again.

Why did the ANC fail to disclose Mnqithi's evidence at the Goldstone Commission? A possible reason emerged two years later, when state advocates got wind of the fact that the ANC was in touch with a key witness. A messy subpoena battle loomed, but on the appointed day, Mnqithi showed up in court, flanked by Caroline Nicholls and an operative from ANC headquarters. At the time, the prosecution's key witnesses – the accomplices – were being battered by insinuations that police had bribed or tortured them into lying. Prosecutors needed independent corroboration of their evidence, and they suspected Mnqithi could provide it.

And so, on 11 August 1993, the ANC's inside source took the stand and identified the perpetrators of the Boipatong massacre: the Inkatha warriors in the dock. That is the man whose Zulu poems whipped the amaButho into battle frenzy, he said. That is the man who administered battle medicine, and that is the induna who distributed AK-47s. Mnqithi insisted that no whites were involved, and that no police were present. He said the only armoured vehicle he saw that night was the SADF Buffel that showed up as the impi was withdrawing toward the hostel, blood-spattered and laden with loot – in Mnqithi's case, a beer-crate full of LP records. His story meshed with a huge mass of corroborating evidence, and the grand conspiracy appeared to have been reduced to ashes.

Smit concluded that the ANC had withheld Mnqithi from the Goldstone Commission 'because he didn't support their case.' In his judgement, he expressed 'shock' at the manner in which 'certain people and organizations' had interfered in the Boipatong investigation. The ANC issued no rebuttal, and the Boipatong drama appeared to have ended – at least with regard to charges of overt police and white complicity.

Which is not to say that a deeper conspiratorial nexus had been ruled out entirely. It had always seemed possible or even likely that shadowy figures from apartheid's security services had secret links with Inkatha fighters. In 1995, the *Weekly Mail* published an article alleging that the massacre had been carried out by black ex-Koevoet operatives now living in an East Rand barracks and guarding Eskom power lines. A frisson of excitement swept the left, but the story fizzled. A year later, *The Observer* of London claimed that Colonel Eugene de Kock's murderous Vlakplaas unit was responsible for the 17 June killings. 'Police set up the Boipatong massacre that nearly derailed South Africa's peace talks,' said the headline. Philip van Niekerk's report went on to claim that the massacre had been 'planned and executed' by De Kock and his 'paid Inkatha collaborators.'

With time, however, this theory also disintegrated. Found guilty of running a 'horrible network' of murderers and dirty tricksters and sentenced to life in prison, Colonel de Kock turned against his former political masters and spilled the beans about all manner of apartheid crimes. But Boipatong was not one of them. 'I was convinced that South Africa was on the verge of civil war,' he told his biographer, Jeremy Gordin. Realising that whites were 'too spoiled to fight for their existence,' he decided to break with De Klerk's pro-peace faction and make common cause with Inkatha. Toward this end, he joined the Zulu movement and provided weapons. He could not discount the possibility that some of his guns may have wound up in KwaMadala Hostel, but as for planning and executing the atrocity with 'paid Inkatha collaborators,' it was nonsense.

And so, by the end of 1997, the Boipatong controversy seemed to be fading into history. The last piece of the puzzle seemed to fall into place when the 17 convicted killers applied to the Truth Commission for amnesty. Among them were Qambeleni Buthelezi, the hostel's chief induna, Bhekinkosi Mkize, the military leader, and Victor Mthembu, deputy leader of the hostel's IFP youth brigade. They portrayed themselves as foot soldiers in a war not of their own choosing, and expressed regret about the death of innocents. Some implicated IFP leaders, some didn't, but on one score they were unanimous: the fleets of Casspirs and hosts of white gunmen who appeared on the world's front pages in June 1992 were a figment of someone's imagination.

Enter the Truth Commission

Let us now turn to Volume Three of the Final Report of the Truth and Reconciliation Commission, where the august body lays out its findings with regard to the Boipatong killings. 'The Commission finds that kwaMadala hostel residents, together with the police, planned and carried out [the attack]. The Commission finds that the police colluded with the attackers and dropped them off at Slovo Park. The commission finds that white men with blackened faces participated ...' And so on, and so on. The grand conspiracy of June 1992 had been resurrected in its most hallucinatory form. As far as I could tell, the Commission hadn't even bothered to read the trial record or the Goldstone papers, let alone refute their contents.

Consider, for instance, the matter of police radio tapes, which the TRC baldly states were 'erased' as part of a cover-up. There was global pandemonium when these charges were first brought up before Judge Goldstone. Pandemonium redoubled when a report drafted by British intelligence confirmed that the tapes had been 'hurriedly erased' with 'masking sound.' There were hundreds of pages of testimony on this issue, and the final outcome was humiliation for both conspiracy theorists and UK spymasters.

Sceptics are invited to consult the record for themselves, but briefly, this is what it states: two months before the massacre, a machine designed to record radio traffic was installed at a riot police base in Vereeniging. It looked like an ordinary double-deck cassette recorder, but it was actually a marvel of high technology and digital sequencing, designed to record on four tracks simultaneously at one-sixth speed. If the vaunted boffins of British intelligence were baffled by its workings, what hope had Constable O'Reilly of Vereeniging, who had no training and barely glanced at the manual? She proceeded as if she was taping songs off the radio, flipping the tapes whenever one side was full. As a result, most of the recordings she made were gibberish. '*Dit klink Russies*' – it sounds Russian, one witness memorably stated. It was a Van der Merwe joke, not a cover-up.

One's judgement might be tempered if TRC investigators had revisited these matters and come up with new evidence, but no investigation was done. Jan-Ake Kjellberg, a senior Swedish policeman seconded to the Truth Commission to beef up its investigative capability, had sight of the TRC's Boipatong file, and said it was empty save for some stray documents pertaining to the provenance of two AK-47s which might at some point have been in KwaMadala's armoury. Otherwise, there'd been no investigation at all. The Swede seemed as perplexed by the TRC's finding as I was. 'Based on what, I wonder?'

A phrase in the report had a familiar ring, so I delved into my files and found the source: a 26 June 1992 article in the *Weekly Mail*, authored by one of the sympathetic reporters granted access to Caroline Nicholls's witness statements in the days after the massacre. Paul Stober's report had the grace to note that claims made in those statements appeared to be contradictory, but the anonymous author of the TRC report had no such compunctions: after borrowing a phrase or two from Stober's article, he or she lifted great chunks verbatim from a post-massacre press release issued by the Human Rights Commission and Peace Action, bodies so close to the ANC that most trial witnesses couldn't distinguish between them. These ill-founded propaganda claims had been fed to the Truth Commission and adopted as legal fact.

For the KwaMadala 17, the implications were Orwellian. They were entitled to amnesty only if they told the truth, but 'the truth' had already been decided – without any investigation – by the body that held their fate in its hands: they had acted in concert with the police and mysterious white gunmen. But they swore they hadn't. At their amnesty hearing, every one of the convicted killers swore that the massacre was 'a Zulu thing,' driven by their desire to avenge themselves on their ANC-aligned tormentors. Advocate Danny Berger, appearing for the Boipatong victims, strove valiantly to break them, but three weeks into the hearings, he'd made no headway at all. To a man, the Zulus insisted there were no white police or soldiers present, and no armoured vehicles. By 9 August, Berger appeared to be on the verge of losing his case.

The following morning, however, he produced a document that purported to shed sensational new light on the killings. This, according to Berger, was an affidavit sworn in June 1996 by one Andries Matanzima Nosenga, a sad, feral creature from the Sebokeng underworld. Orphaned at an early age, Nosenga drifted into political activities in his teens. At some point in the early 1990s, he and his ANC comrades burned down a service station owned by a prominent black businessman. The businessman demanded retribution, and Nosenga found himself on the run from his own side. Like many before him, he pitched up at KwaMadala, begging for refuge. Hostel-dwellers took him for a spy, and he was beaten up and confined. A month or so later, he popped up at an Inkatha rally in Ulundi, where he was paraded on stage as an enemy who had decided to confess and recant.

Nosenga's conversion appeared to be genuine, because he was subsequently convicted and imprisoned for murdering a youth on Inkatha's behalf. After the establishment of the TRC, he filed two amnesty applications, both pertaining to the crime for which he'd been jailed. Boipatong was not mentioned.

According to Berger, however, Nosenga had filed a third affidavit that had somehow got lost inside the TRC. In this document, Nosenga confessed to a leading role in the Boipatong massacre, claiming that he'd marched into the township carrying an AK-47 and personally killed 'eight or nine people.' Moreover, he was willing to name the white policemen who had provided guns as well as four armoured vehicles to escort the Inkatha forces into battle. Here, at last, was the proof for which the anti-apartheid movement had so long yearned. The press went apeshit. Nosenga made front pages countrywide.

Others were less impressed. Amnesty judge Sandile Ngcobo was so sceptical about the last-minute introduction of 'lost' evidence that he took the unusual step of cautioning ANC lawyers to watch their ethics. I dug through the records at the prison where the mystery affidavit was allegedly taken, and Nosenga was not being held there on the given date. I also spoke to Constable Ignatius Ferreira, the detective who'd put Nosenga behind bars on a murder charge. He described

Nosenga as a weirdo who'd walked into Sebokeng police station on 14 February 1993, begging to be arrested.

As Ferreira recalls it, Nosenga presented himself as a KwaMadala resident who knew several notorious Inkatha gunslingers and was willing to spill the beans about killings they'd committed together. Ferreira put him in a car and drove him around Sebokeng, but Nosenga was so vague as to time and place that Ferreira and his colleagues concluded he was lying, if not deranged. They tried to chase Nosenga out of the police station, but he refused to leave. So they gave him another chance, showing him a file of photographs of murder victims in which he came across a face he recognised. This is Sipho, he said. This is one of the people we killed.

Sipho was an ANC comrade who met his death in a drive-by shooting. Nosenga was able to take detectives to the scene of the crime and provide an account that agreed with those of eye-witnesses. Ferreira arranged for him to make a formal confession, and Nosenga was convicted largely on the basis of his own testimony. But Ferreira had nagging doubts. Sipho and Nosenga were of a similar age, and had grown up in the same neighbourhood. Ferreira couldn't rule out the possibility that Nosenga had learned the details of Sipho's demise by other means, and confessed to a murder he hadn't committed. Why would anyone do such a thing? Ferreira said he'd heard that Nosenga was involved in a car-theft racket based in KwaMadala, and that its ringleaders suspected him of informing against them. Remaining in the hostel under such circumstances would have been extremely dangerous, and returning to Sebokeng meant almost certain death. For a man in such a position, a stint in prison might have seemed attractive.

When Nosenga took the stand to give evidence about Boipatong, it was immediately clear that something was wrong. He failed to recognise his own signature on his amnesty applications. He claimed to have relatives in Boipatong whom he'd visited on innumerable occasions, but couldn't remember their names. When the bombshell affidavit was read back to him, he repudiated part of its contents, saying it contained things he would not have said. Furthermore, he said he'd never seen it before, and had no idea where it came from. 'Lots of people came to see me in prison,' he said, mentioning the names inter alia of Caroline Nicholls and an 'ANC Peace Desk' official identified as Mongezi.

Under cross-examination, Nosenga's problems deepened. Shown an aerial map of Boipatong, he misidentified the route followed by the attackers. He said the four Casspirs that allegedly ferried the Zulu warriors into battle were parked near a main road, where scores of previous witnesses would have seen them. He said the armoured vehicles drove the combatants 100 metres before dropping them off again, an action that did not seem entirely logical. Nosenga claimed he then walked into the nearest house and started shooting with an AK-47. Asked to point out approximately where this happened, he indicated a section of Boipatong where no houses were attacked at all. Deepening his own grave, he insisted that all six houses he'd attacked were on that same street. Finally, he swore he'd shot all his victims at close range with his AK-47, but no corpses bore corresponding entry or exit wounds.

Beyond a certain point, Nosenga's demolition was almost too painful to watch. As Judge Ngcobo later put it, 'Mr Nosenga was an appalling witness, to say the least.' Ngcobo went on to list a host of contradictions and improbabilities in Nosenga's testimony, and concluded that, 'We have no hesitation in rejecting his evidence as untruthful.' On that note, the amnesty panel retired to consider its verdict.

So what really happened at Boipatong?

As we have seen, Boipatong changed the trajectory of South African history, and the Truth Commission had already published a finding: the massacre was a Third Force operation, planned and executed by De Klerk's government. To challenge that finding was to challenge a critical fragment of the ANC's political mythology, and I doubted Judge Sandile Ngcobo and his three amnesty committee colleagues were so inclined. They were clearly members of the New Order, at least broadly sympathetic towards the ANC, if not card-carrying members *per se.*

As it turned out, I was wrong. Ngcobo's verdict opened with a scrupulously even-handed description of the state of war that existed between Inkatha and the ANC in the early 1990s. Both movements had established strongholds and no-go areas where political opposition was not tolerated, he said, and both had inflicted severe casualties on the other. 'A cycle of attack and counter-attack ensued,' he continued, 'with each side avenging the killing of its members.' In this regard, he accepted the evidence of Zulu hostel-dwellers who said the massacre arose from their desire to retaliate for their sufferings at the hands of 'the ANC,' even if that entailed murdering innocent women and children. The applicants had furthermore told the truth about their crimes, he concluded, and were thus entitled to amnesty. In other words, Ngcobo found that there was simply no convincing evidence of overt white or police participation.

What then of the ANC-aligned witnesses whose claims to the contrary made Boipatong world-famous? 'It is common cause that shortly after the attack there was chaos and confusion in the township,' he said, with throngs of residents moving about the streets in search of missing relatives even as police armoured cars arrived to investigate. 'It is against this background that the evidence relating to the presence of police vehicles during the attack must be evaluated.' Ngcobo went on to analyse how easy it would have been for key witnesses to misinterpret what they saw in the aftermath.

It doesn't follow that Ngcobo exonerated apartheid's police. He found it extraordinary that an army of nearly 500 men had managed to cross a main road, ransack Boipatong and return to KwaMadala before police intervened. 'The timing of the attack and lack of detection is indeed a cause for concern,' he wrote. 'This strongly suggests that the attackers had information on the movements of police patrols. We need not speculate on how such information could have been obtained. Suffice to say that there is no credible evidence to suggest a conspiracy between the leaders of the attack and the police in this regard. All that is there is a suspicion.'

The verdict was released on 24 November 2000. After eight years, four exhaustive inquiries and stupefying legal expenses, the Boipatong affair had finally ended.

Moral of the story

This has been a cold-blooded exercise, given that most of those who died in Boipatong were defenceless non-combatants whose only crime was to live in an area perceived to be controlled by the ANC. If I have caused offence, I regret it. But the ANC's propaganda campaign was based on the equally offensive assumption that the death of 49 black people was of no consequence unless it could be shown that their blood was on white hands. ANC charges in this regard served their immediate purpose, inspiring a global firestorm of outrage, a significant weakening of President FW de Klerk's position, and a last flickering of militancy on the part of the international anti-apartheid movement.

Unfortunately, the ANC's claims were far-fetched, but nobody wanted to hear that, so the gradual destruction of the ANC's case was entirely ignored by the media. As far as I know, no newspaper reported Judge Smit's charges regarding the ANC's manipulation of witnesses. Flimsy claims implicating Eugene de Kock made international headlines, but no one said anything about their ultimate dismissal. Andries Nosenga's sensational yarn was front-page news in South Africa, but his subsequent annihilation under cross-examination passed unnoticed. As for Judge Ngcobo's final verdict, the only newspaper in the world that covered it was *Die Burger*. For the rest, it threatened one of the myths we've chosen to live by, so it was ignored entirely.

Frontiers of Freedom, vol 20, 1999

6

Love

The Apocalypse that Wasn't

As the story passes into legend, it serves to remember the abyss into which South Africans were staring ten years ago today. De Klerk and Mandela were engaged in a vicious squabble over their shared Nobel peace prize. A sinister alliance of white right-wingers and Bantustan dictators was plotting to subvert the army and stage a coup. Mandela's people were smuggling arms to counter that threat. Buthelezi's people had set up secret military training camps. Political intolerance was absolute. January 1994 was the bloodiest month on record. I knew what was coming on election day. As it neared, I bought a flak jacket, drew up a will and went off to cover KwaZulu, at least half-expecting to die.

Only I didn't. Nor did anyone else. Since the details are familiar, let's just say there was a miraculous reprieve, and by 27 April I was back in Johannesburg, putting my cross on South Africa's first democratic ballot. Outside, the streets were empty and a reverent silence lay on the city. Somewhere in the bush to the north, a white-robed prophet had been praying for days on a mountaintop for salvation, and lo, here it was.

I was suddenly so tired I could barely stand. I walked home and lay on a couch for days, drifting in and out of sleep while pundits bickered on TV and the counting degenerated into an amicable chaos. In this dreamlike state, I saw many amazing things, but none quite as telling as the parable of the lost Afrikaners who sold their worldly goods and took their guns, bibles and families to a gathering point on election eve. When the sun rose on 27 April 1994, every man was at his post, waiting for the blacks to attack. Nothing happened, so they set off in convoy, searching for the war their leaders had prophesied.

By the time the camera found them, they'd been wandering for days, children crying, wives sweaty and ill-tempered, husbands with four-day beards and the dazed, haunted look of men who were beginning to realise they'd made terrible fools of themselves.

No, I'm not mocking them. I was in much the same position, hoist by my own dark prognostications. As I saw it, it was futile to talk of a peace in South Africa. There was too much history, too much pain and anger. 'Civil war is inevitable,' I declared. I wound up shamed and chagrined, with great coagulations of egg on my face.

Unwilling to accept such humiliation, I set out to discredit the outcome. The peace is illusory, I sneered; anarchy is still coming. Look at crime! Rape! Guns and mayhem! Decaying cities! Abandoned factories! Incompetence and corruption everywhere! When our new black rulers dismissed such criticism as racist, I said, fine: if that's the price one pays for speaking truth, I will consider myself honoured and continue. Hospitals that don't work any more! Surly nurses! Drunken teachers! A civil service where the phones just ring!

There was truth in all this, but there came a day when I realised history had marched on and left me high and dry, a middle-aged white male fulminating to no effect to a tiny audience of like-minded bad losers. Anything I said was irrelevant, and I had become utterly ridiculous. This realisation drove me first to the bottle and paralysing depression, and then to some dimly remembered texts from the hippie era.

Buddhist texts, if you must know. 'Be here now,' said Baba Ram Das. I interpreted this to mean, be in Parkview, Johannesburg, in this vegetable garden, with these dogs, fixing this old house, consorting with these old friends, smoking the herb on a sacramental basis and generally attempting to add to the sum of light rather than stink everything up with septic negativism. I stopped reading newspapers and started talking nonsense. If it is true, I said, that materialism coarsens the spirit, and that life itself is something of an illusion, it is surely a blessing to live in a country where you are constantly being relieved of your possessions and risk having your head blown off en route to the shops.

My wife rolled her eyes. We were newly married at this point, and my rehabilitation was greatly assisted by the fact that she was a foreigner who saw everything with fresh eyes. Being American, she placed much store in hygienic bathrooms and bright shopping malls, and Johannesburg had these, along with skyscrapers, freeways and high technology. But it also had noisy bars where 50 African languages were spoken and nightclubs that played Congolese kwassa-kwassa all night. Jo'burg was the envy of all Africa, a magnet for dreamers and success-mongers from as far afield as the Nile. On a good night in Yeoville you'd see more beautiful black people than in all the *Shaft* movies put together, and hear more shooting too.

I loved it, but the Contessa (for this is her nickname) had reservations about the guns and violence, so we'd leave the city whenever we could. For a foreigner, everything out there was a revelation. Wild animals. Deserts. Beaches. Mountains so remote it took days to walk out of them. Landscapes so vast they took your breath away, skies so big they defied belief, cathedrals of cloud towering over yellow plains, and so on. I'd grown blind to these splendours, but whenever she gasped, I looked again and gasped too. I fell in love with the country all over again, eventually softening to such a degree that I agreed to move to the Cape.

You must understand that Jo'burgers regard moving to Cape Town as an admission of defeat. We think of it as a fool's paradise where trendies sip white wine on seaview terraces, congratulating each other for finding the last corner of Africa that is immune to chaos and madness. Naturally, it was this very aspect that the Contessa found seductive. 'It's like Europe or America,' she said, 'only better.'

This is true. Cape Town is impossibly beautiful, improbably clean, and overrun in summer by crews shooting international TV commercials. Parts of downtown resemble London. The Atlantic seaboard is easily mistaken for the French Riviera. Out in the winelands, the oak groves and pastures are somehow Dutch in their gentleness, and the arid west coast easily doubles for Spain. As for the better suburbs, frame your shot to exclude smoke from the shacks where poor blacks stay, and you're in an upper middle class anywhere: Connecticut, Marin County, Surrey, or Neuilly.

Who wants to live in an upper-middle-class anywhere? Not I. I wanted to buy a log cabin out in the wilderness near Cape Point, where we could live a simple life of spartan purity among trees tormented into strange shapes by howling gales. Unfortunately, the Contessa had other ideas, and we wound up with a sensible house in

St James, where the imperialist Rhodes had his holiday pad. From our stoep we can see 60 miles, Cape Point this way, Groot Drakenstein the other, and before us, a giant horseshoe of blue water rimmed by purple mountains. There is an impossibly quaint fishing harbour below us, full of quaint wooden boats and grizzled old salts of the sort beloved by watercolourists. There is also a row of quaint antique shops and galleries, interspersed with trendy boîtes where the cappuccino is served by beautiful girls with rings in their lips and eyebrows. It is a place well-suited to the quasi-Buddhist lifestyle. Every dawn brings an awesome sight – a storm, clouds streaming over mountain crags – that reminds me of my insignificance in the overall scheme of things. Every day I can go fishing, if the spirit moves. On dark stormy nights, I repair to a waterside bar called Polana and wait for high tide, when giant seas heave up in floodlights and come racing towards the picture windows in a great tumult of spume.

Live in Cape Town long enough and you lose interest in the outside world. Visitors from more exciting cities start yawning at your dinner table, but I no longer care. They have no possible conception of the unbearable bliss of fine summer days when the sea is warm and the figs are ripe and you start the morning with a dive into a cool green rock pool, followed perhaps by coffee in one of those impossibly quaint cafes and a spot of light typing, if I can manage to ignore the drama outside my window – tides rising, whales blowing, birds diving, the boats coming back to Kalk Bay. The Contessa and I often walk down to meet them, come home with a fat Cape salmon or snoek. Come sundown, we set the fish to grill on an open fire, uncork a bottle of wine, and, yes, congratulate ourselves for living in the last corner of Africa that is immune to chaos and madness.

In season, tour buses park on the road above our house, disgorging foreigners who gape at the view, dumbfounded, and then turn their binoculars on us, clearly wondering what entitles us to live in this paradise. I often ask myself the same question, and the answer is, nothing. My life is absurd in every aspect. The first Malan arrived in Cape Town in 1688 and owned slaves. His sons trekked into the interior and dispossessed the Khoisan. Their sons moved even deeper into Africa, and by 1840, Malans were spreading like a plague, eating up landscapes, mowing down game, subjugating everyone they came across. My sort wound up owning almost everything and it was nice while it lasted, but by rights we should have been wiped out in the great war of 1994, or at least dispossessed. Instead, here we are, citizens of a stable democracy with an independent judiciary and a constitution that is a beacon unto nations. To be sure, there are problems, but it is not the ending I imagined.

All I can say as the tenth anniversary nears is that the Bible was right about a thing or two. It is infinitely worse to receive than to give, especially if one is arrogant and the gift is forgiveness. The gift of 1994 was so huge that I choked on it and couldn't say thank you. But I am not too proud to say it now.

Sunday Telegraph, January 2004

Postscript: President Thabo Mbeki quoted this article at considerable length in his 2004 'state of the nation' address, a development that provoked rabies in certain circles. The central accusation was that Mbeki had chosen to chosen to elevate me above your average hack as a reward for my writings about Aids, which were said to have 'provided oxygen' for the President's own views on the subject. Pundits like Prof Anton Harber resurrected all the heresies I'd uttered about stuff like the Boipatong massacre, the Truth Commission and the Aids establishment, concluding that I was a 'carbuncular' person whose writings were poisonous. The reaction from my right-wing friends was equally unfriendly. Myself, I think the piece was just a somewhat belated display of good manners.

The People's Republic of Yeoville

Once upon a time in Africa, there was a Camelot that was officially termed 'grey,' even though it was really a vivid and colourful urban village where people said what they felt and did as they pleased in defiance of their hard-hearted rulers. It was a place where forbidden love flourished, where every conceivable rule was broken, and for a brief shining hour, ten years ago, it was the capital of South Africa.

So, then – welcome to Yeoville, founded in 1890 on a rocky ridge just north of the world's richest gold reef. 'Magnificent views,' said the developer. 'Healthy air.' He was a Scotsman named Thomas Yeo Sherwell, and he was hoping to attract the rich. Never quite managed that, but he did get the infant Johannesburg's middle classes, and after the turn of the century, the Jews, who came mostly from the Baltic states and gave Yeoville an intellectual and cultural ambience considerably out of the colonial ordinary. Some Jews went on to become capitalists, but others were Bolsheviks who immediately set about organising revolution, first and rather embarrassingly under the slogan, 'Workers Unite for a White South Africa,' but after 1927, on behalf of 'the natives.'

The presence in Yeoville of this small band of rebels attracted kindred spirits in the form of bohemians (most famously, Herman Charles Bosman), jazz musicians and dope fiends, all of whom lived furtively until 1978 or so, when a gay nightclub called Casablanca opened on Yeoville's main road. In the larger scheme this was a nothing event, but it was one of the first signs that the ruling Calvinists were losing their grip, especially when Casablanca was joined by Rumours, a jazz bar that daringly featured black musicians. When Rumours got away with it, similar joints sprang up nearby, and by 1986, Rockey Street was the hippest place in South Africa – racially integrated in proportions comfortable to whites, lined with fashionable nightspots and overrun by trendies.

Everyone lived in Yeoville. Okay, everyone who was anyone in the alternative society that styled itself the vanguard of political and social change. The pop star Johnny Clegg learned to play Zulu guitar in the 'boy's rooms' on Yeoville rooftops. Barney Simon lay in his bed on Muller Street, dreaming up stories that became world-famous Market Theatre plays. All the seminal anti-apartheid movies were cobbled together in Yeoville. The suburb even had its own Beat poet, Sinclair Beiles, a witty old madman who'd knocked around with Burroughs in Paris. On any given night, Yeoville's entertainment zone was awash with famous actors, human rights lawyers, Marxist academics, gay activists and radical feminists whose unshaven legs were known locally as 'Yeoville stockings.'

Reshada Crouse did not wear Yeoville stockings, but then she was always contrary. Immortally beautiful and talented, she was smitten at an early age by the paintings of grand masters and decided, after art school in Cape Town and London, to become a portraitist 'in the tradition of Goya, Caravaggio and Michelangelo.'

In South Africa, in the eighties, such an ambition was almost insanely inappropriate. Taking their cues from the great overseas, the local art police had declared Eurocentrism a dirty word and figurative painting largely passé. Artists were expected to become 'cultural workers' celebrating the struggle of the masses against racial capitalism. To stand up in such a revolutionary climate and declare yourself a painter in the grand tradition of Dead White Men was a provocation that invited savage retaliation. 'Highly skilled, highly horrible,' said one leftist critic of Reshada's early work. 'Absolutely masterly,' said another, 'but I am reminded of political works done under Hitler.'

One night, at a party, a dogfight broke out on the dance floor. I pulled the slavering beasts apart and got bitten for my trouble, whereupon Reshada offered to take me for a tetanus shot. En route to the hospital, she told me about her war with the art police, and I immediately clocked her as an ally in the struggle against suffocating political rectitude. I moved into her spare room a while later, and we became a team of sorts, roaming from bar to bar in Yeoville's combat zone, picking arguments with art critics and other forms of leftist. The critics were amateurs, but there were real revolutionaries in Yeoville, real guerrillas and trade union organisers plus any number of left-wing journalists who were always game to drink and debate.

By the end of the 1980s, even the hippies and junkies were politicised, and Yeoville was a liberated zone of sorts. Bars stayed open till dawn, defying the liquor laws. Rastas sold dope on the street almost openly. It was almost like Amsterdam in Africa, and it got even better after February 1990, when Mandela was released from prison and the exiles came home from Russia or military camps in Africa. Yeoville was cheap and ideologically congenial, and almost the entire executive corps of the African National Congress settled there. Wally Serote was the movement's cultural commissar, Pallo Jordan its leading intellectual. Also present were Geraldine Fraser, Jabu Moleketi, Derek Hanekom, Albie Sachs, Zola Skweyiya and Muff Andersson, an old girlfriend who'd run an ANC arms-smuggling ring. Communist Party boss Joe Slovo grew up on Rockey Street and returned to live a few hundred yards away.

Living amidst such a dense concentration of political talent was amazing. In the nerve-wracked runup to our 1994 election, insiders started telling me to ignore what I read in the newspapers. A deal has been struck in high places, they said; the revolution has been postponed indefinitely. I found this hard to believe. At the time, right-wing Boers and Bantustan dictators were plotting to take over the military and annihilate the ANC, which was in turn embroiled in a bloody fratricidal war against Inkatha and infested with wild-eyed insurrectionists still bent on FW de Klerk's violent overthrow. One morning, we were woken by war cries. A Zulu impi was marching down Cavendish Street, brandishing spears and clubs and looking to bash Mandela loyalists' heads in. I took this as a sign that the violence was becoming uncontrollable, and would soon engulf all of us. 'Civil war is inevitable,' I wrote. 'We are walking the plank.'

What can I say? I was wrong. Seven weeks later, Reshada and I strolled through the cathedral calm of a bright autumn morning and cast our ballots in SA's first democratic election. Given my erroneous predictions, it was not my proudest moment, but once I'd wiped the egg off my face I had to concede that what was embarrassing for me promised good for others.

Here's the thing, see: at that moment, Yeoville was the epicentre of everything. Six residents of the suburb and its immediate surrounds were about to be drafted into Mandela's first cabinet. Another 40 or so became national or regional Members of Parliament, and hundreds, perhaps thousands, were headed for big jobs in the civil service.

It's hard to convey how odd this was. The Yeoville power zone was so small you could walk across it in 20 minutes, its 35 000 people a drop in the ocean of the nation's 40 million. It was as if a single extended family had taken control of the country, and great things seemed to lie in store for Yeoville residents. In my mind's eye, I saw the suburb becoming a bright shining showpiece of the Rainbow Nation, with fine schools and clinics, an efficient police station and plaques on buildings saying, 'Childhood home of Joe Slovo,' or, 'Here lived Barbara Hogan, first white woman jailed for advocating the overthrow of apartheid.'

Three years later, Yeoville was a hellhole. Read on.

'Let's cartwheel, everybody!' shouted the polished swell with the upper-caste British accent, draining his wine glass and calling for more. It was May 1994, and Reshada and I were in the throes of a party that started on election day and continued without letup for weeks on end. This one took place in a Moorish courtyard, under a big tree, and the polished dark-skinned personage turned out to be Trevor Tutu, wayward son of the famous archbishop.

Like most males, Trevor was smitten by the Aryan siren and became a regular at our semi-daily 'tea parties,' which started around sunset and continued indefinitely. Another courtier was Samuel Johnson, an amiable giant who'd come out from Britain to fight apartheid, only to find himself fighting off white girls who saw him as something of a dream date – big, black and very threatening with his Mohawk and biker leathers, but a gentle poet once you got to know him.

Sam liked to shoot pool. I dimly remember doing a lot of that in the post-election period, also hanging out at the Blue Parrot, a Yeoville bar patronised by the local black nobility and touring celebrities – Mick Jagger, Wesley Snipes, Morgan Freeman, even Hillary Clinton. I think I met Peter Gabriel there one night, but my brain was so addled by booze and euphoria that I wouldn't swear to it. There was a lot of irrational crying in that period, especially on the day of Mandela's inauguration, itself cause for further bouts of indiscriminate celebration.

But all good things end eventually, and there came a day when I woke up sober and noticed that something odd was going on in Yeoville. It suddenly seemed more crowded. Traders were setting up fruit and vegetable stands on any sidewalk they pleased, or knocking holes in garden walls so that they could sell cheap phone calls to passers-by. One day, pirates tapped into Reshada's telephone connection, and she couldn't make any calls for two days on account of voices speaking in tongues on her line. Shortly thereafter, Telkom presented her with a bill for R8 000 to cover hundreds of calls to Ethiopia, Zimbabwe and Nigeria. The *amakwerekwere* had arrived, joining a stream of local blacks pouring into Yeoville in search of cheap accommodation.

Unfortunately, cheap accommodation often consisted of a single room divided by curtains so that eight or ten people could share it. Looking back, Yeoville patriot Maurice Smithers identifies this as the root cause of the suburb's troubles. As apartheid crumbled in the 1980s, laws enforcing residential segregation were ignored, and Yeoville became in official parlance a 'grey area' where racial mixing was tolerated. This caused a huge upsurge in demand for accommodation, which in turn enabled greedy landlords to double or triple their rents. The newcomers, being poor, could only pay by stuffing sub-tenants into every nook and cranny. Overcrowding was illegal, but the municipality – staffed mostly by whites in the pre-democracy period – lost interest in enforcing its own by-laws.

Post-elections, not much changed and the area's housing stock deteriorated further, spurred on by epidemics of apathy in the liquor licensing department, among health inspectors and especially among the police, who seemed to have lost the battle against crime. Until 1993 or thereabouts, it was safe to walk around Yeoville at night. By 1995, walking was almost suicidal. One by one, the trendy bars and restaurants on Rockey Street called it a day, only to be replaced by dank, unlicensed drinking holes whose clientele was young, aggressive and almost entirely male. Reshada and I started staying home at night, flinching at the sound of gunfire and distant screams. And when we ventured out in the morning, we'd inevitably see a removal van drawing up somewhere along Becker Street.

One day they were there, and the next – poof! – they'd vanished. I refer here to the bohemian leftists and art police with whom Reshada and I once sparred so pleasantly. It's a bit unfair to blame the politicians among them for leaving, because parliament was located in Cape Town, but the broad mass of anti-apartheid activists, academics and journalists had no such excuse. They'd spent years jeering at anyone who resisted integration, but now that it had come to Yeoville, they packed their belongings and fled en masse, trailing feeble justifications. 'Couldn't work because of the noise,' they said. Or, 'My daughter's friends' parents wouldn't let them come to play any more.'

I seldom lost an opportunity to tilt an eyebrow and remark on the hypocrisy on display here. On the other hand, I was growing uneasy myself. Two visitors to Reshada's house had their cars stolen. Then Reshada's car was stolen, too, and mine had its windows smashed. I would lie in bed at night, listening to distant gun battles and wondering how big my own balls were. One day, I found my laptop gone, nicked through an open window. I bought a replacement, but within a week, it was stolen too, so I said, that's it, I'm out of here. I invited Reshada to come with me, painting a picture of a rambling commune in some safe, leafy suburb where we could continue to host tea parties behind high walls and an electric fence. But she was made of sterner stuff; I went, she stayed.

And so it came to pass that by 1999, my circle of Yeoville friends had dwindled from hundreds to half a dozen, all of whom were struggling. David Heitner sunk his life savings into an advanced edit suite with plush private cinema attached, only to find that customers were too scared to come to him. Adriaan Turgel was robbed so often that he turned into a vigilante, prowling the streets of night with his Zulu sidekicks, doing work the police were too lazy to do. Tony Richard, a legal aid lawyer, was woken one morning by shouting and pounding on his garden gate. He went out to find an angry mob standing guard over a naked, terrified wretch who'd been caught breaking into cars. 'You're a lawyer,' they said, 'you pass sentence.' Sensing that the crowd was in a murderous mood, Tony presented the captive with a choice: private punishment or the police station. He sobbed, 'Police station! Police station!' and his life was saved.

Still, it was one incident too many, and Tony decided it was time to go. But he'd left it too late. All over Yeoville, houses and flats were on sale, but the area had been unofficially redlined by banks, and there were no buyers at any price. Tony gave his house to a friend and walked away.

Which left Reshada the last white person on her street bar two or three, and harrowingly vulnerable, or so it seemed to me – no gun, no perimeter wall, not even a gate to keep her and her two children safe from the forces of darkness. Visiting her became a nerve-wracking ordeal. I'd drive with knotted guts and white knuckles, chain-smoking, eyes peeled for hijackers. Every time I opened a newspaper, I half-expected to read that she'd been murdered.

Why did she stay? It would have been easier to understand if she'd been a self-flagellating white liberal, but that wasn't the case. She wasn't really poor, either. She was just difficult, in life as in her beautiful but unfashionable paintings. 'I'll do what I want to do when I want to do it,' she said. She wouldn't even admit to being afraid.

And so, as Yeoville disintegrated and white capital fled, Reshada started investing in its restoration. Her house was a grand old Victorian, with generous rooms and high ceilings, but the roof leaked, the wiring was wonky and hot water came from an old coal stove. Reshada rolled up her sleeves and set to work, assisted by an unskilled labourer named Innocent. She fixed the wiring, nearly electrocuting herself in the process. Innocent took some interior walls down. The donkey stove gave way to a rooftop solar geyser, and then came a semi-formal English garden in the back yard, strewn with sculptures and overhung with wisteria. 'It's not a house,' she explained, 'it's a love-affair.' I said, yes, Reshada, but it's in Yeoville. She shrugged and said, 'I'm not willing to leave just for the sake of having white neighbours.'

So then – meet the neighbours. Owen Phiri was a boiler-maker who emigrated to South Africa from Malawi in the seventies, seeking escape from 'low living standards.' He was a sweet, soft-spoken man, very concerned about crime. One night, he woke up to find eight sinister shadows clustered around Reshada's car, tampering with the ignition. 'Go away,' he said. They whispered, 'What's wrong with you? She's white.' Owen shouted, 'Go away or I'll shoot,' and they went.

On the other side was Aletta Khubeka who'd been born in a mud hut on a Free State farm and spent most of her life on her knees, some white madam's maid. Now she and her janitor husband were the burstingly proud owners of a three-bedroom home with tiled bathroom and a kitchen so clean that every surface could be eaten off.

They were also burstingly proud of their son Sibusiso, aged 15, a promising squash player who attended King Edward VII, the school that produced the artist William Kentridge plus any number of billionaires and South African cricket captains. 'It's nice here,' Aletta told me, in a sitting room lined with pictures of the Zulu prophet Shembe, her spiritual leader.

And finally, there was Teresa, who knocked on Reshada's door wearing a frilly hat and an apricot suit, 'looking like something from *Gone With The Wind*.' Teresa wanted a room. Reshada couldn't help her, but she came back twice, and was eventually invited in for a cup of tea. She turned out to be a Kenyan who had worked in a bank and been married to a judge who decided, at the age of 40-something, to exercise the African patriarch's right to a second wife. Mortally offended, Teresa walked out and made her way to South Africa, penniless. Sensing a kindred spirit, Reshada offered her a backyard shack. Teresa stayed for four years, doing Reshada's washing in lieu of rent and furiously striving for success on the side.

She tried selling cosmetics. She did a computer course, but couldn't get a job because she lacked working papers. Eventually, it dawned on her that Yeoville was full of Kenyans aching for chuppattis cooked Nairobi-style, so she established a cottage industry, and next thing, she was an independent businesswoman with a flat of her own and several assistants. 'I don't want to sound like a liberal,' Reshada said, 'but these people have humbled me. They're so decent and hard-working, so determined.'

A while back, a Buddhist dropped in for tea while I was visiting. Patrick Booth was one of those delightful creatures you keep meeting in the New South Africa – a coloured boy from a small country town, largely self-educated, ravishingly charming. In 1999, he moved to the big city, becoming Reshada's protégé and house guest. She introduced him to people who were involved in New Age pursuits, and next thing, Patrick was out in the formerly white suburbs, laying his mystic healing hands on the stressed bodies of politicians and executives in an exclusive health retreat. He lived in Illovo, as I recollect, close to the designer boutiques of Rosebank and the dreamy greensward of Wanderers cricket ground. From this lofty perch, he looked back on Yeoville with something approaching disdain.

'Yeoville is sick,' he informed us, sitting in the lotus position in

Reshada's studio, swathed in robes. 'It's not evolving in a way most people perceive as positive or in keeping with the changes taking place in South Africa.' Reshada's nostrils flared, a sure sign of coming trouble. 'Excuse *me*,' she said, reeling off a string of small acts of kindness she'd recently experienced. One day, for instance, her car broke down some distance from her home. A group of young black males approached, but instead of robbing her, they offered to help and proceeded to push her home. Next morning, a backyard mechanic made a house call, crawled under the car with gun on his hip, reconnected some wires and waved away Reshada's offers of payment.

'Something good happens almost every day,' she said. 'It's like living in an African village. People look after each other. Children play in the street. I bet you don't even know your neighbours' names!'

The Buddhist rolled his eyes. In truth, he and I thought Reshada had long since gone off her rocker, throwing good money after bad in a hopeless slum. The mansion over the road had become a seedy boarding house, crammed full of Nigerians and Congolese who valued the thick steel burglar bars installed by some previous owner. Those bars kept thieves at bay, but they were also the death of twelve people who couldn't get out when the house caught fire. A nearby flat block was tragic in a more ordinary way, abandoned by its landlord and infested now with blank-eyed glueheads and crack addicts who shat in the stairwells and burned trash in Art Deco fireplaces around which I once sat drinking with tormented white revolutionaries, back in the time when playing proletarian was a game. The reality years later was unbearable.

And that is why we don't live there anymore. South Africa has become a country where those who claim to speak for the black poor usually live at the furthest possible remove from them. As far as I know, Winnie Mandela is the only ANC politician who still lives full-time in a township. Her ex-husband has settled among the capitalist robber barons of Houghton. Tokyo Sexwale, the erstwhile revolutionary turned billionaire, lives nearby, and State President Thabo Mbeki is renovating a property just around the corner. These and other black nobles are no longer seen in township shebeens. On Friday nights, they gather at a Rosebank bar called Katzy's, where a whiskey costs R30 and the parking lot is crammed with high-end BMWs and Mercedes-Benzes.

Lurking on the fringes of the Katzy's set, you often hear older cats talking fondly of Yeoville in the old days, but their children are scathing. 'Yeoville?' said a bright young thing, her face disfigured by a sneer. 'Yech. I could never live there.' Such opinions are seized on with glee by whites who fled the area. They say, 'Hey, it's not a race thing. My black friends also regard Yeoville as a no-go area.'

Well, yes: for people like us. People with at least a bit of money. Given half a chance, we'll try to convince you that ours is the real South Africa, but I'm not sure we should be listened to. South Africa remains a country where most people are poor and desperate, and Yeoville has always been a weather vane that points where the whole is going. It was one of the first places where you saw racially mixed couples, one of the first white areas to turn grey, and then one of the first grey areas to topple into what struck me as a typically African state of dysfunctionality. On the eve of democracy's tenth birthday, I returned to Yeoville to divine what next.

Much was as I remembered it – streets clogged with fuming taxis, live chickens for sale on the pavements, formerly illustrious nightspots boarded up or reduced to smoke-blackened holes out of which emerged blasts of kwaito. But here and there, piglets were taking wing. After years of agitation, Joburg's municipality was pulling its socks up. The streets were swept fairly regularly. Council workers were fixing broken street lights. The worst slum buildings were slated for demolition, and nocturnal gun battles had become vanishingly rare. Banks had reversed their no-loans policy, which led, just the other day, to a truly confounding development: Yeoville property prices pulled out of their decade-long nosedive. In Johannesburg, this was greeted with headlines.

All this coincided with the triumphant conclusion of Reshada's renovations, which included, by the time she was done, a rose garden on the front lawn, an imposing palisade fence, and lights to play on the house's ice-white facade. It looked astonishing after dark, a gleaming shrine to some European concept of art and beauty, looming over a street thronged with African prophets, Rastafarians, Senegalese traders in flowing robes and street people in rags and tatters.

Word of this oddity reached certain arbiters of style, and Reshada's house became the subject of a spread in the opulent pages of *Home & Garden*, under a headline reading, 'Artist in Residence.' The rich and famous were rendered green with envy, especially by passages recounting the achievements of Reshada's children. Raised in a slum, they were paragons of art, music and intelligent conversation. One obtained an MBA from Wharton, the world's premier business school, the other won a scholarship to Yale. Reshada looked upon what she had done and pronounced herself satisfied.

'I just hope it doesn't get boring now,' she said. 'I'd hate to have to move away.'

Sunday Telegraph, April 2004

Postscript: In 2009, I took Sir VS Naipaul on what purported to be a tour of Johannesburg's underbelly. I had primed him with stories about Yeoville's glory days and its subsequent degeneration into squalor, but when we got there, humiliation awaited. The government had recently spent R70 million on a World Cup-related urban upgrade. Yeoville looked neat, orderly, stable and even prosperous, so help me God. I suspect the grand old man thought I was a complete bullshitter.

Kind Words for a Mean Town

What's good to say about Johannesburg? I inquired as we drove through a storm towards our dinner. 'Well,' said Kate, 'there's the weather, the weather and the weather.' But it had been raining for days, so the proposition seemed dubious at present. We drove on in silence, wracking our brains. Steve mumbled something about the plethora of golf courses, but drew no takers. The Contessa mentioned street markets, where you can buy artefacts from all over Africa, but someone pointed out that most were faked. As we took our seats in a restaurant called the Smokestack, Steve made a case for South Africa's excellent red wines. I could drink to that, but they're made around Cape Town, so they don't really count.

Stumped, we sipped our cabernet and looked around. The restaurant was brand new and very larney, as we say here, larney meaning fashionable and expensive. The décor was bare bricks and rough-hewn finishes – rather New York 1980s, with a clientele to match: slender young women in cocktail dresses, fat-cats in suits and ponytails, and the races mixed in proportions comfortably familiar to Americans. A row of BMWs and Porsches was visible through the plate glass windows. Everyone had straight teeth, strong bodies and an arrogant air of total self-confidence, and you could bet they all had servants to pick up behind them.

Ja, well, *plus ça change* and all that. Jo'burg has always been world-famous for its vulgar displays of greed and ostentation. I spent the first few decades of my life longing to see the place engulfed by the fires of revolution, but the struggle petered out into a mannered bourgeois transformation, and here we were ten years later, the loyal subjects of Mandela and Mbeki, and richer than ever. The stock market rose 45 per cent last year. The IT sector ran wild. The freeways are clogged with gleaming new chariots. Property prices are rising, while crime threatens to stabilise. For the lucky few, life is more perfect than ever. The same cannot be said for the rain-soaked beggars lining the streets outside, arms waving like sea anemones, trying to earn a few cents by guiding the next Mercedes into a parking bay.

Why raise this at the start of what's supposed to be a love song for my hometown? Just to get it out of the way, I suppose. Johannesburg has always been ruled by grasping elites, and civilised visitors have always recoiled in horror from our vacuous excesses, branding the city one of the ugliest on the planet. Looking back, nobody ever really loved this place except the Voortrekkers, who arrived on covered wagons in the spring of 1837. After trekking for months across harsh, dry plains, they spied a ridge on the horizon, its flanks streaked by gushing streams, hence the name, Witwatersrand, or ridge of white waters. As they drew nearer, clouds of birds rose from marshes, and great herds of antelope thundered away across the savannah. They were on the roof of Africa, almost 6 000 feet high; the sun was hot but the air was cool, and the veld was carpeted with wild flowers. The Boers thought they'd arrived in paradise, so they staked out farms, built crude homesteads out of mud and reeds and idled away the next five decades in a bucolic swoon, blissfully unaware that they were sitting on top of the world's richest gold reef.

The gold was discovered in 1886, and the Boers were instantly overrun by a greed-maddened stampede of Cockney navvies and British imperialists, American freebooters, French brothel-keepers and German Jews. In their wake came Russians, Latvians, indentured Indians, Chinese coolies and armies of sullen Africans, forced off the land by hut taxes. A great city rose out of nowhere. Ziggurats leaped skyward. Mine shafts went down a mile. Fabulous fortunes were made, and fortune-seekers kept coming. In my youth, the mad scientists of apartheid tried to hold back the tide and turn the city into a whites-only moonbase on Africa, a doomed undertaking that came to nothing. The Boers were undermined, overthrown and cast onto the trash heap of history, whereupon the invasion resumed apace.

Peasants decamped from the countryside and settled in shacks around the city. Armies of cheerful opportunists flooded in from elsewhere in Africa – Malians, Ethiopians, gregarious Nigerians, *personnes d'élégance* from Francophone lands. Serbs invaded the cafés of Yeoville. Pockets of Hillbrow became French-speaking. Cyrildene was colonised by traders from Beijing, and the best suburbs have of course been settled by our new ruling class, 'Afristocrats' and politicians who tool around in BMWs and dine in the Smokestack. I pushed my plate aside, daunted by the thought of having to explain why anyone would become attached to such a place.

Well, for a start, there's the weather, clear and crisp in winter, with skies of startling blue, and soft warm springs giving way to burning summers punctuated by violent African thunderstorms. To walk through the aftermath of such a deluge is amazing. The streets are strewn with mauve flowers knocked off the jacaranda trees. Great clouds of red and pink bougainvillea billow over high garden walls, forming a psychedelic arch over the old stone alley that winds up the ridge behind my house. From the summit, it's as if a pastel mist is drifting across the suburbs.

Two decades of convulsive change notwithstanding, aspects of the sweet white life persist down there – the thwock of balls on tennis courts, the click of woods on bowling greens, the clink of ice in frosted glasses borne on trays by loyal African servants. My little corner of the city remains rather British, with Anglican churches, friendly grocers and a ratepayers' association full of crabby ex-Rhodesians and old Africa hands who rail in vain about unkempt pavements, broken street lamps and other signs of the supposedly inevitable slide into anarchy. But all is not lost; not yet. You can still get French pastries and Austrian coffee in the fashionable *boîtes* of Melville, on the far side of the yonder golf course, and the Westcliff Hotel still serves a tolerable cucumber sandwich with afternoon tea. And that, sadly, is about as far as the bourgeoisie ventures, because it's a jungle out there – the most dangerous city in the world. But also the most interesting, if you have the courage to go.

When visitors from outside want to know why I live here, I always take them into the decaying heart of our old downtown, where Africa and the West come face to face across a narrow street called Diagonal. On one side, there's a little African apothecary where a certain K Naidoo does a roaring trade in healing and magical herbs, baboon skulls, lizard feet and tiny vials of crocodile fat. On the other, there's a soaring edifice of blue glass and steel, designed by Helmut Jahn, the great avant-garde architect from Chicago.

I've been there a hundred times, and the juxtaposition has never ceased to amaze and elate me – witch doctors entering one building, accountants exiting the other, and mingling on the street between. It seems extraordinary, but it isn't, because this is the nature of the city: at once an outpost of Western 'civilisation' and a point of entry into a parallel kingdom of African consciousness. Prophets dance around fires in the shadow of skyscrapers. Ancestral cattle sacrifices are conducted in suburban gardens. Mud huts and nuclear power stations occur in the same landscape. University professors smear lion fat on their faces as they set forth to settle faculty battles. In the cafés of Hillbrow, exiles from all over Africa gather in expensive dark glasses to plot coups and comebacks in undertones.

Which is not to say that all Africans are refugees or mystics. The city teems with black merchant bankers and nuclear physicists, black rugby players, black teenagers in the uniforms of colonial Etons called Saint this or King that, speaking English with the same plummy accents as their white classmates, and subscribing to identical values. I once had an African friend who defined hell as 'a place where really bad blacks are sent to spend eternity discussing cricket with white men.' His daughter, a sparkling yuppie of 23, thinks hell is discussing Africa with me, when she would rather be shopping or dancing to kwaito, the Americanised hip-hop that is presently the rage, often sung in Afrikaans, the language of apartheid, by township youths with baseball caps on backwards.

Myself, I remain attached to more traditional musics. It's an indescribable pleasure to tool around the city with the car radio blaring, listening to mbaqanga on this station or mbube on that, with Boer concertina music between. The ether is full of strange languages. The pavements are clogged with al fresco barbershops in the Ghanaian style and traders from Zanzibar and Timbuktu. When the sun goes down, we set forth to eat and drink from the smorgasbord laid out by our many invaders. You can dine on mopani worms and English roast beef, pasta and curry, Congolese delicacies, Mozambican peri-peri and absolutely authentic Szechuan cuisine in the People's Republic of Cyrildene. If you have the stomach, you can repair to Melville in the small hours and argue with black-jacketed intellectuals in a miasma of liquor fumes and marijuana smoke while old African jazz cats blow marabe in the background. You might get hijacked on your way home, but what the heck.

If it is true, as Buddhist sages maintain, that materialism coarsens the spirit and that life itself is an illusion, Jo'burg is a fine place to pursue enlightenment. Theft is so common that it's hardly worth mentioning. Everyone knows a murder victim. You either allow the danger to poison your psyche and deaden your soul, or you learn to be brave, and laugh at the prospect of your own annihilation. It's not necessarily kin to wisdom, but it's a fine quality anyway. I love Jo'burgers. They're loud and vulgar, and the worst of them will shoot you or embezzle your trust fund if you don't watch your back, but they all have something the Boer poet Breytenbach called 'heartspace.' It comes from living on adrenaline, which is, of course, the intoxicant that keeps us here, or draws us back if we try to escape.

And we all come back, eventually. My life here is full of returnees. A toothless old poet who used to knock around Paris with William Burroughs. An ex-terrorist who blew up a nuclear power station. A webmaster who abandoned a career in Silicon Valley. An ex-Oxford professor. Foreigners think we're nuts, coming back to a doomed city on a damned continent, but there's something you don't understand: it's boring where you are. You'll probably live longer than us and acquire more possessions, but there's no ferment in your societies, no excitement, no edge. Your newspapers are bland and your politics are inconsequential, so many storms in teacups. You want crises? We've got real ones – Aids, 40 per cent unemployment, the highest rape and murder rates on the planet and a government that wants to put blacks in our national rugby team, just on principle. We're talking stuff that's really worth fighting about, with real fire in the belly. We're talking about a country where life is an insane gamble that'll end either in blinding light or darkest disaster, and there's absolutely no way of knowing which.

This month, as we have seen, things are looking up, but you can be pretty sure that despair lies ahead, because it always does. We yaw between terror and ecstasy. Every day is an adventure. The only constant is the weather, the African sun that beats down on our backs as we potter around in the garden, digging up rich African soils all red with oxides and squirming with earthworms. Our tomatoes are fat and red. Our Swiss chard grows like trees. Towards evening, we walk the dogs up the old stone path to the crest of the ridge to watch the sun go down. Flights of sacred ibis cross the sky. Lions roar in the zoo nearby. Police chase hijackers on freeways, sirens screaming. We're in the wild heart of Jo'burg, and it's a pretty good place to be.

Sunday Telegraph, 1999

7

Humour

Great White Hyena

||||||||||||||||||||||||||||||||||||||||||||||||||||||||||||||||||||||||||||||||||||||||||||||||||||||||||||||||||||||||||||||||||||||||||||||||||||||||

The Spectator is a grand old British institution; the oldest magazine in the world, in fact, founded in the 1840s. In my imagination, it was a place of dark wood panels where hock-swilling High Tories sat around in leather armchairs, chortling about the glories of empire and the vicissitudes of Her Majesty's subject nations. We never met in person, but on the phone The Spectator's *editors had about them a Churchillian air of absolute self-confidence in the rectitude of their views, which were cynical, intelligent and amusedly sceptical of almost everything. They were conservative, to be sure, but their editorial decisions were mostly guided by other considerations: if an article was witty and made its point without inducing boredom, it went in. I think* The Spectator *generally saw all colonials as some form of savage, but they occasionally made an exception in my case.*

'This is a goer,' declares Deon du Plessis. It's Sunday afternoon, and the Great White Hyena is presiding over a news conference in the Johannesburg offices of the *Daily Sun*, the largest daily in Africa. Mr Du Plessis is publisher and part-owner of this august organ. Seated before him are his editor, Themba Khumalo, an amiable Zulu in a baseball cap, and a cheerful menagerie of subs and hacks. Some weeks ago, they ran a story slugged, 'Dark Secrets of Crime Terror!,' which revealed that unscrupulous sangomas were charging up to R100 000 for magical potions (almost) guaranteed to render robbers invisible to police. Now fate has delivered a follow-up in the form of two criminals caught at a Soweto roadblock with 19 stolen Speedpoint machines in their boot and a bag of supernatural goodies dangling from their rear-view mirror. There are photographs, too. 'I like it,' says Deon. 'This is front page.'

It's also a cue for a bout of reminiscing about similar stories, of which the paper has carried many. 'Penetrated by a python' featured a woman ravished by a snake that came out of the toilet. 'Raped by a Gorilla' told the story of an evil inyanga who conjured a giant ape-like creature to punish a lady who had spurned his love proposals. Deon was particularly fond of the one about a tree with magical penis-enlarging powers. 'A woman from Skukuza revealed to us that if you put your dick in one of this tree's pods, it would grow as the pod grew,' he says. 'Next thing, the Parks Board rang us saying every tree in the area was shaking. An endless stream of *Sun* readers had gone there to stick their members into pods.'

Mr Du Plessis confesses that he acquired such a pod for his own use, but that it had not proved efficacious. This prompts rewrite man Denis Smith, formerly of Paddington, to recall a story about 'stuff in a bottle' that was 'supposed to give you a permanent hardon' but instead rendered a *Sun* editor unconscious for four days. By now everyone in the room is incapacitated with laughter. The Great White Hyena wipes tears from his left eye (the right is presently covered with a piratical eye-patch necessitated by eye surgery) and says, 'What the fuck are they going to make of this in England?'

More to the point – what will they make of it at Rhodes University, where journalism professor Guy Berger wages war against SA's rising tide of journalistic barbarism? Berger would regard this conference as thunderous confirmation of his charges against tabloids, and in a way, he's right: it's a carnival of thought crime. On the other hand, one gets the sense that Du Plessis enjoys playing the bad boy. Either way, it would be remiss to dismiss Du Plessis as a joker, because he's the central figure in a tabloid revolution that has shaken corporate monoliths, lured three million virgin readers into the newspaper market and triggered a furious battle around questions of national identity.

Left-wingers portray South Africa as a painfully politically correct society, imbued with gender sensitivities and what have you. The *Daily Sun* suggests otherwise. It is conservative, at least to the extent that it supports old-fashioned family values and clamours for tough law enforcement. Gay rights make it a bit queasy, and it does not like illegal immigrants who come here to steal our jobs and defile our women. And finally, it is respectful of the cult of ancestor worship and frequently carries stories about miracles and magic. This cocktail has proved enormously popular. Founded in July 2002, the *Daily Sun* now sells 500 000 copies on a good day, utterly dwarfing all competitors.

Several ironies lurk hereabouts. Eleven years ago, when Nelson Mandela came to power, South Africa boasted a dozen or so English-language dailies, all owned by white media conglomerates and deemed to be in dire need of transformation. Within five years, almost all these titles had new owners (often black) and a new ideology – billows of soft-left waffle about women's rights, human rights, gender issues and cultural diversity. Reading these papers became an ordeal for some, but we bore it because this was supposedly what the black masses wanted. Only they didn't, as it turns out. Circulations stagnated. Pundits blamed the internet, but Deon du Plessis knew better.

Du Plessis is the sort of Boer that the English have been caricaturing for centuries, a jovial giant with thighs like tree-trunks and a great raw slab of a face. He likes guns and big game hunting. He eats and drinks to excess, tells dirty jokes, swears. His car licence plates read, 'Beast1,' and his business philosophy comes from Conan the Barbarian: 'Find the enemy, crush him and hear the lamentations of the women.' He and his heiress wife are famous for their outrageous parties. A friend was at one such when gunfire broke out in the backyard. Drunk and bored, Deon was shooting up the shrubbery with a shotgun. On another occasion, trolling for marlin in the Indian Ocean, he came across a boatload of 'wily orientals' fishing illegally in SA territorial waters. He drew his long-barrelled .44 magnum and charged, crying, 'Fuck Japanese emperor! Fuck emperor wife!' through a bullhorn.

Until 1999 or thereabouts, Du Plessis was a senior executive at Independent Newspapers, the local arm of Irish press baron Tony O'Reilly's empire. It was not a happy relationship. Tony's South African acolytes tended to be blow-dried metrosexuals with delicate manners and carefully manicured PC opinions. Du Plessis was a rough ex-war correspondent with a 'rock'n'roll attitude' towards journalism and vivid views about almost everything, including 'the man in the blue overall.' This mythic African hero is a skilled worker with money in his pocket. He's a home owner, thanks to government subsidies. He's saving to buy a car, and even has enough money to go on holiday, an unthinkable prospect for his parents. 'I like the man in the blue overall,' says Du Plessis. 'He's optimistic and positive-minded. He's going places.'

Du Plessis wanted to launch a tabloid for Blue Overall Man, but O'Reilly turned him down, allegedly on the advice of minions who whispered that the Boer was totally out of touch with the mood of black South Africa. Whereupon the Great White Hyena resigned and started pounding pavements with his business plan. Banks turned him down, Rupert Murdoch's organisation likewise, but he eventually secured the backing of Media 24, the erstwhile Nasionale Pers. The first *Daily Sun* appeared on the streets in July 2002, and the rest is history. Today, Du Plessis's paper sells more than all O'Reilly's titles put together.

'The opposition are not happy bunnies,' says Du Plessis. He attributes his success to hard work, good timing and absolute loyalty to Blue Overall Man, a statue of whom stands in the *Daily Sun*'s foyer. Okay, it's a shop window mannequin rather than a statue, but you get the picture. 'The guy in the blue overall comes first,' says Du Plessis. 'If a story doesn't amuse him or serve his interests, it doesn't go in.'

A second Blue Overall Man sits outside the hyena's glass-walled office, grinning broadly as he ploughs through a back issue. Interestingly, says Du Plessis, Blue Overall Man isn't really interested in scandal about celebrities, so the paper's front page is mercifully free of these. Also absent are bare-breasted Page 3 girls (Blue Overall Man finds them offensive), presidential speeches and analysis of government policy. A *Sun* story is about the everyday travails of ordinary people. Domestic squabbles. Struggling to get the children educated. Battling to get lazy politicians to do their duty. Falling victim to crime, or striking back against criminals. 'We call it people's justice and it's a rough thing,' says Du Plessis. 'Mobs turning on suspects and setting them on fire. The police don't come, so people take the law into their own hands.' Another category that resonates is stories about 'strong women who refuse to be pushed around,' and witchcraft stories are routine.

This formula reduces the *Sun*'s critics to apoplexy. Joe Thloloe, a past chairman of the National Editors' Forum, charges that Du Plessis's paper 'exhibits contempt for black South Africans.' University professors complain about 'brainless perpetuation of stereotypes.' Mathatha Tsedu, editor of the broadsheet *City Press*, opines that nobody really believes the guff that appears in the *Daily Sun*, and journalism professor Berger excoriates the paper for its 'caricatural content' and 'crass archetypal narratives.' Berger urges the *Sun* to publish more, rather than less, celebrity gossip, on the grounds that such stories at least offer a 'more-upwardly mobile representation' of black South Africa.

What's interesting is that most criticism emerges from the leftist elite that led the campaign to transform and democratise apartheid media. It galls them beyond endurance to see the masses lining up to buy the *Daily Sun*, but as former Human Rights commissioner Rhoda Kadalie says, they have only themselves to blame. 'The tabloids are a reaction against politically correct newspapers,' she says.

'I don't really give a shit about critics,' says *Sun* editor Themba Khumalo, aka Bra TK. 'If Soweto said, "Bra TK, you're screwing up," I would listen. But not some uptight academic.' Khumalo can afford to be dismissive, because he and Du Plessis are walking on water these days, buoyed up by a triumph that might be unique in the annals of journalism: the *Daily Sun* is so popular that readers are known to sell used copies to neighbours at half price. It employs three typists to record tip-offs and accolades from fans. The volume of incoming calls is such that it sometimes causes the switchboard to crash.

The other day, Khumalo announced that his paper was planning to raise its price to R1.40 and asked readers what they thought. Back came a flood of letters – 'thousands,' says Khumalo – endorsing the move. 'Upping the price is normal,' they said. 'Let's support the People's Paper.' 'Go ahead, Bra Themba! Your hard work deserves reward.' One lamented declining standards of TV news coverage, adding that 'I am left only with *Daily Sun* to console me.' Some went so far as to suggest that an even steeper price rise would be acceptable.

These letters read like a tabloid story to me. I ask Du Plessis if they were fabricated. 'No,' he says, 'they really love us. The day we raised our price, circulation went up 10 to 17 per cent, depending on the area.'

We proceed to a slightly more thoughtful discussion about the paper's critics, who charge inter alia that the *Daily Sun* simply ignores the great issues of the day. 'It's true,' he says. 'We don't do traditional politics. We do real politics. Real politics is shit flowing past your front door because the municipality won't fix the sewerage. It's work-men leaving open holes for kids to fall into. It's police ignoring calls for help. Last year, every day, we did a thing called the Hall of Shame. Every day, we invited people to send us details of government failing them, then published the names and addresses of those responsible. I think that campaign contributed to the emphasis Mbeki's government is now placing on local government delivery, and that's where the rubber hits the proverbial road. Don't say we're not political.'

He also bridles at suggestions that it is racist to air stories about magic and ancestral spirits. 'I'm not going to slag off these beliefs,' he says. 'We once carried a picture of a bed on a roof in the township of Mangaung. The owner insisted that he woke up there. His neighbours told our reporter there was a white horse hanging around, and that the horse and the removal of the bed were connected by magic. Are we supposed to go to Mangaung and tell people they're talking shit? I'm not going to do any such thing. We'll report it as it was told to us.'

With that, he blows an ear-splitting blast on a Vuvuzela, summoning the troops to daily conference. On the agenda this afternoon we have, 'Three Die in East Cape Road Horror,' an ordinary traffic accident story, and 'Sex Maniac Flattened!' about a would-be rapist who tried to jump a woman on a crowded station platform and was beaten to a pulp for his trouble. Next up is the tale of Fikiwe Godo (38), whose Eastern Cape home was invaded by a swarm of killer bees. A sangoma, Nogazi Ntoni (46) informed Mrs Godo that the bees had been sent by her ancestors, who were upset because the family had failed to perform certain rituals. She advised them to slaughter a cow to appease the spirits, and presented them with a bill for R3 000. The Godo family did as instructed, but the bees refused to leave, and when they asked for their money back, the sangoma said sorry, I spent it on booze. Whereupon the angry family dumped buckets of cold water on her head.

This latter detail causes great perplexity. Normally, an offender in this position would be thrashed or worse. 'They should come to Diepsloot for lessons,' quips editor Khumalo, referring to a township famed for do-it-yourself law enforcement. There is also a dispute about the headline, occasioned by a sub who suggests something along the lines of, 'Evil ancestors send killer bees.' 'Never!' thunders the Great White Hyena. "This is not the *Surbiton Times*! This is Africa! Ancestors are never evil!' Bees on the other hand are fair game, so the gathering eventually settles on, 'Cursed by evil bees!'

In a few hours, 'Cursed by Evil Bees!' will be on the news stands, battling for attention against an array of imitators. Du Plessis's partners in Media 24 have launched *Die Son*, a national redtop in

Afrikaans. *The Sowetan*, which suffered a catastrophic drop in circulation after the *Daily Sun* appeared, has fired the self-regarding
editors who presided over its decline and returned to the mass-market
battlefield. Broadsheets have been forced to brighten their news holes,
and Tony O'Reilly has struck back with *The Voice*, a racy Cape Town
tabloid edited by an Irishman named Karl Brophy. One gathers that
Mr Brophy simply cannot believe the stories one gets here – mystery,
magic, Jesus appearing in people's bathrooms and man-eating sharks
in the surrounding seas. (The latter gave rise to the immortal headline,
'Great Sharks Eat Whites.') A friend who used to work for him says
Brophy believes he has died and gone to 'tabloid heaven.'

And so we come to the moral of the story. According to *Media*
magazine, the tabloids have added 1.3 million to the combined circulation of SA dailies. Since readership per copy is very high, this
translates into five million readers, some three million of whom were
reading nothing a few years ago. That's an awful lot of readers, and
an awesome degree of influence. Does President Mbeki lie awake at
night, worrying about it? Is he haunted by memories of British Labour
Prime Minister Jim Callaghan, cast into the wilderness in 1979 after
Rupert Murdoch's mass-market tabloids convinced the working class
it was okay to vote Tory?

Deon du Plessis defers these questions to Blue Overall Man, saying that the *Daily Sun* will be guided by his interests and desires. As
for political parties, they seem curiously indifferent; according to Du
Plessis, the only politician who has come courting his endorsement
is Patricia de Lille, and she didn't get it. But watch this space; Jim
Callaghan also believed the tabloids were neutral, only to wake up one
morning with a knife in his back.

So there you have it. A once stagnant newspaper market has turned
into a 'thunderdome' (Khumalo's phrase). Intellectual snobs are be-
side themselves, but I am rather enjoying the spectacle. Missionaries,
Marxists and Great White Masters have always sought to feed South
Africa's natives what they thought was good for them. It's nice to see
Blue Overall Man at last spitting out their tepid medicine.

The Spectator, December 2005

British Banks Make Me Glad to be South African

||||||||||||||||||||||||||||||||||||||||||||||||||||||||||||||||||||||||||||||||||||||||||||||||||||||||||||||||||||||||||||||||||||||||||||||

'Tis the season to be jolly and so on, and then to stand on Boxing Day beneath wilting boughs of holly, contemplating gifts you don't know how to work, like, for instance, a new laptop, or a Bluetooth cellphone. What follows is always unpleasant. I consult manuals, admit defeat and pick up the phone, invariably to find myself listening to computer-generated Christmas carols while a disembodied voice says, 'Your call is important to us; please hold for the next available operator.' This rapidly dims the glow brought on by brandied eggnogs, but what can you do? Almost all large companies have call centres now. They are lean and efficient. They cut costs, boost profits. They are also, according to the Future Foundation, the leading cause of frustration in the British Isles, topping rush-hour traffic and delayed trains as the UK's most stressful experience.

This story is therefore dedicated to all those facing a Christmas-related ordeal by call centre. It opens on a sunny morning three months ago. I am pacing my office in a state of mounting agitation while the phone in the crook of my neck offers the umpteenth rendition of National Westminster Bank's theme song. I owe NatWest's credit card division a splodge of wonga but cannot pay because NatWest's Online Banking setup is a fiasco and my NatWest cheque book is empty. Ergo, I want a new cheque book, but NatWest won't post one to Africa because they fear it will be nicked in the mail. They want me to collect a new cheque book at my branch. I keep saying, 'But the branch is in Notting Hill Gate, and I am in Cape Town.' Whereupon the call centre operators say, 'Hold on,' and force me to listen to more muzak.

My first call in this regard consumed 28 ruinously expensive inter-continental phone minutes and got me nowhere. This one has already lasted eight minutes, and I am beginning to get angry.

When I opened a NatWest account, I would routinely ring the branch and talk to someone who knew me, but that was before the advent of call centres, which enabled banks to shave backroom costs by up to 30 per cent and boost profits to their present record levels. The only thing rising faster than bank profits (up 15 per cent in 2005) is complaints about bank service, up 50 per cent in the same year, according to the Banking Standards Board. One gathers that many of these complaints involve call centres, and that bank bosses are concerned. In a better world, they would simply improve their service, but that would cost money, so they have turned instead to 'queueing theory,' a branch of mathematics that enables them to calculate precisely how much torture a call-centre customer will endure before exploding.

In my case, the timing is perfect: seconds before detonation, a soothing voice materialises, and I find myself talking to Amira, a senior customer services officer. 'I'm so sorry, Mr Malan,' she says. She listens sympathetically, takes details and promises to find a solution.

Amira has just tranquillised me with a shot of CARE, call-centre jargon for Consideration, Active listening, Responsiveness and Empathy. A well-CAREd-for customer will become supine and passive, but his predicament will not necessarily be attended to; Amira promises to phone back, but doesn't. Over the next ten days, I place three more calls to NatWest. On each occasion, I speak to a call centre staffer who doesn't know what to do but promises to get back to me. They never do.

At this point, I must introduce my wife, a stylish Latin-American whose jet-black hair and fighting spirit hark back to the Chibcha, an Andean tribe famed for slitting the throats of early Jesuit missionaries. We call her the Contessa. Earlier this year, the Contessa needed a new ATM card. NatWest refused to send one to a country where the post was likely to be pilfered, so she agreed to pick it up in London. But when she got there – no card. One does not treat a Chibcha thus. The ensuing tantrum left the bankers so shaken that they not only apologised but offered 50 quid in atonement. Imagine that – a bank offering compensation for slack service! Amazing.

In any event, this formidable woman returned to London in the

midst of my fruitless search for the caring Amira. She saw an ad claiming that NatWest customers are now allowed to call their branches
directly again, just like in the old days. This was news to us colonials,
but it seemed a step in the right direction. She provided two numbers
for the branch where our accounts are held. One just rang. The other
rang through to a call centre. I said, why don't you courier a cheque
book to me? I don't care how much it costs. I can't stand this. I will
pay anything. The young woman on the other side of the conversation
agreed to look into it and have someone call me. Never happened.

One morning, 16 days after my first call, there comes a letter from
Mr Michael Smith, NatWest's Care Team Manager. Mr Smith regrets
my difficulties and is pleased to announce that he's found a solution:
'I can confirm that I have today ordered you a new cheque book to
come directly to your home address.'

Hallelujah! For the next several days, my thoughts about NatWest
are kindly, but the promised item fails to arrive, so I phone to find
out what's gone wrong. The number dialled is Mr Smith's, but the call
winds up at yet another call centre. A girl called Heather looks me
up on her computer. 'Hmmm,' she says, 'Your cheque book has been
ordered and sent out to Notting Hill Gate branch. We need to find out
what the branch has done.' I say, 'Yes, that's a very good idea, because
my wife is in London at the moment, and if it is at the branch, she
can pick it up.' Heather says she will ask the branch to ring me, but
the call never comes.

Three days later, I phone again. Heather's not there, so I start all
over again with Indo. She looks me up on her machine. 'Hmmm,' she
says. 'Your cheque book went out to the branch. They must have sent
it to you in South Africa.'

I say, 'Yes, that's what I was told, but it hasn't arrived.'

'Well,' says Indo, 'these notes say it shouldn't be a problem for your
wife to go in to the branch to collect it, so long as she has proper ID.'

I say, 'This is ridiculous. A moment ago, you were telling me it had
been sent to Africa. Now you say it's in London. Are you sure it's at
the branch?' She isn't, but she's willing to give me the branch's direct
line. I say, 'Sorry, you can't fob me off with that one. I've been calling
that number for weeks, and I never get through.'

Indo says, 'Okay, I will call the branch.' She puts me on hold. Muzak
plays.

Two minutes later, she's back. 'Nobody is answering the phone at the branch, sir.'

I am tempted to scream, 'What did you expect, you stupid bitch!' But I control myself, because I have Googled the call centre racket and acquired a measure of sympathy for the techno-serfs who work in it. A call centre is typically located in a depressed area (North England, Bangalore) and staffed by desperate people who work for almost nothing under the lash of evil supervisors who dock their pay if they fail to handle the required number of calls per hour. In the worst centres, staff are required to raise their hands like school children if they want to use the lavatory. Derided, stressed, exploited and dehumanised, call centre workers are allegedly succumbing en masse to a previously rare condition called 'acoustic shock', caused by 'a sudden spike of noise' in their headphones. Close to 40 per cent of the UK's million-odd call centre serfs are so afflicted. Management blames techno-gremlins, but I beg to differ: these people have surely been deafened by the demented screams of millions of irate customers. I do not want to deafen Indo, so I grit my teeth and beg her please to find out where the cheque book is and call me back.

I spend the following day staring at the phone, waiting for it to ring. It is the Contessa's second-last day in London. Time is running out. The call doesn't come. Towards evening, I ring Indo again. 'Did no one call you?' she says. 'I'm so sorry. I tried five times and couldn't get through. I'm going to call again now.' She puts me on hold. I listen to corporate Muzak. After three minutes or so, Indo returns to say, 'I'm sorry, Mr Malan. They are closed.' She swears blind to make sure they ring me in the morning.

And lo, they do, but I am out when the call comes. When I phone back, a girl says, 'Hello, Notting Hill Gate branch,' but she's not really there, she's at a call centre. Ergo, she cannot put me through to the manager. All she can do is send a message, asking someone to call me. I sit by the phone, waiting. The clock is ticking. The Contessa is packing. At 4 pm, she leaves for Heathrow. At 4.15, the phone rings. It is Amrit, calling from Notting Hill Gate branch. She says, 'Hello, Mr Malan. We have your cheque book here. They said your wife was going to pick it up.' I lower my head into my hands. I say, yes, that was discussed, but she is boarding a plane even as we speak. Amrit says, 'No problem, we can post it to you.'

Things got a bit ugly at this point. They could, after all, post the bloody thing. If I'd been able to talk to Amrit on day one, none of this would have happened. So I let go and had a rant, but I won't go into details. Instead I will say, Merry Christmas! Hope you enjoyed my tale, and that it gives you something to chuckle about when your own hour of torment comes.

There is of course a moral lurking hereabouts. *Spectator* readers are probably accustomed to my gripes about the deteriorating state of South Africa, but NatWest has forced me to reconsider. There are advantages to living in a backward country. For instance, South Africa still has real bank clerks. Mine is called Fiona. If I have a problem, I phone her and say, 'Hello, Fiona.' She says, 'Hello, Rian.' Then we chat for a while about the weather and crime before getting down to business.

Such quaint relationships are extinct in the civilised world, victims of corporate greed and so on. South African bankers are also greedy, but they get their pound of flesh by charging nearly a pound to cash a cheque or use an ATM. Ten pounds a month in banking fees is a lot of money, but is not too great a price to pay for being able to phone the bank and say, 'Hello, Fiona.'

I think every Briton should ask Father Christmas to bring their Fionas back. If it goes on like this, someone will be murdered.

The Spectator, December 2006

The Warring Tribes of White Suburbia

||||||||||||||||||||||||||||||||||||||||||||||||||||||||||||||||||||||||||||||||||||||||||||||||||||||||||||||||||||||||||||||||||

This is an Anglo-Boer War story, and it begins on a gold mine west of Johannesburg in January 1959. It's little Ernest Oelofse's first day at school. He's waiting at the garden gate for the school bus to pick him up while mommy and daddy beam and take pictures. Mommy and Daddy are English-speaking. So's little Ernest. The school bus, on the other hand, is full of tough little Dutchmen whose eyes light up with malevolent glee as Ernie steps aboard, a lonely little rooinek, branded an enemy by his green Arthur Matthews Primary School blazer. As soon as the doors close behind him, poor little Ernest gets *dondered*. In fact, he gets *dondered* every morning for the next six years.

The *dondering* is so bad that Ernest acquires a psychopathic streak. By standard five, he's nine inches taller than the biggest of his former tormentors, and it's their turn to suffer. Now, when Ernest boards the bus, they have to scramble off the back seat and sit on each others' laps. If they don't, they get *dondered*. Sometimes he *moers* them any- way, on the grounds that you have to *moer* the Boers while you have the chance because you know they'll *moer* you when the odds shift back in their favour. For instance, if they catch you alone on your way home from school. Or when they find you occupying their favourite fishing spot on Florida Lake. They *donder* you in bars and in army barracks, and you *moer* them back whenever you can. Looking back, it's as if your entire youth was a replay of the battle of Colenso.

As I write, a tidal wave of Boer War centennial stories is breaking over our heads, but nobody is saying anything about this post-war history of inter-white loathing and violence. Why not? Such passions were a force of destiny in the South African twentieth century. All whites were mildly concerned about 'the native question,' but then again, almost all whites agreed that some form of white domination was necessary and inevitable. Until the seminal black uprising in Soweto, 1976, the real divide among whites was tribal. Politics was about English versus Afrikaners, and English vs Afrikaners was about the war and its legacy.

Consider my father, born in a dusty sheep town in the Great Karoo and brought up on Boer War atrocity stories, at least some of which were probably true. A handful of young rebels from his hometown were captured by the British and hanged as traitors. Everyone had relatives further north who'd been thrown into concentration camps or had their farmhouses burned down and livestock shot during the scorched earth campaign. Having drunk deep of this cocktail of re- sentment, the old man went off to Stellenbosch University in 1939 and promptly signed up with the Ossewa Brandwag, an ultra-nation- alist movement that sought to oust Smuts, capture the British High Commissioner and join the war on the German side. Towards this end, he and his friends did mock military training on midnight rugby fields and walked out of bioscopes when 'God Save The King' was played. Conventional wisdom has it that they did this for Hitler, or to hasten the coming of apartheid, but I doubt it. They did it because they were full of rage and pain about what they called *Die Tweede Vryheidsoorlog*, the second freedom war, and because they knew that the English regarded them as backward white trash.

Yes! White trash! The English watched their words in public, be- cause the imperialist gameplan required rabid Boer national-socialists to be kept in check, which in turn required English-speakers to sup- port moderate Afrikaners of the Smuts ilk and mask their true feelings with hypocritical cant about broader South Africanism. One of the few *rooineks* to break ranks and speak truth in this regard was Drury Pifer, an American poet who grew up in various Anglo/De Beers mining towns in the thirties and whose autobiography contains some aston- ishing insights into the way Afrikaners were really perceived by their English-speaking bosses and betters. We had no doubt, says Pifer, that Afrikaners were stupid, dirty, drunken and violent. 'Everything about them,' he says, 'was inferior.'

Pifer had a point. Afrikaners were inferior. Englishmen controlled all the mines, all the cities, all the fancy golf and country clubs and every last company listed on the Johannesburg Stock Exchange. Afrikaners earned, on average, barely 60 per cent of what the English did, placing them at about the same social level as the American Negro. For my father's generation of Afrikaner nationalists, all this was directly attributable to greedy imperialists who'd engineered an unjust war, crushed the Boers by any means necessary, seized riches that were rightfully theirs and then spat on them.

My mother was one of the spitters. On one side, her family were English 1820 Settlers who'd made good in Johannesburg selling bicycles and later, horseless carriages. On the other side were parsimonious Scots who came out for the gold rush and made money running transport for the British Army between 1899 and 1902. The Gays and Connocks, for those were their names, subscribed to Victorian values, worshipped the Royal family, and observed the essential British rituals of tea, straight bats and stiff upper lips. Their sons – educated, of course, at colonial sub-Etons called Saint this or King's that – considered it a privilege to fight and die for the Empire. They did it in 1899, and again in 1914 and 1939. There was no doubt in their minds that Britain was the source of all things worthy and superior, and that the bloody Dutchmen were uncouth and backward. I doubt that my mother had ever met one socially until she met my father.

And he really was the enemy, my old man. He'd spent the war plotting with Jerry, while her brother fought him in the Western Desert and her sister sat in a lookout post above the Indian Ocean, scanning the sea for German U-boats. He was a member of the Broederbond's youth wing; her family were Masons. His entire being was dedicated to throwing off the yoke of British imperialism. She turned out to squeal and wave the Union Jack during Royal Tours. The only thing in my old man's favour was that he was quite good-looking, but even so, my mother's friends were horrified when she agreed to a date, and then another, and another.

At the time, such love affairs were 'interracial' in the newspaper parlance, and frowned-upon by both tribes. The mater was denounced by her other suitor, an RAF pilot with handlebar moustache. The family began to ostracise her. The headmistress of the rather posh English girls' school where she taught gym hauled her onto the carpet and ordered her to drop the Dutchman, on the grounds that dating him just wasn't ... done. As for the old man, he was cornered by his comrades from the Boer nationalist movement and bullied to tears for his treachery.

In the end, social pressure was such that they parted. My father was a shy and fundamentally decent man, seldom given to displays of emotion. He said nothing when his English rose left town, and uttered no rebuke when he heard she was planning to marry a gentleman farmer in the Eastern Cape. But on the day her train passed through Queenstown, he got on his bicycle and, driven by a force whose name was never spoken in our family, rode to the station and fell on his knees, begging her to reconsider. She got off the train, and that was that. They were married in 1948, and paid a mild price in terms of social awkwardness, and in my father's case, excommunication from the Afrikaner secret societies.

Unto this should be added the probably considerable pain of discovering that he'd fathered a *volksvyand*, a traitor. I was mortified to find myself branded with an Afrikaner name, and wanted more than anything else to be Captain John Black, MC, preferably wounded in heroic battle against Jerry while Scottish bagpipes skirled in the background. I hated obligatory attendance at the Dutch Reformed Church on Sundays, and cringed whenever the old man opened his mouth in public, because his English was heavily accented.

By the age of twelve, I'd discovered that the best way to irritate the old man was to mock and scorn his beloved National Party and write letters to English newspapers, condemning apartheid. My left-liberal credentials thus established, I wormed my way into a progressive private school, where, to begin with, I was the only pupil with an Afrikaans surname. Modelled on AS Neill's Summerhill, Woodmead was without a doubt the most fashionable educational establishment in South Africa, the first school to flout apartheid and admit black pupils.

I am sorry to say that the high moral tradition of English South African left-liberalism was contaminated from within by a rather low strain of crude anti-Afrikaner racism. In theory, our callow politics were driven by love for blacks, but I'd say, looking back, that all we really wanted was to see the Boers come short. All my classmates were extremely liberal and anti-racist except when it came to Afrikaners, who were universally disparaged as rockspiders and hairybacks, and much mocked for their short hair, concertina music and mangling of English, as in the case of the speed cop who said, 'Did you got a licence,' or the Boer woodwork teacher who used to cry, 'Both you three came here.' No wonder the Dutchmen stepped on our faces with their studs on those rare and terrifying occasions when we had to face them on the rugby field.

We retaliated by growing our hair long and supporting anyone and anything that was against the National Party, from Helen Suzman to the KGB. In theory, we were doing this because we yearned for freedom, but as I say, all we really wanted was to see the Dutchmen punished for such atrocities as banning the Beatles on state radio and outlawing Sunday movies. The 1976 Soweto riots put an end to this idyll, rocking the white establishment to its core and prompting me to undertake a nine-year draft-dodging excursion to safer places. By the time I came back, everything had changed.

For a start, Afrikaners had grown richer, more confident and sophisticated, the fruit of decades of superior education and ethnic nepotism in the civil service. Afrikaners everywhere were growing ponytails, smoking dope and buying African art to grace the distressed walls of their suburban homesteads. As for the arrogant English liberals next door, they'd been brought down a peg or two by the dismaying realisation that they, too, were on the black power menu, or as the African National Congress once phrased it: 'There is no difference between Helen Suzman, John Vorster and PW Botha. They are just different teeth in the same white mouth that is grinding the workers down.' In times of terror, one seeks alliances wherever one finds them. Anti-Boer racism became less and less virulent as liberation neared, and just the other day it vanished.

The defining moment came in the run-up to our recent general election. My father's beloved National Party was foundering, fouled beyond redemption by the Truth Commission. Into the vacuum stepped the liberal and traditionally English Democratic Party, assiduously courting the confused Boer voter with a campaign calculated to appeal to his baser instincts. DP leader Tony Leon began appearing at agricultural shows in the Boer heartland, ankle-deep in cow-dung, urging thickset farmers in halting Afrikaans to stand firm and 'fight back' against the omnipotent ANC. And lo, they heeded his call, elevating an English-speaking Jew to leader of the opposition and thus supreme leader of most white people. The unthinkable had happened. Ancient animosities had been buried. Most whites wound up in the centre, holding hands somewhat apprehensively. And that's when the Boer War really ended: 2 June 1999.

The Spectator, October 1999

House Going Cheap in Doomed Country

||||||||||||||||||||||||||||||||||||||||||||||||||||||||||||||||||||||||||||||||||||||||||||||||||||||||||||||||||||||||||||||||||||||||||||||

When the winter rains closed in on Cape Town I thought, bugger this, I'm selling up and moving somewhere sunny. Toward this end, I asked the char, Mrs Primrose Gwayana, to come in and help spruce up the house. We were scrubbing and painting and what have you when Primrose's broom bumped the dining table, and crack – a leg snapped off, rotted from within by woodborers. I thought, uh-oh, here's an omen. Something awful is going to happen. And it has.

Nine months ago, South Africa seemed to be muddling through in a happy-go-lucky fashion. The economy was growing, albeit slowly. Trains ran, if not exactly on time. If you called the police, they eventually came. We thought our table was fairly solid, and that we would sit at it indefinitely, quaffing that old Rainbow Nation ambrosia. Now, almost overnight, we have come to the dismaying realisation that much around us is rotten. Nearly half our provinces and municipalities are said to be on the verge of collapse. A murderous succession dispute has broken out in the ruling African National Congress. Our Auditor-General reportedly has sleepless nights on account of the billions that cannot be properly accounted for. Whites have been moaning about such things for years, but you know you're in serious trouble when President Thabo Mbeki admits the 'naked truth' that his government has been infiltrated by chancers seeking to enrich themselves and 'plunder the people's resources.'

I knew in my bones that it would come to this, but somewhere along the line I got tired of stinking up my surroundings with predictions of doom, so I shut up and went with the flow. Ergo, I cannot say, told you so. But I have a pretty good idea why things went wrong, and it all began with transformation, a euphemism for ridding the civil service of whites, especially white males. Under apartheid, those chaps ran everything. Clearly, this had to change, but white males carried the institutional memory in their brains, and blacks who replaced them tended to flounder. This led to what we call 'capacity problems,' a euphemism for blacks who couldn't or wouldn't carry out the jobs for which they were paid. Capacity problems in turn led to crises in electricity supply, refuse removal, road maintenance, health care, law enforcement and so on. Again, white malcontents have complained about such things for years, but you know you're in trouble when an eminent black journalist like Justice Malala dismisses the Mbeki administration as an 'outrage,' characterised by 'a shocking lack of leadership' on the part of a cabinet riddled with 'incompetent, inept and arrogant' buffoons.

In short, we're in crisis. Everyone acknowledges it, but somehow, we never see firm corrective action. Previously we were told it was awkward for a black liberation movement to purge black appointees, even if they were useless. This year, a new excuse emerged.

Back in April, around the time of the ominous table-leg incident, the actress Janet Suzman and I dined with a bossy American woman who bit my head off when I opined that our recently deposed deputy president, Jacob Zuma, would one day step into Nelson Mandela's shoes. For a foreign feminist, it was unthinkable that a man with four years of schooling and rape and corruption charges pending should become president of anything. My explanations to the contrary were dismissed as racist rubbish, but let me air them anyway.

Zuma is a Zulu, and when he became a target for criminal investigation, many fellow tribesmen suspected he was being stitched up by President Mbeki, who was reputedly keen to eliminate him as a potential successor. Conspiracists noted that Mbeki was a Xhosa, and that various members of what we call the 'Xhosa nostra' had become billionaires as a result of their political connections, whereas Zuma's allegedly improper payments were limited to a trifling £100 000. They found it even more fishy that the sad and desperate young woman who invited herself to spend a night in Zuma's home, only to accuse him of rape in the aftermath, was acquainted with Minister of

Intelligence Ronnie Kasrils, a KGB-trained master of the dark arts of espionage, presumably including honey traps.

Zulus are a warlike bunch, as we know, and the Zuma affair got their blood up. Thousands turned out to cheer their homeboy at his rape trial, and to denounce his accuser as a harlot bribed to bear false witness. Zuma's acquittal sparked riotous celebrations, and when his corruption trial started last month, the crowds were even larger. '100% Zulu Boy' T-shirts were still evident, but now there were red flags too, because radicals had started rallying to the Zuma cause. First to join were the young lions of the ANC Youth League. They were followed by the Young Communists, then by large sectors of the trade union movement and the Communist Party proper. All that remained was for Winnie Mandela to take sides, and lo: when the judge dismissed Zuma's corruption charges in late September, she materialised among the jubilant masses, praising the Lord for answering her prayers.

These developments dumbfounded naïve left-liberals, who had repeatedly assured us that Zuma was politically dead. Feminists recalled how a dalliance with Ms Lewinsky almost destroyed Bill Clinton. Aids activists were scandalised by Zuma's failure to use a condom during the rape-case escapade, even though the woman involved was HIV-infected. Moralists contended that even though criminal charges had proved unsustainable, there were enough facts on the table to show that Zuma was sorely lacking in probity. For such people, it was unhinging to see Zuma become the leading contender for SA's presidency, greeted at every turn by adoring supporters who informed reporters that the Ten Commandments were an alien invention that didn't apply to African males. Their campaign song was even more unnerving: 'Bring me my machine gun.' A Serbian journalist presently resident here took one look at this and wrote a piece headlined, 'Time to Panic?'

Hmm. My friend Steve, a capitalist who golfs with the black elite, says this is nonsense. 'Zuma is charming,' he says. 'Things will settle down. We can do business with him.' Maybe so, but the next general election is three years away, and meanwhile, government is incapable of acting against the borers in our woodwork

Let's look at law enforcement, one smallish aspect of the growing problem. After years of slow decline, crime surged earlier this year, with insurance companies reporting a 20 per cent rise in claims. Some blamed a strike by security guards, who took to looting shops they had previously guarded and throwing scabs off trains. Others pointed the finger at feral refugees from Zimbabwe. 'Capacity problems' in the police were certainly a factor, too. In the midst of all this, a convoy of expensive cars carrying senior ANC dignitaries rolled up at a prison outside Cape Town. Uniformed warders swarmed out of the gates, and the gathering turned into a revolutionary song-and-dance extravaganza in honour of Tony Yengeni, a popular ex-MP about to start serving four years for fraud.

Is this not bizarre? A politician accepts a discounted Mercedes from an arms contractor, lies about it, gets nailed – and several of the ruling party's most prominent leaders hail him as a hero, a staggering insult to their own criminal justice apparatus. In her eagerness to charm the rabble, National Assembly Speaker Baleka Mbete went so far as to claim that Yengeni had never committed fraud, even though he pled guilty to same. The main opposition party, the Democratic Alliance, termed her behaviour 'disgraceful,' but there was no retribution.

Why? Because a crackdown by Mbeki might cause figures like Mbete to defect to Zuma, who is not particularly punctilious about whom he accepts as allies. Don Mkhwanazi, for instance, got into hot water after hiring a 'well-known crook' to assist him in his duties as boss of the Central Energy Fund. Mkhwanazi claimed racists were defaming him, but fell silent when it emerged that his bent chum (who earned £300 000 a year) was channelling money into a bank account that paid Mkhwanazi's mortage in a posh Jo'burg suburb. Mkhwanazi resigned in disgrace. Today he is a trustee of Zuma's unofficial election campaign.

My pal Steve says one shouldn't take such things too seriously, noting that respectable people have also cast their lot in with Zuma. Maybe so, but Zuma's core supporters are scary. The other day, they put on a spectacular display at a conclave of Cosatu, South Africa's mighty Congress of Trade Unions. Whenever an incumbent cabinet member appeared, delegates surged to their feet, waving red flags and chanting, 'Tell us, what has Zuma done?' One minister was jeered off the podium. The Deputy State President was 'humiliated and degraded' by hecklers, who went on to sing, 'It is better for us to take over this country, we will go with the Communists.' President Mbeki wisely kept his distance, but they had a song for him too: 'We will kill this big ugly dog for Zuma.'

Alas, poor Thabo. I'm no great fan of our remote and autocratic president, but the charges emanating from the red brigade – 'betraying the poor' and 'tolerating inequality' – are asinine. A former Communist, Mbeki saw the light in the late 1980s and cajoled his comrades into a historic compromise with capitalism. His saturnine manipulations of business and labour led to a massively increased tax harvest, which in turn financed the creation of a welfare state, with 11 million poor now receiving subsistence grants of one sort or another. This is amazing. A welfare state in Africa!

Unfortunately, such goodies are the fruits of gradualism, and I can't see us staying the course. Jacob Zuma wants the big job, so he promised to resurrect the ANC's revolutionary tradition, and the movement's most dedicated activists immediately rallied to his standard. As I see it, the only way for Mbeki loyalists to block him is by promising even more loot to the masses, and once they do that, Zuma will surely move even further leftward. Nobody (save opposition leader Tony Leon, who is white and therefore irrelevant) is going to stand up and say, 'Sorry, folks, this isn't the answer, we have to work harder, exercise self-discipline and bring white technocrats back into government so as to make things work again.'

And besides: if by some miracle Mr Leon started swaying the electorate, would our rulers put up with it? The ANC dominates almost everything else, but it has never won an election here in Cape Town. This enrages the city's black power faction, which has prevailed upon the ANC to oust DA Mayor Helen Zille and impose a multi-party government. The stated reason for this initiative, launched two weeks ago, is that Zille's coalition is weak and unstable. Maybe so, but we all know it's really a power grab, inspired at least in part by fears that Africa's last white- and Creole-controlled city will continue to prosper while all else hurtles into a black hole of dysfunctionality. What can we do? Some in the ruling party have a peculiar view of democracy. They see it as a system designed to put themselves in power. If voters fail to understand this, their mistakes must be corrected by fiat.

No, there won't be civil war. Whites are finished. According to a recent study, one in six of us has left since the ANC took over, and those who remain know their place. For apartheid-era police minister

Adriaan Vlok, this turned out to be on his knees, washing the feet of those he sinned against during the struggle. Truly! He carried a briefcase and a basin into various government buildings and performed acts of abject contrition in public. No doubt Mr Vlok's bones were warning him to repent before the end came.

Ah well. Let's look on the bright side. Osama bin Laden has no beef with us, we are not sinking into a Mesopotamian quagmire and the weather is wonderful in summer. Anyone want a house here?

The Spectator, October 2006

Rock of Ages

IIIIIIIIIIIIIIIIIIIIIIIIIIIIIIIIIIIIIIIIIIIIIIIIIIIIIIIIIIIIIIIIIIIIIIIIIIIIIIIIIIIIIIIIIIIIIIIIIIIIIIIIIIIIIIIIIIIIIIIIIIIIIIIIIIIIIIIIIIIIIIIIIIIIIIIIII

Rian Malan decided to become a rock star at the age of fifty. Rian Malan came short very quickly.

Okay, picture this. Me and my band are gearing up to do a show at the rock festival part of last year's Klein Karoo National Kunstefees in Oudtshoorn. We're supposed to be doing a sound check, but some other band is blasting away on the stage right behind us and we can't even think, let alone hear what we're playing. My bassist, an unsentimental pro named Dr Hook, says, 'This is ridiculous. You should just walk out.' Then he downs his Fender and does just that. One by one, the other musicians follow suit, and I'm left on stage all on my ace.

Five minutes later, the band behind us falls silent, and the stage manager comes running up to say, 'You're on. Start now.' I say, 'I can't. My musicians have buggered off to the bar.' I step up to the microphone and shout, '*Manne! Woza!* We're on!' About 50 punters are milling around, trying to figure out what on earth this *ou top* is doing on stage at a rock festival, but they lose interest when Valiant Swart opens up on the adjoining stage, and by the time the boys show up, most have drifted away.

I have only one song that's really suitable for a rock festival, so we start with that. It's an ominous heavy metal thing about Zimbabwe-style land reform, played in the unsettling time signature of 9/8. Our drummer is a jazz cat who supposedly knows all about odd time signatures, but he's been smoking something so he kicks off in straight 4/4. The result is aural chaos. I'm screaming at Dr Hook, who is screaming at the drummer, who is screaming, 'What? What?' He can't hear us, so he eventually stops playing entirely, and the song grinds to a halt amidst derisory applause. The last fans leave to listen to a band that can actually play, and we are left with an audience of two: Dr Hook's girlfriend, and the sound engineer. I think, holy smoke, what a mortifying fuckup. How on earth did I get here?

It's a long story, and it begins with my high-school china Roy 'Maggie' McGregor. He and I were in the same class from standard six onwards, and we both wanted to be ... no, not pop stars. Pop stars were commercial. We only liked obscure artsy bands nobody else had heard of, like Henry Cow, early seventies' practitioners of what was known as 'head music.' A head musician was a cool dude who smoked dope, had shoulder-length hair and prefaced every sentence with the word, 'Like.' By the time we left school, Maggie and I were, like, head musicians.

After a year or two of aimless jamming in hippie digs, I cut my hair and got a job in the real world, but Maggie was a mad Scot who lacked the gene for compromise. He worked in advertising for a while, but it didn't last, and when I met up with him again, 30 years later, he was still a longhair who owned nothing but a guitar, an old desktop computer and a cellphone. Didn't even have a car. He was 48. You might think he was a failure, but the converse was true: Maggie had organised his life so that he could spend every waking hour doing exactly what he wanted to do, which was play head music.

By 2005, head music had come to mean strange collages of whale sound and eerie guitar figures. Maggie created this resolutely anti-commercial music in a cheap flat near Kalk Bay harbour, using a single microphone and some primitive music-recording software he'd downloaded off the internet. The sign on his door said, 'Dr Oom Voodoo.' He was also known locally as 'King of the WABIs,' WABI being short for, 'What a brilliant idea.' Maggie was full of WABIs. He thought money should be outlawed, along with cars and most forms of industry. He thought one could make better movies than Hollywood with R250 and a hand-held digital camera. One fateful night, he had a WABI about me.

I hadn't played guitar in decades, but Maggie urged me to have a go on his machine, so we bought a box of Tassenberg and set to work on a song that chronicled President Mbeki's struggle to suppress his internal black man, who kept threatening to burst out of the presidential anus and embarrass His Eminence by dancing to *Meadowlands*. It was called 'Styf,' or stiff, and I saw it as a serious piece of political commentary about our president's proclivity for leaden solemnity. Maggie, on the other hand, thought it was screamingly funny, and our friend Pedro laughed so much he couldn't sing backup. That's when Maggie was stricken by a WABI. 'Mealie,' he said, for that was my high school nickname, 'you could do this for a living, you know.'

For a man in the throes of a grave midlife crisis, those words were fatal. I was nearly fifty. My hair was falling out, my eyesight fading, and I'd dug myself into a rut so deep I couldn't see the sky anymore. I'd look at myself in the mirror in the morning and scheme: this is not my life; this is not me. All males eventually reach this point, whereupon many go *bossies*. They commit suicide, or run off with a woman half their age, or grow ponytails and start hanging out at trance parties. Others buy sports cars or motorcycles, but thanks to Maggie, I developed a better plan than most. My wife rolled her eyes when I announced it. Friends laughed out loud, but I didn't care. I wanted my youth back. I wanted to be a rock star.

In truth, my secret yearning was to become a member of the Hantam Klipwerf Orkes. If you're English, you've never heard of these guys, but they are like Afrikanerdom's Grateful Dead. According to my friend Warwick Sony, who works in the music business, the Hantam boys (all *dik*, grizzled Afrikaners of approximately my vintage) spend weekdays in the Great Karroo, looking after sheep on their various farms. Come Friday, they pile into a van and drive off to play boeremusiek at rugby club dances or agricultural shows. They make good money, answer to no man and have an army of fans that buys them drinks in smalltown bars countrywide. For all I know they even pull groupies.

This struck me as a hugely enviable lifestyle, so Maggie and I started crafting songs that would conceivably go down at rugby club dances. 'Hoender is Eintlik 'n Vegetable' – Chicken is actually a vegetable – was about the hardcore braai culture. 'Renaissance' was about affirmative action, 'Onverskrokke' – Dauntless – about rugby. We sent eight or so songs off to Jo'burg, where friends were putting together an Afrikaans album for 'Boet en Swaer,' properly the actors Ian Roberts and Norm Anstey, who starred as Boer hillbillies in those Castrol ads that ran forever on SABC TV. The songs wound up on a CD called 'Stoomradio', by the Radio Kalahari Orkes, and next thing the critics were saying we'd invented a new genre called 'nouveau-boeremusiek.'

Rendered delirious by this modest success, I started working on a solo album consisting mostly of dark tunes about such cheerful subjects as suicide, farm murders and trying to get off in a bar when you're fifty. Shifty Records, the leading underground rock label of the 1980s, saw fit to issue these on a CD titled 'Alien Inboorling,' which means 'resident alien' in Afrikaans. I was trying to say something clever about being white in Africa, but my wife thought the title meant space cadet and decamped to France, vowing never to return unless I came to my senses. Sadly, the reviews rendered this unlikely. 'A very fine songwriter,' said *Business Day*. 'Afrikaans album of the year,' said a critic at Litnet.

Eish. Stand aside, Mick Jagger! I was on my way. In my mind's eye, I saw stadiums full of adoring fans holding cigarette lighters aloft as they swayed in time to my immortal ballads. I started doing 400 situps a day, spent hours studying the wreck of my face in a mirror. What to do? I shaved my head, hoping this might hide the fact that I was grey, and bought myself an Eminem-style hip-hop beanie. I mean, I was about to become a rock star, and you have to look the part, not so?

Unfortunately, I was up against real stars, like, for instance, Steve Hofmeyr, a luminously charismatic oke who has probably shaken the hand of every Afrikaner south of Windhoek in the course of his career. He has also kissed their babies, signed autographs for their grannies and in certain instances, seduced their daughters. In the season of my debut, Steve was himself facing a serious challenge from Chris Chameleon, who started off singing punk rock in a mini-skirt and high heels but achieved stardom with a set of haunting folk songs based on the poems of Ingrid Jonker. Below Steve and Chris there were thousands of good-looking young Afrikaners jostling for attention, all of whom could sing and dance and hold an audience, whereas I was so decrepit I had to sit down while playing. I couldn't even sing in tune, but there was no stopping the geriatric rock-star manqué. I assumed my 'profound' words would carry the day.

And so they might have, if the words had been audible. But they weren't. Next time you see a live band, check it out: unless you know the words of a song, all that really registers is noise. In the case of real stars, it's an agreeable noise. In my case, it was more like the low, gravelly rumble of a mudslide, emanating from a weird old dude in a beanie. Audiences were deeply perplexed, so I tried to spice things up with witty between-songs patter. 'It's great to see young South Africa here in all its beauty and racial variegation,' I told a student bar in Pretoria. 'I've been studying you and wondering what we have in common. The answer is ... fuckall.' Nobody laughed. Maybe they didn't find it funny. Maybe they couldn't hear. Maybe they were too drunk to care.

And that gig, let it be said, was one of the higher points of my career. We played to eight people in Pretoria East, about ten in Stellenbosch. One night, an agent booked us into a restaurant that was anticipating a lounge act that played suave background muzak. I obliged by introducing songs in dog Spanish – 'La musica de Led Zeppelina!' When that didn't work, I sharpened the joke by saying, 'La musica de Sex Pistales,' then playing '30s boeremusiek. Nobody laughed, because nobody was listening. Nobody even noticed.

Then came the KKNK, where we shared a bill with Fokof Poliesiekar and Chris Chameleon. This was the big time, but it was also our nadir. As the band broke down in chaos to the desultory claps of an audience of two, I found myself thinking about Digby Prior, my best friend at the age of seven or so. Digby used to come over in the afternoons to play war. We had a redoubt near the compost heap, and the orchard at the bottom of the garden was infested with imaginary Jerries who would cry, '*Achtung*,' as they charged us, only to be mown down – da-da-da-da – by our plastic Mattel Tommy-burst machine guns. Then we moved away for a year. On the day of our return, Digby showed up, wanting to play war as usual. I took my toy gun and followed him into the garden, but I'd lost my capacity for fantasy: where enemy soldiers once swarmed, there were only peach trees. The game was ridiculous. I'd grown out of it.

My rock star idyll came to a similar end. One moment I was on the brink of stardom, and then next – poof – paralysed by recognition of my own absurdity. All that remains is to pluck a moral from the ruins, and it is probably this: life is nice, and there's much too little of it to waste any. Most of us spend our middle years making compromises so we can be presently comfortable and have enough to live on when we're old, so we slave away at jobs we hate until we reach a point where we can no longer tell if we're content or dead already. I woke up one morning and realised that what I really, really wanted was to be a wild and free troubadour, roaming the veld with a *konsertina*, so I made a break for it, only to see my *gat*. So what? 'Tis better to have tried and failed than not to have tried at all, and besides: I had some great times along the way, and wound up with this story.

Best Life, 2007

Postscript: This story ends on a slightly misleading note. After the humiliations described above, I went on to become an anonymous sideman in various bands, most notably the Ensemble Borsalino, whose slogan is 'Gypsy Boer Jew,' and the Hot Club d'Afrique, a Jo'burg-based outfit dedicated to resurrecting the darkly glamorous music of Parisian nightclubs in the pre-World War II era.

8

God

The Messiah of the Mealie Fields

||||||||||||||||||||||||||||||||||||||||||||||||||||||||||||||||||||||||||||||||||||||||||||||||||||||||||||||||||||||||||||||||||||||||||||||||||||||||||||||||||||||||||||||||||||||||||

A miracle in the mealie fields

O ye of little faith, ponder the parable of Michael Rosen, a holiday-maker who was travelling across Zululand on Friday, 8 April, heading towards a game farm on the upper Tugela River. Rosen thought he'd reach his destination in time for dinner, but he's a creature of the secular world, and had no idea of the tribulations awaiting. Some 20 km short of Greytown, he ran into the rearguard of a giant traffic jam. Assuming there had been an accident, he turned on his radio, but there was no mention of any such thing, so he got out and asked the men in the van behind him what was up.

'They were Boers,' he says. 'Big tough okes in khaki who said they'd driven all the way from the Kalahari to hear a preacher called Uncle Angus.' Same applied to the men in the buses, the leather-clad bikers revving past on the verge, and even the light planes passing overhead. Like most residents of the secular world, Rosen had never heard of this Angus person. Like most residents of the secular world, he was heading towards a revelation.

Angus Buchan is a white African of Scots extraction, born in Zimbabwe and raised in Zambia, where he farmed as a young man. When Zambia's economy collapsed in the 1970s, he sold out for a pittance and bought some wasteland near Greytown. He built a crude mud house in the Zulu style and set forth to hew a living from the soil, but it was tough: no water, just one tractor and too little capital to clear the fields of alien vegetation. He says his neighbours thought he was 'some sort of gypsy' who'd soon give up and drift away.

For a while, it was touch and go. Buchan started dropping

tranquillisers, drinking heavily and taking out his frustrations on his labourers. Shamed by his actions, he turned to the Lord on 18 February 1979, and lo, miracles ensued. His crops flourished. Boreholes struck water. Rain quenched a bush fire that threatened to ruin him, and a Zulu woman struck by lightning was raised from the apparent dead by prayer. These and other wonders were recounted in *Faith Like Potatoes*, his 1998 autobiography, made into a movie seven years later by Frans Cronje, brother of the ill-fated cricket captain.

By then, Uncle Angus had become a minor star on the evangelical circuit, with tours pending in several countries, but the Lord was not entirely pleased with him. Indeed, the Lord spoke to him at a bush retreat, instructing him to scrap other plans and become a light unto the lost men of his native land. Toward this end, in 2004, he staged the first Mighty Man Conference on his farm. It drew 170. The next year, some 600 turned up, and the year after, 1 060. In 2007, the crowd swelled to 7 500.

Angus was 'petrified' by his success, but the Holy Spirit warned that even greater things were coming, so he went to Johannesburg and hired 'the largest tent in the world' for this year's event. A tent that took three weeks to erect, and seated 30 000. People thought he was nuts. Not even Billy Graham could pull that many to a mealie field in the middle of nowhere. But as the event neared, it became clear that Buchan's prayers were yielding abundant results. With three days to go, his webmaster informed him that registrations were coming in at the rate of one per second. Shortly after, the server crashed, and it became clear that a huge army was converging on Greytown. 'We panicked,' says Buchan, but it was too late to do anything but pray.

This then was the crisis into which Michael Rosen drove on that fateful Friday evening. He sat in bumper-to-bumper traffic for three hours, hugely irked that his pleasure should be disrupted by something as anachronistic as a revival meeting. And when he reached the turnoff to Shalom Ministries, he did not go in. If he had, he would have seen something amazing: a tent the size of a cathedral, and beneath it, on stage, an unlikely figure in baggy jeans and farm boots, yelling himself hoarse about the coming transformation.

'God is looking for Mighty Men,' thundered Angus Buchan. 'God is looking for valiant soldiers! The tide is turning in South Africa because the Holy Spirit is here! It's here!' Buchan is 60, but when the spirit moves him, he skips around the stage like a child, his excitement barely containable. 'There's enough men at this conference to change the destiny of this country! Do you understand that? *Do you*?' In response came an uncanny rumble: the sound of 60 000 mostly white males saying, 'Amen.'

Sixty thousand men. By several reckonings, it was the largest gathering of white males since the 1938 Voortrekker centenary celebrations. Every third farmer in the country was there. One in 20 adult white males. English-speaking South Africans tend to be embarrassed by this sort of thing, but Afrikaans papers splashed Angus across their front pages, causing furious debate on a thousand websites. Some thought Angus was the real thing. Others dismissed him as a money-grubbing charlatan. Progressives were horrified by his Old Testament views on almost everything, and right-wingers wondered if he might be The One whose coming was prophesied nearly a century ago by Siener van Rensburg, a wild-eyed Boer holy man. The One who would defeat the forces of darkness and restore the Afrikaners' freedom.

As for cynics like Mr Rosen, they yawned. It was wildly inconceivable that a country as advanced and complex as South Africa could be swayed by a mere evangelist. But Angus was not done yet. One of his followers, a Middelburg farmer named Paul du Toit, heard a voice in his dreams instructing him to fill the nation's largest rugby stadium for the Lord. Everyone laughed at him too, but Du Toit did as he was told, and lo: by early July, advance bookings had accounted for every seat in Loftus Versveld's towering stands, along with 14 000 on the sacred field itself. This suggested – God help us – that Angus was a bigger draw than rugby.

This was an event of seismic dimensions. I set forth to investigate it.

In which the narrator assesses his relationship with God (such as it is)

We're on the stoep of a farmhouse overlooking a row of vineyards and a line of bluegums that marks the banks of the Orange River. This place has no name, as far as I know, but it's 70 clicks downstream from a village called Grootdrink, bounded on one side by the Kalahari desert, and on the other, by the arid wastes of Bushmanland. I'm drinking tea with FJ Nesar, a bearded Boer with broad shoulders, calloused hands and a face as open as this landscape. FJ is desperate to sell his farm and I'm a potential buyer, but he's one of those religious Afrikaners who can't quite bring themselves to dissemble. Fertiliser prices have risen 150 per cent in the past year, he says. Diesel is up 70 per cent. This has shaved margins to almost nothing, he says, and now the raisin price is collapsing because of foreign competition, and because South Africans are becoming too poor to buy.

FJ is a man in anguish. He has three children under ten, and wants to save them from the apocalypse that is surely coming in South Africa. He has a visa for New Zealand, but can't leave until he sells his land, and who in their right mind would buy a farm at this time? You will bleed here, he says. I suspect that's true, but I can think of worse things. The climate of paranoia in Johannesburg, for instance. Crime. Corruption. Pogroms against foreigners. A government that seems to be foundering on most fronts, and a state president who seems to support the murderous Robert Mugabe. And atop all this, a surge in food prices that threatens to sink tens of millions below the breadline, with consequences that can't fail to be grim.

This Jeremiad pushes FJ even closer to despair, and he starts talking about God. Faith is the only answer, he says. I tell him I have none, and then I tell him about Tolstoy, who wrote that there are four kinds of human beings. Those too dumb to ask themselves, 'What is the meaning of life?' Those who ask the question, find it disturbing, and numb themselves with drink and debauchery. Those who ask the question, and find an answer in God. And finally, those who find no answer at all, and ought by rights do the rational thing and kill themselves. I find myself in the latter category these days, but lack the courage to act consequentially.

In short, I'm just another white man rolling down a road that seems to disappear in darkness around the next bend. When I heard about the miracle of the mealie field, I thought Angus was talking directly to me, and I wasn't put off by the antediluvian tenor of some of his views. On the contrary: it was amusing to see someone giving the progressives a go on issues like family values (Angus believes they're critical), abortion (Angus thinks it's murder) and the position of women (Angus says husbands should be 'king, prophet and priest' in their homes). He also thinks corporal punishment is good for unruly children, and that homosexuality is an aberration that can be cured by love and prayer. Yes, these are terminally unfashionable positions, but so what? South Africa is a nation of conservatives presided over by a tiny elite that seems to imagine it's in Sweden. If you despise what Angus stands for, you despise most South Africans.

That said, you probably despise me, too, but the hour is late and I'd rather not waste time arguing about social rights and gender issues. For me, the astonishing thing about Angus Buchan was that he seemed to have found seeds of optimism on the hard and stony ground of our present realities. 'There's enough men at this conference to change the destiny of this country! Do you understand that? *Do you*?' I didn't. But I liked the sound of it.

A crash course in the theology of Born-Agains

Joy! magazine is created in Cape Town by evangelical Christians for evangelical Christians, and the news it carries is sometimes strange to the layman. There are world-famous Christian rock bands the secular world has never heard of. Famous Christian movies and novels likewise. It turns out that South Africa is awash with bible colleges whose names ring no bells, and miracles that pass unnoticed by the mainstream media. (On 22 November 1998, for instance, Bill Weise of Cape Town spent 23 minutes in hell, and has now written a best-seller about his experiences there.) *Joy!* has no discernible political stance, but the magazine seems to enjoy the support of the tiny African Christian Democratic Party, which runs an ad in every edition. 'It is time for change,' reads one such. '*When there is moral rot within a nation, its government topples easily* – Proverbs 28:2.'

Angus Buchan's face often graces the cover of *Joy!* and its pages bring news of his services and offerings. He has published nine books over the years, and filmed more than 300 episodes of 'Grassroots', a show carried by five cable or satellite TV channels. The entire body of work is available by mail order, but time enabled me to absorb only a tiny fraction of it – one book, and a boxed set of six DVDs chronicling the most recent Mighty Man conclave. These open with an eerie trance-like soundtrack and visuals of clouds boiling over the cathedral tent in time-lapse slow motion. 'Faith is the ability to believe things you cannot see,' intones the disembodied voice of Angus, 'and the reward of that faith is to see the things you believe in.'

The music ends, sunlight floods the screen and Angus appears, sitting astride a horse in a jaunty Stetson. He tells the camera of the extraordinary venture he has embarked on, and then we cut to footage of pick-ups and buses streaming into the Mighty Man campsite. Most of the attendees are sunburned farmers, but there are also many surprises: shaven-headed bikers, youths with body piercings, long-haired Christian heavy metallurgists, executives with soft hands, and a fair smattering of persons of colour. These men are shown hugging each other and choking back tears as they contemplate the enormity unfolding around them.

In due course, the sun sets and Angus appears on stage, wearing his trademark farmer's work clothes and carrying a battered red bible, which he refers to as 'my agricultural manual.' He raises both hands to acknowledge thunderous applause, opens The Book and starts preaching. Most of his parables involve the land, and are populated by tractors and harvesters, dry boreholes, and strong men rendered desperate by adversity. No, not farm murders or land claims. Drought is the eternal theme of African prophets. Sun beats down, crops wither, humans face ruin and starvation. Then a man of God arises to purify the community, and salvation comes in the form of rain.

Buchan has a vast repertoire of such stories, all of them riveting. At Mighty Man 2008, he came up with a cracker involving a visit to the Eastern Cape, then in the throes of a crippling drought. Angus flew down there in a sponsored light plane, and when he beheld the suffering of his fellow farmers, made a rash promise: 'Boys,' he said, 'before I leave here, it's going to rain.' Not, it will rain, God willing. His promise was categorical: if you repent your sins, rain will come before next Monday.

Word spread, and at every stop, more people turned out to hear the good news. Angus picks up the story: 'Guys said, "Where's the rain?" And I said, it's coming. But it didn't. Thursday, no rain. Friday, no rain. Saturday, not a cloud in the sky. Come Sunday night, I was lonely and scared. I died, boys. I died. I was sitting in a tin-roof sheep-shearing shed in a place called Kroomie. In the cow dung, like Job. I said, Lord, I have sullied everything, because I got a heart for these men. They going bankrupt, Lord, their sheep and cattle are dying. That's why I shouted my mouth off, Lord. Not because I want to be a hero. Because I want them to prosper. But there was no sign of rain.

I wanted to run. The way farmers were looking at me, I could see they were thinking, *ja*, big mouth, liar. I could hear cars coming for the last service. I said, Lord, you never let me down before, and I got to preach in ten minutes. What am I going to say?'

Angus's voice sinks to a whisper and 60 000 men lean forward in their chairs as he describes slinking out onto the stage, dreading what's to come. And then, just as he starts preaching, rain starts drumming on the tin roof. At this point in the telling Angus goes messianic, eyes bulging and neck tendons straining. 'Do you hear that?,' he shouts. 'DO YOU HEAR THAT? That's the King! That's my Lord! He's the rainmaker and He's coming!' The roar that follows is so loud the earth seems to tremble.

My neck hairs are standing on end by now, and Angus is only just hitting his stride. 'We're in a war here,' he thunders. 'This is not a Sunday school picnic! This is the real thing! We will leave here as an army ... 60 000 men! Sixty battalions signed up for Jesus!' And later, 'We are not taking no for an answer! We are claiming this country!' In context, these statements pertain to the war against Satan, but I could almost swear I heard something else there – a veiled call to militancy directed mostly at people like myself, and aimed at inciting us to rise against the Romans of our time and place.

Was this farmer Buchan's underlying message? There was only one way to find out. I packed my bags and set forth to kneel at the prophet's feet.

Among the faithful

Buchan's Shalom Ministries stands on a rise five miles south of Greytown, the surrounding land falling away in all directions in a tapestry of green fields and pine plantations. There is a towering cross that lights up at night, and at its feet, a small chapel and a white building that seems to have done previous service as a dairy or stables. As I enter, the receptionist is talking to a distraught woman in the UK, who says her niece is threatening suicide. Chantal slips the details into a folder bulging with prayer requests, three or four of which arrive daily.

On her desk, there's a glossy magazine with a cover featuring two blow-dried grotesques of the sort that typically populate American televangelism, but otherwise, there's no sign of Elmer Gantryism. The women who work here look like hippies with their long straight hair, mostly unmade-up faces and sensible jeans and sweaters. The cars outside are humble, and there's a plaque on the wall in which Uncle Angus disavows all interest in money. 'We are committed to preaching the word of God to a dying world,' it says. 'God has promised He will provide for our needs. We are therefore against fund-raising of any description.'

There are those who say this is too good to be true, but if Angus Buchan owns a gold-plated Cadillac, he keeps it well-hidden. His wife Jill is a serene, other-worldly creature whose style runs to simple cotton frocks and sandals. Her nails are unvarnished, and if she ever had a soap opera hairdo, it grew out years ago. They still live in the mud house Angus built when he first came here, still cook on the cast-iron wood stove that dominates their lounge. The roof is bare corrugated iron – no ceiling, and no insulation. In winter, the cold in that house must be unbearable, which is possibly why Angus showed it to me. The prophet is at pains to present himself as a simple rural everyman, clad in working clothes and forever pausing to scrape dung off his boots. 'I'm just a farmer,' he says. 'I didn't even finish school, man. I'm nothing special.'

In the flesh, Buchan has a bluff hello-howzit manner that is initially slightly disconcerting. He slaps you on the back, calls you *boet*, and spices his talk with clumsy jokes and Zulu phrases. His smile is impish, his enthusiasm contagious. 'I've got one hour,' he says as we sit down to talk. 'One hour. That's it.' Then he launches into a spirited description of all he's up to. Newspaper interviews. Calls from Christian radio stations. Preparations for the forthcoming Loftus Versveld rally, and the national stadium tour that follows. 'Is this really happening or am I dreaming?' he says. 'It's awesome, man. Awesome.'

Agreed, I say, but what does it mean, and why is it happening now? Angus turns serious. 'I'm telling you my heart now, Rian. I believe it is God. If revival doesn't come, this nation is doomed.'

But how will revival save us?

'Good question,' says Angus. 'We talking reality here. We not talking froth and bubbles. I'm not into that, hey. I'm a farmer. Feet on the ground.' He pauses to gather his thoughts. I sit back, anticipating visions of righteous Christians flogging Pharisees and so on, but all that comes forth is a slightly lame anecdote about a coal mine where workers and managers pray together, and an even lamer one about a man who broke off an adulterous affair after hearing Angus preach. 'That,' says the prophet, 'is the fruit of revival.'

It's not quite what I had in mind, so I inquire about his politics. 'No,' says Angus, 'that's one thing I will not be drawn into. I'm not a politician. Can't even spell the word.' How about race? 'Apartheid was not God's will,' he says. 'Definitely not. I want to make that straight and clear. There's white racialism in this country, and as much racialism in reverse, maybe more. But God has set me free from that. A man is a man. Treat him with respect. My biggest desire is that this thing should be multiracial.'

Oddly, this longing for interracial love and understanding lies at the root of the only act of dishonesty I can lay at the door of Angus Buchan's organisation. Last year, *Joy!* magazine published a photograph purporting to show a multiracial crowd hanging on Buchan's lips. On closer inspection, the image had been doctored, with several Indian and African figures inserted into the sea of white faces. Some might be dismayed, but it was a forlorn and hopeful little sin, so let's let it pass.

By now, I'm thinking a spot of confession might hasten our progress to the heart of the matter, so I start telling Buchan about my own despair. He nods sympathetically. 'Lots of people are in despair,' he says.

I observe that in my case, hopelessness seems to breed a spiritual infection that manifests itself in poisonous racial tirades. Angus chuckles sympathetically. 'Well said, Rian!' he cries. 'That's exactly right, my *boet*! If you hang around negative guys long enough ... *ja*, the blooming country's in a mess, there's no manners on the road, there's hijacking, the blooming economic situation, the government's gone to the dogs, this and that, let's drink because tomorrow we die. And the guys just pull each other down. We got to draw the line somewhere, *boet*. We can't let this carry on.'

But how do we stop it? With marches and strikes? With guns?

'No,' says Angus, 'there's no victory in that. I want to tell you the good news – there's Christians in every political party in this country, and there's lots of strong African Christians in government.' He says the head of the South African Air Force attended Mighty Man 2008 in mufti, and that this black man was so moved by the experience that he's decided to bring his friends to the upcoming Loftus Versveld affair. 'This is fantastic,' says Angus. 'Hatred is not the answer. Retaliation is not the answer. We got to find a common denominator.'

And that is?

'His name is Jesus,' says Angus. 'I'm telling you now, his name is Jesus.'

Is that it? All this talk of war, soldiery and determining the destiny of the nation ends right here? *Eish*. I came looking for John Knox, the Calvinist whose political sermons made Queen Mary tremble, or Martin Luther, who shook the Catholic Church to its rotten foundations. I am bitterly saddened, but then it's not Buchan's fault that I'm blind to the revolutionary power of his sort of holy rolling. 'I believe,' says Angus, 'that when a man's heart turns to God, he's going to feed the poor and treat his subjects with respect. He's not going to be racialistic. He's not going to steal. He's going to be just, compassionate and merciful. That's what I believe.'

Buchan is right; a non-racial government of law-abiding and God-fearing Christians would be a considerable improvement on our present one. Let us therefore pray that his revival brings our politicians to their knees, promising to walk the straight and narrow and never sin again.

My friend Rosen was appalled to hear that I thought Buchan was a good man and should be supported. 'He's a televangelist!' he shrieked. 'They're all the same! At some time he'll start collecting. First it will be power, then money. They prey on desperate people who clutch at any straw in the hope that somehow tomorrow things will be better. It's a symptom of confusion and dire despair.' I sighed and said, 'You're right, Mike. Dead right.'

Unpublished, July 2008

Postscript: This article was commissioned by *Maverick*, the late and much lamented 'business' magazine founded by Branko Brkic, a Yugoslav who arrived in Johannesburg in 1993, on the run from Slobodan Milosevic's murderous regime and speaking not a word of English. *Maverick* was on its death-bed as I wrote, and died before the story saw the light of day. I never got paid, but that's small potatoes:

I wasn't following Angus for the money. I was hoping for spiritual salvation. I didn't find it.

The demise of *Maverick* was by far the greater tragedy. *Maverick* and its sister publication, *Empire*, were magazines that prized good writing above all else, and tried to give writers enough space and money to soar. That of course is why they failed. I warned Branko that his seeds were unlikely to flourish in South Africa's arid and stony soil, but he wouldn't turn back. Alas, poor Branko: his dream was heroic, and his failure was noble.

9

Mutations

Those Fabulous Alcock Boys

||||||||||||||||||||||||||||||||||||||||||||||||||||||||||||||||||||||||||||||||||||||||||||||||||||||||||||||||||||||||||||||||||||||||||||||||||||||||||||||||||||||

We're en route to an advertising shoot and I want to know if GG is carrying a gun. Anywhere else in the world this would be a wretched pun, but here in Soweto, it seems a legitimate and fairly pressing question. I know GG owns a Colt, and that he usually stuffs it down the back of his pants. Personally, I would be reassured to know that at least one of us is armed, but I don't want to display my cowardice by saying, 'Trust you're carrying your gat, GG.'

In the bad old days, I would have been chain-smoking at this point, dreading what lay ahead. Soweto was bandit country, home to two million angry black people corralled in a grim and depressing labour barracks by the mad scientists of apartheid. Anything could happen here, but today, under the bright autumn sun, it looks oddly cheerful. Liquor billboards line the highway. The landscape is scarred with building sites where developers are erecting a billion rand's worth of shopping malls. Old Potch Road is clogged with gleaming new cars, all presumably piloted by members of the Black Diamond tribe, a dark-skinned bourgeoisie whose numbers have grown ten-fold since Mandela came to power in 1994. The Unilever Institute, which coined the term, says Black Diamond spending power is about £12 billion a year, and growing at the dumbfounding rate of 50 per cent per annum. Unilever reaches for terms like 'economic tsunami' to describe the consequences. Judging by what I see out the window, Unilever is on to something.

GG is a white male, aged 39, with muscled forearms, bulging biceps and a square jaw topped off by a crew-cut. On the deceptive surface, he looks rather like a Boer cop from the apartheid era. This is not exactly a style associated with Soweto, but GG loves this place.

He is jabbering like a cokehead about its glories. That there is The Back Room, a dance club owned by one of his buddies. The dam over yonder is where GG stages the annual 'Soweto Beach Party,' of which more later. This is the route followed by the Tour de Soweto, a GG-organised bicycle race that drew international attention two months ago. And this is Pimville.

In the struggle years, my heart would sink into my boots as I turned into Pimville. It was less dangerous than other zones of Soweto, but you were still liable to encounter feral comrades who threw stones if they saw white skin in a passing car. Back then, Pimville was a sea of identical matchbox houses, all dusty and unpainted, marching over the horizon in all directions. Now it's a suburb.

When apartheid ended, residents were given deeds to their houses, and with ownership came pride – trees, lawns, rose gardens, cars in every second driveway, every third house undergoing renovation. Here and there, the old apartheid matchboxes have been torn down entirely and replaced with double-storey monstrosities that resemble nothing so much as the houses Afrikaners built when apartheid first lifted them out of poor white squalor. 'Ja,' chuckles GG, 'there's no difference between the Boers and the Bantu. Wait till you see Mrs Phetlo's house.'

Mrs Catherine Phetlo is in many respects your classic Black Diamond. Her husband made money in the transport business. She is a super-market supervisor. In her living room, leather-upholstered sofas face a giant TV set. Her display cabinets are crammed with china, crystal glasses and pink porcelain ducks my middle-class mother would con-sider 'nice.' The walls are lined with photographs of children in mortar boards, and a brass plaque offers a Victorian platitude – 'Bless this house, O Lord we pray, make it safe by night and day.'

The lady of the house is a matronly person who exemplifies the Black Diamond virtues. She is optimistic and resourceful, keeps an im-maculate house, prides herself on her five children's achievements and keeps up with the Joneses. That is why Mrs Phetlo has been selected to appear in a TV advertorial sponsored by Sunlight washing powder, a brand eager to win the Black Diamonds' favour.

She woke up this morning to find a film crew in her driveway. They're setting up gear, preparing for the shoot. Mrs Phetlo has gotten herself up for the occasion in a silky beige pants suit with gold accessories. Her neighbours, equally resplendent, have turned out in force to support her. One is adjusting her hem, another helping with make-up. A third is making tea. 'This is why I will never move to the white suburbs,' says Mrs Phetlo. 'Things are not right there. There is no neighbouring.' Her neighbours go, eh-heh. White suburbs are cold. Black people who move there get homesick and sad. One last touch of the powder puff, and Mrs Phetlo is ready. GG nods to a young man with a clipboard, who cries, 'Action.'

The shooting of Mrs Phetlo gets underway, and GG and I step outside to smoke and catch up. 'By the way,' I ask, 'have you got that Colt on you?' He laughs and says, 'Nah, I hardly ever carry a gun anymore. Soweto is safe these days.'

What a strange day this is turning out to be – Soweto booming, Black Diamonds turning up their noses at the white suburbs, GG telling me once-mean streets are now quite tame. Would you mind if I resurrect that painful old saw about Africa's knack of always producing something new? Well, here it is. I should have seen it coming. Let's dig up its roots and examine its nature.

It's the winter of 1986 and I'm sitting on a mountaintop overlooking the Tugela River, discussing the art of war with an ancient Zulu named Mankomaan Mabaso. Mabaso prefers to live here, three hours'walk from the nearest road, because his business is illegal. He has an anvil, a hand-cranked drill, a file and a pile of scrap metal that he fashions into homemade rifles. Technically, his guns are about two centuries behind the times, but they are much in demand in this wild valley where maidens still go barebreasted and women crawl on all fours in the presence of kings. Mabaso himself is a grand old savage. He has an old .303 hunting rifle secreted somewhere and is said to be deadly with it, capable of hitting an enemy from a thousand yards away. This makes him a man of distinction in the Thembu clan of the Zulu nation.

All Zulus enjoy in a warlike reputation, but the Thembu and their neighbours, the Mchunu, were arguably more warlike any other. Their territory was known as Msinga, and it was notorious for opaque feuds that sometimes boiled over into full-scale fratricidal warfare, with armies of warriors armed with spears, home-made rifles and the occasional machine gun hunting one another in the canyons and broken hills that lined the slow brown river. There were jets in Msinga's skies and buses crawling along its dusty roads, but in many respects, it was a place of the Iron Age. Women wore traditional regalia – purple cloaks, leather skirts, great coagulations of beads and bangles around wrists and ankles. Their husbands sported huge coloured discs in their earlobes. Everyone was poor and hungry. And everyone save the Alcocks was black.

Neil Alcock was a rural development worker who came to Msinga with dreams of turning a poverty-stricken apartheid dumping ground into a land of green and plenty. It turned out to be a greater challenge than he'd anticipated. Drought and war ruined his agricultural projects. His water-wheel was washed away in a flood. His white neighbours, outraged by his interference in their medieval labour practices, were constantly threatening to kill him. In the end, though, the bullet came from a different direction – he was caught in the crossfire while attempting to broker a truce between warring Thembu and Mchunu factions, and was murdered for his trouble.

I'd come to Msinga to talk to his widow, Creina, a strange and bewitching creature who spoke mostly in riddles. She conceded that she and her dead husband had largely failed in what they came to do in Msinga, and yet, there were tiny increments of progress. She said she'd recently seen a Zulu child building play-play soil-retaining walls on an eroding footpath. Saving the topsoil was an idea Neil had brought here, and it had taken root in the child's consciousness. It wasn't a big thing, but it was something.

Another thing Neil left behind was two teenaged sons, one of whom once asked his father what his future would be. 'I can't afford to send you to university,' said Neil, 'but I will prepare you for life in Africa.' Colonial Africa was full of whites who grew up playing with piccanins in farmyards, but there were only two who grew up in a mud hut, with no running water, no electricity, no TV, no lights, no windows even – just rafts of logs lowered against holes in the walls to keep out the winter cold. For the Alcock boys, hunting small game with their Zulu peers wasn't sport. They did it because they were hungry, like everyone else.

One cringes at the term 'white Zulu,' which has been much debased by urban fakers whose Zuluness consists largely of dreadlocks and tribal bangles. The Alcock boys were strangers to such self-indulgence. Their Zulu peers regarded them as Zulus, and when it came to the boyhood ritual of stick-fighting, they were expected to stand and fight, never flinching in the face of blood and pain. They learned the Zulu warrior code – hammer anyone who messes with you – and the allied art of shooting straight. And they learned the Zulu language.

The Alcocks had the only phone for miles around. When Zulu migrant workers in distant cities needed to communicate with relatives, they would call to leave messages with the Alcocks. Sometimes they found themselves speaking to creatures whose Zulu was so immaculate that they refused to believe the person on the far end of the line was white. In South Africa, a handful of white farmers and policemen speak Zulu, but their accents betray their race. With the Alcock boys, you couldn't tell. Such a thing was unheard-of, and Mabaso found it unsettling. 'Those boys are dangerous,' he said.

He was laughing as he spoke. Indeed, one of the Alcock boys was sitting beside me, translating. Mabaso loved the Alcock boys, but still, the language thing was troubling. A Zulu could penetrate the white world more or less at will, provided he was willing to adopt an alias (John or Peter), learn a bit of English, and take a job as a house boy. But whites couldn't enter the Zulu world, because they were too arrogant to learn the language. This gave Zulus a huge strategic advantage in certain situations. You could stand a yard away from a white man and openly plot picking his pocket, so long as you spoke only Zulu. You could crack jokes about him, admire his wife's breasts, plan his overthrow, and he'd be totally clueless.

Ceding this advantage to anyone, even to boys he liked, did not appeal to Mabaso. But what could he do? The boys were there. They were growing big and tall, with unruly mops of blond hair. They were squabbling with their mother, chasing girls and developing attitude. Soon they would finish school and go out into the world, armed with the only legacy their dead father could bestow on them: the skills to live in Africa.

One wonders if Neil Alcock understood the riches he was bequeathing. He began life as a commercial farmer, but got increasingly involved in liberal politics as apartheid blighted the lives of his Zulu neighbours. In the sixties, he became a sort of secular missionary, obsessed with the idea that hunger would be wiped out if African peasants could be taught to use their land effectively. Towards this end,

he and Creina moved to Msinga, where they planned to live among
Africans, like Africans, until such time as Africa's pain became their
own. Only in this way, said Neil, could you earn the peasants' trust
and begin to make progress.

The boys born into this insanely idealistic social experiment are
now in their thirties. The younger was named Rauri, but Zulus called
him Khonya. The other was GG. This is his story.

The Palace bar is located on the ground floor of a highrise in Randburg, a suburban business district just north of Johannesburg proper.
Once upon a time, Randburg was strictly whites-only, but as apartheid
crumbled the area was infiltrated by blacks who liked the low rents
and made the Palace their watering hole. Initially, owner Lance Smith
was thrilled to have the extra business, but as time passed, his white
clientele vanished entirely, and Lance grew paranoid in his isolation.
As he mounted the stairs to open his doors, he'd find dozens of black
customers waiting to get their hands on a cold beer. Lance was sure
it was just a matter of time before the blacks killed him, so he was
ecstatic when a madman offered to take the business off his hands.

GG spent his first several years out of school doing upliftment work
in rural areas, but didn't like it much – too many limp-wristed pieties
from the NGO types, no adventure, and above all, no money. Having
grown up in a mud hut, GG did not find poverty glamorous. Most of
his Zulu brethren shared this view and trekked to Johannesburg as
soon as they were old enough, dreaming of smart clothes, fast cars
and big money. In 1990 or thereabouts, GG gave up the struggle and
joined them.

He worked on a construction site before linking up with businessmen who wanted to install manned phone booths in black areas.
Elsewhere in the world, this would have been easy, but in those
anarchic times, doing business in Johannesburg's townships was almost impossible. White-owned companies routinely had their vans
stoned or burned, their employees robbed or shot. As a rule, white
civilians never set foot in the townships. There were areas where
even policemen were scared to venture, but the white boy from
Msinga had seen worse. He cruised the city's hellholes in jeans and
a T-shirt, setting up phone shops at the rate of two or three a day
and installing tough Msinga homeboys to run them. The grateful

businessmen gave him five per cent of the takings, and GG moved on to bigger things.

For a man accustomed to hellholes, Randburg held no terror at all. GG bought Lance out, repainted the place, put paper in the toilets and reopened it as The Palace of Kwaito. Again, his Msinga homeboys were a critical part of the operation. One is at pains to acknowledge that the Zulu nation has produced its share of poets, cowards and gentle intellectuals, but they do not feature in the great legend of Zulu militarism. In Jo'burg, a certain kind of Zulu – especially a rural Zulu, and *especially* a rural Zulu from Msinga – is held to be very dangerous. You do not cross these guys. You do not even look at them askance. You view them as Romans viewed Asterix and Obelix, because they are presumed to be capable of beserkery when their blood is up.

There are a thousand yarns in this regard, but for the moment, one will suffice. The Palace of Kwaito's manager was Fana Dlada, a 22-year-old who'd grown up in a mud hut a few hundred yards from his own. Fana was definitely that certain kind of Zulu. One afternoon, he looked up from his newspaper to find four robbers levelling weapons at him. He dropped the paper and charged, bellowing frightening Zulu war cries. The robbers ran, one in such a state of terror that he broke an ankle leaping down a staircase. According to GG, Fana was sorely disappointed at this outcome. He hadn't had a scrap for ages, because locals were terrified of him. He thought the four-to-one odds would stiffen the robbers' resolve, but no such luck.

While Fana and his crew kept anti-social elements at bay, GG was holding down a day job with a company that owned a fleet of gaily-coloured trucks whose appearance in rural villages would cause all normal activities to cease. Thousands would gather in the town square, whereupon staff would drop the sides of the truck, revealing a stage. The show that followed featured pop music, comedy sketches, morality playlets, beauty pageants and every now and then, a word from the sponsors, who ranged from soap manufacturers to Aids awareness campaigns.

GG started as a lowly organiser, but his unique African skills soon elevated him to a directorship in a company that was turning over around R65 million a year. As such, he took it personally when gunmen started hijacking company trucks. 'We went through a patch where we had 23 trucks hijacked in three months,' he says. 'We were being targeted by an organised crime syndicate that was threatening to murder our drivers if they refused to cooperate. We knew exactly who was doing this. Not the big guys – they had whites and Indians moving the vehicles out of the country – but the operators we knew. So we went to the police and said, what can we do? They said, get a court interdict. The criminals would have laughed at us. So we tried the politicians, but they had succumbed to white liberal weakness and said, "Be vigilant, not vigilante." We thought okay, let them dream, this is our Africa.

'So I talked to these guys I grew up with – Fezela which means scorpion, and Dumisani which means thunder. They were famous for not taking shit. They organised four or five others and we went to the East Rand at three am. When we arrived at the first house, the guy wouldn't open his door until he saw there was a white guy in the group. He thought I was a cop, so he said, "Wait, wait, I will open, I want to talk to the sergeant."

'He opens and says, "Sergeant, where is your search warrant?" I shove the barrel of my shotgun up his nose, and he realises he's in trouble. Scorpion says, get out of the way, you don't want brains on your clothes. Then he cocks his pistol and shoves it into this guy's ear. The guy thinks he's going to die. He starts peeing. Please, please please. We said, okay, take us to your boss and we'll let you live.

'It was like a Western, all these heavily armed okes walking down the road with our captive in front. We arrived at a nice house, surrounded it. They wouldn't open the door, so we shot out the lock. The owner comes out in his underpants, saying, "I don't even know this guy." We knew he was lying, but it was getting light and we were worried about the cops coming, so I gave them all a business card and said, "If you ever see this logo in a truck you hijack, we will come back and there will be a war like you have never seen before. You will all die."'

Later that week, Thunder and Scorpion visited several houses in Soweto, where they distributed more business cards and similar messages. The hijackings stopped immediately.

Meanwhile, in Msinga, Khonya Alcock was building himself a mud hut a few hundred yards downstream from his widowed mother's. Khonya is the younger and some say gentler of the brothers, although I would dispute that assessment. Let's just say Khonya is the more cerebral of the two, and seems to have inherited his parents' indifference to worldly comforts. Like his mother, he reads avidly, and writes letters full of vivid descriptions and wise insights. Like his father, he's interested in the land and the Zulu peasants who live on it.

The lot of those peasants changed radically after 1994, when Nelson Mandela's government announced that land taken from blacks under discriminatory laws would be returned to its original owners. Zulus responded by laying claim to vast swathes of territory along their border with white South Africa. Their own land was barren and eroded, ruined by overgrazing. The white farms were verdant, and Zulu cattlemen couldn't wait to drive their scrawny herds over the apartheid boundary. But first, there were disputes to settle. Some white farmers threatened to shoot anyone who tried to take their land away. Some Zulus claimed land to which they weren't entitled. In some instances, rival clans laid claim to the same farm and threatened violence if the prize was denied them.

The authorities were at a loss. How to control the process and quell the looming anarchy? They needed someone who could explain the Zulu position to white farmers, and vice versa. Someone willing to venture into remote areas where the locals were armed and sometimes dangerous. In short, they needed Khonya Alcock.

If this was a sentimental Hollywood movie, it would now evolve into a story of the good brother versus the bad, Khonya striving for racial justice in the heartland while the violence-prone GG pursues a variant of capitalist gang warfare in the distant and sinful city. Well, yes. The Alcock boys are indeed prone to rivalry. GG admires Mitsubishi off-road vehicles. Khonya feels the Toyota is more rugged. GG favours the Colt, whereas Khonya swears by the Glock. GG feels one owes criminals the courtesy of a warning shot, whereas Khonya jokes about 'two warning shots through the heart.'

On the page, this sounds rabidly racist, but in context, it's something else entirely. The Alcock boys are almost always surrounded by blacks who seem to enjoy their company hugely. The laugh, spar, crack jokes about you in a language you can't understand, then turn to you and say something outrageous, like, 'Hey Rian, we're just talking about the solution for crime. Two warning shots through the heart, hey. What do you say?' Everyone falls silent and watches your reaction. They find it particularly amusing if you turn red and start sputtering liberal nonsense about constitutional rights and due process.

This is about the only subject the Alcock boys agree on – the inanity of white liberals who think all Africans are humble Christians or kindly practitioners of *ubuntu* but flee the country as soon as anyone points a gun at them. Such liberals admire the results of Khonya's land reform work, but tend to be disconcerted by his methods. He drives into a dispute with his guns and his dogs, dazzles the opposing parties with his language skills and charms them into a deal. If that fails ... On one occasion, rival claimants started threatening to kill each other rather than compromise. Khonya slapped his Glock on the table and said, 'I'm the only armed man in this room.' By sunset, he had a signed settlement.

One imagines nostrils twitching in Hampstead as liberals digest this, but that's Hampstead for you. South Africa is a frontier state where the rules are still being written and the state is struggling to impose its progressive values on an unruly populace. What would you do if you lived here? Weep? Bow down before the hard men? Emigrate? The Alcock boys are made of sterner stuff. As far as I know, they've never actually shot anyone, but they exist in a world I can only liken to 1940s Hollywood westerns. The town has been taken over by evil men. Widows and orphans are suffering, but the good citizens are too timid to resist until a lone rider shows up to save them.

In the outside world, such men would be regarded as deranged fantasists, but here, they seem saner than most. 'They have their own moral universe that they almost chopped out of the rock they grew up in,' says Christine Hodges, a film editor who has known the boys for years. 'It is very hard-core but there is no black and white about it, excuse the pun. They never muddy things with doubts about moral worthiness and relative merit, because they've already decided that. They just do it.'

Do what, exactly? Over the past decade, Khonya has reclaimed an area half the size of Wales for landless people. His brother figures his labours have altered the lives of 200 000 Zulus, but Khonya is reluctant to claim credit. He just shrugs and says, 'Ah, change the subject.' GG owns a company called Minanawe (you and me) that does advertising and promotions in black communities, employing up to 500 people at peak periods. Both boys are married with children, and both concede the other's achievements, within limits.

'As far as I'm concerned,' says GG, 'the one with the most toys wins.' He lives in a ranch house in a suburb favoured by the black nouveau riche because Soweto is just ten minutes down the freeway. He owns a Mitsubishi pick-up, a VW Toureg, 1200 cc BMW motorcycle, a motor boat, sundry mountain bikes, several kayaks and a paraglider. Khonya lives in a modest Pietermaritzburg flat and might in crassly materialistic terms be judged a failure, but a far more profound assessment lurks hereabouts. Let's seek it.

Can we talk about market research for a moment? One hears yawns, but South Africa is a country where research commissioned by soap powder firms often reveals truths that elude the daily papers. In the 1980s, for instance, journalism gave the impression that black South Africa was a seething hotbed of Marxist insurrection, four-square behind the then-Sovietist ANC. Market research told another story entirely, finding massive levels of admiration among urban blacks for all things American, including capitalism. The sole exception was a tiny segment of university-educated black women, who thought Maggie Thatcher's UK was the finest country on the planet.

Today, South African newspapers are full of stories about crime, unemployment and the decay of our electricity supply network, which is increasingly prone to plunge us into days-long blackouts. On bad days, you get the impression of a doomed nation, septic with despair. But market research reveals blinding optimism in places like Soweto. Upwards of 80 per cent of the black middle class feel life is great and getting better. They have money in their pockets, access to well-paid white-collar jobs. Some own cars, and take seaside holidays.

Johannesburg's advertising companies are naturally keen to talk to these people, but it is not easy. Advertising was traditionally a white industry, staffed by cosmopoles who took their cues from New York and London. When the new dawn broke over SA, these cosmopoles turned their gaze on the black market, assuming that cool was a non-racial thing and that blacks were prey to exactly the same status cravings as whites. The result was an epidemic of TV ads featuring slender African models with long straight hair and English accents, consorting with Armani-clad beaux in 'international' settings.

Blacks were not impressed. Indeed, the aforementioned Unilever research project found that two-thirds of Black Diamonds disliked the way they were portrayed in advertising. They did not want to see trendies mimicking whites. They wanted real Africans. 'People like us,' with African accents and African attitudes.

GG was delighted by the resulting consternation, because he'd been telling advertising agencies this for years. In fact, his career is built on rubbing white noses in white ignorance. 'There was a time when the agencies hated us,' he says, 'because we were always telling them their campaigns were absurd. They'd say, ah, rubbish, and commission research which would always confirm the answers we'd already given.'

We're driving around Soweto in bright sunshine, talking about market research and the light it sheds on the African female derrière. This is no small thing, pardon the pun. A certain sort of white South African has always maintained that black men love big butts, but you'd never see a big behind in advertising. 'Whiteys don't want to show large African women because they think it's a stereotype,' says GG. 'I've been telling them for ages that large African women are very happy with themselves. They don't need whitey's approval.'

This was precisely the sort of sentiment that advertisers found offensive, but research recently commissioned by Levi Strauss shows GG was right: African prejudice in favour of the ample derrière is real and widely held. African woman are not ashamed of their large butts. On the contrary, they want skin-tight jeans that show them off to best advantage. Levi's obliged by introducing a brand called Eva, cut to suit African requirements, and laughed all the way to the bank.

Levi Strauss is not one of GG's clients, but this is the sort of thing he does for a living – tells First World companies who their African customers are and how to talk to them. A soup company hires him to find out why blacks wouldn't buy their minestrone. Answer: a strong cultural aversion to the mushrooms pictured on the package. Captain Morgan rum wants to sell its product to blacks but doesn't know how. GG says, well, your advertising is based on palm trees and Caribbean beaches, and black South Africans don't get it. But this can of course be changed.

Then he and his men dump 400 tons of white sand on the banks of a power station dam, moor eight ocean-going yachts offshore and invite Soweto's elite to a 'Soweto Beach Party,' which subsequently turns into an annual event. Last year, they had the nation's hottest pop stars on stage, 12 000 fans inside the fence, another 15 000 clamouring to get in. Traffic was gridlocked for five km in all directions. Captain Morgan was ecstatic.

We pull up outside a joint called Masakeng, a Sotho term for cattle kraal. In the bad old days, this would have been a shebeen, an illicit drinking spot, but now it's an upmarket entertainment venue frequented by Soweto's upper class. We are here to meet Billy Chaka, a dashing, dark-eyed playboy who quit a job in academe to become GG's partner. Billy drives an Audi 180 turbo, dates celebrities, and seems to know everyone. 'I work, he networks,' jokes GG. Billy recently lured Doctor Khumalo, the greatest striker in SA football history, to spearhead a soap powder promotion. Last year, every impresario in town was battling to book Kelly, a sexy pop tart who surged to megastardom when the tabloids revealed she was performing on stage without panties. Billy convinced her to headline the Beach Party.

Billy and GG have actually come to confer with Masakeng owner Sonwelo Mautloa about their next wild party, but today's newspapers feature a story that has aggravated them hugely. Foreigners are saying South Africa is too disorganised to stage the 2010 Soccer World Cup. Indeed, Australia is reportedly plotting to take our World Cup away on grounds that football fans will never set foot in a country so dangerous. 'Preposterous,' says Billy. 'Racist,' says GG. 'Completely uninformed crap.'

'Look,' says GG, 'nobody's denying that there's crime, but we've repeatedly shown that we can run world-class events and make sure there's no shit.' Minanawe's last beach party drew 27 000 punters, most of whom were drunk. Video footage of the event shows thousands of half-naked bodies writhing in firelight while fireworks detonate in the sky and a dark human tide batters the perimeter fence, begging to be let in. And yet, thanks to 'strong local boys' doing the security, the event passed off with less aggro than an English folk festival; two fans cut themselves on broken glass, and some guy bit his girlfriend's face when he found her dancing with someone else.

Last March, GG and Billy pulled off a similar feat with the inaugural 'Tour de Soweto.' You must understand that cycling is a lily-white sport in South Africa, and that most whites view Soweto with terminal dread. At the outset, GG and Billy thought they'd be lucky to lure a few dozen white cyclists, but they formed an alliance with Soweto's taxi associations, who agreed to provide marshals. Soweto's taxi men are hard; nobody messes with them. When word of the arrangement got out, GG started getting tentative inquiries from nervous white cyclists. Will I be safe? Can women participate? Will police line the route? And so on. GG cajoled them into taking a chance, and on the day, two thousand showed up and had a wonderful time. The sun was bright, the roads great, crowds friendly and cheerful. A few punctures and traffic jams aside, there wasn't a single problem.

Perhaps the bosses of international soccer should talk to GG about the appropriate African response to crime. Towards sunset, he and I ran into Archie Sepoyo, chairman of the Soweto Cycling Association. Archie said some of his chums had recently fallen victim to muggers as they rode across a stretch of open land. This prompted GG to tell a story about the day someone tried to rob him of his mountain bike on a lonely footpath north of Jo'burg.

'This guy shot at me from point blank range,' he says. 'I was so shocked I fell off and this guy takes off with my bike.' Interestingly, GG never carries a gun in Soweto, but he finds it advisable to pack a gat on the mostly white and supposedly safe side of town. He draws the Colt, fires a shot in the air. The robber abandons the bike and runs, but it is too late: he's reawakened the Zulu beserker in GG's corporate breast. GG screams, 'Someone is going to die today,' and gives chase.

When the robber realises he's being followed, he stops and shoots. GG shoots back. The race resumes, but GG's losing because he's wearing clumsy cycling shoes. Then two offroad motorbikes appear. The riders want nothing to do with this madness, but GG says, 'Just get me close,' so they give him a ride. Now they're gaining on the robber, who keeps turning to fire at them. The bikers are terrified, but GG urges them on.

'When he's maybe 50 metres away,' says GG, 'I jump off and aim. I'm waiting for him to turn and fire at me. As he starts turning, he sees I've got him covered. He drops the gun and says, "Sorry." I say, lie down. I go over, take his gun. It's still got one bullet in. I give it back to him and say, in Zulu, "Pick up the gun." He says, "No, you're going to kill me." I say, "*Pick up the fucking gun!*" The two whitey bikers get between us at this point, shouting, "Hey, no ways, 'bru, stand back, you can't just shoot this guy!" I wasn't really going to. I just wanted to scare him, but things are getting out of hand so I lower the Colt and say something very stupid. I say, "Don't worry, I'm a white liberal."'

Archie and I howl with laughter. GG says, 'I don't know what I meant.' Nor do we.

And so we come to the end of this story and consider its moral. Some years ago, in Tanzania, I met an old Afrikaans lady who, in 1950 or thereabouts, committed the unforgivable sin of getting herself knocked up by a black lover. The trekboer community under Mt Kilimanjaro expelled her, and Tannie Katrien Odendaal spent the rest of her life as a peasant farmer, living in a mud hut with her African family and, when the occasion presented itself, making soap out of hippopotamus fat. Tannie Katrien was a mutant. The Model C schoolgirls who congregate at my local shopping centre are mutants too. They are black, but their English accents are entirely Rosebank, and as far as I can tell, their interests are as vacuously suburban as were mine at that age. The Alcock boys are of course mutating in the opposite direction.

It is hard to say where all this mutation is leading, although the trend seems generally promising. A century hence, historians might look back and identify the Alcock boys as primitive incarnations of a new African life-form. On the other hand, there might not be a posterity at all, so let's just say Neil Alcock's experiment has produced hybrids whose world is infinitely more interesting and optimistic than the gloomy one I inhabit. For them, just visiting the supermarket can turn into an extraordinary experience.

Picture this: you're in a shopping mall in northern Jo'burg. African ladies man a line of tills. They're chatting in Zulu, assuming their white customers don't understand a word. A white man reaches the head of the queue, laden with groceries. One of the ladies says, in Zulu, 'Look at the hair on this one's arms. It's a baboon, I tell you.' Her friends titter. The white man says nothing. He's writing a cheque. He rips it out, hands it over. He says, 'Ever see a baboon write a cheque?'

The till lady freezes. She says, 'Oh God. Sorry, baas.' The white man laughs and says, '*Senge suki kwe mfene ngaya kubasi?* – so I've gone from baboon to baas in a couple of seconds?' This is seriously weird; the skin is white, but the voice is African. The till lady shrieks, claps a hand over her mouth and runs to hide behind a pillar.

By now, the rest of the till ladies are convulsed with merriment, and the entire supermarket is paralysed. A supervisor appears, apologising profusely. GG says, 'I don't mind. I think it's funny.' The guilty till lady is coaxed back to her post and finishes the transaction amid gales of laughter and ribald Zulu banter. GG gathers his groceries and waves goodbye. As he leaves, they give him a standing ovation.

The Observer, June 2007

Postscript

When this collection was first mooted, I said, sure, but only on condition that I get to write a postscript in which I settle old scores, gloat over my enemies' humiliations and exhume all the stories I couldn't get published because nobody wanted to know. Having laid waste to all around me, I intended to stand on their corpses and render a magisterial final verdict on the South African situation. But writing is a process of discovery, and I have discovered that I have nothing worth saying. I've been sitting here for weeks, typing furiously, but it's all rubbish. The same old what-ifs chase the same if-onlys around the same old obstacle course, usually working their way toward conclusions so dismaying that I want to shoot myself.

So I just hit delete and liquidated all of it. What a relief. I sounded like an old Africa hand with skin cancer on his bald spots, holding up the bar in Salisbury or Nairobi and complaining about the way the natives are buggering things up. They *are* buggering it up, for the most part, but I can't stand myself when I slip into that mode of virtuous outrage. Besides, I'm tired of writing demented tirades about the declining state of the nation. What's the point? We all know where we came from, and where we're going. Empires are always rising and falling. The empire I was born into – the empire of white males – was a mighty thing until a few decades back, but now it's in decline everywhere, and the end is likely to be messy. But what can I do? What can anyone do? We're all at the mercy of forces beyond our understanding. Myself, I'm just trying to enjoy the downhill part of the ride.

Beyond that, I take solace in the long view. I've always loved the passage in the opening pages of *Heart of Darkness* where Marlowe eyes the mud flats lining the Thames estuary and says, 'This too was once a place of darkness.' Conrad was of course looking through the eyes of Caesar and Claudius, who arrived to find the banks of the Thames thronged with half-naked Celts in blue war paint. The Romans subjugated those savages with ease and introduced them to the benefits of empire: level roads, comfortable villas, advanced systems of social organisation and so on. In due course, the Roman empire succumbed to the laws of entropy, and the Romans sailed away again.

The results, as Churchill noted, were catastrophic: Roman roads were overgrown; Roman villas crumbled; Britain was without central heating or indoor plumbing for centuries. And when Britons pulled themselves out of the slump known as the Dark Ages, a hallucinatory sight awaited the visitor to Oxford or Cambridge: descendants of the blue-painted savages of yore wearing togas and declaiming the classics in Latin, the tongue of their ancient oppressor. And not just that: venerating the Romans as a higher form of life, poring over their texts for clues as to their greatness, and lamenting their downfall. The Britons went on to formulate a culture that combined naked self-interest with early Roman ideals of public service and self-sacrifice, and lo: they wound up with an empire of their own, while the descendants of Caesar and Claudius became a jokey nation of waiters and ardent swains.

I suspect the gods of irony are planning similar reversals for all of us. Johannesburg as we know it will vanish, and something new will arise in its place. Many centuries hence, visitors to this New Jerusalem will encounter something presently inconceivable – Africans wearing OK Bazaars-style safari suits with combs in their socks, struggling to decipher the crumbling texts of a race that once lived here, planting mealie-fields that stretched further than the eye could see, splitting atoms and making the trains run on time. That race will be gone, of course, but the New Order will preserve and venerate its ruins, in much the way that Europeans preserve Roman roads and aqueducts. Outside the universities, Afrikaans will be a ghost that rattles its chains in the depths of some new African tongue, and white and black skins will have given way to something closer to golden. The issues that divide us now will seem absurd in retrospect. The good that white men did will be acknowledged, the evil forgotten. The wounds of history will be healed. I scheme it will be quite lekker.

'I ache to move beyond this time'
– Jefferson Airplane, 1967